Psychological Dimensions
of the Self

Psychological Dimensions *of the* Self

Arnold Buss
University of Texas

Sage Publications
International Educational and Professional Publisher
Thousand Oaks ■ London ■ New Delhi

Copyright © 2001 by Sage Publications, Inc.

All rights reserved. No part of this book may be reproduced or utilized in any form or by any means, electronic or mechanical, including photocopying, recording, or by any information storage and retrieval system, without permission in writing from the publisher.

For information:

Sage Publications, Inc.
2455 Teller Road
Thousand Oaks, California 91320
E-mail: order@sagepub.com

Sage Publications Ltd.
6 Bonhill Street
London EC2A 4PU
United Kingdom

Sage Publications India Pvt. Ltd.
M-32 Market
Greater Kailash I
New Delhi 110 048 India

Printed in the United States of America

Library of Congress Cataloging-in-Publication Data

Buss, Arnold H., 1924-
    Psychological dimensions of the self / by Arnold Buss.
      p. cm.
    Includes bibliographical references and index.
    ISBN 0-7619-2020-X (hardcover: alk. paper)
    ISBN 0-7619-2021-8 (pbk.: alk. paper)
    1. Self psychology.   I. Title.
  BF697 .B864 2001
  155.2—dc21   00-013200

This book is printed on acid-free paper.

01   02   03   04   05   06   7   6   5   4   3   2   1

Acquisition Editor:	Jim Brace-Thompson
Editorial Assistant:	Karen Ehrmann
Editorial Assistant:	Cindy Bear
Indexer:	Teri Greenberg
Cover Designer:	Jane Quaney

Contents

Preface	ix
Acknowledgments	ix
1. Introduction	**1**
Early Psychologists Examine the Self	3
The Concept of Self	4
Elements of the Self	6
Dimensions of the Self	9
Who Has a Self?	14
Summary	20
Dichotomies	21
Glossary	21
2. Body Focus	**23**
Private Body Self	24
Body Image	30
Public Self	35
Development	38
Causes of Body Dissatisfaction	40
Disorders	42
Summary	44
Dichotomies	44
Glossary	45

3. Self-Esteem — 47
- Sources — 48
- The Trait of Self-Esteem — 59
- Cognitive Mechanisms — 67
- Development — 76
- Value of Self-Esteem — 80
- Culture: North America and Japan — 82
- Summary — 83
- Dichotomies — 84
- Glossary — 84

4. Identity — 87
- Self-Esteem Versus Identity — 87
- Social Identity — 90
- Personal Identity — 100
- Culture and Identity — 109
- Development — 111
- Individualism and Collectivism — 116
- Summary — 118
- Dichotomies — 119
- Glossary — 119

5. Self-Consciousness — 121
- Private Self-Focus — 124
- Public Self-Consciousness — 131
- Private Versus Public Self-Focus — 134
- Two Factors of Private Self-Awareness — 137
- Theory — 140
- Summary — 150
- Dichotomies — 151
- Glossary — 151

6. Embarrassment — 153
- Blushing — 153
- Other Nonverbal Aspects — 156
- Causes — 159
- Development — 165
- Theories — 169
- Summary — 175
- Dichotomies — 176
- Glossary — 176

7. Shame and Guilt — 177
- Causes of Shame — 178
- Shame Versus Embarrassment — 182
- Theories of Shame and Guilt — 184
- Adult Theories — 185
- Developmental Theories — 201
- Evolutionary Theories — 203
- Summary — 207
- Dichotomies — 208
- Glossary — 208

8. Boundaries I: Privacy — 211
- Self-Disclosure — 212
- Motivation to Self-Disclose — 216
- Personality Traits — 221
- Sex Differences — 226
- Personal Space — 228
- Privacy Components — 229
- Summary — 232
- Dichotomies — 233
- Glossary — 233

9. Boundaries II: Empathy and Altruism — 235
- Empathy — 236
- Determinants of Empathy — 240
- Altruism — 243
- Cost and Benefit — 249
- Development — 250
- Evolution — 251
- Sex Differences — 253
- Summary — 254
- Dichotomies — 254
- Glossary — 255

10. Self-Concepts — 257
- Empirical Self-Concept — 258
- Self-Schemas — 259
- Self-Discrepancies — 263
- Possible Selves — 267
- Self-Presentation — 269
- Summary — 272
- Dichotomies — 273
- Glossary — 273

Glossary	275
References	281
Author Index	313
Subject Index	323
About the Author	334

Preface

This book presupposes some background in psychology, perhaps a few undergraduate courses. I need to write a few words about the construction of the chapters. Each one starts with a brief outline of the chapter. At the end of each chapter, there is (a) a summary, (b) a list of the dimensions/dichotomies that help us understand the facets of the self dealt with in the chapter, and (c) a glossary of terms used in the chapter. (In the text, these are set in bold.) And throughout most chapters, compare-and-contrast tables summarize particular topics.

At the end of the book, there are also features to look for: an overall glossary, a subject index, an author index, and a "References" section, which includes all the references cited throughout the book.

Acknowledgments

Jim Brace-Thompson, my editor, has been encouraging and helpful from the start, and Karen Ehrmann has offered editorial assistance. The book has been improved by the efforts of several reviewers—Daniel M. Ogilvie, Joachim Krueger, and others—who of course are not responsible for any problems that remain.

But the largest debt is to my wife, Ruth, to whom this book is dedicated.

1

Introduction

Early Psychologists Examine the Self
The Concept of Self
Elements of the Self
Dimensions of the Self
Who Has a Self?

In his book, *The Singular Self,* Rom Harré (1998) suggested two underlying ideas about the self: that we have a particular point of view on the world and that we have a sense of being the same person over time and across situations. Brewster Smith (1978) offered a different set of characteristics:

> Selfhood involves being *self-aware* or *reflective;* being or *having* a body; somehow taking into account the *boundaries of selfhood* at birth and death and feeling *continuity* of identity in between; placing oneself in a *generational* sequence and *network of other connected selves* as forebears and descendants and relatives. (p. 1053)

These citations list aspects of the self that surely seem familiar, so much so that we might assume that the self has always occupied a crucial place in human existence. Perhaps not. St. Augustine advanced the belief in a private self that could be self-reflective: "Do not go outward; return within yourself. In the inward man dwells the truth" (quoted in Taylor, 1989, p. 129). But this essentially theological argument had no particular impact on most of the population, who were locked into the rigid constraints of life in the Middle Ages.

The subsequent course of the concept of self in Europe and America has been offered by Roy Baumeister (1987, 1997), who used history and literature to trace how the self became a salient issue. In his view, the modern emphasis on the self in Western society appears to be the most recent stage of a historical sequence that started in the Middle Ages. Then, each person was rooted in an assigned role within the rigid structure of medieval society. There was no place for individualism and therefore no sense of selfhood.

However, during the latter part of the Middle Ages, the religious focus shifted from collective salvation to individual salvation. Such salvation depended on the totality of one's life, which of course is different for each person. From the 16th to 18th centuries, people increasingly became preoccupied with the notion that appearances could be deceiving. There is an underlying, hidden self not known to others but that might be discovered through introspection. The Romantic period of the early 19th century emphasized love and creativity. People were encouraged to look "inside" to discover the true self. In the Victorian era, the remainder of the 19th century, people tended to introspect more, and they became more sensitive to the discrepancy between an outer and inner self.

In the 20th century the trend of introspection continued, and as psychotherapy become pervasive, the need to know oneself intensified. This century saw a waning of religion. Another trend in 20th-century Western life is a sharp drop in stable, extended families, thereby diminishing what might be called the *collective self.* This trend, together with greater choices and opportunities for many people, has strengthened the belief in personal uniqueness. In America especially, our cherished individuality is rejected as immature by those who live elsewhere: "Other cultures do not insist on so sharp a separation of the self from the nonself. The I of Western man sticks out like a stubbed thumb. In other cultures it blends more readily with nature and society" (Allport, 1961, p. 116).

Riesman (1950) suggested another 20th-century trend. Modern industrialized societies function better when people are attuned to others' cues, more influenced by *inter*personal needs and group goals than by personal needs and goals. Such people, called **other-directed,** have a predominantly *social* self. Their identity is defined principally by social roles, relationships, and affiliations. They have no internal gyroscope but instead tend to "go along to get along."

The self as other-directed fits neatly into a sociological perspective, so it is not surprising that sociologists have defined the self this way. At the turn of the 20th century, Cooley (1902) developed the idea of the **looking-glass self.** Presumably, you use the reaction of others to determine precisely who you are, just as you appraise your appearance in a mirror. Mead (1934) took the idea one step further, assuming that who you are derives from taking the perspective of others toward yourself. Then you regard yourself as others regard you, internalizing what was once an external audience. Later, Goffman (1959) added the stage metaphor, suggesting that the self develops through self-presentation in a manner analogous to a stage actor playing a role. These ideas, collectively called *symbolic interactionism,* have strongly influenced psychologists, especially social psychologists, who study the self.

Early Psychologists Examine the Self

William James (1890), who wrote extensively about the self, analyzed it in two different ways. First, there is the I-self versus the me-self. The *I-self* is the knower, taking in information and processing it. If the I-self represents cognitive *processes,* the *me-self* represents the *contents* of the self: our feelings and evaluations about our bodies, our talents, and about ourselves in general. More of this distinction later.

James had an alternative analysis, dividing the self into three components. There is the **material self,** which consists of possessions in the home and elsewhere. Why are these listed as part of the self? Presumably, they are part of the self because they offer psychological meaning to the word *mine.* Thus, some men treasure their cars enough to take pride in them and to grieve when they are damaged or wither with age. And for some women, household possessions are similarly valued. Thus, these material goods may represent *extensions* of self.

The *social self* refers to the various social roles we adopt when with others: parents, children, friends, and coworkers. In this sense, we have many selves, one each for the various people we deal with. This kind of Jamesian self surely influenced Cooley (1902) when he formulated the looking-glass self, as well as today's sociologists.

The *spiritual self* consists of thoughts and feelings about who we are, how we originated, and what our ultimate destiny is. Typically, these thoughts are associated with wonder and awe and tend to occur in the context of religion and God. This spiritual component may be regarded as an inner or private self, in contrast to the outer material and social selves.

James was credited by Gordon Allport (1961) with anticipating his own more detailed analysis of the self into seven aspects. The *bodily self* consists of sensations arising from inside the body, which establishes the difference between me and not-me:

> Picture yourself sucking the blood from a prick in your finger; then imagine sucking blood from a bandage around your finger. What you perceive as belonging ultimately to your body is warm and welcome; what you perceive as separate becomes instantly cold and foreign. (p. 114)

Self-identity refers to the feeling of continuity over time that all of us experience. Biologically, you are not the same person you were as a child, for most of the cells of your body have turned over. And your adult appearance surely is different from your childhood body and face. Yet you feel as though you are the same person now as then.

Next on Allport's list is *self-esteem,* which refers to how much or how little you like yourself, value yourself, or feel confident about yourself—a concept so familiar that it needs no elaboration here.

Extension of self incorporates James's material self but also encompasses possessions and family members and those close to you. What happens to them is to some extent vicariously experienced by you, as manifested in empathic feelings and altruistic behavior.

By **self-image,** Allport seems to refer to the ideal self: what your parents and other socialization agents want you to be. This ideal self is compared with what you actually are, the discrepancy tending to buffet your self-esteem. This conception is related to another idea of James: the ratio between aspiration and achievement.

Allport's sixth aspect of the self is *rational coper,* which appears to be the adolescent version of the issue of identity, as revealed by the following questions that are presumably asked by adolescents: "Just who am I?" and "Am I a child or adult?" (p. 124).

Allport's last aspect of the self is **propriate striving,** meaning some sense of purpose, a central theme of life. Perhaps a few people possess such a dominant, overarching purpose in life, but most do not.

The Concept of Self

The writings of James and Allport continue to influence some current approaches to the self. James's distinction between the I-self and the me-self is still alive. Thus, the I-self may be viewed as a constructor of the me-self (Harter, 1988). A slightly different approach sees the I-self as being aware that we are perceiving and thinking versus the me-self as involving the self-referent thoughts themselves (Brown, 1998). An earlier version of the I-self is Allport's (1961) idea of the self as rational coper, which assumes that each of us tries to use reason in dealing with the environment.

The problem, as I see it, is that the concept of the I-self implicitly equates self with person. Indeed, one of the several dictionary definitions of self is *person*. In everyday usage, we might say, "I'm not myself today." Or we may behave differently toward a boss than to a worker, differently in a courtroom than in a tavern, which might be interpreted as our having several selves. But we know that a chimpanzee behaves differently with a dominant animal than with a subordinate animal, differently with a male than with a female, yet we do not refer to chimpanzee *selves*. We should not equate self with person in humans for the same reason we do not do it in chimpanzees: It blurs the distinction between self-related behavior and other behavior.

At issue here is how to define self-related behavior, which in my view must be done in a way that distinguishes it from nonself behavior, for otherwise there would be no reason for a book devoted to the self. So the self as knower, the I-self, will be considered in this book only when the focus of knowing is directed toward the me-self (more of this issue shortly).

Defining the Self

I suggest two defining characteristics of self-related behavior. The first involves the *boundary between me and not me*. Each of us knows that we have sensations that are not open to observation by others: the tastes, smells, and pains that are part of private experience. These sensations are part of the self as knower but with the restriction that we are aware that the sensations are entirely private, not shared with others. In addition to these sensations, the self-boundary is also *spatial*: an area around our bodies, personal space, which is narrow or broad (Hall, 1966). And there is Allport's (1961) idea of the *psychological* extension of self, which involves identifying with others or sharing experiences vicariously. It bears repeating that in an individualistic society such as the United States, the self is sharply defined:

> We think of ourselves as people with frontiers, our personalities divided from each others as our bodies visibly are. Whatever ties of love and loyalty may bind us to other people, we remain centrally aware that we have an inner being of our own, a unique biography and consciousness—that we are individuals. (Kitzinger, 1992, p. 228)

The second defining characteristic of self-related behavior is *focusing on oneself.* For example, if I evaluate you, that is social behavior, but if I evaluate myself, I am the evaluator and the person being judged. If I listen to you, that is ordinary perceptual behavior, but if I listen to an audiotape of myself, I am the listener and the person being listened to. More generally, the self as knower is relevant to self-related behavior only when the process of knowing is directed toward the me-self. Simultaneously being the cognizer and that which is cognized is precisely the *self-reflexiveness* that attracts us to the study of the self, differentiating it from other areas of psychology.

These two characteristics, boundaries of the self and self-focus, are regarded here as hallmarks of the concept of the self. They serve to demarcate self-related behavior from other kinds of social behavior, personality-related behavior, or general cognitive processes. And this concept of self serves to limit what is included in this book.

An example of the difference between *self-directed* behavior and behavior directed toward the social or physical environment may be found in how we construe ourselves versus how we construe others (McGuire & McGuire, 1986):

1. Being aware of an inner self, we focus more on the *covert* aspects of ourselves, but we focus more on the *overt* aspects of others.

2. Similarly, knowing about our own *cognitions,* we think about them more than *emotions,* which can so easily be observed in others.

3. Being aware of ourselves when alone, we are relatively more aware of the *physical* actions we take (e.g., eating). Being aware of others only in social contexts, we focus more on their *social* actions (e.g., talking).

4. The self is familiar to us, which means we can more easily think about ourselves in terms of *what we are not.* Thinking in affirmative terms is known to be much easier, and others are much less familiar to us, which is why we tend to think of others mainly as *what they are.* The importance of familiarity was confirmed by Prentice (1990).

Elements of the Self

To understand how the body works, we must regard it as a conglomeration of organ systems: digestive, cardiovascular, respiratory, and so on. These elements comprise physiology. Similarly, to understand the self, we must regard it as a conglomeration of different contents or facets; they are the elements that comprise the self. In what follows, I am adhering to the twin characteristics used to define the self: boundaries and self-reflexiveness.

Body Focus

The first and perhaps most basic sense of self is the distinction between self and other: the boundary where your body ends and the environment starts. This knowledge starts in infancy, but only much later is it discovered that your voice sounds different to you than it does to others, the reason being that each person benefits from bone conduction of vibrations from the throat. Even at this basic level of what is heard, we have a sense of our own bodies that is not available to others. And each of us has a body image, a vague idea of what our body looks like, which is not necessarily the same as what others see. Thus, some young women see themselves as overweight when others see them as slim. The point is that reactions to other persons' bodies are different from self-reactions to one's body, with such reflexivity being one of the two defining features of the self.

Self-Esteem

This is the evaluative component of the self, which involves several questions. How worthwhile am I? Do I feel like a success or a failure? Do I like myself? Am I satisfied with the way I am or do I want to change? Am I confident or unsure of myself? My answers to these questions may be different from the assessments others make of me, the extremes of such discrepancies being humility and conceit.

Identity

Some time during adolescence the following question arises: "Who am I?" There may be several answers to this question: a feeling of uniqueness, being special and different from everyone else; a feeling of belonging to a family or other social group; awareness of one's ethnic heritage; or being so involved with others or with a cause that there is a kind of merging of oneself with others. Any of these answers is likely to lend meaning to life. For some social scientists, awareness is crucial:

> Identity is a coherent sense of self. It depends upon the awareness that one's endeavors and one's life make sense, that they are meaningful in the context in which life is lived. It depends also upon stable values, and upon the conviction that one's actions and values are harmoniously related. It is a sense of wholeness, of integration. (Wheelis, 1958, p. 19)

However, some people are so totally submerged in their social identity—as members of a family or of a tight, traditional culture—that they are unaware of their identity but nevertheless are strongly bound by it.

Self-Consciousness

Attention may be focused on ourselves, but what is the target of such focus? It may be on inner life: sensations, emotions, motives, and fantasies that may remain a secret to anyone else. We are especially aware of this inner self when it conflicts with the demands of social behavior—for example, when the food is bad but it is a social necessity for a guest to compliment the cook. More typically, though, awareness of the private aspects of the self occurs when we are alone, for when we are with others, our senses and attention are directed mainly to events outside ourselves.

Alternatively, the focus may be on appearance and social behavior, which may be observed by others. An important part of the **socialization** of children is training them to become aware of themselves as social objects. As a result, social behavior often involves a split focus: on what we see in others (nonself) and what we think others are seeing in us (self).

Embarrassment

When with others, we sometimes feel conspicuous and therefore embarrassed. Or we are the focus of attention, which may cause blushing. Or we make a trivial social error and experience embarrassment. Common to these reactions is an acute awareness of the self as a social object, together with a mild negative emotion.

Shame and Guilt

These intense, self-focused emotions involve negative self-attributions that range from "I have done something seriously wrong" to "I am a bad person." This is the essence of self-reflexiveness: You are both the prosecutor and the accused. How people develop such self-accusations is a matter for further inquiry.

Boundaries I: Privacy

The nonobservable parts of the self may remain hidden or they may be made available to others, which implies that there is a boundary between self and nonself. Why would I reveal contents of my inner life to others?

One reason is to test reality by disclosing inner emotions, memories, or ambitions. Another reason is to reciprocate another person's disclosure because mutual disclosure enhances friendship and intimacy. Or perhaps I am simply bursting to tell someone else about my private thoughts and feelings.

What are the reasons for keeping quiet about one's private self? Perhaps others are just not interested and would be bored by a recital of body sensations, esthetic feelings, or private thoughts. But there may be a more serious reason for remaining silent: a history of ridicule or shaming behavior from others, which would make you become secretive about your inner life.

How important is privacy: not being seen or overheard? How much of my body may be seen or touched by others? The answers to these questions involve whether the boundary between ourselves and others is tight or loose, whether one is closed or open.

Boundaries II: Empathy and Altruism

The boundary of the self is also an issue here in the sense of extension of self. We may empathize with the plight of another person or vicariously share another's happiness. And we may reach out beyond self-interest to engage in altruistic behavior.

Or we may not extend ourselves, maintaining a sharp distinction between self and other, as reflected in being unsympathetic, being uncaring, and behaving selfishly.

Self-Concepts and Self-Schemas

Some of us have imaginary selves, which may never become realized but are different from the "real self" we implicitly or explicitly know. One example is the ideal self, a goal of our aspirations. Discrepancies between any of these imagined selves and the real self may serve to motivate change or may reflect maladjustment.

Dimensions of the Self

An excursion into maps will introduce this section. Imagine a map of the United States. If we impose weather conditions on this map, there is a temperature dimension that runs from the cold of Minnesota southward to the heat of Texas, and there is a moisture dimension that runs from the wetness of Florida to the dryness of Nevada.

Now apply the mapping metaphor to the self. I am postulating particular *psychological* dimensions that may serve as cognitive tools, helping us to understand different facets of the self. For ease of exposition, they will be discussed as dichotomies, just as temperature may be discussed in terms of the extremes of hot and cold.

Personal-Social Dichotomies

The term *personal* refers to issues of concern to you and usually no one else. The term *social* refers to self-related issues that in some way involve others. If there is a single dimension that applies to virtually all aspects of the self, it is reflected in the personal-social dichotomy. This overarching distinction includes several subordinate dichotomies.

As mentioned earlier, when you attend to yourself, you may focus on aspects of the self that only you know about. Or you may focus on your dress, demeanor, or social behavior, which can be observed by others. In both instances, you may be keenly aware of yourself, but the direction of your attention is different: on the observable versus the nonobservable aspects of yourself. This is the *private-public* dichotomy. The private self

> consists of somewhat different material for every person—past experiences, feelings about the self and others, latent fears or personal needs.... But this sort of knowledge is not ordinarily shared unless the need is great or confidence in the other person is high. (Barnlund, 1975, p. 33)

The public self consists of the behavior and appearance open to observation by others. Barnlund (1975) suggested that the Japanese self consists more of the public aspects, whereas the American self consists more of the private aspects.

Subsequent research provided a factual basis for the private-public distinction. Participants were asked to write about their thoughts, feelings, or emotions (private) and their observable behavior and actions (public). The descriptions of the private self were fuller, more distinctive, and written more quickly than the descriptions of the public self.

Like most people, you probably believe that you are in some ways different from everyone else. Yet, each of us is at least partially defined by belonging to collectives of people: family, community, ethnic group, and nationality. The dichotomy here involves self-definition: *individual-group*. This distinction is crucial in our attempts to understand identity: Is it largely defined by your individuality and feeling of uniqueness (personal) or by your membership and feeling of affiliating with a group (social)?

It is a truism that nevertheless must be stated: Pleasant events and rewards make people happy. But you may also share the happiness of someone else who is rewarded. Thus, at a wedding, the happiness of the bride and groom is shared by relatives and friends. This distinction is reflected in the *direct-vicarious* dichotomy. You may be happy, sad, or angry because of events that befall you (direct), or you may experience these emotions because they are occurring in someone else (vicarious); an example of the latter is empathy. Vicarious feelings typically occur when there is a social bond among people but may also occur among strangers.

These three dichotomies—private-public, individual-group, and direct-vicarious—should help us understand several aspects of the self. As will be seen, they come up in a number of chapters. However, they do not exhaust the dimensions underlying the personal-social dichotomy. Two other dichotomies assume importance for only one or two topics.

Let us start with the *open-closed* dichotomy. Why do you reveal contents of your inner life to others? You are aware of your own subjectivity, which may distort your perception of events. One way of testing reality is to disclose thoughts, memories, or ambitions.

Some people who do not wish to reveal themselves to others may hide their true self, the way an actor does when playing a role on stage, which involves the *inner-outer* dichotomy. For example, some children and adults play the role of clown when with others, and this surface presentation, something like a mask, conceals the personality underneath. This dichotomy is also relevant to body focus: internal sensations (inner) versus body image (outer).

The inner-outer dichotomy is made more salient when emotions are inhibited and when private cognitions remain secret. An intense awareness of self occurs when the urge to reveal a private aspect of the self is opposed by counterpressure to keep the private aspect covert. The underlying assumption here is that *any* discrepancy or conflict between different aspects of the self results in a greater self-awareness.

The personal-social dichotomies are summarized in Table 1.1. The three at the top of the table are broad in scope in the sense of applying to several areas of the self. They are basic dimensions of the self. The two at the bottom of the table apply to only one or two areas of the self.

General Dichotomies

Beyond the personal-social dichotomy, there are other dimensions of the self, which I have gathered under the heading of *general dichotomies*.

TABLE 1.1 Personal-Social Dichotomies

> Broader in scope
> Private-public: self-consciousness
> Individual-group: identity
> Direct-vicarious: empathy
>
> Narrower in scope
> Open-closed: self-disclosure
> Inner-outer: body focus

Is there one self or are there many selves? Both William James and Gordon Allport referred to several different selves, and sociologists suggest that there are as many selves as the social roles we play in everyday life. But what about the experiencing person? Do you feel as though you possess several selves or just one?

At issue here is the *unitary-multiple* dichotomy. Some scholars insist that the self is multiple:

> A unitary "self" has philosophical charms, but can hardly embrace all the modes of reflexive thought and conduct that we refer to by "self-" and "-self" terms. All that such compound terms have in common is reflexivity: instead of having someone else as a target, the thoughts and actions in question, *in some way or other,* turn back on the agent. The specific target of this "turning back" is not the same in all cases: it may be directed at any feature of an agent's habits or feelings, personality, body or skills. (The terms "self-esteem," self-awareness," and "self-abuse" point to quite different features of the individual concerned!) (Toulmin, 1986, p. 52)

Clearly, there are multiple aspects of the self, as may be seen in the various chapters of this book. These are separate elements of the self, each requiring different approaches and methods of study, but each of us has a feeling of being a unified self. Let me make the point with another example: self-esteem. As you will see, there are several different sources of self-esteem—for example, achieving success, belonging to a group that achieves success, or being liked by others. At the same time, each of us has a sense of global self-esteem, an overall self-evaluation, which is more than the sum of the sources of self-esteem. We should therefore consider self-esteem from both perspectives, examining it as both multiple and as unitary. This issue may also be relevant to identity:

> The challenge of identity demands that the modern adult construct a narrative of the self . . . to suggest that (1) despite its many facets, the me is coher-

ent and unified and (2) despite the many changes that attend the passage of time, the me of the past led up to or set the stage for the me of the present, which in turn will lead to or set the stage for the me of the future. (McAdams, 1997, p. 63)

This quotation makes the case not only for unity but also for continuity, a feeling that you are the same person now that you were last year or a decade ago. But in some respects, you are not the same person. This example involves the *continuity-discontinuity* dichotomy. There may be discontinuity, for example, if you have moved from childhood to adolescence, your body has assumed a very different shape, and you have acquired secondary sex characteristics. Yet you are the same person. Is this an illusion? Perhaps, but consider this:

For anyone who experiences annihilation anxiety, who fears that his or her sense of self is disintegrating, the existence of self is not a matter for philosophical debate. The feeling that the self is becoming fragmented, transformed, or annihilated evokes the most terrible anxiety that anyone is likely to experience. The apprehension of self that is continuous over time is thus not any illusion . . . but something that is essential to our existence. (Modell, 1993, p. 12)

Some issues involving the self are more important than others. This is the *central-peripheral* dichotomy, which may be traced to the writings of William James (1890). Consider various sources of self-esteem. Athletic ability is sure to be crucial to the self-esteem of a professional football player, but musical ability is likely to be trivial. For a violinist, musical ability is surely a strong determinant of self-esteem but not athletic ability. If you were forced to choose which body part would be surgically removed, you might say the little toe of the left foot (peripheral) but certainly not the left kidney (central). And there are likely to be sex differences in which parts of the body are more central.

A philosopher once suggested that an unexamined life is not worth living. Is this true, or are there people who appear to have a good life though they pay no attention to themselves? And we know that some depressed people introspect often, perhaps too often. So perhaps there is no connection between examining your life and its being worthwhile. Of greater relevance here is the fact that people differ greatly in their self-attention. The appropriate dichotomy is *aware-unaware*.

In addition to these four general dichotomies, which apply to several areas of the self, minor dichotomies are particularly useful in understanding a single area of the self or, at most, two areas. One is the *dependable-undependable* dichotomy. Some people are entirely confident that they can deal with any situation, but others cannot trust them-

TABLE 1.2 Dichotomies of Self: General

Broader in scope
- Unitary-multiple: self-esteem
- Continuous-discontinuous: identity
- Central-peripheral: body
- Aware-unaware: self-consciousness

Narrower in scope
- Dependable-undependable: body
- Positive-negative: identity

selves to cope. Consider the body. We rely on our bodies to sustain us and not let us down, but people with diabetes do not have the same confidence. We expect our bodies not to betray us, but some people are never sure when they will blush or sweat excessively or even faint.

If you can depend on yourself, you probably like who you are. If you cannot depend on yourself, you might devalue yourself. This dichotomy is *positive-negative,* which of course is a basic dimension of self-esteem. The dichotomy is also relevant to identity. You may affiliate with a highly regarded group such as high school merit scholars or the winning college football team. Or you may be a member of a group that is scorned by many people (a motorcycle gang) or despised by most people (Ku Klux Klan). A negative social identity may be strong because the group is attacked (circle the wagons), but continued censure from society may eventually erode a negative identity, rendering it less stable and less dependable.

The general dichotomies of the self, with examples, are summarized in Table 1.2. Again, the dichotomies are divided into two categories. The first four are broad in scope—basic dimensions underlying several areas of the self. Thus, the unitary-multiple dichotomy may be usefully applied to understanding body focus, self-esteem, identity, self-disclosure, and self-concepts. The second group of two dichotomies is narrower in scope, applying to one or two areas of the self.

Who Has a Self?

Do animals have a self? Do human infants? The answer to both questions is yes. But do they have the same kind of self as adult humans? My answer

Introduction 15

is no. I distinguish between two kinds of self: a primitive self that human adults share with infants and animals versus an advanced self that is unique to older human children and adults.

Primitive Self

Body Boundary

As mentioned earlier, you are aware of the boundary of your body: where your feet end and the floor begins, where your fingers end and this book begins, and where pain arises inside your body versus where pain originates outside your body. This distinction between you and not-you, which is acquired during infancy, involves a particular kind of awareness. Awareness of external stimuli can be studied without recourse to a concept of self, but awareness of the private events that can be sensed only by you is special. It is one reason why self-related behavior is studied differently from other behavior.

Double Stimulation

If someone were to put a hand on your arm, you would duly record being touched. If you put your right hand on your left arm, the left arm registers being touched, and the right hand registers that it is touching the left arm. In this self-induced stimulation, part of you is active and part of you is passive. Clearly, such double stimulation is different from the single stimulation of being touched by another person or of touching another person.

Mirror Image Recognition

When you look in a mirror, you know that the image is yours. What does this capability of self-recognition involve? Gallup (1977) assumed that a sense of identity is required:

> The unique feature of mirror-image stimulation is that the identity of the observer and his reflection are necessarily one and the same. The capacity to correctly infer the identity of the reflection must, therefore, presuppose an already existent identity on the part of the organism making the inference. (p. 334)

In pioneering research, Gallup (1970) demonstrated that chimpanzees are capable of self-recognition when presented with a mirror. He and others had informally observed chimpanzees behaving as though they recognized themselves in a mirror. Young, wild-born chimpanzees were placed in a small room that had only a mirror in it. For the first few days, they responded to the mirror image with social behavior, which implies that they perceived the mirror image as another animal. Thereafter, they groomed parts of the body they could not otherwise see, picked food from their teeth, blew bubbles, and made faces—behavior that strongly suggests recognition of self.

Gallup (1970) continued with a more controlled experiment. Older chimpanzees were anesthetized and red dots were placed above one eyebrow ridge and at the top of the opposite ear of each unconscious animal. After the chimpanzees regained consciousness, the mirror was again introduced. They repeatedly attempted to touch the red dots on their own heads and spent an inordinate amount of time looking at themselves in the mirror.

Gallup's (1977) summary of his own and others' experiments on **mirror image recognition of self** in other animals revealed that it had been demonstrated in chimpanzees and orangutans but not in baboons or any species of monkeys. Since then, mirror image recognition has been studied in detail across a variety of species, and, according to an entire volume on the subject (Parker, Mitchell, & Boccia, 1994), self-recognition is limited to these nonhuman higher primates: chimpanzees, bonobos, orangutans, and gorillas.

Does it follow, as Gallup implied, that these animals have the same sense of self that humans have? Not necessarily:

> Sometimes mirror self-recognition is viewed as indicative of the whole array of the diverse types of self-awareness found in humans—imagining ourselves recognizing others' perspectives on us, and evaluating ourselves according to their perspectives. . . . It is more parsimonious to suggest, however, that the kinesthetic-visual matching likely responsible for MSR [mirror self-recognition] creates a self-representation of a very specific and more limited sort—one that can be used to imagine and recognize ourselves. (Mitchell, 1994, p. 90)

Research on humans has shown that recognition of mirror images follows a developmental sequence in early childhood. Amsterdam (1972) placed infants of different ages before a mirror and observed their reactions. At 14 months of age, one or two infants started to admire themselves. Five of 12 infants in the 15- to 17-month age range displayed this reaction, 7 of 12 infants in the 18- to 20-month range, and 11 of 16 infants in the 21- to 24-month range.

Bertenthal and Fischer (1978) confirmed these findings. At about 6 months, they found that infants could touch a part of themselves while looking at their mirror image. At about 8 months, when an infant is placed in front of a mirror while dressed in a vest with a hat projecting over the head, the infant immediately looks up or tries to grab the hat. At roughly 10 months, when a toy that can be seen only in a mirror is lowered from the ceiling, an infant turns directly toward the toy rather than looking at the mirror image. At approximately 18 months of age, when a dot of rouge is applied to the infant's face and the infant looks in the mirror, he or she touches the face and says that there is something different about it. Finally, 2-year-old children, when asked, "Who's that?" (indicating the child's mirror image) say "me" or state their name. It seems reasonable to conclude that the norm for recognition of oneself is roughly 18 to 24 months of age (see also Asendorpf & Baudonniere, 1993; Cameron & Gallup, 1988; Lewis & Brooks-Gunn, 1979).

Though mirror image recognition is a primitive sense of self in comparison to the advanced senses of self to be described, it occurs only among the great apes and appears in humans only during late infancy. It therefore represents the outcome of a higher level of intellect than awareness of **body boundary** and **double stimulation.**

Advanced Self

The facts of body boundary, double stimulation, and self-recognition provide a rationale for a concept of self: a self that is shared by humans and the great apes. If only body boundary and double stimulation are considered, other mammals may also share this kind of self. But it is a primitive kind of self, at least in relation to the **advanced self** that is seen only in humans and, among them, only in older children and adults who possess the necessary cognitive capabilities. Three kinds of behavior sustain the need for the concept of an advanced self, each kind being a cognitive parallel of the more sensory behavior that defines the primitive self we share with animals.

Covertness

The first, parallel to body boundary, is *covertness*. Each of us is aware of a private self, consisting of cognitions among other things: daydreams, feelings, memories, and grandiose ambitions that no one else can know directly. Early in childhood, we learn to keep most of these cognitions to ourselves. We also gradually learn that covert feelings of affection or love may cause embarrassment if expressed openly and that the emotions of fear and anger may cause ridicule or anger from others if they become aware of them. When we are suppressing cognitions, feelings, or just opinions (laughing at the boss's unfunny joke), we become especially aware of the dichotomy between the private self and the public self.

Self-Evaluation

Another example of an advanced self is cognitive or affective *self-evaluation*. When another person praises you or thinks you are worthwhile, the evaluator and the recipient are two different people. But in self-esteem you are both evaluator and object of evaluation. In this respect, self-esteem is analogous to double stimulation (your hand touches your arm). Double stimulation is sensory, representing a primitive self, but self-esteem is cognitive, representing an advanced self. Animals are aware of double stimulation but lack the advanced cognitions needed for self-esteem.

Though there is no evidence of self-esteem in animals, might they still be capable of such self-evaluation? Admittedly, animals might have more cognitive abilities than we know, but we must be wary of the seductive trap of attributing human qualities such as self-attributions to animals. A conservative approach seems best here: Until there is evidence that animals have the self-esteem we know that humans have, we must assume that they do not.

Identity

The last example of an advanced self is *identity*. Humans tend to know who they are or try to discover who they are. The search may involve discerning your affiliations, the nature of your character, or the continuity of your life. It may extend into seeking the meaning of your life or descend into existential anxiety. Thus, attempting to establish your identity is in one respect parallel to self-esteem: You are both the searcher-evaluator and the recipient.

The issue of identity is also parallel to mirror image recognition, but there is a crucial difference. In self-recognition, there is a *perceptual* match between one's own body and the image in the mirror, an example of a primitive, **sensory self.** In identity, there is a higher-order cognitive characterization of oneself or a search for such a characterization that goes beyond perception and into *conception*. Animals and human infants do not possess the cognitive ability required for this kind of advanced, cognitive self, but older human children and adults do.

Introduction

TABLE 1.3 Primitive Versus Advanced Self

	Primitive	*Advanced*
Kind of self	Sensory	Cognitive
Bases	Body boundary	Covertness
	Double stimulation	Self-esteem
	Mirror image recognition	Identity
Occurs in	Animals, human infants	Human children, adults

Primitive Versus Advanced Self

In brief, there are three instances of an advanced self, each analogous to an instance of a primitive self (see Table 1.3). Among humans, the primitive self develops in infancy. The earliest distinction is between me and not-me. Once this body boundary has been established, the infant can become aware of the difference between stimulation and double stimulation. The last aspect of the primitive self to appear is (mirror) self-recognition, which occurs during the second year of life. Such self-recognition represents a higher intellectual achievement than the first two aspects of a primitive sense of self, for as we have seen, mirror self-recognition occurs only in the great apes and develops in humans only in the second year of life. Thus, mirror self-recognition represents the peak of a primitive sense of self, but it does not imply the presence of an advanced, cognitive self.

This conclusion, first suggested some time ago (A. H. Buss, 1980), now has been sustained by research important enough to be described in detail. Povinelli, Landau, and Perilloux (1996) pointed out that recognizing oneself in a mirror involves only *simultaneous* recognition but not the kind of self-recognition present when there is a *continuity of self over time*. In the first experiment, children played a game in which the goal was to find small stickers. When a child found one, the experimenter patted the child's head, surreptitiously planting a sticker on the front of the child's hair. This sequence was videotaped and played back to the child. Would the child reach up for the sticker on his or her head? These were the results:

2-year-olds—0 of 10 reached up

3-year-olds—4 of 16 reached up

4-year-olds—12 of 16 reached up

In the second experiment, a Polaroid photo was taken of the experimenter secretly placing the sticker on the child's head. Then the child was shown the photo, and these were the results:

35 to 40 months of age—2 of 15 reached up

41 to 46 months of age—9 of 15 reached up

47 to 52 months of age—12 of 15 reached up

53 to 58 months of age—14 of 15 reached up

The two experiments converge on roughly 4 years as the age at which most children (12 of 15) can accomplish recognition of self when it is delayed: about 2 years later than immediate mirror image recognition. This 2-year difference, Povinelli et al. (1996) concluded, "is the result of a developmental lag between the emergence of an 'on-line' self-concept and a self-concept that includes the temporal contiguity of the self" (pp. 1551-1552). Evidently, it requires advanced cognitions to link what happened to the self earlier in time—in the experiment, just a few minutes—to what the self is now. Two-year-olds lack such advanced cognitions; 4-year-olds have them. Similarly, 2-year-olds cannot remember events that occurred many months earlier, but 4-year-olds possess this ability, called *autobiographical memory* (Nelson, 1993).

These issues are linked to the period of *representative intelligence* (Piaget, 1950) that starts in children at about 2 years of age and is well on its way by 4 years of age. During this period, autobiographical memory develops, enabling the 4-year-old child to link present self with past self. At the same time, a sense of covertness develops, as the child becomes keenly aware of the discrepancy between the private self and the public self, between covert truth and overt lies. Self-esteem probably emerges next, followed by an interest in identity. These developments gradually accumulate to form the advanced sense of self present in older children and adults.

SUMMARY

1. The concept of self has changed during the past several hundred years of Western history, attaining its modern form late in the 19th century when William James outlined a material self, a social self, and a spiritual self.

2. Gordon Allport's list of components of the self included bodily self, identity, self-esteem, extension of self, self-image, and propriate striving.
3. The domain of the self, as distinguished from other behavior, is defined by two features: *self-reflexiveness* and a *boundary* between me and not-me.
4. A set of dimensions of the self, framed as dichotomies, may be used as aids to understanding the self. The most comprehensive dimension of the self is personal-social.
5. We share with other animals a primitive sense of self, which includes body boundary, double stimulation, and mirror image recognition.
6. Only humans possess an advanced sense of self, which includes self-evaluation, identity, and understanding covertness.

DICHOTOMIES

aware-unaware: for example, self-consciousness
central-peripheral: for example, body image
continuity-discontinuity: for example, identity
dependable-undependable: for example, embarrassment
direct-vicarious: for example, empathy
individual-group: for example, identity
inner-outer: for example, self-disclosure
open-closed: for example, privacy
personal-social: for example, identity
positive-negative: for example, body image
private-public: for example, self-consciousness
unitary-multiple: for example, identity

GLOSSARY

advanced self   the self observed in older children and adults (e.g., identity)

body boundary me versus not-me

double stimulation you are both the perceiver and the object of perception

looking-glass self the idea that the self is based on others' reactions to you

material self the self extended to one's possessions

mirror image recognition of self part of the primitive self

other-directed a predominantly social identity—go along to get along

propriate striving seeking a central theme of life

self-image the self that you might be

sensory self the primitive self seen in animals and human infants

socialization preparing the young for adult social life

2

Body Focus

Private Body Self
Body Image
Public Self
Development
Causes of Body Dissatisfaction
Disorders

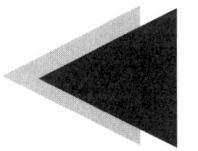

> *The image of the human body means the picture of our own body which we form in our mind, that is to say, the way in which the body appears to ourselves. There are sensations which are given to us. . . . Beyond that there is the immediate experience that there is a unity of the body. This unity is perceived, yet it is more than a perception. We call it a schema of our body or bodily schema. . . . The body schema is the tri-dimensional image everybody has about himself. We may call it the "body image."*
> —Schilder (1950, p. 11)

In current usage, there are more psychological aspects of the body than are included in Schilder's (1950) "body image," so this chapter has a more inclusive title: "Body Focus." Body Focus encompasses cognitions about identity, physical condition, and strength. These topics will be discussed in the section called "Body Image." We also have perceptions and cognitions about our bodies that no one else may ever discover: the private body self. And cognitions about the appearance of the body and evaluation of it are also part of body focus. Accordingly, the chapter is divided into three major sections: private body self, body image, and public body self.

Private Body Self

Body Boundary

We are all aware of where the body ends and the environment begins, but this boundary was assumed to be especially important by psychoanalysts early in the past century. For example, Federn (1926) speculated that the body boundary is crucial to the development of reality testing. This and other psychoanalytic ideas spurred research on the exterior versus the interior of the body, summarized in two books (Fisher, 1970, 1986). Some people focus on the interior: heart, lungs, and digestive system. Others focus on the exterior: muscles and skin. They are typically not aware of these tendencies, and it usually requires instructions or manipulations to get most people to focus on the inside of the body. Virtually all the research on the interior-exterior of the body has used responses to the **Rorschach** ink blots. Fisher (1986) called them *barrier responses,* in which a surface is covered or protected: "The Barrier category embraces references to clothing, animals with unusual skins, overhanging or protective surfaces, buildings, vehicles, animals with container characteristics (e.g., kangaroo), and enclosing geographical formations" (p. 331). People with many of these Rorschach responses are assumed to focus on the exterior of their bodies, and people with few such responses are assumed to focus on the interior. These assumptions were tested in different ways.

Fisher and Fisher (1964) described four experiments, all with college students.

1. Participants were given a list of these terms: *skin, muscle* (both exterior), *stomach,* and *heart* (both interior). During a 5-minute period, they were to check whenever one of these body areas produced a sensation. The sum of interior sensations was subtracted from the sum of exterior sensations, and this score was correlated with Rorschach **barrier scores.** For two samples of participants, the correlations were both .33.

2. Participants were asked to *recall* sensations, and again the exterior minus interior score was correlated with barrier responses. The correlations for two samples were .15 and .47.

3. Participants were told that a drug they ingested would cause physiological changes, and they were to report which changes occurred. The exterior minus interior changes were correlated with barrier scores. The correlations were .33 for men and .11 for women.
4. Participants were shown a list of phrases describing skin, muscles (exterior), heart, or stomach (interior) and later asked to recall the phrases. Exterior minus interior recall correlated .52 and .38 for the two samples.

Notice that some of the correlations are so low as to suggest no relationship between barrier scores and relevant variables. But most of the findings indicated a significant relationship between focusing on the exterior versus interior parts of the body and barrier responses. As to why there are variations in the findings, one possibility is that some individuals are so unaware of their bodies that attempts to relate their body focus to Rorschach responses must fail. Do individuals vary in such awareness? Yes, as we shall see shortly.

In a different approach, objective measures of physiological activity were related to barrier scores (Davis, 1960). Participants were divided into those with many barrier responses (Highs) and those with few such responses (Lows). Their pulse rates (heart) and muscle action potentials (muscles) were recorded while they were first at rest and then when they were stressed by failing a task. At rest, the muscle action potentials of the Highs (exterior focus) were greater than the Lows (interior focus), and the pulse rates of the Lows (interior focus) were higher than those of the Highs (exterior focus). Next, the elevations of these physiological measures from rest to stress were compared for the two groups. Participants with an exterior focus had greater increases in muscle action potentials, and participants with an interior focus had greater increases in heart rate.

Suppose individuals were induced to focus on the exterior versus the interior of the body. Would their Rorschach barrier responses be affected? To find out, Van de Mark and Neuringer (1969) had one group of participants hold arms and then legs horizontally for a minute; use an electric vibrator on the neck, shoulders, and arms; and immerse a hand in cold water (exterior focus). Another group of participants swallowed a little crushed ice, drank warm cola, and listened to their heartbeat (interior focus). When they were subsequently administered the Rorschach ink blots, the participants induced to have an exterior focus had higher barrier scores than the interior focus participants.

A concern with the exterior of the body should also be related to a concern about the public (exterior) aspects of the body, a topic soon to be discussed. The expected association is there: Barrier scores on the Rorschach correlate .39 with self-rated (exterior) body dissatisfaction (Zakin, 1989). By and large, these various studies have confirmed the assumption that a focus on the interior versus the exterior of the body is associated with barrier responses on the Rorschach and, by implication, the importance of the inner-outer dichotomy.

Aware-Unaware

Most of our senses are oriented toward the environment, so we ordinarily ignore stimuli arising from inside the body. However, there are times when these stimuli command our attention. During exercise, we become aware of a racing heart and rapid breathing. Of course, while resting in a quiet room, we may also become cognizant of these sensations if we concentrate on the insides of our bodies. And at rest we may suddenly sense a skin itch, tired muscles, a dry throat, or a full stomach.

These examples are neutral stimuli in the sense that they occur in the absence of emotional turmoil or pain. The body reactions that accompany fear demand our attention, whereas neutral stimuli may stay in the background. We are interested in individual differences in awareness of both kinds of stimuli, starting with neutral body stimuli.

Neutral Stimuli

Awareness of neutral body stimuli has been assessed by a body consciousness questionnaire, which measures both private and public body consciousness and body competence (Miller, Murphy, & Buss, 1981). (The public *body* consciousness scale was so closely related to the broader trait of public *self*-consciousness, the correlations being .71 for men and .66 for women, that the two measures must be regarded as assessing essentially the same trait. Public self-consciousness will be discussed in Chapter 5.) We focused solely on awareness of neutral body stimuli. A factor analysis yielded five items loading on the private body consciousness factor:

1. I am sensitive to internal bodily tensions.
2. I know immediately when my mouth or throat gets dry.
3. I can often feel my heart beating.
4. I am very aware of changes in my body temperature.
5. I am quick to sense the hunger contractions of my stomach.

The factor was the same for women as for men, but during pilot work, an interesting sex difference emerged. The last item, on stomach contractions, was originally written this way: "I am aware when my stomach is empty or full." This item loaded on the private factor for men but on the public factor for women, who interpreted it as meaning their stomach would stick out when full and everyone would notice (public self-awareness). Men ignored the public aspect of a full stomach, so for them the item measured only the private aspect of the body. The new item loads on the private factor for both sexes.

The questionnaire was then used to divide college students into the top third (Highs) and bottom third (Lows) of the distribution of private body consciousness (Miller et al., 1981). Some details are necessary to understand the experiment. All participants drank a cup of hot chocolate, which contained either the amount of caffeine in about two cups of coffee (experimental group) or no caffeine (control group). There was no difference in taste. Before drinking the hot chocolate and 30 minutes afterward, the participants filled out a questionnaire about sensations known to occur after drinking coffee: alert, stimulated, exhilarated, shaky, jittery, restless, not fatigued, nervous, and heart pounding. Composites of the ratings of these nine terms were converted into change scores from before drinking the beverage to 30 minutes afterward. For participants in the control group (no caffeine), there was no difference in reported sensations between those high and those low in private body consciousness. But for those in the experimental group (caffeine), the Highs reported significantly more sensations of alertness, stimulation, and so on. Private *self*-consciousness did not affect awareness of the caffeine; thus, the effects were specific to private *body* consciousness.

For those high in private body consciousness, would their greater awareness of internal events allow them to detect the absence any internal changes? To answer this question, Brockner and Swap (1983) gave an inert pill (placebo) that the participants were told would strongly affect them. In the arousal condition, participants were told that the pill would cause their heart and mind to race and body temperature to increase. In the relaxation condition, other participants were told that the pill would slow down heart rate and body temperature and also calm down their mind. Then the participants left and slept at home for two nights. One night they took the pill; the other night they did not. Subsequently, they returned to the laboratory and reported on the effect of the pills.

Those low in private body consciousness (Lows) were affected by the suggestion that they would feel warm (arousal condition) or cold (relaxation condition), but the Highs were not. The Highs tended to be suspicious that the pill was indeed a placebo; the Lows were not. Furthermore, the Highs reported sleeping less during the night they took the pill than the night they did not. This is an example of the reverse placebo. If these changes do not occur, the individuals worry about why they are still awake, which itself leads to more insomnia. Those high in private body consciousness, being alert to their insides, knew that the pill was not affecting them, so presumably they worried and therefore slept less. Bearing in mind that Highs also resisted suggestions about becoming warm or cold, we can see that Highs are unlikely to be fooled by a placebo because they are keenly aware of the events going on inside the body.

There is a downside to being high in private body consciousness, though. Participants reported on daily stresses and life experiences, labeling those they considered bad (Baradell & Klein, 1993). Private body consciousness correlated .32 with life stresses and .37 with the number of bad experiences. Participants also completed an analogies task. Among participants who reported considerable life stress, those high in private body consciousness made many more errors than the Lows. Using the abbreviation PBC for private body consciousness, the authors speculated that "High PBC persons may be so concerned with monitoring their internal sensations that they are distracted from the problem at hand. Distraction could divert their attention from effective problem solving strategies" (Baradell & Klein, 1993, p. 272).

A special group of people are keenly aware of the inside of the body—hypochondriacs, who believe they are ill in the absence of any medical evidence. They have been aptly described as individuals who "scrupulously monitor their normal body sensations and functions; they react to these perceptions with apprehension and alarm; they readily attribute them to physical disease" (Barsky & Klerman, 1983, p. 280).

Clearly, hypochondriacs are high in private body consciousness, by definition, but are people high in private body consciousness also hypochondriacal? There is a hypochondria scale on the Minnesota Multiphasic Personality Inventory (MMPI) that, not surprisingly, has several items that overlap those on the private body consciousness scale. This overlap guarantees a built-in spurious relationship between the two scales. We therefore eliminated the overlapping items from the hypochondria scale of the MMPI and then correlated it with private body consciousness (Miller et al., 1981). The correlations were .10 for men and .21 for women. These very modest correlations tell us that people high in private body consciousness are not necessarily hypochondriacs. Hypochondriacs appear to be slightly more aware of internal body events, but what differentiates them is their attributing the body sensations to physical illness. What you or I would regard as muscle tightness in the chest, a hypochondriac might think is a heart attack.

Stimuli Accompanying Anxiety

The elements of bodily arousal during fear were described many decades ago (Cannon, 1929). Awareness of these stimuli depends primarily

Body Focus 29

on how intense they are—that is, if your heart is pounding like a trip hammer, you will know it. However, when the bodily reactions of fear are milder, some people recognize them and others remain unaware. Furthermore, individuals vary in which body reaction they attend to. Thus, one person might focus on heartbeat and another on breathing rate.

Such individual differences are important to investigators who study anxiety, so they have constructed questionnaires for use in research on therapy. Typically, they inquire about frightening body feelings such as a rapid pulse, tightness of the chest, shortness of breath, upset stomach, tight throat, dizziness, and sweating. These stimuli often accompany anxiety, but they also occur in vigorous exercise, sudden movements, or even breathing too rapidly. What would happen if these neutral stimuli were confused with anxiety-related bodily reactions? Presumably, the person would have a panic attack. That is the hypothesis underlying a behavior modification treatment for panic:

> At the heart of our treatment program is systematic structured exposure to feared internal sensations. At the outset, patterns of fear are assessed by having patients engage in a variety of exercises designed to produce different physiological symptoms. To activate cardiovascular symptoms, we use exercise. For respiratory symptoms, we induce voluntary hyperventilation. (Barlow, 1988, p. 451)

Thus, treatment begins with making patients aware of the internal sensations. Then, by producing the symptoms by themselves, they recognize the internal sensations as deriving from safe, everyday events. They can distinguish between neutral and anxious body stimuli. This self-awareness technique seems to help panic patients. Even when they are treated in groups, the recovery rate is 85% immediately after treatment and 64% after 6 months (Telch et al., 1993).

This discussion of panic patients and hypochondriacs suggests that awareness may be just the first stage of a series of cognitive processes that all of us carry out. The typical sequence is part of a model of somatic interpretation. It starts with a change in physical state, say a tightness of the chest, which may or may not reach awareness. If noticed, it will be labeled, perhaps with a term such as *indigestion*. Next, a cause is assigned—for example, nothing more than something I ate, which is minor and leads to merely eating easily digestible foods. But the label might be "my heart hurts," suggesting a heart problem as the assigned cause. This attribution typically is taken seriously, leading to seeking of medical help, or it might be dismissed as something that can be lived with. The particular attribution made, trivial or serious, depends in part on personality characteristics—for example, a tendency toward hypochondria or a fear of doctors and hospitals. Furthermore, one may be aware of any stage in the sequence: the body event, the label, the attribution, or even the consequences of the attribution.

Body Image

Dependability

Private-Public Barrier

Some body sensations or reactions are entirely private. One familiar sensation is a full bladder, which remains private unless it is revealed by a mad dash for the restroom. It may also be inferred from a child's hopping up and down in an attempt to control the urge to urinate. The menstrual cramps of women are of course entirely private, but the accompanying bleeding may sometimes be observed or inferred.

Other quite personal reactions would best be kept private, but they are observable. Some people blush easily and therefore frequently, the red face signaling embarrassment to anyone present. Others sweat profusely and therefore back off from shaking hands or touching others and worry that sweat will be revealed through their clothes. They tend to become fearful that they will have to remove their shoes and expose others to the odor. Another possibility for a body event being revealed through clothes, seen especially in young men, is the penile erection. There is a double awareness: of the distended penis itself and the possibility that others will notice, which involves the public self: the public-private dichotomy.

Some people have a tendency to faint, perhaps because of low blood pressure or low blood sugar, and are so anxious about this possibility that they avoid social situations when possible. Worse still is epilepsy, the extreme of lack of body dependability, for epileptics never know when they might have a seizure.

Everyday Functioning

Recall the last time you were bedridden with an ailment. The hours dragged on slowly, and even a few days of the nagging symptoms seemed forever. But once you recovered and returned to daily activity, the memory faded, and you did not think twice about the fallibility of your body. Furthermore, the fact that your body healed itself is another reason for implicitly depending on it as a source of health. But what if your body healed only slowly and painfully? Then it would be a source of instability in your life.

Just as there are people who can fall several stories and not break a bone, there are others whose minor slip to the ground results in a broken bone. Older women, many of whom have fragile hip bones, often break them. Older people also bruise easily, whereas young people do not. When cut, most of us develop a scab, but a minority of people (hemophiliacs) have difficulty in stopping the bleeding and without medicine will bleed to death. Those with diabetes must continually monitor their diet and insulin intake or risk the debilitating extremes of too much or too little sugar in the blood. Those with heart disease must be careful of overexertion, which might cause a heart attack. Some middle-aged men, after being diagnosed with heart disease, give up sexual intercourse because of a fear of dying during it.

A different sexual problem concerns male potency. Most healthy men have no difficulty in having or sustaining an erection, but a minority experience occasional trouble in doing so. For a long time, the problem was believed to be entirely psychological, but now it is recognized as a biological problem—penile circulation, which can be dealt with medically. However, the men who have this problem are keenly aware of bodily failure and feel "less than a man."

These examples illustrate the extremes of dependable-undependable dichotomy. At one end are people who, without being aware of it, implicitly assume that their bodies will resist disease or breakage and will recover from illness. Their bodies are metaphorically like an old friend who can be relied on and taken for granted. At the other extreme are people who are painfully aware that they cannot rely on their bodies, for they may fail to perform as expected, not resist ailments, recover from illness only with great difficulty, or fail to perform as required. Their bodies are like a friend too erratic to be trusted and therefore a matter of continued attention and concern.

Identity

Do we know who we are in the sense that the image we have of our face and body is a true image? One way of answering this question is ask if we can recognize ourselves. Participants looked at their face in a distorting mirror and were to adjust the mirror to make the image look like themselves (Schneiderman, 1956). They accepted large distortions unless they were first shown a picture of their face. Another kind of mirror distorts the image of the entire body, and participants again own up to images that deviate from the true image of their bodies (Orbach, Traub, & Olsen, 1965).

However, when participants are asked to pick out their own pictures from an array of pictures, the outcome is different. Several studies converge in finding that virtually all participants recognize their faces (see Fisher, 1986, chap. 1). When specific parts of the body are shown, there are errors of recognition. Thus, we can easily recognize our face and body, but when presented with photos of specific parts, say an arm or a leg, we make more errors, indicating a weaker image. With respect to recognition, then, our facial identity is clearer than our body identity.

Transsexuals

For virtually everyone, sexual anatomy corresponds to the feeling of being male or female, but for a tiny minority, the two are discrepant. The relevant dichotomy is unitary-multiple. Some feel they are really men trapped inside the body of a woman. Many become transvestites, cutting their hair short in the masculine style and wearing trousers and other garments associated with being male, flattening their breasts, and padding their crotches (Lindgren & Pauly, 1975).

In the alternative kind of discrepancy, some feel they are women trapped inside the body of a man, and they also tend to cross-dress. They attempt to conceal their maleness and present themselves as women by wearing a wig and a padded bra and by using women's makeup. Some of them have surgery that alters the body to conform to female anatomy, and they are given female hormones. One group of 28 was followed up 3 to 14 years after surgery (Rehman, Lazer, Benet, Schaefer, & Melman, 1999). On the basis of reports on a body image scale specifically for body image in **transsexuals** (Lindgren & Pauly, 1975), all but one reported high satisfaction with the quality of their lives after surgery, saying that life was easier and more comfortable. One said that she now felt like a total woman; her body image now matched her feeling of being a woman.

Integrity of the Body

What happens to the **body image** when part of the body is missing? It depends on when it occurs. For example, those born with no left arm below the elbow know they are missing a body part but grow up with an intact body image because it is the body they started with. And if a part is removed early in childhood, again the body image is likely to develop in the same way that it does for most people.

If surgery for a body part is necessary in adulthood, however, whether body image is affected depends on which part is excised. Losing a tooth is obviously of little consequence. Suppose the loss is much larger and more serious: a lung, a kidney, or part of the digestive tract. Paradoxically, such surgery has little effect on body integrity.

Removal of an arm or leg is another matter. Virtually all amputees react initially to the loss by feeling that they are no longer whole. Many of them report feeling pain in the missing limb, so with respect to body image, it is almost if the limb is still there. But *almost* is not the same as complete intactness, and some of them never regain the implicit belief in body integrity. Others do regain a sense of body integrity, for there is a remedy: Artificial limbs have become technologically so sophisticated that they can function reasonably well for hands, arms, or legs. After years of use with the prosthesis, many patients report that they feel incomplete without it, suggesting that their body image now includes the prosthesis.

Loss of gender-related parts also threatens body image. Many women who have had a **mastectomy** mourn the loss of breasts, feeling they are "less than a woman." A more recent breast-conserving surgery has been developed, which retains most of a woman's breast. A review of the literature found that women's body image, whether assessed through self-report questionnaires, perception of appearance, or shame about the body, was not as bad after breast-conserving surgery than after mastectomy (Moyer, 1997).

What about women who have had a hysterectomy and therefore can no longer have children? The answer depends largely on age. Women in their late 40s typically are beyond childbearing age, so their felt loss is minimal. For younger women, however, the loss of ovaries may well threaten their gender identity.

For men, the major threats to sexuality are castration and removal of the penis. These removals may be analogous to mastectomy in women, resulting in a loss of body integrity. But castration is perhaps more of a threat to male identity than the absence of sexual parts is to women's identity in that it affects male potency.

The relevant dimension for body integrity is central-peripheral. With respect to body parts that typically are lost, limbs are central for most people, as are breasts and ovaries for women and testes for men. With the exception of the heart, much of the anatomy inside the torso—appendix, gallbladder, stomach, and intestines—though anatomically central, is psychologically peripheral, as fingers and toes are for most people. There surely are individual differences in the centrality of body parts. For a painter or pianist, fingers would be essential; for a runner, legs; and for a professional car racer, arms and legs.

Assessing Body Image

Body image questionnaires started with the Body-Cathexis Scale (Secord & Jourard, 1953), which assessed positive or negative feelings about a large variety of body parts. It was modified to form the Body Esteem Scale by Franzoi and Shields (1984), who extracted three factors for each sex. For women, they were sexual attractiveness (body scent, lips, breasts), concern about weight, and physical condition (speed, strength, stamina). For men, they were physical attractiveness (body scent, chest, body hair), upper body strength, and physical condition.

This questionnaire is merely one example of a flood of questionnaires on body image (see Thompson, Penner, & Altabe, 1990). Subsequently, one of the leading researchers of body image, Thomas Cash, developed several more. The Multidimensional Body-Self Relations Questionnaire (Brown, Cash, & Mikulka, 1990) yielded factors dealing with fitness, appearance, and health. The Appearance Schemas Inventory (Cash & Labarge, 1996) contains factors of vulnerability (body is defective and socially unacceptable), self-investment (body is central to identity), and appearance stereotyping (being attractive is crucial). The Body-Image Ideals Questionnaire (Cash & Szymanski, 1995) inquires about ideals for complexion, hair, face, body proportions, and so on. Participants say how important the ideals are and how closely they resemble them. Importance of the ideals correlated .48 with the public self-consciousness scale (Fenigstein, Scheier, & Buss, 1975), a measure of awareness of oneself as a social object (see Chapter 5).

How do people react when their ideal body image is so much better than the present state of their bodies? Szymanski and Cash (1995) used the Body Ideals Questionnaire to study the discrepancy between actual and ideal body image in college women. These participants also completed a checklist of two kinds of adjectives: *dejection* (disappointed, sad, hopeless) and *agitation* (annoyed, anxious, disgusted). The discrepancy between actual and ideal body image was highly correlated with both sets of adjectives: .63 for dejection and .60 for agitation. Clearly, the women were upset when their body ideal was far from their present body image.

Silhouettes of the women's bodies have been used in body image research for decades, but Thompson and Gray (1995) added one for men. Nine women's silhouettes range from emaciated to shapely (ideal) to fat, and nine men's silhouettes range from emaciated to muscular (ideal) to fat. Singh (1994) specified precisely what makes the shapely body ideal for women. He presented silhouettes that varied in waist-to-hip ratio from .6 to .8 for slim bodies and from .9 to 1.1 for heavy bodies. A waist six or seven tenths of the hip was selected as ideal by a large majority of participants.

What is the ideal body shape of men? As judged by women, the ideal waist-to-hip ratio of men of normal weight is overwhelmingly .9. The reason this ratio is higher in men, though their weights are larger than women's, is that male hips are relatively small. It would seem reasonable that a fair percentage of women would find ratios of 1.0 or even .8 to be ideal also, but they did not; a mere .1 difference was decisive. Ideals for body shape are important in establishing the standard people use to evaluate their own bodies. Most of the population cannot meet this standard, so those who value the appearance of the body are likely to have a negative body image.

Public Self

Appearance of the Body

Large-scale surveys of feelings specifically about the *appearance* of the body started showing up in the 1970s. There was overall satisfaction with the body, but many people were concerned about their weight (Berscheid, Walster, & Bohrnstedt, 1973). In the next decade, in a sample of more than 30,000 respondents, of those who were of normal weight, almost half the women and less than a third of the men said they were overweight (Cash, Winstead, & Janda, 1986). Of those who were underweight, 40% of the women and 10% of the men believed they were of normal weight. Clearly, there is a tendency for people to believe they are fatter than they really are. In a national survey, in the next decade, again almost half the women said they were overweight and were generally dissatisfied with their appearance (Cash & Henry, 1995). Apparently, many people are coming down on the negative side of the positive-negative dichotomy as it applies to appearance.

Research throughout the 1980s and 1990s, culminating in two books on body image (Cash & Pruzinsky, 1990; Thompson, Heinberg, Altabe, & Tantleff-Dunn, 1999), documented considerable body dissatisfaction by a significant minority of adult men and almost half of adult women. But discontent with the body starts long before adulthood. Indeed, two national surveys revealed that adolescents view the appearance of the body as more important and feel more negative about it than do older persons (Berscheid et al., 1973; Cash et al., 1986). And the body ideal of young women is thinner that that of women a generation older (Lamb, Jackson, Cassiday, & Priest, 1993).

Face

Good looks are important in everyday life, a fact not lost on psychologists who have produced a body of research on attractiveness and personality traits. Hundreds of relevant studies were subjected to meta-analyses in a review by Feingold (1992). Let us start with the relationship between body image (self-ratings of attractiveness) and self-reports of personality variables. Meta-analyses reveal that attractiveness correlates .22 with sociability (strong preference for being with people), .25 with dominance, and .32 with self-esteem. Clearly, people who believe they are good-looking tend to like being with others, are assertive with others, and think highly of themselves, though these relationships are moderate.

But self-ratings of attractiveness are entirely subjective and do not necessarily represent what others would consider good looks. Is facial attractiveness, when evaluated not by the person but by others, related to these same personality traits? Feingold's (1992) meta-analyses reveal that judge-rated attractiveness correlates .04 with sociability, .07 with dominance, and .06 with self-esteem. Thus, attractiveness in itself is unrelated to these personality traits. Rather, it is the belief in one's own attractiveness that accounts for the links with sociability, dominance, and self-esteem. Self-rated attractiveness correlated –.29 with dating anxiety and .31 with popularity. Body image—in this instance, about the face—does matter. Objectively rated attractiveness correlated –.28 with dating anxiety and .31 with popularity: Good looks matter too.

The focus on facial appearance is so prevalent in everyday life as to escape notice, but virtually everyone pays close attention to what the mirror reveals. The minority of women with barely discernible facial hair periodically rid themselves of it. Most women apply at least some cosmetics, and some indulge in the extensive change called makeover. Some dye their hair, especially as they age. And in a minority, the onset of wrinkles and sagging muscles causes them to seek cosmetic surgery (Sarwer, Wadden, Pertschuck, & Whitaker, 1998).

At least as common is surgery to reduce or straighten the nose. Some Asian women have adopted the Caucasian facial ideal and resort to surgical modification of the epicanthic fold, which makes their eyes look Asian (Hall, 1995).

More serious plastic surgery is not merely cosmetic but a necessity for those with harelip. Those with prominent facial scars, birthmarks, or crossed eyes are destined to go through life being stared at and feeling ugly unless they receive the necessary surgery. Consider what it would be like to want to hide your face because strangers might be shocked at the sight.

Hair

Some men dye their hair as they age, and a few have cosmetic surgery to remove bags under the eyes and smooth out the skin. Male pattern baldness affects most older men, but a significant minority start to lose their hair in their 20s. This development is doubly vexing, for loss of hair signals not only aging but also a loss of attractiveness. Photos of bald men and men with hair were presented to college students, who rated them for various characteristics (Cash, 1990). Bald men were perceived as less attractive, less assertive, less likable, and older. Notice, though, that these were the judgments of college students, not those of middle-aged or older adults (see below).

This message has not been lost on bald and balding men. Most of them, especially younger and single men, report being very upset and strongly interested in getting some hair back on top (Cash, 1989). As a result, there is a thriving industry in patent medicines and recently some worthwhile substances that will regrow scalp hair. Dermatologists are busy transplanting hair, and hairpieces sell well.

One group of men might be especially sensitive to being bald—namely, those high in the trait of public self-consciousness (Fenigstein et al., 1975), which is essentially being keenly aware of oneself as a social object (see Chapter 5). This hypothesis was tested on men waiting for an airplane in the Milwaukee airport: "Balding men high in public self-consciousness were significantly more concerned about hair loss than were balding men low in public self-consciousness . . . and were more likely to be interested in using a prescription hair-growth product" (Franzoi, Anderson, & Frommelt, 1990, p. 215).

Torso

Those who are dissatisfied with their bodies tend to ignore legs and arms and instead concentrate on the region from the chest to the hips. There is a Breast-Chest Rating Scale, consisting of five sizes that range from small to larger (Thompson & Tantleff, 1992). Both sexes had smaller chests or breasts than the ideal. In a later study, more than half the women had an ideal chest size larger than their actual one, but for almost a third, the ideal was smaller than the actual chest size (Tantleff-Dunn & Thompson, 1999). There was no relationship between the actual-ideal discrepancy and body image or self-esteem. The results for men were different. Three quarters of them had a higher ideal than actual chest size, and less than 5% rated the ideal less than the actual (presumably this small percentage was overweight). The correlations between the actual-ideal discrepancy and both body image and self-esteem were in the range of .30 to .43. Thus, among college students, chest size appears to be more of body image problem for men than it is for women.

For other adults, however, women appear to be more concerned about chest size than men, as revealed by what they do about it. A trivial number of men have had mass added to the pectoral region, but millions of women have had breast augmentation. When asked why, the women gave these reasons: breasts are too small, want to improve appearance and sex appeal, and want to increase self-confidence (Kaslow & Becker, 1992). Women rate their breast size as smaller than the ideal, and they overestimate the ideal size chosen by men (Jacobi & Cash, 1994).

The lower torso is also a matter of concern for those who consider themselves overweight and perhaps even those who do not. Recall the ideal waist-hip ratios (Singh, 1994, 1995), which for both sexes emphasize a waist much slimmer than the waist most of us possess. The presence of such an unattainable ideal sets up the potential for a negative body image. This problem is especially acute for obese people. As might be expected, they have a very poor body image (Thompson & Tantleff-Dunn, 1998).

Body Builders

Adding muscle mass through weight training is the goal of body builders. One reason for such training is a desire for better health, which includes slowing down the progressive weakening of muscles that occurs in aging. The other reason, of particular interest here, is to promote a better-looking body. In addition to working out, some body builders use steroids to achieve better muscular definition. For men especially and even for some women, there is a burgeoning interest in having well-defined abdominal musculature ("abs"), which offers the look of a washboard, as seen on the bodies of models.

There is no evidence that most male body builders have a negative body image, but there is a problem for such women. In one study, a large majority of women body builders believed that they were weak and puny when actually they were large and muscular, and most used steroids to bulk up (Pope, Gruber, Choi, Olivardia, & Phillips, 1997).

Development

Childhood

Preadolescent children were presented with outlines of seven figures, ranging from emaciated to obese, and asked to identify the ideal figure (Collins, 1991). Girls chose figures slimmer than their own size and slimmer than what most boys selected. Boys chose as ideal a figure heavier than themselves.

Most 8- to 10-year-old girls are dissatisfied with their bodies but only roughly a third of the boys are (Wood, Becker, & Thompson, 1996). Of the girls and boys who were dissatisfied, most wanted to be thinner. During adolescence, the 12- to 18-year age range, the picture changes (Kostanski & Gullone, 1998). Now 80% of the girls and 40% of the boys were dissatisfied. Again, most of the dissatisfied girls wanted to be smaller. The dissatisfied boys were more realistic, however: Those who were overweight wanted to be slimmer, and those who were underweight wanted to be larger.

These facts make sense when we consider the teasing that marks the childhood of many children. They may be teased for being too fat or too thin, for being too short or too tall, for having freckles, or for having crossed eyes. The ridicule comes mainly from other children, but some adults join in. As a result of years of such jeering, one residual of childhood may be negative feelings about the body.

Adolescence

In a longitudinal study, adolescents' body satisfaction was evaluated at ages 11, 13, 15, and 18 years (Wright, 1989). Overall, boys were more satisfied with their bodies than girls, and 18-year-olds were more satisfied than those at the earlier ages. Also, girls were more concerned about their weight, and boys concentrated on the size of their shoulders.

Another longitudinal study revealed how sex differences develop during adolescence (Rosenblum & Lewis, 1999). Participants rated 23 parts of the body, and the dissatisfaction score was the number of body parts rated moderately or very dissatisfied. At age 13 years, there was no sex difference. By 15 years of age, the girls were more dissatisfied than before, but the boys were slightly more satisfied, yielding a clear sex difference. There was little change over the next 3 years for boys and girls, with the girls remaining more dissatisfied than the boys.

The explanation for the development of the sex difference in body image may reside in cultural ideals:

> Girls' bodies change physically in a manner that is not reinforced by prevailing cultural standards, that is, the preference for a thin, noncurvaceous shape. Boys, however, live in a society that values a large and muscular physique in its men; therefore, the natural physical changes that occur during this epoch for boys are supported by current mores. (Thompson et al., 1999, pp. 30-31)

The findings reviewed so far apply to heterosexual youth, but what about homosexuals? In a survey of more than 36,000 adolescents in the 12- to 20-year age range, lesbians were *less dissatisfied* with their bodies than heterosexual females (French, Story, Remafedi, Resnick, & Blum, 1996).

Evidently, this finding suggests that lesbian youth have not been influenced as much by prevailing body ideals as most young women.

Adulthood

Homosexual men are more dissatisfied with their bodies (Gentleman & Thompson, 1993) and have more eating disorders (Yager, Kurtzman, Landsverk, & Weismeier, 1988) than heterosexual men. And in the large-scale study, gays reported more dissatisfaction with their bodies than heterosexual males (French et al., 1996). But there are differences in body dissatisfaction *within* the gay population. During childhood, many gays dislike sports and prefer girls as playmates, and some like to dress as girls—a combination known as *childhood gender nonconformity*. Such gays, who presumably suffered considerably from being teased, have more body dissatisfaction than do heterosexual men; other gays are no more dissatisfied with their bodies than are heterosexual men (Strong, Singh, & Randall, 1999).

From adulthood to old age, the body weakens and loses firmness as muscles sag. In one study, young people who averaged 19 years of age were compared with old people who averaged 74 years of age (Franzoi & Koehler, 1998). As expected, the young men were more satisfied with their bodies than the old men. And young women were generally more satisfied with their bodies than the old women, but there was an exception: Old women were more satisfied with their thighs and weight than young women. This exception occurred despite older women being shorter and heavier: "Compared to young women today, the elderly women of the present study were born during a time (1920s and 1930s) when thinness was not as important of a cultural beauty standard" (Franzoi & Koehler, 1998, p. 8).

Causes of Body Dissatisfaction

Where does the ideal for body shape come from? One obvious source is the models presented in magazines and on television. Though television contributes to **body dissatisfaction** (e.g., see Heinberg & Thompson, 1995; Tiggerman & Pickering, 1996), researchers have concentrated more on magazines.

Magazines tend to offer pictures of tall, excessively thin models. A large-scale survey revealed that 27% of women compared themselves to models in magazines very often or always (Garner, 1997). The impact of models starts early in adolescence. The ideal shape portrayed in magazines was found to influence a drive for being thin among 11- to 14-year-old girls (Levine, Smolak, & Hayden, 1994). Adolescent girls in the 13- to 17-year age range signed up to read the magazine that portrays thin models, *Seventeen,* and were followed for 15 months (Stice, Spangler, & Agras, 1999). Negative affect increased only for the girls who were initially dissatisfied with their bodies.

Laboratory research has confirmed these findings. College women rated body satisfaction, viewed photos of either models or women of average appearance, and again rated body satisfaction (Posavac, Posavac, & Posavac, 1998). Body dissatisfaction increased in some of the women who looked at the models' pictures, specifically only in women who were low in body satisfaction at the start of the experiment. Evidently, exposure to beautiful women in the media poses a body image problem only for those who are already vulnerable.

Can we resist cultural stereotypes? College students' body dissatisfaction was measured before and after a series of messages (Stormer, 1998). The messages were (a) how ideals for beauty have changed over many decades, (b) the thin ideal for women is both abnormal and biologically out of reach for most women, (c) the ideal images in the media are unrealistic and sometimes due to retouching, and (d) comparisons with models lead to body dissatisfaction and occasionally to eating disorders. Body dissatisfaction decreased from before to after these messages, suggesting that cultural stereotypes can be counteracted.

Another cause of body dissatisfaction, mentioned earlier, is a past history of teasing and negative feedback about the body. In the 1970s, an early national survey offered evidence that people who are dissatisfied with their bodies are likely to have been teased about them during childhood (Berscheid et al., 1973). Two decades later, a national survey revealed that more than a third of men and women said their body image was shaped by being teased as youngsters (Garner, 1997). These two surveys bracket a host of studies confirming that being teased, especially by family members and peers, contributes to dissatisfaction with the body (Thompson et al., 1999, chap. 5). For example, adult women recalled parental teasing about weight from ages 6 to 15 years (Schwartz, Phares, Tantleff-Dunn, & Thompson, 1999). Parental feedback correlated .35 with body dissatisfaction. Of course, being dissatisfied with their bodies may have caused them to recall more teasing.

Once girls become concerned about their bodies, this focus might become reinforced by their friends. A study of high school girls who were in cliques found that those with body image dissatisfaction and who wanted to lose weight (a) compared their bodies to those of other girls more often and (b) were teased more about weight (Paxton, Schutz, Wertheim, & Muir, 1999, p. 262).

One way to get a better handle on causation is to use the longitudinal method. Girls were tracked once early in adolescence and again 3 years later (Cattarin & Thompson, 1994). Being teased at Time 1 predicted being dissatisfied with the body 3 years later, which establishes that teasing does cause body dissatisfaction.

As to who is teased and derided, it is likely to be those who are considerably overweight, especially women. After reviewing research showing an association between obesity and dissatisfaction with the body, Friedman and Brownell (1995) suggested that it was because of societal pressure to be thin or at least not overweight.

Disorders

Anorexia

Anorexia is listed as a psychiatric disorder in which people, mainly young women, deliberately eat so little that their bodies are malnourished; some die of it. Is it a problem in estimating the size of the body? No, some anorexic women do overestimate their body size, but others underestimate it (Collins, 1987) Other research has shown that anorexics do not necessarily overestimate the size of their own bodies. Yet they starve themselves to attain emaciated bodies, so perhaps they do have an abnormal body image.

The answer to the paradox came from a study that used *morphing,* a process borrowed from motion picture technology (Smeets, 1999). Women were presented on a television monitor with the body of a thin woman who became successively fatter at the rate of four frames per second. They were instructed to use a pointer to mark the transitions from thin to normal to fat to obese with references to their own bodies. Compared with normal controls, anorexic women marked the transition from thin to normal earlier, suggesting that some of the normal-looking women appeared thin to them; they also regarded more of the frames as obese. A few of the anorexic women complained that the thinnest picture was not thin enough. The participants also marked off transitions as they applied to other women; again, the transition from thin to normal occurred earlier for the anorexics. Clearly, the body image problem in anorexics appears to reside not in distorted perception of body size but in *how thin is visually defined,* that is, leaner than most people would define it.

Shame

Inner-city, middle-aged women were asked at the start of an interview if they were ashamed of their bodies, concealed specific parts, or felt mortified when others commented about their bodies (Andrews, 1995). They were also asked about being depressed and, toward the end of the interview, whether they had been abused as children (being punched, kicked, or hit with a stick or belt). Regression equations established first that child abuse was related to current depression and, of special relevance here, that this relationship was mediated by bodily shame. A later study on the daughters of the women in the first study confirmed these findings (Andrews, 1997a), and a study of depressed women again found a relationship between child abuse and bodily shame (Andrews, 1997b). This research tells us (a) that child abuse is a source of bodily shame and (b) that the link between child abuse and depression is bodily shame.

A small percentage of men believe that their penises are tiny because they are somehow retracting into the abdomen. Called Koro, it is limited mainly to Asian men who are likely to seek medical or other help for what they perceive as a terrible threat to their masculinity (Yap, 1965). One speculation about its cause involves the difference in the angle of inspection of a man's own penis and that of other men, which the inspection angle may render larger. And there is enough scatological joking about the size of a penis to make men with smaller penises feel inferior.

Body Dysmorphic Disorder

Body dysmorphic disorder appears to be the pathological extreme of common and well-documented normal dissatisfaction with the body. The disorder is classified as a psychiatric category having these features: imagined ugliness or distorted perception of a minor defect in physical appearance. A study of 30 diagnosed cases revealed that many patients said that they spent several hours a day thinking about their defects (Phillips, McElroy, Keck, Pope, & Hudson, 1993). Some said that such thoughts dominated their lives, and a few were so distraught that they became housebound. Most of the concern focused on the nose, eyes, and hair, but some patients were obsessed with imagined abnormality in breasts, genitals, and buttocks.

It has been suggested that the consequences of body dysmorphic disorder are devastating to self-esteem:

> The typical thought pattern is, "I look defective, other people notice and are interested in my defect, they view me as unattractive (ugly, deformed, devi-

ant, etc.), and evaluate me negatively as a person, and consequently my appearance proves something negative about my character and worth to other people." (Rosen, 1996, p. 152)

SUMMARY

1. People vary in whether they focus more on the interior or on the exterior of the body, as determined by Rorschach responses.
2. They also vary in awareness of the private or the public aspects of the body, as determined by a questionnaire.
3. Body dependability consists of (a) keeping internal events private and (b) relying on normal body functioning.
4. A small minority of people suffer an identity conflict between their gender anatomy and their psychological sense of gender.
5. Integrity of the body becomes an important issue when it is threatened or when a body part is eliminated.
6. Body image consists of a mental picture of the body, which may not be accurate; it also includes a hoped-for ideal. A minority of people have a body image so distorted as to lead to abnormal behavior.

DICHOTOMIES

aware-unaware: the extent of sensing internal body events

central-peripheral: some parts of the body are more important than others

dependable-undependable: the body can be relied on to function versus not being relied on

inner-outer: focusing on the inside versus the outside of the body

positive-negative: feeling attractive versus feeling plain

private-public: concealable versus observable aspects of the body

unitary-multiple: the body feels whole or as having parts missing

GLOSSARY

anorexia abnormal dieting to excessive thinness

barrier scores Rorschach indicators of an external body focus

body dissatisfaction wanting the body to be better looking

body dysmorphic disorder an abnormally distorted, negative body image

body image a mental picture of the body

mastectomy the removal of a woman's breast

Rorschach a set of ink blots that have been used in research on body focus

transsexuals people who feel trapped in a body of the wrong sex

3

Self-Esteem

Sources
The Trait of Self-Esteem
Cognitive Mechanisms
Development
Value of Self-Esteem
Culture: North America and Japan

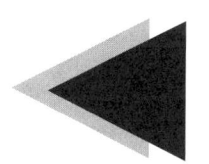

Our understanding of self-esteem derives from research mainly on North Americans. Thus, what is to be discussed applies mainly to Western culture, and only at the end of the chapter will self-esteem be examined in the context of Asian culture.

We know from casual observation of everyday life and from laboratory research (see the reviews by Dunning, 1999; Taylor & Brown, 1988) that people tend to view themselves favorably. Generally, people say that many more positive traits are characteristic of themselves than negative traits. Too many describe themselves as above average, too few as average or below average. When self-ratings of behavior are compared with the ratings of observers, the self-ratings are considerably better. The abilities people possess are perceived as rare and distinctive, the abilities they lack as commonplace. They see improvement in the abilities they deem important even when there is no change in performance. When asked to predict academic, social, and recreational events in their lives, they are supremely confident, and the more overconfident the predictions, the less accurate they are (Vallone, Griffin, Lin, & Ross, 1990). Worse still, the tendency to inflate one's own abilities seems to be strongest among those who are least competent: Participants who scored in the bottom quarter on tests of logic, grammar, and humor had the largest gap between their performance and their estimates of their own abilities (Kruger & Dunning, 1999). Exaggerated self-worth is not merely self-presentation, promoting oneself in the eyes of others, for it occurs even when the self-evaluation is made in private (Greenberg, Pyszczynski, & Solomon, 1982).

This account of a favorable bias emphasizes self-esteem as unitary, that is, a generalized tendency to put a positive spin on matters pertaining to the self. Thus, global self-esteem is a crucial determinant of how we deal with the positive and negative events that bear on our self-worth. This is a top-down approach to self-esteem. The emphasis here is on how the level of global self-esteem influences our interpretation of success and failure, acceptance and rejection, and upward and downward comparison with others. The major focus is on individual differences: how those high in global self-esteem differ from those low in self-esteem, especially in the cognitive mechanisms that maintain self-esteem.

But the unitary, top-down perspective on self-esteem presents only one side of the unitary-multiple dichotomy. There is an alternative perspective that views self-esteem as having multiple sources: We evaluate our appearance, talent, performance, and likableness, each being a source of global self-esteem. The chapter starts with a discussion of how these specific sources contribute to overall self-worth, a bottom-up approach to self-esteem.

Sources

Various components or sources of self-esteem have been listed by several psychologists. After interviewing participants and noting previous research, Coopersmith (1967) came up with four components: being able to influence or control others, attention and affection from others, being moral, and achieving success. Since then, several other lists have been suggested in research on possible factors of self-esteem or the importance of any single source for global self-esteem (Fleming & Courtney, 1984; Fleming & Watts, 1980; Hoge & McCarthy, 1984; Wells & Marwell, 1976). The larger the list, the more specific the items are on it. For instance, some of the items on Marsh's (1988) list are extremely narrow: physical, appearance, opposite sex, same sex, parents, emotional, spiritual, honesty, verbal, math, academic, and problem solving. But most lists are broader and shorter—for example, achievement, influence, acceptance, and virtue (Mruk, 1999).

Underlying all these lists, however, a distinction may be discerned between two kinds of self-esteem (Diggory, 1966). One kind involves **confidence** in issues that involve evaluation: appearance, ability, and power, for example. The other kind involves a feeling of **self-worth,** which derives mainly from interaction with others and what may be described as the issue of character. Bear this distinction in mind as the various sources of self-esteem are described. What follows is a discussion of six sources of self-esteem, distilled from previous lists.

Appearance

The epigram "What is beautiful is good" summarizes a body of research on facial appearance (Berscheid & Walster, 1978). Beauty is considerably more important in adults, especially between men and women, but it also affects judgments of children's personalities (Langlois & Downs, 1979) and even which infants are preferred (Langlois, Roggman, Casey, Reiser-Danner, & Jenkins, 1987). Attractiveness elicits a strong first impression that tends to endure.

It would seem to follow that physical attractiveness must therefore be a source of self-esteem. The correlations between the two have ranged from a low of –.08 (Major, Carrington, & Carnevale, 1984) to a high in the 70s (Harter, 1993). Does appearance determine self-esteem or the opposite? To find out, Harter (1993) asked adolescents to say which came first. They were split evenly, some saying that appearance determined self-esteem and others saying that self-esteem determined their evaluation of appearance. Interesting as this finding is, the problem remains that the same person who reports on self-esteem also evaluates his or her own appearance, a confound present in virtually all studies on this topic.

The confound can be removed by having others rate participants for attractiveness. When this procedure was followed, the correlations between attractiveness and self-esteem were .24 for women and –.04 for men (Mathes & Kahn, 1975). Thus, when the confound is removed, there is no relationship for men and a modest one for women. This sex difference should come as no surprise, especially in light of the fact that across a wide variety of cultures, physical attractiveness is an important feature in mates for men but not for women (Buss, 1994).

When does the sex difference first show up? In her cross-sectional research, Harter (1993) answered this question by plotting self-ratings of physical appearance over the course of development. In the third grade, there was no sex difference, but starting with the fourth grade, girls' self-ratings dropped gradually through the eleventh grade, whereas boys' ratings remained high, leading to this conclusion: "Beginning in junior high school and continuing into high school, self-esteem is consistently lower for females as compared to males. Decreased perceptions of attractiveness among females would appear to contribute the lowered esteem of females" (Harter, 1993, p. 97).

Ability and Achievement

Ability

In discussing ability, it is important to point out that it may be narrow or broad. At one end is highly specific competence, say doing an algebra problem. This narrow end of the spectrum defines the concept of **self-efficacy** (Bandura, 1986). Bandura and others have shown that confidence about completing a particular task often leads to success, and lack of confidence often leads to failure. Such self-efficacy refers directly to perceptions about performance on highly specific tasks.

The other end of the narrow-broad spectrum is defined by competence over a wide range of tasks, and the most general ability we possess is probably intelligence. If you are aware that you are bright, that should boost your self-esteem because intelligence is highly valued in our culture. It follows that intelligence might be strongly correlated with self-esteem. The correlation varies from nearly zero to .50, but typically it is in the .30s (Wylie, 1974).

Why is the relationship not stronger? Ability is only one source of self-esteem, and other sources may contribute to self-esteem when intellectual prowess is weak. Furthermore, intelligence is only one of a list of abilities available as sources of self-esteem. Vocations such as truck driver and mechanic require manual skills. Talent beyond intelligence is a requisite for painting or sculpting; playing or composing music; writing plays, novels, or poetry; and acting and directing. And social skills are important in everyday life, especially so in politics.

Standards

The focus here is on standards, not ideals. Ideals are what we strive for, but they are distant and perhaps unattainable. For example, the ideal of complete and unwavering honesty can be met only by a saintly few. A standard is more realistic and more tolerant than the ideal: We are allowed little white lies. Standards also differ from ideals in being more specific, especially when they relate to ability and performance.

Talent, skill, and performance can be a source of self-esteem only when measured against a standard of comparison. Criteria for judging performance vary. Thus, we have low criteria for young children, praising them for being barely able to read or for producing drawings that only a mother could love. With each passing year, performance norms escalate. Similarly, in athletics we do not judge women by the same criteria as men, and professional athletes are expected to perform better than amateurs. Usually, when competition is organized, each person competes only with those on the same rung of the competitive ladder. If a person loses to a higher-ranked opponent, self-esteem is not damaged.

Standards are routinely acquired during the course of development. In the innocence of youth, young people may think they will succeed in anything they attempt. They have little idea of the talent and hard work required for what appears to be simple accomplishments. Some children are trained to have excessively high standards, which they are unlikely to meet.

Dimensions of Achievement

The impact of performance or achievement on self-esteem depends on the cause assigned to explain the outcome and on the person's goals. In attributing causality, there are several possibilities (Weiner & Kukla, 1970). An achievement may be attributed to innate talent or to a combination of motivation and hard work. Some people derive self-esteem from being blessed with talent, and they need not work at what they do well. It is as if they are wearing a badge proclaiming their talent; for example, those with a sufficiently high IQ may join an organization for such people, Mensa.

Ability and performance are of course related, but the correlation is far from perfect. Some people of high intelligence, for example, do not approach the potential expected of them. This discrepancy between ability and performance may cause no drop in self-esteem because several excuses are available: bad luck, lack of opportunities, excessively high standards, and reference to other talented people who were late bloomers. **Attributions** about oneself need not be veridical, for they are subjective and typically motivated by a need to maintain self-esteem.

The distinction between ability and performance is also prominent in a conception by Dweck and her colleagues (Dweck & Leggett, 1988; Elliott & Dweck, 1988). They hypothesized two kinds of individuals and confirmed their presence with self-reports. The first kind uses performance to make judgments about their ability, which is assumed to be stable and enduring. Called **entity theorists,** they seek evidence that they are able. They feel smart when the work is easy and when they perform better than others or make no mistakes—evidence of fixed ability. **Incremental theorists** feel smart when they work on difficult problems and when they figure things out for themselves without any help—evidence of personal mastery or improvement.

Hong, Chiu, and Dweck (1993) demonstrated that the distinction is also important among college students, who in answering the following statement—"You have a certain amount of intelligence and you really can't do much to change it"—either agreed (entity theorist) or disagreed (incremental theorist). Then the participants sampled items from aptitude tests and were asked to give a percentage of correct answers that would satisfy them. Entity theorists required a higher percentage of correct answers to feel satisfied; they were setting a higher standard for themselves, presumably because they needed evidence of their fixed ability.

Another dichotomy, skill versus luck, applies mainly to competition. Breaks may determine who wins, offering an explanation that can maintain self-esteem. Thus, if I win, it was because of skill; if I lose, it was due to bad luck. A closely related dichotomy is temporary versus enduring: If I lose, I had a bad day; if I win, it was because of enduring skill.

A sex difference has been found in these attributions (Dweck, Davidson, Nelson, & Enna, 1978). When boys failed, they said it was because of bad luck. When girls failed, they said it was because of a lack of ability. As we shall see later, the boys' attributions are typical of those who have high self-esteem, and the girls' attributions are typical of those with low self-esteem. However, we must bear in mind a sex difference in the *sources* of self-esteem: Males derive more self-esteem from success at tasks, and females derive more self-esteem from social rewards.

The issue of recognition leads to a personal-social dichotomy. There are talented people whose performance or skill is appreciated only by few others. There have been occasions when one person has stolen another's invention and received credit for it. The rare brilliant speech delivered by a president typically is not written by him but by an unknown speechwriter. Virtually all the "autobiographies" of prominent professional athletes are the work of ghostwriters. In Hollywood, stunt men and women replace actors in dangerous scenes, and there are singers whose glorious voices emerge on the screen from actors who merely mouth the words.

The personal-social dichotomy is especially relevant when there is a contrast between team performance and individual performance. For example, if a women's basketball team succeeds, the esteem of each player is enhanced, a boost that may endure because of trophies and memories of past achievements. But what about a member of the team who plays below the level of the others and contributes little to the team's success?

Self-Esteem 53

TABLE 3.1 Dichotomies of Ability and Achievement

Basis of Comparison	Dichotomy
Standards	Personal versus social
Performance	Innate talent versus discipline, hard work
Evidence sought	Of fixed ability versus mastery of challenge
Attribution	Me (skill) versus not-me (luck)
Recognition	Personal (not recognized, though I achieve) versus social (recognized, though I do not achieve)
Who achieves	Individual (I achieve) versus group (my team achieves)

Her self-esteem will escalate only if she depends mainly on social sources of self-esteem. In the opposite case, a superb basketball player is on a team with poor players. She feels good about herself because those with talent tend to rely mainly on personal sources of self-esteem, but she derives no esteem from the team's performance.

Let me summarize (see Table 3.1). Standards may be individual, applying only to oneself, or they may be group standards, established by a consensus and applying to everyone. Performance may be determined mainly by innate talent or by training and discipline; both contribute to self-esteem. If the goal is to demonstrate fixed ability, good performance increases self-esteem, and one defends against evidence of poor, unchangeable ability. But if the goal is mastery over a difficult challenge, self-esteem is enhanced by attempting difficult tasks or by showing improvement over previous performance.

Self-esteem can be elevated by attributing successful performance to yourself, or it can be defended by attributing poor performance to luck. You can demonstrate considerable talent that receives no public recognition, a personal source of self-esteem. Or you can receive credit for another's talent, with public acclaim being a social source of self esteem. And self-esteem can be enhanced by personal success in the midst of group failure (personal source) or by group success to which you contributed little or nothing (social source).

Whether ability and performance contribute to self-esteem depends on prior learning. As we try various activities, we discover those that fit our talents and tend to stick to them, improving performance as we practice. As a result, we tend to like what we are good at and are good at what we do, a situation that holds mainly for persons whose self-esteem is positive. But some of those who are low in self-esteem may seek activities for which they lack talent and simultaneously devalue.

Morality

To be moral is to treat people fairly and honestly, but such behavior may contribute little to self-esteem. A more potent asset may be altruistic behavior, but the component of morality most frequently used to boost self-esteem is probably religiosity. A person who is deeply involved in religion, worships faithfully, and scrupulously follows religious tenets can claim to be a good person, one who is worthy in the eyes of God. And if the particular deity is regarded as compassionate, previous sinful behavior will be forgiven, and the restoration of grace is likely to repair any damage to self-esteem.

Influencing Others

In everyday life, we control others and are controlled by them. The relevant personality traits are dominance (telling others what to do) and leadership (showing initiative and decisiveness). As might be expected, these traits are related to self-esteem (Buss, 1995, p. 164). The correlation between dominance and self-esteem is .30 for men and .25 for women. The correlation between leadership and self-esteem is .48 for men and .42 for women.

Dominating or leading is expected to elevate self-esteem, and being submissive or being a follower either lowers self-esteem or has no impact. It requires at least a modicum of self-esteem to attempt to dominate another person or to try for leadership. The direction of causality might go either way, and we might reasonably expect a cascade: self-esteem to dominance to more self-esteem.

Social Rewards

At issue here are the rewards that occur mainly when there is a relationship—among friends, family, spouses, or coworkers—and that tend to intensify any social relationship. The most powerful of these rewards is love. Children are loved by parents and doting grandparents, adolescents and adults may be loved by an infatuated romantic partner, and there is the more realistic affection of siblings and spouses. The effect on self-esteem appears to be straightforward. In effect, the recipient says, "If others like me, I must be worthwhile; if others love me, I must be a special person to deserve it."

Self-esteem obviously can also be enhanced by praise. Why are people admired? Several of the attributes have already been discussed: appearance, talent, superiority in competition, and leadership. These qualities can be observed by oneself, but making such self-evaluations is known to be self-serving. Praise from others is more objective and realistic, and recipients of praise rarely question the motives of others. Again, the contribution to self-esteem is straightforward: If others admire me, I must be praiseworthy.

The last social reward that influences self-esteem is respect. Just as praise is linked to ability or performance, respect is linked to status. When the status is earned, for instance, by election or by winning the Nobel Prize, there is more respect than when the status is ascribed.

Vicarious Sources

Why do people boast about meeting or shaking hands with well-known athletes? Why do people want autographs of famous people? Why do they pay considerable sums to own letters of historical figures? Cialdini and his colleagues wrote about "the tendency to bask in reflected glory (BIRG). That is, people appear to feel that they can share in the glory of a successful other with whom they are in some way associated" (Cialdini et al., 1976, p. 366). After the Arizona State University football team won, more students wore buttons, jackets, sweaters, or shirts with the name or insignia of the university than after a loss. When describing a victory, they used the pronoun *we* more often than when describing a loss. One advantage of this source of self-esteem is that it is mainly positive. After their team's success, students basked in reflected glory, but after a defeat, they quickly dissociated themselves from the team: We won; they lost.

However, among true fans who are closely identified with the team, there are costs as well as benefits (Hirt, Zillman, Erickson, & Kennedy, 1992). College students, who were selected as true fans, watched a live broadcast of their team's basketball game. Then they were assigned a laboratory task and asked to indicate their temporary level of self-esteem and to predict their own subsequent performance and their team's subsequent basketball performance. If the team had won, self-esteem rose and so did predictions of their own and the team's performance. If the team lost, self-esteem dropped and so did predictions of the their own and the team's performance. And the personal costs after team failure were greater than the benefits after team success.

When the affiliation is interpersonal, such as being a family member, the involvement is even more intense, and again, failure is not easily ignored. When the famous family member fails, the close association may diminish the self-esteem of the rest of the family (although, as we shall see, whether this occurs depends on the closeness of the relationship and the relevance of the activity). Parents have a larger stake in their children than the reverse; after all, the parents have contributed genes and child rearing. Similarly, vicariousness is a more important source of self-esteem for teachers and coaches than for their students or athletes.

Another source of **vicarious self-esteem** is possessions. Some people are proud of their cars; others, their homes and clothes. And some men, regarding their wives as possessions, are proud of their wives' beauty. Others collect valuable paintings, stamps, or rare books, all of which are a source of pride. The underlying psychological rationale appears to be as follows: The excellence of my collection reflects on me, establishing that I am a worthwhile person.

Six Sources

The six sources of self-esteem—appearance, ability, morality, social rewards, social influence, and vicariousness—first occur at different times during childhood. Very young infants accomplish little, but they can receive social rewards. Affection comes first, followed by praise. Attractiveness is the next component, probably by the second year of life, and then vicariousness, as young children borrow esteem from parents and older siblings. As children develop skills during the preschool period, they can derive self-esteem from demonstrated ability. The clear assertion of dominance starts later in the preschool period, but morality awaits later developments in cognition.

There is relevant research on many of these sources of self-esteem (Buss & Perry, 1991). College men and women rated seven attributes for their importance as sources of self-esteem (see Table 3.2). In Table 3.2, ability is represented by intelligence, social rewards are represented by being liked, and dominance is represented by the ability to influence others.

For men, intelligence is the most important source, followed at a distance by character/morality. For women, intelligence and character/morality are the two most importance sources. After these first two sources, both sexes agree that being liked (due to social rewards) is more important than physical attractiveness, which is more important than the ability to influence others (which includes dominance). There is an expected sex difference for the least important sources: Women value artistic ability more than men do, and men value athletic ability more than women do.

TABLE 3.2 Sex Differences in Sources of Self-Esteem

	Men	Women
Intelligence	8.6	8.2
Character/morality	8.0	8.3
Being liked	7.8	7.9
Physical attractiveness	7.3	7.0
Ability to influence others	6.6	6.4
Artistic ability	5.1	5.9
Athletic ability	5.2	4.8

SOURCE: Buss & Perry (1991)
NOTE: Based on 499 subjects, who rated these from 1 to 9, with 9 being the highest in importance.

These data are averages, and individual differences are to be expected. We would not be surprised if bright students overvalued intelligence and good-looking students prized appearance. Those who are deeply religious surely place character/morality at the top of the list. And for those who cannot depend on themselves, vicarious sources may be the most important. Furthermore, age is probably important. Thus, a 60-year-old would be expected to assign a lower rating to appearance as a source of self-esteem than an adolescent does.

Personal Versus Social

The personal versus social distinction neatly divides the six sources of self-esteem discussed earlier. Appearance, ability, and morality are attributes of individuals and therefore are personal sources. Social rewards and the vicarious claim of esteem through association are social, by definition, and so is social influence.

This dichotomy has been linked to a sex difference, with men being more individualistic and women more socially centered (Bakan, 1966). As applied to self-esteem, men would depend on "being independent, autonomous, separate, and better than others. For women, feeling good about one's self . . . should derive, at least in part, from being sensitive to, attuned to, connected to, and generally interdependent with others" (Josephs, Markus, & Tafarodi, 1992, p. 392). It follows that (a) men with high self-esteem would *differentiate* themselves from others in ability more than would men low in self-esteem, and (b) women high in self-esteem would feel *more connected* with others than would women low in self-esteem. The authors tested these hypotheses in two experiments.

In the first one, participants wrote down their best skill among four (social, athletic, academic, and creative) and the percentage of local students who were good at that skill. The lower that percentage, the more participants would regard themselves as possessing superior abilities. Then participants high in self-esteem (Highs) were compared with those low in self-esteem (Lows). For men, those high in self-esteem believed that they were superior in every ability, which indicates differentiation. For women, there was no similar difference between those high and those low in self-esteem (no differentiation).

The second experiment involved memory for words, and again Highs were compared with Lows. For women, Highs remembered words involving friends or groups better than did Lows, indicating that the Highs were more connected to others. For men, those high and low in self-esteem did not differ. In brief, men derived more of their self-esteem from personal sources, whereas women derived more of their self-esteem from social sources.

Stigma

The focus so far has been mainly on the positive sources of self-esteem, though there is an implication that lack of these sources would lower self-esteem. But there is an explicit source of low self-esteem. It is *stigma,* which is most apparent in physical anomalies such as crossed eyes or a misshapen body. And members of groups may be stigmatized for being different and deemed inferior. It would seem that the most characteristics regarded by others as negative or inferior would cause the greatest drop in self-esteem.

But just because a minority is regarded as inferior by the majority does not necessarily mean that the minority's self-esteem will be low. Blacks, for example, have a level of self-esteem equal to that of Whites (Crocker & Major, 1989). One reason for the apparent paradox may be how conspicuously different the minority group is. On the basis of self-reports, students at a prestigious private college were divided into two groups (Frable, Platt, & Hoey, 1998). The *conspicuous stigmatized* group consisted of Blacks, obese individuals, and stutterers. The *concealable stigmatized* group consisted of bisexuals, gays, lesbians, bulimics, and individuals whose families were poor. The conspicuous stigmatized participants had self-esteem roughly equivalent to control participants (those not stigmatized), but those whose stigma was concealed had a much lower level of self-esteem. These results suggest that self-esteem is driven down not so much by the *presence* of a stigmatized characteristic but by the fact that people find it necessary to *hide* it from others.

The Trait of Self-Esteem

The most popular measure of the trait of self-esteem is a questionnaire that inquires about feelings of self-worth and confidence in oneself (Rosenberg, 1965). Since 1965, several other questionnaires have been published, all of which are highly correlated. The high correlations are not surprising because their items overlap considerably.

Some of the questionnaires ask whether the self-esteem-related behavior occurs *never, seldom, sometimes, often,* or *very often.* Some ask respondents to compare themselves with others: *below average* in the behavior, *average,* or *above average.* It has been assumed that the terms *sometimes, somewhat,* and *average* occupy a conceptual midpoint on questionnaires (Baumeister, Tice, & Hutton, 1989). When distributions reveal a mean or median that is higher than this midpoint, as they do, it means that most people have relatively good self-esteem. It also follows that some of the people labeled as low in self-esteem might have a moderate or intermediate level of self-esteem.

However, there are no objective criteria for deciding what is average in self-esteem, only criteria for what respondents say about themselves. The only empirical basis of a midpoint of self-esteem is the mean of the distribution of the scores on self-esteem questionnaires. Researchers are free to locate the "conceptual midpoint" of self-esteem as being indicated by the term *sometimes,* for example, but this is an arbitrary decision based on an assumption that this word is precisely the same psychological distance from *seldom* as it is from *often.* This assumption may not be true.

One solution to this problem is to select participants from the high and low extremes of the distribution of self-esteem, which would guarantee that those labeled low in self-esteem really are low. This solution has been employed in most of the research to be reviewed.

Self-Esteem and Other Personality Traits

We start with a self-esteem questionnaire (Cheek & Buss, 1981) that correlates highly with Rosenberg's (1965) questionnaire. The items are the following:

TABLE 3.3 Correlations of Self-Esteem With Other Personality Traits

Optimism	.64
Social loneliness	−.59
Shyness	−.51
Hostility	−.49
Sociability	.28

NOTE: $N = 912$, except for optimism, which has an n of 499.

1. I have a good opinion of myself.
2. Overall, I'm glad I'm me and not someone else.
3. I'm fairly sure of myself.
4. I am basically worthwhile.
5. I'm satisfied with who I am.
6. I often wish I were someone else. (reversed)

Most of the items refer to being worthwhile, but one especially deals with *comifence* (sure of myself). This questionnaire was correlated with questionnaires tapping personality traits that might be related to self-esteem (Buss & Perry, 1991, 1992). The participants were college students, and for the most part, there were only trivial sex differences in the correlations, so the data for the sexes were combined. The correlations are shown in Table 3.3.

The optimism questionnaire refers only to events that might happen to you, not events in general (Scheier & Carver, 1985). Concerning the outcome, you may feel positive (optimism) or negative (pessimism). The correlation of .64 between self-esteem and optimism means that they are closely related. This linkage makes sense. If you feel confident, you should be optimistic; if you lack confidence, you are likely to be pessimistic. So in a sense, optimism might be regarded as a cognitive consequence of believing that you are worthy and pessimism a consequence of feeling unworthy. However, some people with high self-esteem might set such lofty goals that they might be pessimistic about reaching them. And some people with low self-esteem might set such modest goals that they might be optimistic about reaching them. So though self-esteem and optimism are closely related, they are not necessarily identical.

Social loneliness is defined as lacking contacts with friends or acquaintances and missing the sharing of activities that occurs in social gatherings (Weiss, 1973). Socially lonely people report "not feeling part of a group of friends and not having a lot in common with other people" (Russell, Cutrona, Rose, & Yurko, 1984, p. 1317). This trait also shows a strong relationship with self-esteem, –.59, and the reasons are not hard to find. Friends must like being with you or else they would not bother getting together with you; knowing this fact must contribute to self-esteem. But if you are lonely, you do not receive this attention and affection from friends, which means that a social source of self-esteem is missing. Of course, the causation might flow the opposite way, from self-esteem to loneliness. If you have low self-esteem, your lack of self-worth leads you to believe that others might not find you appealing. Expecting not to be accepted or liked, you may be tentative and reticent when with others. Worse still, you might not be socially assertive enough to make friends and seek out acquaintances, who are possible sources of self-esteem.

Social tentativeness and reticence are to be expected in shy people, which means that if my explanation of the relationship between loneliness and self-esteem is correct, shyness should correlate negatively with self-esteem. It does: –.51. To elaborate, part of having low self-esteem is lacking confidence in social situations. As a result, you may be so tense and inhibited that others do not enjoy your company. Then, if they neglect you, that further diminishes your self-esteem. As may be seen from these explanations, the direction of causality might go either way: from self-esteem to shyness or social loneliness or from these traits to self-esteem.

The hostility questionnaire used here derives from a factor analysis of a large number of aggressiveness items (Buss & Perry, 1992). Two kinds of items loaded on the hostility factor. One set consisted of resentment items—for example, "I am sometimes eaten up with jealousy" and "Other people always seem to get the breaks." The other set consisted of suspicion items—for example, "I am suspicious of overly friendly strangers" and "When people are especially nice, I wonder what they want." Thus, **hostility,** at least as a personality trait, appears to consist of ill will toward others, as manifested in resentment and suspicion.

Hostility correlates –.49 with self-esteem. My after-the-fact explanation assumes particular cognitive mechanisms that derive from being low in self-esteem. Such persons, feeling that they are below average in appearance, ability, or agreeableness, cannot believe that others will find them good-looking, able, or interesting. When others react positively, those low in self-esteem become suspicious of their motives. Lows also tend to be jealous of those who appear to be more confident of themselves. Lows may feel that fate has dealt them a poor hand; that is, other people get the breaks. Thus, being low in self-esteem lends itself to resentment and suspicion.

What about those high in self-esteem? As we shall see below, they possess a variety of cognitive mechanisms that enhance or maintain self-esteem. However, being assured and confident, they have no particular reason to be resentful or suspicious and therefore are not more hostile than the average person. In brief, I suggest that the negative correlation between hostility and self-esteem is explained mainly by the cognitions of people who are low in self-esteem.

The last correlation, between self-esteem and *sociability,* is a modest .28. Sociability, the tendency to prefer to be with others, varies from people who are strongly motivated to be with others to those who would just as soon be alone (Buss & Plomin, 1984). Those who are high in self-esteem expect to be accepted by others and so may seek them out. Those low in self-esteem, expecting not to be accepted, may be less motivated to be with others. Or, turning the explanation around, highly sociable people tend to be warm in their interactions with others and therefore may derive self-esteem from others; low self-esteem people are less likely to derive self-esteem from others. Whatever the direction of causality, we need to bear in mind that sociability and self-esteem are only moderately correlated. The social interaction trait more crucial to self-esteem is shyness.

Self-Descriptions and Attributions

People high in self-esteem are expected to describe themselves in more flattering terms than those who are low in self-esteem. Several studies have unequivocally established this fact by having college students rate themselves on personality-related adjectives.

Baumgardner (1990, Study 1) had participants make the best guess in percentage terms (0% to 100%) of where they stood in relation to the general population. Those high and low in self-esteem were drawn from the top and bottom thirds of a distribution of scores on Rosenberg's (1965) self-esteem questionnaire. Highs offered clearly higher percentages for these terms: *able, bright, clever, enterprising, happy, likable, overconfident, smart,* and *talented.* The Lows had higher percentages than those Highs for these terms: *incapable* and *unpopular.* For these last two terms, the percentiles for all participants were low, indicating that they believed that most people were much higher in these negative traits. The two lists tell us two things. First, high self-esteem people rate themselves better than most people and better than low self-esteem people on a group of traits that are admirable. Second, low self-esteem people are willing to admit that for some admirable qualities, they are higher than most people. Thus, their percentile for *likable* was a better-than-average 65% but lower than the 85% for high self-esteem participants.

A later study had participants rate how well a set of adjectives applied to them (Brown, 1993). High and low self-esteem participants were selected from the top and bottom of the self-esteem distribution. The Highs rated themselves clearly more favorably than the Lows on these positive terms: *attractive, capable, good-looking, kind, smart, talented,* and *well liked.* The negative terms were generally not endorsed as much, but the following were endorsed *less* by high self-esteem participants than by Lows: *inadequate, incompetent,* and *insensitive.*

Campbell and Fehr (1990) used a median split, which may not separate Highs and Lows in self-esteem as precisely as we would like. However, even with a median split, they found that high self-esteem participants rated themselves higher on positive adjectives and lower on negative adjectives than did Lows. In a related experiment by these authors, observers watched participants get acquainted and rated their personalities. The self-ratings of participants high in self-esteem were more positive than the ratings they received from observers, but the self-ratings of the Lows were no more positive than the ratings of the observers. Thus, not only do those high in self-esteem admire themselves much more than Lows do, but they also admire themselves more than objective observers do. To anticipate findings to be discussed, those high in self-esteem tend to put a positive spin on most things that happen to them; Lows are more realistic in that their self-ratings tend to agree with objective observers.

We expect Lows to lack self-confidence, and they do so even in the *process* of describing themselves. When they are asked to describe themselves on two occasions roughly 2 months apart, the descriptions are more variable (less stable) than those of Highs (Campbell, 1990). Indeed, stability correlates –.50 with self-esteem: The lower the self-esteem, the more unstable it is (Kernis, Cornell, Sun, Berry, & Harlow, 1993). And the descriptions of Lows are less complex (Campbell, Chew, & Scratchley, 1991), which, taken together with the other findings, suggests a link between self-esteem and identity (more of this issue in the next chapter).

When compared with those high in self-esteem, Lows are not only more realistic but also too hard on themselves. Unacquainted men and women were paired and asked to get acquainted (Brockner & Lloyd, 1986). They completed likability questionnaires on themselves and their partners. Compared to Highs, those low in self-esteem not only liked themselves less, as expected, but also believed that their partners liked them less. The Lows were too self-critical, for the partners liked them just as much as they liked the Highs. These participants had little time to get to know each other, but what about dating and marriage partners? Again, Lows underestimated how their partners regarded them (Murray, Holmes, & Griffin, 2000).

What about self-descriptions after self-esteem is threatened? In one of the earliest experiments, participants took a test purportedly measuring social sensitivity (Shrauger & Rosenberg, 1970). Negative feedback had no effect on the Highs, but after positive feedback, they rated themselves as more socially sensitive. Positive feedback had no effect on the Lows, but after negative feedback, they rated themselves as less socially sensitive. In other words, Highs responded favorably to positive feedback, and Lows responded unfavorably to negative feedback.

In a similar vein, participants were given a test that presumably measured intelligence, and they were divided into three groups (Brown & Gallagher, 1992). One group was told that they succeeded, another was told that they had failed, and a control group was told nothing. Then they evaluated themselves, using trait adjectives, and the Highs evaluated themselves better than the Lows in all three conditions. The participants also evaluated others, revealing an interesting pattern. Compared with the success condition, after failure Highs devalued others, presumably as a means of demonstrating that although they had not done well, they were still better than others. Lows did not use this tactic, their evaluations of others being no different after failure than after success.

In line with these findings, those high in self-esteem tend to take credit when they succeed, but when they fail, they blame others (Roese & Olsen, 1993). Lows display the opposite pattern. The contrasting tactics of Highs and Lows are especially evident after failure (Brown & Smart, 1991). After failing an intellectual task, Highs exaggerated their sincerity, loyalty, and kindness, thereby counteracting the intellectual failure by exalting their interpersonal qualities. Lows, however, disparaged their own interpersonal qualities, which implies that they regarded failing the intellectual task as just more evidence that they are not worth much generally.

These various findings converge on a clear difference between those at opposite ends of the self-esteem dimension. In the face of failure, Highs typically adopt tactics designed to compensate for the failure, demonstrating they are still competent. Lows, however, often passively accept the verdict of failure and see themselves as incompetent. This difference is not restricted to failure but is part of a more general tendency on the part of those high and low in self-esteem.

These facts are relevant to a theory called *self-affirmation* (Steele, 1988). Presumably, each of us possesses a self-system that sustains the integrity of the self. When threats to self-integrity occur, the self-system acts to restore an image of self-adequacy. But such threats pose a serious problem for those low in self-esteem:

> These individuals have fewer and less distinct positive aspects of their self-image ... and therefore fewer specific self-aspects with which to affirm a sense of global self-integrity. Thus when they are threatened, it may be more difficult for them to restore feelings of adequacy by recruiting valued self-aspects. (Spencer, Josephs, & Steele, 1993, p. 23)

As we shall see, one consequence of this difference is that Highs and Lows tend to use different cognitive mechanisms in dealing with self-esteem.

Performance Outcome

If those low in self-esteem tend to put themselves down, does this affect how they actually perform? Anecdotes from everyday life suggest that the answer is yes. Professional tennis players of lower rank start a match knowing that they will probably lose, and this lack of confidence causes two problems: They do not try the difficult shots they need to win, and they make mistakes on crucial points in the match. Based on prior failure, they expect to lose and they do. What is the research evidence on this issue?

A review of laboratory experiments conducted in the 1970s and 1980s concluded that failure typically deteriorates the subsequent performance of people low in self-esteem (Brockner, Derr, & Laing, 1987). These researchers extended the earlier findings to a real-life situation, college students' exams. Doing poorly the first exam did not affect the performance of those high in self-esteem on the second exam, but it caused a significant drop in the second exam's scores for the Lows. The Lows, presumably devastated by the negative feedback from the first exam, lost confidence and did even worse on the second one. Incidentally, doing well on the first exam had no particular consequences on the second exam for either the Highs or the Lows, a typical finding.

One reason that those low in self-esteem perform so poorly after failure is that they *overgeneralize,* concluding that they are bound to fail in anything they try (Kernis, Brockner, & Frankel, 1989). These researchers used an overgeneralization questionnaire, sample items of which are as follows: "How I feel about myself overall is easily influenced by a single mistake" and "If something goes wrong—no matter what it is—I see myself negatively." This questionnaire correlated –.61 with self-esteem: The lower the self-esteem, the more overgeneralizing. Said another way, each failure is just one more confirmation of the global lack of worth experienced by those low in self-esteem.

Lows are so sensitive to failure as to be affected even when it is not real but only *hypothesized* (Campbell & Fairey, 1985). The task was anagrams, arranging letters to make up a word. In the experimental condition, participants were shown the anagrams, and they were asked to imagine that they had taken the task and done poorly and asked to explain their failure. Then they worked on the task. Control participants merely performed the task, nothing else. Experimental participants low in self-esteem performed worse than controls; Highs performed better than controls. So even imagining failure is so devastating to Lows that they lose confidence and perform poorly. Highs, however, try harder after imagined failure and perform better.

We expect emotional reactions after failure, but self-directed emotions play a crucial role for those low in self-esteem (Brown & Dutton, 1995). After success or failure, participants high or low in self-esteem rated how they felt on two sets of emotions. Only Lows felt ashamed and humiliated when they failed.

In a related experiment, participants were initially separated not only on the basis of global self-esteem but also after they sampled items from a specific task, on the basis of the self-evaluation of the specific ability required for the task (Dutton & Brown, 1997). After succeeding or failing on the task, they rated the validity of the task and whether their performance was due to their task-specific ability (cognitive reaction). They also rated the self-directed emotions used in the previous study. Global self-esteem predicted the participants' emotional reactions, confirming the results of the previous experiment, and the task-specific self-evaluation predicted participants' cognitive reactions. Humiliation after failure occurred even among those low self-esteem participants who believed they had many positive qualities.

Recall that global self-esteem may be divided into worthwhileness and confidence. Do both affect performance? To answer this question, Tafarodi and Vu (1997) used questionnaires to obtain four kinds of participants: high or low in self-liking and high or low in self-competence. The participants worked on one set of anagrams, received high or low scores (success or failure), and then worked on a second set. After failure, those low in self-liking persisted less on the second set than those high in self-liking, but self-competence had no effect on persistence.

In a subsequent experiment, participants were again divided into the same four groups (Tafarodi, 1998). This time, participants were asked to remember personality trait terms applied to them and to interpret ambiguous statements about them. The low self-liking/high-competence participants tended to remember more negative trait words and were more negative in the interpretation of ambiguous material about themselves, that is, had a *negative* bias; the high self-worth/low-competence participants had a *positive* bias. Evidently, self-worth is more crucial to self-evaluation than is competence.

Cognitive Mechanisms

Social Comparison

Social comparison has played a major role in social psychological research since Leon Festinger (1954) proposed his theory. Social comparison is involved in one of the sources of self-esteem—namely, a boost in self-esteem deriving from the success of a familiar member (vicarious self-esteem). The success of a family member, however, might also decrease self-esteem because the comparison might indicate inferiority.

To deal with this complexity, Tesser (1980, 1991) offered a theory of **self-evaluation maintenance,** which starts with family dynamics. If I do not compete with my more successful brother, I can bask in reflected glory, enhancing my self-esteem. If I compete with my more successful brother, my lack of success diminishes my self-esteem. One way to compete and not suffer a loss of self-esteem is to put psychological distance between him and me. Of course, if I am the more successful sibling, I will feel close to my rival, for closeness enhances the value of my superior performance.

Tesser (1980) tested his theory in several ways. College men and women were asked how much they resembled their siblings in ability and ways of thinking. When men performed better than siblings, the men reported being closer in ability and feeling, thus intensifying rivalry and elevating their self-esteem. When they performed worse, they reported feeling closer to a more distant sibling than the successful one, thereby minimizing rivalry and maintaining their self-esteem. There were no comparable findings for women, suggesting that this formulation holds only for men.

Next, biographies of eminent scientists were examined to discover whether a less successful father and a more successful son were close or did not get along. When their occupations were dissimilar, they tended to be close, but when their occupations were similar, there was friction.

Tesser (1980) referred to similarity of occupations or of tasks requiring ability as *relevance*:

> When relevance is high, comparison processes are relatively important. A good performance by the other is threatening to self-esteem, and the close-

ness of that other increases the threat. When relevance is low, the reflection process is relatively unimportant, and the other's good performance will bolster the person's self-esteem, especially when the other is close. (p. 78)

Subsequent research has been consistent with this formulation (Tesser & Campbell, 1983), including evidence that the most pleasant affect is observed when a participant is outperformed by someone close on a task low in relevance, a situation favoring vicarious self-esteem (Tesser, Miller, & Moore, 1988).

The theory has been extended to dating couples (Pilkington, Tesser, & Stephens, 1991). Participants filled out questionnaires listing a variety of activities, rating each for importance—in Tesser's terms, "relevance." They also evaluated whether they or the partner performed each activity better. Self-esteem was maintained by claiming superiority for relevant activities, but

when relevance was high for one partner and low for the other, the superior performance was most often attributed to the first partner. This allows the "high relevance" person to benefit from the comparison of performance and the "low relevance" person to bask in the reflected glory of his or her partner. (Pilkington et al., 1991, p. 500)

By using this kind of strategy, couples can boost or maintain each other's self-esteem and avoid conflict. Further evidence for the theory came from research on married couples. There was evidence for the extended self-evaluation maintenance model; when one spouse performed better and partner relevance was high, there was less satisfaction in performing better (Beach et al., 1998; Mendolia, Beach, & Tesser, 1996).

What happens when relevance is high and there is no relationship—for example, when one student receives clearly higher grades than another student in a course? This question was answered in an article, aptly called "The Person Who Outperforms Me Is a Genius" (Alicke, LoSchiavo, Zerbst, & Zhang, 1997). In one experiment, after a confederate scored higher on a bogus intelligence test, participants rated the confederate's intelligence higher than did neutral observers. This inflation of the confederate's ability presumably minimized the threat to self-esteem by saying, in effect, that the other person is so talented that anyone would suffer by comparison. This rationale for being outperformed should help to maintain self-esteem.

Alicke et al. (1997) also investigated what happens when the participant performs better than the confederate. Surprisingly, the participants again magnified the ability of the confederate. The authors suggested that praising your inferiors serves to boost your own self-esteem.

The various experiments just reviewed dealt with downward and upward comparison but not with participants who varied in the level of self-esteem. How are both kinds of comparison related to global self-esteem?

Downward and Upward Comparison

Students report an experience that may have happened to you. When inspecting your grade on an exam, you discover that you have received a disappointing C. When you discover that two friends have received Ds, somehow you feel better. Downward comparison often improves subjective well-being (Wills, 1981).

Crocker and Gallo (1995) failed participants in a task and then had them list groups that either they were glad *not* to belong to (downward comparison) or groups they *would like* to belong to (upward comparison). Downward comparison led to an elevation of mood and life satisfaction in Lows but not in Highs, who benefited from upward comparison. Subsequent research confirmed the finding for Lows but not for Highs (Gibbons & Gerrard, 1989; Gibbons & McCoy, 1991). And in one study, self-esteem, in itself, did not lead to benefits from downward comparison (Aspinwall & Taylor, 1993). When the measures were frustration/discouragement and relative adjustment, only the low self-esteem participants who had had a recent academic setback benefited from downward comparison; those without such a setback did not benefit from downward comparison.

When do people *seek* social comparison? To answer this question, experimenters had participants succeed or fail in relation to another person; then the participants were given the opportunity to obtain information about this other person (social comparison) (Wood, Giordana-Beech, Taylor, Michela, & Gaus, 1994). Those with high self-esteem wanted *upward* comparison after failure. Those with low self-esteem wanted *downward* comparison after success.

As experimentation continued, more complex findings emerged about the relationship between level of self-esteem and the direction of social comparison, but there were general trends. A review of research (Collins, 1996) supported the following conclusions: (a) downward comparison benefits mainly those low in self-esteem or those who have been threatened, and (b) compared to Lows, Highs tend to react to upward comparison with more positive moods.

Self-Enhancement

Versus Self-Protection

Perhaps Highs and Lows react differently to upward and downward comparison because Highs have a different strategy for dealing with threats to self-esteem than Lows (Arkin, 1981; Baumeister et al., 1989). Those high in self-esteem exude confidence and seek to enhance their self-esteem by accepting challenges, though the strategy is risky. Thus, just before Super Bowl III, Joe Namath, quarterback of the underdog New York Jets, calmly predicted a victory. To everyone's surprise, the Jets won.

Those low in self-esteem typically lack the confidence to attempt enhancement and therefore settle for protecting the self-esteem they possess. It follows that Lows should be less likely to take risks. Participants were told that they would gamble for real money and allowed to choose risky or safe options (Josephs, Larrick, Steele, & Nisbett, 1992). Lows selected safer bets than Highs.

In a related experiment, participants practiced a video game and then bet on how well they would do when they played it again (Baumeister, Heatherton, & Tice, 1993). Highs set higher goals and met them, winning more money than Lows. In an additional experimental condition, the experimenter suggested that participants might choke under pressure and therefore should make safer bets. Under this ego threat, Highs bet too much and wound up losing more than Lows, who hedged their bets. Presumably, in the face of ego threat, Highs tried to rise to the challenge by being big bettors, a self-enhancement tactic. Lows reacted to ego threat by betting more cautiously, a self-protective tactic.

Having one's performance evaluated may be threatening, which may elicit the strategy called **self-handicapping**: placing barriers to performing well, which can then be used as an excuse for poor performance (Jones & Berglas, 1978; Rhodewalt, Saltzman, & Wittmer, 1984). In addition to protection against failure, self-handicapping can enhance self-esteem when barriers are overcome and the successful performance demonstrates ability.

Tice (1991) allowed participants to decide how much time they would practice for a forthcoming performance. One group of participants was told that the task would identify only those extremely high in ability. Then they answered questions about the meaning of their future performance. High self-esteem participants endorsed this attribution much more than low self-esteem participants: "If I do not practice much and do very well on the evaluation, that suggests that I have extremely high ability." This tactic uses self-handicapping for enhancement of self-esteem.

In the other condition, participants were told that the task would identify only those extremely deficient in ability. Lows endorsed this attribution more than Highs: "If I do not practice much and do very poorly, that does not say much about my ability because I might have done better if I had practice longer." This tactic uses self-handicapping to protect against a drop in self-esteem.

There is evidence that men may self-handicap more than women do (Hirt, McCrea, & Kimble, 2000). Men practiced less for an oncoming task (self-handicapping) when observed by a camera than when not observed. Further analysis revealed that only the men who felt threatened while being observed tended to self-handicap. There were no comparable findings for women; they simply did not self-handicap.

Another way of dealing with threats to self-esteem is managing impressions. Participants accounted for their performance under conditions of high or low motivation to impress another person (Schlenker, Wiegold, & Hallam, 1990). When motivated to impress others, Highs tried to impress others by bragging, but Lows became more modest.

The behavior of those high in self-esteem after failure may lead to their being disliked. Participants were either failed or received no feedback on performance (control) and then interacted with another subject who rated them for likability and being antagonistic (Heatherton & Vohs, 2000). After failure (but not in the control condition), Highs were rated as less likable and more antagonistic (rude, unfriendly, and arrogant) than the Lows. Evidently, the Highs' tendency to compensate for failure may be annoying to others.

Such compensatory behavior means that when their self-esteem is threatened, Highs also act to protect it. Notice that they do not passively accept failure but actively engage in behavior designed to convince themselves and others of their competence. And when they are not threatened, Highs' general tendency is toward enhancing self-esteem.

Versus Consistency

In addition to **self-enhancement**, many people strive for **consistency**. To be consistent, those high in self-esteem should prefer positive feedback, but those low in self-esteem should prefer negative feedback or at least not prefer positive feedback. In an early experiment, participants were either flattered or evaluated neutrally and then asked to rate the evaluator (Colman & Oliver, 1978). Highs, as might be expected, rated the flattering evaluator more favorably than the neutral evaluator. But Lows rated the neutral evaluator more favorably than the flatterer, presumably because the neutral evaluation was more consistent with their self-evaluation.

A more recent study demonstrated that the need for consistency may also shape memory for self-relevant information (Story, 1998). College students filled out a personality self-report, were given either favorable feedback or unfavorable feedback about their personality, and subsequently asked to recall the adjectives that comprised the feedback. Those high in self-esteem remembered the favorable feedback as more favorable than it had been, and those low in self-esteem remembered the unfavorable feedback as more unfavorable than it had been.

Psychologists who emphasize one or the other of these perspectives—self-enhancement or self-consistency—have offered evidence that sustains their respective positions. Many years ago, Shrauger (1975) was able to reconcile the two approaches. After reviewing the literature on this topic, he concluded that when *cognitions* were assessed, the data supported the consistency position, but when *emotions* were assessed, the data supported the enhancement position.

Later findings confirmed this hypothesis (Swann, Griffin, Predmore, & Gaines, 1987). Participants low in self-esteem reported that unfavorable feedback was more self-descriptive than positive feedback. At the same time, they were depressed and distressed after receiving unfavorable feedback. Swann et al. (1987) concluded that "cognitive reactions to social feedback conform to self-consistency theory and affective reactions conform to self-enhancement theory" (p. 886).

Thus, self-esteem has both affective and cognitive components. When people with insufficient self-esteem succeed, they feel good just as anyone would, but they cannot believe that they really are competent. When people with adequate self-esteem succeed, they feel good and construe the success as further evidence of their competence.

But what happens when people fail? Highs, after failing in an achievement task, exaggerated their positive social characteristics (e.g., being altruistic), but Lows depreciated their social characteristics (Brown & Smart, 1991). Thus, people high in self-esteem do not challenge the fact of failure. Instead, in line with self-affirmation theory (Steele, 1988), they maintain self-esteem by exaggerating their accomplishments elsewhere, saying, in effect, "I may not be good here but I'm great elsewhere." People low in self-esteem do not use this compensatory mechanism, presumably because they do not believe that they are great elsewhere, and failure depresses their self-esteem even further. They say, in effect, "Failure is just more evidence that I'm no good."

What happens if, after failure, individuals are given another opportunity to demonstrate ability? College men and women were given tests that ostensibly measured two kinds of ability (Josephs, Markus, & Tafarodi, 1992). One kind supposedly involved *independent* thinking: uniqueness and ability to achieve individually. The other kind presumably assessed *interdependent* thinking: capable of nurturance and group achievement. After being told that they scored low in these abilities, participants guessed their improvement if they took the test again. As might be expected, Highs predicted much more improvement than Lows, but there was also a sex difference: "Evidence of poor independent thinking ability prompted the highest predictions by high self-esteem men, whereas evidence of poor interdependent thinking ability was answered with the highest predictions by high self-esteem women" (Josephs et al., 1992, p. 399). Among Highs, in accord with traditional sex roles, men respond more to failure when it involves individual achievement, and women respond more to failure in the interpersonal sphere. Lows, as might be expected, predict little improvement, for low self-esteem persons of both sexes are more ready to accept failure as being consistent with their self-views.

It bears repeating that most people maintain their enduring level of self-esteem. Those with high self-esteem develop mechanisms to sustain it in the face of threats to their self-worth. They believe that what they are good at is important to them and what they are poor at is not. Those with low self-esteem seem unable to deny the importance of whatever they are poor at and deny the importance of what they are good at, thereby sustaining their low level of self-esteem.

Swann (1984) suggested that all of us seek information that confirms who we think we are, a theory of **self-verification.** This variant of self-consistency theory predicts that Lows prefer people who confirm that they really are low in self-esteem. Participants who were either socially confident or not confident were allowed to choose one of two partners with whom they would spend several hours (Swann, Stein-Seroussi, & Gieseler, 1992). They were told that one partner thought he or she was high in social confidence (favorable), and the other partner thought he or she was low (unfavorable). Those who were socially confident chose the favorable partner 72% of the time, and those who lacked social confidence chose the unfavorable partner 78% of the time. The participants verbalized two main reasons for making the choice. One was a preference for someone who confirmed their views of themselves. The other was the expectation that a partner who agreed with their self-views, even when these were negative, would lead to more harmony in the interaction. The motives for self-confirmation and harmony sometimes outweigh the desire to obtain positive feedback.

Other research, however, has demonstrated that the need to self-enhance may be stronger than the need to self-verify. Sedikides (1993) had participants select questions they would be asked about their own personality traits. The traits were either positive or negative and either central or peripheral to the participants' personality. The questions varied in diagnosticity, that is, how much they distinguished between people high in the trait from those who were low. In several experiments, participants selected questions high in diagnosticity more when the traits were positive than when they were negative. This is evidence for self-enhancement.

The self-verification view assumes that individuals prefer information about central traits rather than peripheral traits, even when the traits are negative. It follows that they would select questions about central traits, even when the traits are negative. This prediction was supported in only one experiment; in the other five experiments, it was not supported, suggesting that "the self-enhancement motive is more influential than the self-verification motive in steering the self-evaluation process" (Sedikides, 1993, pp. 334-335).

Theories

Much of the research on the cognitive mechanisms of those high and low in self-esteem has been guided by the various theories I have been discussing. These theories are summarized in Table 3.4.

High Versus Low Self-Esteem

The differences between people low in self-esteem and those high in self-esteem are summarized in Table 3.5. A warning: The differences are being exaggerated a bit for the sake of exposition, and there are exceptions. Lows avoid challenges because they are insecure about their abilities. They seek sure bets, tasks that are so easy as to guarantee success. If those with high self-esteem take the offensive in the expectation of success, people with low self-esteem adopt a defensive strategy of not failing. They do not take chances and desperately seek to avoid mistakes that, in their pessimism, they believe are likely to occur. They play it safe, for example, preferring a secure job to a riskier one with greater potential. When confronted with a specific inability, they cannot deny its importance. When confronted with failure, they perform worse and assume that they will fail in everything. They find consolation in the fact that others are inferior (downward comparison) but seem not to benefit from upward comparison.

Those with high self-esteem, being optimistic, seek to enhance their already high self-esteem. Highs are likely to seek challenges because they are secure in their own abilities. Confident of success, they are willing to reach for the brass ring, seeking a risky job but one with a potential for

Self-Esteem 75

TABLE 3.4   High Versus Low Self-Esteem

	Low Self-Esteem	High Self-Esteem
Outlook	Pessimistic	Optimistic
Self-cognitions	Protective	Enhancing
Goals	Set low	Set high
Specific low ability	Deemed important	Deemed unimportant
Reaction to failure	Poorer performance	Trying harder
	Overgeneralization	Compensation: other successes
Downward comparison	Benefit	No benefit

TABLE 3.5   Cognitive Theories of Self-Esteem

Self-affirmation: maintenance of the integrity of the self-system

Social comparison: impact of our own performance depends on how well others do

Self-enhancement: we seek to elevate our self-esteem

Self-esteem maintenance: impact of another's performance depends on both our relationship and the relevance of the task

Self-verification: we seek to confirm our stable level of self-esteem

personal advancement. They dismiss evidence of inability as being unimportant. Only when they fail are they self-protective, by telling themselves and others of their other abilities and successes; otherwise, they are self-enhancing. Already feeling superior, they cannot benefit from knowing that others are inferior, but they do value upward comparison.

These descriptions, which follow from decades of research, suggest that Highs and Lows follow different paths over time. Those low in self-esteem set themselves up for failure or at least not to succeed, and they are ready with excuses when they do fail. They believe that they are not worthy and respect people who agree with them. Avoiding challenges, they are less likely to acquire the skills needed for success and the confidence that might accompany it.

Those high in self-esteem expect to succeed, are willing to take chances to do so, assume that any failure is transient, and have cognitive mechanisms for maintaining or even enhancing self-esteem. Thus, even if Highs and Lows initially were not much different in self-esteem, the respective cascades just described should lead to increasing divergence between them.

Development

It is not clear whether preschool children have the requisite cognitive ability and experience needed for an enduring, global sense of self-esteem, but it is present in elementary school children (Harter, 1982). Harter (1982) constructed a questionnaire that has four correlated factors. *Cognitive competence* refers to intelligence and doing well in school. *Social competence* refers to having lots of friends, being liked, and being popular. *Physical competence* refers to ability in sports and games, and this was the only factor to show a sex difference: boys were higher. And there is a factor of *general worth*: being sure of oneself, being happy as is, and being a good person.

As with adults, most children practice self-enhancement. Most of them readily claim their achievements in school but take less responsibility for their failures, and this tendency increases from the third through the ninth grade (Harter, 1988).

In other cross-sectional research, Harter (1982) found that self-esteem held steady from Grades 3 through 6, dropped slightly at Grade 7, and then held steady through Grade 9. The gradual increase in self-esteem was confirmed in a longitudinal study by Simmons (1987). She also verified the drop at Grade 7, but only for girls who were starting junior high school. Simmons (1987) argued that girls start puberty at about when Grade 7 begins, and that event, together with the shift from elementary school to junior high, caused the drop in self-esteem. Seeking confirmation, she counted the potential major transitions in girls at the start of adolescence: entering junior high school, puberty, early onset of dating, geographical mobility, and death or divorce of parents. As the number of transitions increased from one to three, self-esteem dropped sharply. Such changes had virtually no effect on the self-esteem of boys, however, perhaps because they enter adolescence later.

In the 1980s, many farmers in Iowa suffered an economic crisis, which offered an opportunity to study the effect of financial strain, parents' self-esteem, and parental support on the self-esteem of the children when they reached adolescence (Mayhew & Lempers, 1998). Adolescent daughters with lower self-esteem were affected by lack of support by their fathers and by both parents' low self-esteem. Adolescent sons' self-esteem was influenced by lack of support from both parents but not by parental self-esteem.

In a rare longitudinal study on self-esteem, Block and Robins (1993) followed adolescents from an average age of 15 to 23 years. There was moderate consistency over the 8-year period, with some individuals being stable and others changing considerably. When the personality of those who changed was examined, there were sex differences. Fluctuations in self-esteem among the females was linked to earlier changes in warmth and nurturance. Changes in the self-esteem of the males was related to earlier inability to control anxiety. Consistent with cross-sectional research on younger participants (Harter, 1982), over the 8-year period the males increased slightly in self-esteem but the females dropped slightly.

Aside from global self-esteem, some particular sources may have a greater impact than others on the self-esteem of older children and adolescents. Harter (1986) developed another self-competence measure consisting of five factors (sources) of self-esteem. A higher-order factor analysis yielded two clusters: (a) appearance, peer likability, and athletic competence, and (b) scholastic competence and behavioral conduct (Harter, 1993). Children and adolescents judged the first cluster to be more important to the self than to parents, which may reflect the idea that peer acceptance—presumably based on looking good, being likable, and being athletic—is crucial to self-esteem. The second cluster was judged to be more important to parents than to the self, which suggests that good grades and good behavior are less important to the self because they do not lead to acceptance by peers.

In other research by Harter (1986), children rated their competence in school, athletics, social interaction, appearance, and conduct. The average score was compared with average ratings of the *importance* of each of these domains. For those high in self-esteem, the most competent domains were rated as more important than the least competent domains. The Highs dealt with low competence by dismissing it as unimportant, thereby maintaining their high self-esteem. For the Lows, the least competent domains were rated nearly as important as the most competent domains. The Lows were not able to dismiss low competence, thereby maintaining their low self-esteem. These mechanisms in children are similar to the ones discussed earlier in adults.

The question remains about whether school grades play a role in self-esteem. For students in the seventh through ninth grades, the correlation between academic achievement and self-esteem was found to be .25 (Dubois, Bull, Sherman, & Roberts, 1998). So grades do affect self-esteem, albeit modestly. We know from research discussed earlier that those low in self-esteem expect to fail, so the direction of causation might also work the opposite way: The lack of confidence of Lows affects their schoolwork, leading to lower grades.

Core-Periphery Theory

If we add up all the sources of self-esteem, does the sum equal a person's global self-esteem? First, consider research. College students rated themselves for components of self-esteem such as intelligence, appearance, leadership, and emotional stability, and a composite of these sources was found to correlate only .50 with global self-esteem (Pelham & Swann, 1989). It might be argued that if they had included more sources of self-esteem, the correlation would have been higher.

Perhaps. First, consider Harter's (1999) summary of global self-esteem versus specific sources in this country and others among children and adolescents. Only appearance correlated higher than .50 with global self-esteem. The correlation coefficients between global self-esteem and particular sources were the following:

appearance (in the 60s),

scholastic competence (in the mid-40s),

social acceptance, liking (in the mid-40s),

behavioral conduct (in the mid-40s), and

athletic competence (in the low 30s).

Second, compare people's self-esteem with the way they are regarded by those who know them. Even if these two evaluations match for perhaps a majority, there is a significant mismatch for a minority who are either conceited or humble.

Third, what happens when self-esteem is buffeted by rejection, failure, or humiliation? Some people with an adequate level of self-esteem crumble in the face of a psychological onslaught, and their self-esteem plummets. Others are more resilient and can fall back on an internal reserve of self-esteem that does not depend so much on external support.

Fourth, consider a distinction drawn by Deci and Ryan (1995). For them, **contingent self-esteem** depends on meeting standards that are usually imposed by others. Because one does not always live up to these standards, contingent self-esteem tends to be variable. *True self-worth* consists of an intrinsic, secure, stable sense of self. Such self-worth does not have to be earned, for it is a given. In line with this distinction, recall the research demonstrating that self-liking (self-worth) is related to persistence, but confidence (contingent self-esteem) is not (Tafarodi & Vu, 1997).

Core and Periphery

The theory assumes a *core* of self-esteem that cannot be observed by others. It is metaphorically surrounded by a *periphery* of self-esteem that consists of the various components or sources of self-esteem already discussed. If these external sources were stripped away, there would still be an inner residual of self-esteem, a feeling of being intrinsically worthwhile. How would such a feeling develop?

One possibility is that some people are born that way, but in the absence of any evidence, this hypothesis will not be further discussed. Another possibility is the social reward of love. However, the affection may be too inconsistent to be relied on, for in close relationships, there is often friction and dislike. And the affection may depend on one's attractiveness, ability, or agreeableness. What is needed is affection that endures even when one does not display the positive qualities valued by others. Intrinsic self-worth accrues only if love is delivered *consistently* and *without conditions,* what Carl Rogers (1951) called "unconditional love."

Such love is available in early infancy. Infants are tiny and helpless, eliciting nurturance from parents. But most newborn infants tend to be bald and wrinkled, display little of the physical attractiveness they may later have, and wear out parents with their need for constant care and their nighttime waking. Infants are intensely loved by their parents simply because the infant is theirs. Needing no beauty or accomplishment, the infant merely has to exist to receive generous love and care.

During the first year of life, the infant learns that the two most important and powerful figures treat the infant as the most special person in the world. The learning process is assumed to be imitation, with the parents being the models and the infant being the observer and copier. Such imitation is different from most observational learning in that what is learned is self-directed. There is an implicit, unverbalized attitude: "If they love me, I must be great." From another perspective, that of symbolic interactionism (Mead, 1934), there are reflected appraisals coming from the parents, and these are internalized by the infant.

The infant need not do anything to be loved, just be there. Under this benevolent regime, the infant acquires a core of self-esteem that does not depend on any specific source. Infants who are loved unconditionally and consistently during the first year of life are expected to develop a robust core of self-esteem. In rare instances, parental unconditional love continues well beyond the first year of life, producing an insufferably conceited child who expects to be liked regardless of selfishness and nastiness. However, if the period of unconditional love is too short and parental love becomes conditional too early, the core is expected to be smaller and weaker. Such children do not develop a sufficient intrinsic feeling of being worthwhile and must depend largely on external sources of self-esteem.

By late infancy, unconditional love ends, and mere existence is no longer sufficient to generate praise and affection. Hugs and kisses are less spontaneous and more in response to the child's good behavior, causing young children to learn the contingencies of social reinforcement. Parental love is now mainly conditional, and any subsequent additions to the child's self-esteem depend on the sources discussed earlier.

These external sources may potentially be lost, which means that they contribute only to peripheral self-esteem. However, such sources may develop an *enduring* periphery of self-esteem. Most mature adults can contemplate a background of at least a modicum of attractiveness, ability, status, affection, praise, respect from others, morality, and the value that comes from being part of successful groups. Thus, peripheral self-esteem does not have the postulated permanence of core self-esteem, but in the face of threats to self-esteem, the peripheral self-esteem of an adult might be battered but not shattered.

The theory requires an additional assumption to explain conceit and humility: The size of the core partly determines the size of the periphery. The woman with a large core engages in self-serving judgments about herself in excess of the normal tendency to favor oneself. She values the external sources of self-esteem as they apply to herself more highly than would neutral observers. Her periphery thereby becomes larger in her own eyes than it is when judged by others. As a result, her self-esteem is higher than the esteem she receives from others; she is judged to be conceited.

The woman with a small core does not value herself intrinsically and therefore downgrades her appearance, ability, and other sources of self-esteem; she displays humility. Others may wonder why she is so self-deprecating. The reason for her being seen as humble is a weak core of self-esteem.

Value of Self-Esteem

Implicit in **core-periphery theory** is the familiar distinction between self-worth and confidence. In speculating about the existence of self-esteem, some social scientists have leaned toward adaptiveness, which necessarily emphasizes the confidence aspect of self-esteem. Greenwald

(1980) began his account with the self-centeredness that marks virtually all humans—specifically, that we take too much credit for success and too little for failure, that self-related events are remembered better than other events, and that we rewrite personal history. He suggested that the self-centeredness helps us persevere to reach goals: We keep going because we are confident of succeeding.

Self-esteem has also been placed in the context of the evolution of our species beyond its primate origins, emphasizing adaptiveness:

> I am going to argue that natural selection has transformed our ancestors' general primate tendency to achieve high social rank into a need to maintain self-esteem. With the development of a sense of self, our ancestors' primate tendency would have been transformed. Having a sense of self means that self-evaluation is possible. The social dominance imperative would have taken the form of an imperative to evaluate the self as higher in rank than others: *To evaluate the self as higher than others is to maintain self-esteem.* (Barkow, 1975, p. 554)

And we know from their behavior that dominant animals move among others with an air of confidence.

The idea of self-worth underlies two other theories about the value of self-esteem. **Terror management theory** assumes that humans, knowing they will eventually die, develop what has been called "existential anxiety" (Greenberg et al., 1992; Harmon-Jones et al., 1997). Presumably, the mortality terror is so intense that it paralyzes and therefore thwarts your attempts at self-preservation. Self-esteem comes to the rescue through a belief that you are a valuable person living in a meaningful universe. There is a place for you, and you are important; that is, you have self-worth. Once your worldview is so organized, it resists a change, an assumption that harks back to an earlier cognitive-experiential theory of the self (Epstein, 1980).

Mortality salience is induced by having participants report their emotions when they think of dying or of being dead, and typically, participants experience at least some anxiety. Greenberg et al. (1992) found that being high in self-esteem reduces not only self-reported anxiety but also physiological arousal. In a recent experiment, participants high in self-esteem (but not those low in self-esteem) reacted to mortality salience with increasing identification with their bodies (Goldenberg, McCoy, Pyszczynski, Greenberg, & Solomon, 2000). A growing number of experiments have yielded results consistent with the theory; they are summarized by Greenberg, Solomon, and Pyszczynski (1997).

The self-protective nature of self-esteem is also assumed in the **sociometer hypothesis** (Leary, Tambor, Terdal, & Downs, 1995). As a

TABLE 3.6 Theories of Self-Esteem
Self-centeredness: leads to confidence and perseverance, which are adaptive
Social dominance: immediately establishes self-esteem
Mortality salience: self-esteem allays the fear of dying
Sociometer: self-esteem protects against feeling rejected or excluded
Core-periphery: explains conceit and humility by invoking developmentally early unconditional affection

highly sociable species, we have a strong need for affiliation, which is linked to self-esteem this way:

> A person's feelings of state self-esteem are an internal, subjective index or marker of the degree to which the individual is being included versus excluded by other people... and the motive to maintain self-esteem functions to protect the person against social rejection and exclusion. (Leary et al., 1995, p. 519)

Though being included may elevate transient self-esteem, the sociometer mechanism is assumed to respond mainly to the threat of being excluded. Having self-worth deals with this threat. So far, the only research relevant to this theory used *imagined* scenarios involving positive or negative evaluations (Leary, Haupt, Strausser, & Chokel, 1998), so the theory awaits further research.

These theories and the earlier core-periphery theory are summarized in Table 3.6.

Culture: North America and Japan

North America, which here will be restricted to the United States and Canada, has an individualist culture, whereas Japan has a collectivist culture. The details of this distinction will be spelled out in the next chapter. For now, it suffices to introduce the cultural difference with two quotations from an article by Heine, Lehman, Markus, and Kitayama (1999). North Americans value "independence, freedom, choice, ability, individual control, individual responsibility, personal expression, success, and happiness" (p. 4). Japanese value "self-criticism, self-discipline, effort, perseverance, the importance of others, shame and apologies, and balance and emotional restraint" (p. 4).

Recall that for North Americans, the distribution of self-esteem scores is skewed, with most people reporting that they are above average in self-esteem. Such overestimation enhances self-esteem, especially among Highs. The distribution of self-esteem scores of Japanese shows that almost as many people report below-average self-esteem as above-average self-esteem, and the average self-esteem score for Japanese is substantially lower than that for North Americans (Heine et al., 1999).

The difference is cultural, not racial. Japanese who have lived in North America for three generations have the same score as Americans (cited in Heine et al., 1999). It is the Japanese who live in Japan who are so different from North Americans. A related finding, reported earlier in the chapter, showed that Americans tend to believe that they can perform better than the average person. The result was repeated for Canadians; after being told they failed on a task, they still believed they were better than the average person; that is, they self-enhanced (Heine, Takata, & Lehman, 2000). But the Japanese, after being told that they were successful on a task, did not believe they were better than the average person; they did *not* self-enhance.

North Americans and Japanese react differently to success and failure. North Americans predicted that success would increase their self-esteem more than failure would, but Japanese predicted that failure would increase their self-esteem more than success would (Kitayama, Markus, Matsumoto, & Norasakkundit, 1997). After North Americans succeeded on a task, they regarded the task as more accurate than after they failed, but Japanese regarded the task as more accurate after they failed (Heine, Kitayama, Lehman, Takata, & Ide, 2000). North Americans tend to discount failure feedback, not allowing it to affect their subsequent self-rating, but Japanese self-criticize and rate themselves lower after failure (Heine, Kitayama, & Lehman, in press). North Americans defend against admitting failure; Japanese self-criticize.

In brief, we err in assuming that there is universal need for self-esteem and that good self-esteem necessarily is adaptive. The theories discussed in the last section, "The Value of Self Esteem," may apply only to particular cultures. If self-esteem varies from one culture to the next, we are left to wonder whether the same holds for identity.

SUMMARY

1. Most North Americans view themselves favorably.

2. Self-esteem consists of self-worth and confidence.
3. The major sources of self-esteem are appearance, ability and achievement, character, influencing others, social rewards, and vicarious success.
4. Being low in self-esteem has been linked to pessimism, shyness, emotional loneliness, and hostility. Lows (a) admit negatives about themselves, (b) generalize from their failures, and (c) typically give up after failing.
5. People high in self-esteem (a) describe themselves in admirable terms, (b) excuse their failures, and (c) struggle to do better.
6. The cognitive mechanisms that deal with self-esteem are social comparison, self-enhancement, self-protection, and self-verification.
7. The major theories of the origin of self-esteem are core-periphery, evolution, terror management, and the need to be included.
8. Self-esteem is not as crucial an issue for Japanese as it is for North Americans.

DICHOTOMIES

central-peripheral: crucial versus unimportant sources of self-esteem
dependable-undependable: confident versus lacking in confidence
direct-vicarious: experiencing your own accomplishments versus basking in reflected glory
personal versus social: sources of self-esteem
positive-negative: a high versus low opinion of yourself
unitary-multiple: global versus particular sources of self-esteem

GLOSSARY

attribution   a guess about the cause of behavior or who caused it

confidence   the belief that you will succeed

consistency   the urge to logically square divergent cognitions

contingent self-esteem   self-esteem that depends on comparing yourself with others

Self-Esteem

core-periphery theory   a developmental explanation of humility and conceit

entity theorist   one who seeks evidence of being able, competent

hostility   resentment and suspicion of others

incremental theorist   one who seeks evidence of improvement or mastery

self-efficacy   confidence that you can perform a specific task

self-enhancement   the attempt to boost self-esteem

self-evaluation maintenance   a theory about when to bask in reflected glory

self-handicapping   using an advance excuse for potential failure

self-verification   trying to confirm your own views about yourself

self-worth   an intrinsic feeling that you are of value

social loneliness   a feeling of insufficient contact with others

sociometer hypothesis   the assumption that self-esteem equals a feeling that others include you

terror management theory   the idea that self-esteem protects against the fear of dying

vicarious self-esteem   basking in reflected glory

4

Identity

Self-Esteem Versus Identity
Social Identity
Personal Identity
Culture and Identity
Development
Individualism and Collectivism

Understanding identity starts with the question, "Who am I?" This question may be answered in different ways, which implies multiple sources of identity. In this respect, identity is like self-esteem, but there are other similarities. Ascribed status adds to self-esteem and is a source of identity. Environmental impact (e.g., being an architect) is a source of both self-esteem and identity. And the personal-social dichotomy is relevant to both self-esteem and identity. However, identity and self-esteem also differ, and one way to introduce identity is to contrast the two.

Self-Esteem Versus Identity

Self-esteem involves evaluation: "How worthwhile am I?" As we saw in the last chapter, the answer depends in part on the various sources of self-esteem: appearance, ability, power, social rewards, morality, and vicariousness. The answer also depends on how much residual or core self-esteem developed during infancy and how much peripheral self-esteem was added subsequently. The basic question relevant to identity is, to repeat, "Who am I?" The answer depends in part on an awareness of one's own uniqueness and in part on one's **social roles** and affiliations.

If the answer for self-esteem is positive—that is, having good self-esteem—it adds pride and confidence in oneself. If the answer for identity is positive—that is, a strong sense of who one is—it lends meaning to life. If the answer for self-esteem is a lack of self-esteem, the result is self-effacement. If the answer for identity is a weak sense of identity, the result typically is a feeling of rootlessness and perhaps a fear of one's own mortality.

What happens when all memory is lost? I assume that one's self-esteem is an implicit sense of worthwhileness, which means that amnesia has no effect on it. But in the absence of memory, how can one answer, "Who am I?" Thus, amnesia destroys identity. Amnesics do not know who they are, but they might still feel more or less worthwhile.

Self-esteem is enhanced by romantic love, which offers unconditional love from a valued partner: If that special person adores me, I must be worthwhile. Is such love relevant to who I am? Is being a lover a source of identity? I suggest that it is not, because *lover* is not a recognized social role, though some of my students have protested that it is. However, identity is changed by marriage. Being single involves no particular social role, but being married establishes a special place in the eyes of the community, a role that starts with wedding rites and is followed by social expectations. Husbands and wives are *committed* to these roles, which means that marriage adds to identity.

Being married is only one of many social roles involving family and work that are enacted by adults. With respect to self-esteem, the question is, "How good a mother am I?" With respect to identity, the question is, "How committed am I to motherhood?"

Being a member of a group may add to self-esteem through sharing vicariously in the group's triumphs. Being a member of a group can add to identity through a feeling of belonging to an entity larger than oneself, an entity typically accorded recognition by the community. If the group is attacked, vicarious self-esteem is weakened and self-esteem is thereby diminished. However, if the group is attacked, members come to its defense with a stronger sense of belonging, thereby enhancing identity.

The differences between self-esteem and identity are summarized in Table 4.1. Clearly, there are sufficient bases for distinguishing between the two, and doing so outlines the boundaries of the concept of identity. Within identity, the right side of the table, there is a shift in content from the first four items to the second four. The first four are issues of concern

Identity

TABLE 4.1 Self-Esteem Versus Identity

Self-Esteem	*Identity*
How worthwhile am I?	Who am I?
Positive: adds pride in self	Positive: lends meaning to life
Lacking: self-effacement	Weak: rootlessness
Amnesia has little effect	Amnesia obliterates it
Romantic love adds to it	Marriage adds to it
How well a role is played	Commitment to a role
Group: vicarious self-esteem	Group: a feeling of belonging

only to the person and not necessarily to anyone else: who I am, the meaning of life, a feeling of rootlessness, and the destruction of identity. This is the *personal* part of identity.

The second three items involve others: marriage, commitment, a feeling of belonging, and group identity. This is the *social* part of identity. These two sources of identity may come into conflict, for as one psychologist suggested, there may be a

> tension between our "individual," private, interior, unique selves, and the "social," public, exterior, collective world. That dichotomy and its resultant dilemmas have a powerful hold on the Western imagination. From the individual/society dichotomy springs the question "who am I?" (or "who am I really?"), and the tormented search for "the real me" as distinct from social roles, the struggle to find, to truly know and fully actualize the inner self. (Kitzinger, 1992, p. 223)

This distinction between personal and social identity traces back to an early theory of personality (Angyal, 1951). Angyal (1951) assumed that we have two strong and at times conflicting motives. We want to pursue our individual goals free of social constraints, thereby clearly separating ourselves from others (personal identity). At the same time, each of us "strives to surrender himself willingly to seek a home for himself and *to become an organic part of something he conceives is greater than himself*" (p. 132), which approximates social identity. Angyal's distinction was largely ignored until it reappeared, stated explicitly as personal versus social identity in the theory of Henri Tajfel (1981) (more of social identity theory later).

Social Identity

Social identity derives from a variety sources, which may be divided into two classes. The first consists of face-to-face groups in which each of us plays a *social role*. The second class consists of broader social entities in which we are immersed in a mass of people that may run into the millions.

Roles

Kinship

Marriage. In all societies, marriage is marked by ceremony. Until recently, in our society, we regarded it as the natural consequence of reaching adult status. Older single women were regarded as "old maids," incapable of attracting a man. Divorce was difficult, and children born out of wedlock were demeaned. Now, many women choose not to marry and are not censured for it, even when they become single parents.

However, for most adults, being a husband or wife is still a major way of defining themselves. This fact is underscored when a marriage is dissolved. Married people have a secure place in the community, which recognizes them as basic to the core family. After divorce, the man and woman revert to the now-unfamiliar identity of a single person. For some people, especially those raised in traditional families, there is a loss of social identity. And whenever there is such a loss or the threat of such a loss, the issue of identity becomes salient: What was previously taken for granted now breaks into awareness, an example of the aware-unaware dichotomy. In divorce, a woman again is faced with the issue of her surname. Retaining her married name implies a partial retention of the married identity. Returning to her maiden name represents a rejection of the marriage and any identity attached to it.

Parents. Like the role of a married person, the role of a parent is recognized by the community and its laws and strongly supported by both. In all societies, boys and girls are socialized to become parents, a role that is willingly adopted by most adults. It is a potent source of identity; for many parents, it is a source so powerful that they work harder just to make a better life for their children.

Which is generally a stronger identity, that of mother or father? Women have a much greater biological investment in their children, typically breast-feeding them and traditionally doing most of the child rearing. Many more fathers abandon their children than do mothers. Evidently, women generally have a stronger parental identity than men do.

The single parent, who must be both mother and father to the children, bears a much larger share of responsibility for them than a married parent does. It follows that parenthood is a stronger source of identity for a single parent than for a married parent.

Children. For children of an intact family, it is a strong source of identity, for they have yet to develop the other sources that will accrue later. Thus, divorce may be as much of a problem for the identity of children as for that of their parents. Certainly, there is some confusion and a diffusion of roles and relationships. If the mother remarries, the children now have both a stepfather and a biological father. If the mother assumes the name of her new husband, do they change their name or retain the name of their biological father? If the children are young and the stepfather assumes the paternal role with them, do they now identify with this new family, retain their previous familial identity, or, more likely, have a split familial identity? Whatever the outcome, familial identity is chaotic while they adjust to the new reality.

Familial identity is more problematical for adopted children who know that they are adopted. If they are adolescents when they discover that they are adopted, there may be an identity crisis. In an English study called "Now I Know Who I Really Am," such adopted children split on their reaction (Haimes, 1987). One group was profoundly affected and changed their name back to that of the biological parent. Then they reconstituted the sequence of their life this way: original (birth) identity, which was altered by adoption to a false identity; when they discovered the truth, they reappraised the situation and returned to their original, true identity. The other group was minimally affected. They merely added their original identity to their foster family identity and reported that the discovery of their adopted status made little difference in who they were.

Extended Family. In these days of great mobility, many people lose contact with grandparents, aunts, uncles, and cousins. Those who do maintain a continuing, close relationship because of geographical proximity or regular family reunions tend to develop a strong sense of their place in the context of a broader familial unit. This identity is especially strong in families who trace their roots over a number of generations, the extreme in this country being those whose ancestors came over on the *Mayflower.* Such identity is further strengthened by organizations such as Daughters of the American Revolution, Daughters of the Confederacy, and similar groups that band together families who can trace their heritage to events of long ago. In this respect, Americans are newcomers.

I once received a letter from a woman who was tracing those with the Buss name back 900 years to migrants from Holland to England.

An adult member of an extended family has a network of relationships. A woman, for example, can be a wife, mother, sister, daughter, cousin, aunt, niece, and granddaughter. These varied relationships have posed a problem for some women. As one woman reported, "I was a daughter, then a wife, and then a mother. My identity was defined by my relationships with others. When do I get to be an individual in my own right?" Clearly, the sources of her identity were mainly social, and she was appealing for personal sources of identity.

Vocation

Why is vocation a source of identity? The answer starts with medieval guilds, when a young man would apprentice to a master, perhaps a stonemason. After years of apprenticeship, increasing skill and maturity, the man would eventually be admitted to the guild. It was a life appointment; only members of the guild were allowed to engage in stonemasonry. Being a stonemason became a crucial part of his social identity.

One analogue of guilds in our time is the professional societies that oversee licensing. Thus, no one can practice law without having completed the special education required and passing a licensing exam. Generally, people who enter a profession must pass through a selection process and a period of study. Like immigrants who want citizenship in the United States, they have to work to become professionals. Licensed plumbers, for example, must first apprentice somewhat in the way their forebears did in the Middle Ages.

Once people attain the required skills, most of them work in that job or profession for decades, probably most of their adult lives. What is the relevance for identity? Ask teachers this question, and most of them will offer this kind of reply: "I have a strong commitment to helping students to learn, and I make my living doing that. Having done it for years adds to my sense of sameness. Commitment and continuity contribute strongly to my social identity: Ask me who I am, and an important part of the answer is teacher."

Organized Social Groups

Fraternities and sororities are a prime source of social identity. For ease of exposition, I shall discuss only fraternities. College students live together almost like siblings, and there is an analogue of the extended family: the national fraternity. Once a student becomes a member, he is there for life. Fraternity brothers, even when they are strangers, are expected to help each other.

The feeling of belonging is enhanced by the selection process ("You have been chosen") and the punishment of initiation. The more severe the initiation rites, the more the group is liked (Aronson & Mills, 1959). There are secret ceremonies and secret handshakes. Athletic rivalry is prominent, and the competition intensifies commitment and the group feeling. Members are expected occasionally to subordinate personal needs to the needs of the fraternity. For some members, especially officers, the fraternity is a major component of their social identity.

Despite some obvious differences, there are similarities between fraternities and gangs. Just as fraternities offer a place for students who might get lost in the crowd, gangs offer a place for adolescents who wander unprotected in poor neighborhoods. Like fraternities, gangs have initiation rites, a hierarchy of older and newer members, access to women, pressure for individuals to subordinate personal goals for group goals, and competition with peer groups. Like fraternities, they engender a strong sense of belonging to a group, often identifying themselves by the jackets they wear and the territory they stake out.

Next, consider educational organizations. For some people, the college experience is one of life's highlights, and the particular college contributes to their social identity. For some students, the college may be regarded as an extension of themselves, and this is especially true of die-hard fans of athletic teams. At Indiana University, basketball is the major sport, a fact that was used to study how students identified with the university (Hirt et al., 1992). Students watched a live basketball game on television, during which their team either won or lost. The team's success or failure significantly affected only the truly dedicated fans:

> [Their identity] is so integral to their sense of self that they respond to team outcomes as if they directly affected the self. Success on the part of their team led these fans to assess *their own* abilities more positively, whereas team failure resulted in lower estimates of *their own* abilities. (Hirt et al., 1992, p. 736)

This is an example of the direct-vicarious dichotomy. Incidentally, when the Indiana University basketball coach, Bob Knight, was fired in the year 2000 for the culmination of years of uncontrolled anger and aggression, there were student riots and death threats to the university president who fired him.

Broader Social Entities

Ethnicity

We start out life as members of an ethnic group, a nation, and a religion. We can alter our original nationality and religion, but ethnicity is almost always permanent. One's physical characteristics, especially facial features and skin color, lead to immediate labeling by others, a major contributor to ethnic identity. But there is also a more private aspect. At issue here is not how others regard a person but the feeling that one belongs, as reflected in verbalizations such as, "My fate and future are bound up with my own group," "I feel attached to my group," and "I feel strong bonds toward my group" (Phinney, 1990, p. 504). But there are marked individual differences in this commitment to ethnic identity.

Most White Americans tend to be unaware of their ethnic identity because they swim in a sea of White people. Housing in our society is still largely segregated, with each ethnic group having its own enclave. However, at school, there is some mixing of the races, which is expected to cause those in the minority to become more aware of their ethnic identity. When schoolchildren were asked to tell about themselves, White children hardly mentioned ethnicity at all, whereas minority children mentioned ethnicity with some frequency (McGuire, McGuire, Child, & Fujioka, 1978).

The feeling of belonging is strengthened when the minority group is subjected to bigotry by the group that predominates. Though this country has the reputation of being a melting pot, non-Whites have never been truly integrated. Here, the ethnic identity of Caucasians is weak, except for members of hate groups (more about this later). There is a much stronger group identity among Blacks, Asians, and Indians. Why?

There appear to be two reasons. First, their different physical characteristics make them immediately identifiable and therefore quickly labeled. Whenever they mix with the White majority, their ethnicity is brought home strongly. Second, as mentioned earlier, attacks on a group lead to a circling of wagons to defend the group against the attacks. This we-versus-them attitude strengthens group identity.

Religion

Virtually everyone is born into a family that has a specific religion. This country is predominantly Christian, and within this religion, there are enormous variations in the strength of this identity. There are people who not only attend church regularly but also read the bible daily, contribute money by tithing, and would not consider marrying outside the

Identity

faith. At the other extreme are those who have drifted away from the church, which has no special hold on them, and they often intermarry.

Religious identity is expected to be stronger when the particular religion commands obedience in the details of everyday life. The everyday life of Orthodox Jews is specified in great detail: the time of prayer, the allowable food and how it is prepared, and the precise dishes and cutlery to be used. Muslims obey similar customs.

Religious identity is magnified when two religions occupy the same country and contend for dominance, as may be seen in Ireland. When both religious and cultural backgrounds clash, group identity is even more intensified: Witness the struggles within Israel between the ruling Jews and the subordinate Palestinians, most of whom are Muslims. Or recall that a few years ago in Yugoslavia, the Christian Serbs practiced genocide on the Muslim Croats.

Place

The title of this section, "Broader Social Entities," includes more than identity with one's country, but nationalism is surely the more pervasive of the sources of identity involving place or citizenship. Most Americans—indeed, citizens of most countries—have a strong feeling of patriotism, for our children are brought up to feel that way. We are taught to salute the flag. Some people burned American flags as a protest against international policies, especially during the Vietnam War. This flag burning elicited a storm of patriotism and demands for punishment of the protesters.

Patriotism demands that we sacrifice in the name of our country, not only in war but also in any competition. College men were tested for tolerance of painful electric shocks and then told that Russian men had been found to tolerate more pain than American men (Buss & Portnoy, 1967). American men responded by tolerating more intense electric shock.

Negative Identity

Most social identities are part of mainstream society and are regarded as positive or at least neutral. But some groups are outside the mainstream, and their members are branded as outcasts. They may be said to have a **negative identity,** and it typically is a stronger identity than the positive identity of those in the mainstream because they are continually being attacked.

The largest group may be homosexuals, who have a social identity thrust on them because they are branded as deviants. Most of them react

TABLE 4.2 Social Identity

Interactive
  Core family: spouse, parent, child
  Organized social groups
    Fraternity
    Gang

Larger entities (usually not face-to-face)
  Ancestral family: roots
  Vocation
  Alumni
  Race
  Place
  Religion

Negative identity
  Sexual orientation
  Hate groups
  Criminals

by keeping quiet about their sexual preference. Some react by flaunting their homosexuality by their dress and outrageous behavior. In the past few decades, many have become militant in fighting against prejudice, which of course strengthens their social identity.

Homosexuals are innocent victims of prejudice, but there are several groups that deserve the negative label: skinheads, American Nazis, members of the Ku Klux Klan, and other hate groups. They are easily recognizable by their haircuts, uniforms, or sheets. The Nazis and KKK members tend to have initiation rites and secret ceremonies, which help solidify the group. And their social identity is further enhanced by the opposition they encounter, which engenders a we-versus-them attitude.

Summary of Social Sources

The sources of social identity are summarized in Table 4.2. We are born into kinship and race and cannot escape from them. We are born into a nationality and a religion, but we can relinquish both or change them. These first four components may be regarded as our roots.

Identity 97

The last three components are voluntary, except for the negative identity of homosexuality. The rest of these components may be transitory, ending with adulthood: fraternities and gangs, for example. Organized social groups, vocation, and negative identity do not involve our roots and therefore are expected to be less important aspects of social identity for most people, though of course there are individual differences.

These various components also differ along several dimensions. We are *born into* kinship groups, a religion, and a nationality but *voluntarily* join clubs, vocational groups, and outcast groups. Some of them involve *face-to-face* contact. Kinship certainly does, and so do fraternities, gangs, hate groups, and groups of criminals. Ethnicity, religion, and place are more *distant,* enormous affiliation groups (more of this distinction later). The closeness of contact, however, does not determine how *powerful* the source is as a contributor to social identity. Thus, for some people, the most important source is religion, and for others it is national identity.

Awareness of any source of identity varies from person to person. Awareness also depends on events that can render it salient, especially attack from outside. A related question is the following: How aware are most people of their identity (the aware-unaware dimension)?

Searching for an answer, Turner (1975) asked people in Los Angeles how often they asked, "Who am I really?" In round numbers, 4% said often, 14% said sometimes, and 82% said never. The more education people had, ranging from grade school to college, the higher the frequency of awareness of identity, but even for college students, it was a minority. However, awareness does not equal importance. For example, in this country, we hardly ever think about being American until we visit a foreign country, but national identity is important to most of us.

In brief, there are four dimensions of social identity:

1. Origin: innate versus voluntary
2. Interaction: close versus distant
3. Commitment: intense versus casual
4. Awareness: keen versus vague

There is no research on all the sources of social identity, but two studies come close (Buss, 1992; Buss & Portnoy, 1967). The earlier one was conducted at the University of Pittsburgh, the later one at the University of Texas, each with more than 300 participants. Reference groups appropriate to college students were selected, and participants were instructed to rank them for how strongly committed they were, how important it was to belong to the group, or how strongly they felt as members of the group.

The groups were listed in alphabetical order: age, American, club, college, gender, religion, state, and vocation. For age, they were to contrast their peer group with those younger and older. For club, they were to consider current, past, or future fraternities, sororities, or other meaningful clubs. For vocation, they were to consider the one they were aiming for.

The rankings, presented in Table 4.3, are in order of the ranking for men in the 1967 study. In 1967, the strongest identification was for nationality, followed by gender and religion, and then age and vocation, with club and state being the lowest ranked. The only sex difference was for vocation, with women ranking it higher than men did.

The pattern was different in 1992, so let us compare the two sets of ranks that are separated by 25 years: the rows of the table. Being American dropped sharply, and so did religion. The peer group (age) became more important, and so did gender. Could these differences be due to different regions of the country, North versus Southwest? It is hard to believe that patriotism and religion are weaker in Texas than in Pittsburgh, and there is no obvious reason why the peer group would be stronger in the Southwest than in the North. Therefore, these shifts in sources of identity are probably due to changes over more than a generation, not to differences in geography.

There were shifts that might be attributed to geography. Thus, for women only, vocation became less important, perhaps not because of a difference between generations but because women might be more traditional in Texas. Among the lower-ranking reference groups, college and state were ranked higher by Texas students than by Pittsburgh students. Again, geography probably played a role. Texas residents identify more with the state than do Pennsylvania residents, and as one of the prime universities in the state, the University of Texas may be more valued than the city University of Pittsburgh. Notice, however, that none of these reference groups was ranked especially high for social identity.

Now examine the right-hand column, particularly the sex differences in the current rankings for identity. A rank difference of .5 appears to be meaningful. On this basis, women ranked gender much higher than men did. For men, the highest ranks were for American and gender, with little difference between them. For women, gender received the top ranking, with American far behind. The only other sex difference was a minimal one, with women ranking age a little higher than men did.

A few words of caution are needed. First, these are college students and a very limited sample at that. People with only a high school education of the same age might have a different kind of social identity, and even college students are expected to shift as they mature. Second, these are average rankings, with a fair amount of variability. Third, if we sampled a church group, religion would be assumed to have a higher ranking;

TABLE 4.3 Rankings of Social Identity

Reference Group	Pittsburgh (1967)	Texas (1992)
American		
Men	2.3	3.5
Women	2.5	4.0
Gender		
Men	3.3	3.3
Women	3.2	2.0
Religion		
Men	3.3	4.8
Women	3.0	4.6
Vocation		
Men	4.3	4.6
Women	3.0	4.9
Age		
Men	5.0	4.2
Women	5.2	3.7
College		
Men	5.3	4.2
Women	5.0	4.5
Club		
Men	5.7	5.8
Women	6.4	6.2
State		
Men	6.5	5.5
Women	6.2	5.8

NOTE: Rankings based on a scale from 1 to 10.

if we sampled a military group, American would rank higher; and if we sampled fraternity officers, clubs would rank higher.

The past several decades have seen women stream into the workforce, and today's women seem much more aware of what are called women's issues. These facts may account for gender being as such a strong source of their identity. In 1967, the Vietnam War made most people aware of their patriotism, whether or not they were opposed to the war, which may account for nationality being preeminent then. The events since then have made many Americans wary of the excesses of patriotism. Young people are no longer as proud of America, nor do they identify with it as strongly, though it still ranks relatively high, especially for men. And religion has dropped as a source of identity.

Two studies overlap the social identities just discussed. Jackson (1981) used a questionnaire that included these social identities: group members, kinship, occupation, friendships, recreation, religion, and romantic attachment. The other study focused on whether in fact there are different types of social identity (Deaux, Reid, Mizrahi, & Ethier, 1995). College students sorted 64 social identities for how similar they were to each other, a procedure yielding five clusters. With an example in parentheses, these were the following: relationships (wife), vocation/avocation (musician), political affiliation (Republican), stigma (lesbian), and ethnicity/religion (Asian American).

Personal Identity

Personal identity may be roughly equated with individuality: how each of us is different from everyone else. In this age of machines, computers, telephone answering machines, and automatic mailing systems that send letters to "occupant," many people assume that they are regarded as nothing but ciphers. In our crowded cities, many citizens feel that their individuality is buried beneath the weight of hordes of people. Even without these modern tendencies toward deindividuation, many people are motivated to regard themselves as special and take pleasure in the feeling of uniqueness. This feeling derives from two sets of characteristics.

Public

In Chapter 1, the personal-social dichotomy was seen as including the private-public dichotomy; thus, *personal* tends to be linked to *private* rather than to *public*. If so, how can personal identity include public aspects of the self? The answer is that observable characteristics can be used to differentiate oneself from everyone else, that is, to establish the sense of uniqueness that is a hallmark of personal identity.

With rare exceptions, each person has a distinctive *appearance.* Most people can recognize their face and body, which means that they are distinctly different from others. The need to be different may also be seen in women's use of cosmetics, hairstyle, and clothing, not only to enhance beauty but also to help establish individuality. At a party or other social event, a woman is likely to become mildly distressed to discover another woman wearing exactly the same dress. As a generality, individuality of hair and clothing seems to be less important for men, as may be seen in the comparatively limited range of hairstyles and clothing for men.

The desire for individuality in appearance is tied closely to freedom of choice, a particularly salient issue among adolescents. Most schools have dress codes, some of which specify length of hair for boys, length of skirts for girls, and details such as whether shirttails must be tucked into blue jeans. Parents may also restrict the hairstyle and clothing of their children. Adolescents tend to rebel against such regulations because they want the freedom of choice that allows them to establish their individuality. Consider the hairstyle called *punk,* in which adolescents of both sexes dye their hair in exotic colors and have it cut in a manner regarded as bizarre by most people. But that is the point: "My hair gets noticed and serves to set me apart from everyone else."

Next, consider *personality traits.* Contrast an extreme extravert and a shy person. Both typically tend to accept the way they are without any particular awareness of personality. But as they become acquainted, the enormous personality difference emphasizes the individuality of each. The shy person wonders how anyone can forge ahead and talk easily with strangers without being concerned about being intrusive. The extravert is puzzled about why anyone would be so self-conscious and constricted in social behavior. When a person is at the extreme end of a personality trait dimension, that fact highlights individuality and so contributes to personal identity.

Twins

An essential part of personal identity is a feeling of uniqueness, which depends on a combination of appearance and personality traits. But if you share all of these characteristics with your identical twin, the feeling of uniqueness is more difficult to sustain. One solution is to diverge in hairstyle and clothing and to emphasize different interests, vocation, and even personality. Thus, some twins may establish a distinct, *individual* identity despite their sameness by focusing on the few differences between them.

However, other identical twins cherish their sameness, deliberately dressing alike and enjoying the fact that others mistake one for the other. They often decide on the same college and the same career, and they may even marry spouses who are similar. Clearly, they share a personal identity and are delighted to do so. Being special as individuals is obviously not important to them, but they may still have a sense of being special as a duo. And as identical as they are in most respects, their inner lives may be entirely different.

Private

Infants express every irritation, every pain, and, generally, every experienced feeling. As the years pass, children gradually suppress some emotions and learn the value of secretiveness. They become aware of a private self, aspects of which are unknown to others. They experience body sensations and private feelings that remain unshared. Most people at one time or another develop a crush or generate an intense hatred for another person, experience awe at the grandeur of a scene at sea or in the mountains, or feel a communion with God. There are people who talk to God, have fantasies of God or other heavenly beings appearing before them, or have related religious epiphanies. Such cognitions are assumed to contribute to personal identity, whereas religious *affiliation* is assumed to contribute to social identity.

These various feelings are difficult to express and typically are not expressed, hence the need for poets. And some of these experiences are not revealed for fear of ridicule. But we are intensely aware of these various aspects of a rich inner life and know that they belong to ourselves and no one else. These experiences and the recognition of their covertness contribute to personal identity and the associated feeling of individuality.

Linked with feelings but nonetheless separable are *daydreams*: voyages to remote areas of the earth or to distant stars. More often, they are romantic fantasies that involve a partner, sometimes with sex and sometimes not. And who has not had a fantasy of vaulting ambition: winner at the Olympics, Nobel Prize recipient, president, internationally known actor, painter, or inventor? Most dreams of glory are so farfetched and self-serving that they risk ridicule when made public. By keeping them private, we not only avoid embarrassment but also maintain the myth that our fantasied goals are singular or at least rare, thereby enhancing personal identity.

Identity

TABLE 4.4 Sample Items From the Gender Identity Scale for Men

I often wonder what it would be like to be a woman.

I feel like part of me is male and part of me is female.

At times, people in stores and restaurants have mistaken me for a woman.

I feel more comfortable around women than men.

In general, I understand women better than men.

People think I should act more masculine than I like to.

I preferred to play with girls when I was a child.

As a child I was a "sissy."

It would be fun to go to a costume party dressed as a woman.

SOURCE: Adapted from Finn (1988).

Gender identity starts with anatomy, which in turn starts with the action of sex hormones during prenatal development. Boys and girls differ not only in anatomy but also in hormones that in part determine how the brain develops. Thus, there is a biological basis for the private side of gender identity: the feeling that one is male or female. There is also a psychological basis for private gender identity. From birth onward, boys and girls are labeled appropriately, treated differently, and develop slightly different personality traits. And by adolescence, they are expected to become attracted to the opposite sex. Presumably, these lessons of socialization are internalized such that by the end of adolescence, each of us *feels* masculine or feminine.

Private gender identity has been assessed by questionnaires for each sex, the items deriving from a factor analysis of a large number of items relating to masculinity and femininity (Finn, 1988). Some examples of the scale for men, which assesses their *feminine* gender identification, are presented in Table 4.4. Most of the items are the same as those on the women's scale, except for sex-appropriate substitutions. Thus, the first men's item, "I often wonder what it would be like to be a woman," becomes "I often wonder what it would like to be a man" for women. And the women's scale assessed *masculine* gender identification (for ease of exposition, the men's and women's scales will be called *gender misidentification*). Only a minority of college men score high on the scale for men, and only a minority of women score high on the scale for women. But for this minority, the way they feel about their sex identity conflicts with the way they are identified by others: Males are not sufficiently masculine, and females are not sufficiently feminine.

As might be expected, high scores on these scales are associated with low scores on traditional scales of masculinity and femininity. For men, the correlation between gender misidentification and masculinity is −.41; for women, the correlation between gender misidentification and femininity is −.27 (Finn, 1988). Having a gender-inappropriate identity is also associated with homosexuality (Finn, 1988). The correlation between gender misidentity and homosexual tendencies is .58 for men and .34 for women. Clearly, men with a feminine orientation tend to be homosexual, whereas for women with a masculine orientation, this relationship is much weaker. These two sets of correlations can be explained by the assumption that socialization of masculinity is more stringent than socialization of femininity. If boys dress up in girls' clothes, they are reprimanded more severely than if girls dress up in boys' clothes. Blue jeans are available to girls, but dresses are forbidden to boys. It is merely mild teasing to call a girl a tomboy but strong ridicule to call a boy a sissy.

It is a reasonable guess, then, that gender identity is more crucial for most men than for most women, with the masculine role being more sharply defined and more valued by society than the feminine role. Therefore, any boy who resists masculine socialization and tends to adopt a feminine gender identity must be more strongly driven to do so than a girl who resists feminine socialization and adopts a masculine orientation—hence the above sex difference in correlations between gender misidentity and masculinity/femininity. Similarly, boys who are seen as sissies are more likely to become homosexuals than are girls who are seen as tomboys—hence the sex difference in the correlations between gender misidentity and homosexuality.

Public and Private

The public and private components of personal identity are summarized in Table 4.5. Notice that gender identity is in the middle, for it is both private and public. The novel part of the table is the addition of a sense of *continuity,* which also includes both public and private aspects of personal identity. Children in the age range of 6 to 9 years can already sense the ways in which each is the same person since birth (Guardo, 1971). Girls tend to emphasize personality and boys masculinity.

Adults, of course, have a clearer and more articulated sense of identity. We can recognize not only current photographs of ourselves but also those taken many years ago. We sense that much of our personality is highly similar to that of years or even decades ago. For most of us, gender identity is a constant over decades. Feelings, daydreams, and ambitions

Identity

TABLE 4.5 Personal Identity

Public		Private
Appearance		Body image
Behavioral style		Feelings
Personality traits		Daydreams
	Gender identity	
	Sense of continuity	

can be recalled with amusement, sadness, pride, or regret. These memories and memories of events that are specific to each life history offer evidence of a continuity of one's personal identity.

Which of the various aspects summarized in Table 4.5 are more important for personal identity? A sense of continuity would seem to rank first, for how can one maintain a personal identity if it is momentary and disconnected from one's past life? The crucial role of continuity may explain why amnesia so devastates identity. Next in importance may be one's inner life: body experiences, feelings, daydreams, and ambitions. Awareness of one's behavioral style and personality traits would seem to be next. Last would be one's appearance, which undergoes considerable change and therefore offers the least continuity, making it the weakest source of personal identity.

Personal and Social Identity

If our identity derives from both personal and social sources, in some people, the personal sources will predominate; in others, the social sources predominate. When the personal sources largely determine identity, the person tends to feel special and different from others. But there is an unfortunate consequence of this tilt toward a personal identity. If you are indeed unique, your death completely cancels you. Thus, the stronger the emphasis on personal identity, the greater is existential anxiety. But if there are important social sources of identity, part of you is not wiped out by death: yourself as part of a family, a religion, a nation.

There may well be a sex difference in whether personal or social components prevail in determining identity (Josselson, 1988). Men tend to seek independence and strive to achieve, both of which are related to a sense of distinctiveness and, more broadly, personal identity. Women tend to seek affiliations and try to imbed themselves in a network of personal relationships, which are related to social identity: "Intimacy, or interpersonal development, among women *is* identity" (Josselson, 1988, p. 99). If this view of a sex difference in sources of identity is correct, it follows that men will have greater existential anxiety than women do.

So far, each component has been described as a source of either personal or social identity. This either-or dichotomy holds for most of the components, but a few are the source of *both* personal and social identity. Homosexuality, mentioned earlier, is one example. Religion is another. It is a source of social identity, one that most of us are born into and retain throughout life. But religion may be more than just belonging to a particular sect or attendance at a particular house of worship. Some people maintain a personal relationship with God. They talk to God and believe that He reveals Himself to them in direct or indirect ways.

Continuity-Discontinuity

Continuity of identity, the feeling of sameness over time and across situations, can be either personal or social. As evidence of personal continuity, feelings, daydreams, and ambitions can be recalled with amusement, sadness, pride, or regret. These memories, alone or together with the autobiography that each of us constructs, whether veridical or fictional, elicit a feeling of continuity that defies changes in appearance, values, and even personality: "As memory alone acquaints us with the continuance and extent of this succession of perceptions, 'tis to be considered, upon that account chiefly, as the source of personal identity" (Hume, 1777/1949, p. 269).

Recall the foster children who discovered their true, biological parents (Haimes, 1987). Some of them saw the event as part of a continuous identity, with new knowledge merely supplementing the same identity. Others saw it as discontinuous, which they marked by changing their names.

But there are also social sources of continuity: the same set of relatives, perhaps of friends, the same race, nationality, and religion. The commitments we make to social roles, social organizations, and vocation tend to change little in adulthood. Most adults settle into a life that is organized around the various social groups they were born into and those they chose. One's place in these stable entities offers a sense of being the same now as decades ago.

The other side of the coin is discontinuity: the sense of a break with one's past identity. Discontinuity tends to occur when threats to one's personal identity trigger defenses of it, changes in appearance or the in-

Identity

side of the body, or a desired change in identity, the extreme of which would be a sex change operation. And there are other causes. Death or divorce challenges the identity of the remaining spouse and any children. Emigrating from another country raises the issue of national identity: single or double, harmonious or conflicted? A person's belief in the family religion or faith in God may be shaken and religion abandoned. Body integrity may be threatened by amputation of a limb or mastectomy.

Aside from such adventitious events, there are two times during life when identity is likely to be unstable. One is during the teenage years, when adolescents are leaving childhood and in the process of establishing an adult identity. The other time is the 40s, when the makeup of the family is changing, there may be career problems, and the aging process starts to take its toll.

A real-life example of feelings of both continuity and discontinuity may be found in Janusz Kaminski, a filmmaker associated with movies such as *Saving Private Ryan* and *Schindler's List*. He reflected about his youth in Poland:

> Of course I can see that we are the same person.... But it is a person who has evolved from being a teenager in a Communist country in a very protected environment to a man who is in his 40s who lives in a different country, in a different system, but who still has many of the same values. Now I am in America, but I am still idealistic; I am still romantic, money still does not dominate my world. I am the same person, but I am still searching. (Lyman, 2000, p. B26)

Unitary-Multiple

There also may be a sense of diversity across the various social roles that adults assume during everyday life. Some people see themselves as behaving very differently as they move from one role to another (multiple), but others see consistency and integration of behavior across roles (unitary). Linville (1985) called these individual differences *self-complexity*. People who see themselves playing many different roles (multiple) are assumed to maintain more distinctiveness among these subidentities. When any particular subidentity is threatened, the threat presumably does not spill over into others, which would be adaptive. However, in research bearing on this idea, participants with self-reported multiplicity across roles tended to be low in self-esteem, anxious, depressed, and neurotic (Donahue, Robins, Roberts, & John, 1993). This was no transient phenomenon of early adulthood, for these relationships between multiplicity and maladjustment tended to be stable over several decades. Evidently, multiplicity in identity is not an advantage but a disadvantage.

A more severe maladjustment, **multiple personality,** represents a bizarre, abnormal kind of discontinuity of identity. Perhaps the best-known case was described by Thigpen and Cleckley (1954), later made into a movie, *The Three Faces of Eve*. Eve originally had two separate identities, each with its own personality features. These merged into one, but years later she reported more than 20.

Social Identity Theory

As mentioned earlier, Henri Tajfel's (1981) social identity theory was the modern forerunner of the distinction between personal and social identity. Tajfel wished to correct what he saw as a tendency by American social scientists to emphasize individuality and personal identity. So he pointed up the social sources of identity, not so much social roles but membership in groups. He came up with the idea, which may seem obvious in retrospect, that when a person identifies with members of a group, *who I am* becomes *who we are*. The motivation and the expected outcome of such social identity are enhanced self-esteem. The process involves social comparison between one's one group and other groups.

But how does a person move from *me* to *us*? The answer was supplied by the *self-categorization* theory of Turner and his colleagues (Turner, 1982; Turner, Hogg, Oakes, Reicher, & Wetherell, 1987; Turner & Onorato, 1999). They assume that the particular and unique features that mark personal identity are pushed into the background during the process of identifying with a group. This *depersonalization* involves categorizing oneself as a member of the group, which results in group cohesiveness and seeing others in the group as similar to oneself.

The motivation for social identity may be more complex than just self-esteem. One possibility is the need to reduce uncertainty (Abrams, 1994). The world, especially the social world, is sufficiently complex to baffle people, which is one reason that social comparison is such an important cognitive process. Presumably, by identifying with a group, a person adopts the group's attitudes and understanding of the world, rendering it easier to understand.

Two other motives were suggested by Brewer (1991) in her *optimal distinctiveness* theory. One is the need to be different from others (uniqueness and individuation), and the other is the need to have social validation and be similar to others (inclusion and assimilation). These needs involve, respectively, personal and social identity, which are regarded as not differing qualitatively but rather being on opposite ends of a continuum (Brewer & Pickett, 1999).

Culture and Identity

Some History of the Western Self

Now that we understand something about identity in our time, it is appropriate to amplify the history of the concept of self that was introduced in Chapter 1, starting with the work of David Riesman (1950). In the Middle Ages, virtually every aspect of life was controlled by a rigid set of rules. Identity was more or less fixed at birth by one's gender and social status, lending stability and a strong sense of continuity, for little changed over generations. People were so immersed in society that they just belonged, and no one was aware of the issue of identity any more than a fish is aware of water. Nevertheless, people had an identity that was determined by tradition. In Riesman's words, "The tradition-directed character hardly thinks of himself as an individual. Still less does it occur to him that he might shape his own destiny in terms of personal, lifelong goals" (p. 17).

When the Renaissance and the Industrial Revolution tore apart the fabric of medieval society, the changes wrought increasing mobility and opportunity for individuals. Now there were fewer rules and more choices. Parents and other authority figures trained their children to move toward goals, which became internalized. Riesman (1950), using the metaphor of an internal gyroscope, suggested that these people set their sights on achieving and making individual choice, but the gyroscope is established by adolescence, and their choices are limited by it. Called *inner-directed,* their identity is defined by their individual commitments and achievements.

As industrial societies became centralized and populations were located mainly in dense cities during the 20th century, people came into close contact with each other. Inner-directed people, who tend to be rugged individualists, might have caused too much friction. Furthermore, family and local community waned as important influences and sources of stability. Now people needed to be more sensitive to others, more attuned to cues emanating from others. Such *other-directed* persons have their identity defined by their peer groups and other affiliations: "*What is common to all other-directeds is that their contemporaries are the source of direction for the individual—either those known to him or those with whom he is indirectly acquainted, through friends or through the mass media*" (Riesman, 1950, p. 22). Thus, their identity is defined by their social roles, relationships, and affiliations. These three types correspond roughly to the three sources of identity mentioned earlier: traditional with being born into a category, inner-directed with individual achievements and a unique history, and other-directed with roles and affiliations.

Recall that Roy Baumeister (1987) also presented a history of the self in Western culture. Again, in the medieval era, identity was defined by gender, kin, and social status. Gradually, these waned as determinants of identity, and during the middle and late 19th century, the upheavals of political and economic change made absolute guidelines obsolete, and this trend has continued to the present.

In his book, Baumeister (1986) offered two criteria of identity in Western culture that should now be familiar: continuity and uniqueness. After specifying the sources of identity during the Middle Ages, he concluded that they have been undermined by two processes: *destabilization,* meaning change over time, which weakens the sense of continuity, and *trivialization,* meaning that the difference between you and others is no longer recognized or important. Here is most of his list of medieval sources and what happened to them:

1. *Geographical home.* Once people stayed more or less where they were born, but now mobility tends to be the norm, diminishing continuity.

2. *Ancestral family.* The family tree was once crucial, but now virtually no one cares about the family tree, trivializing this source of identity.

3. *Marriage.* Marriages once endured for decades, often until the death of a spouse, but now divorce is common, weakening continuity.

4. *Jobs.* In the Middle Ages, after an apprenticeship, you stayed in one job for life, but now people change jobs regularly, which denies continuity.

5. *Social rank.* Class status was once fixed for life, and those of higher social rank were thought to be superior, but now there is considerable social mobility (destabilization), and it is no longer believed that those higher in social class are necessarily better persons (trivialization).

6. *Gender.* Women had virtually no rights in the Middle Ages, but now they are nearly equal to men in their rights and opportunities (trivialization).

7. *Moral goodness.* Morality was crucial for identity in the Middle Ages, but with the impersonality of the modern business world, trustworthiness is no longer valued (trivialization).

8. *Religion.* In the Middle Ages, religion established the meaning of life, gave it coherence, and presented ideals to strive for. Now most people live in accord with secular goals (trivialization).

Baumeister (1986) was of course contrasting the Middle Ages with current life. But a century ago in this country, many of the sources of identity he listed would have been neither destabilized nor trivialized. And with respect to today's world, he may have overstated how much the social sources of identity have deteriorated. However, he has enlightened our understanding of identity in today's world by placing it in a historical context. His account may be especially relevant for adolescence. He suggested that adolescents now have to arrive at an identity on their own, through commitments made with the knowledge that change is inevitable and that the world is not the stable place it once was. He was referring to what is now known as the adolescent identity crisis. The idea of an adolescent identity crisis was popularized by Erik Erikson (1950) when he referred to an adolescent stage of development called *identity versus role diffusion*.

Development

The first step in establishing identity is differentiating between me and not-me. During the first year of life, infants learn the boundary between self and nonself, between their bodies and the external world. The fact of a separate body establishes that they are different from other things and other people.

During childhood, an analogous differentiation between self and nonself occurs, this time based on psychological features: behavioral style, personality traits, gender identity, and a private, inner world. These features are recognizable as the components of personal identity, which also contribute to a sense of continuity.

Childhood Through Adolescence

In a developmental study, participants were asked to describe themselves (Peevers, 1987) All the 6-year-olds mentioned continuity, especially lack of change over time. The percentage mentioning continuity dropped to 70% in 9-year-olds, bottomed at 50% in 13-year-olds, and rose only slightly among 17- and 21-year-olds. Few participants at any age mentioned distinctiveness, perhaps because distinctiveness is not salient in free reports.

An alternative is to ask individuals directly about distinctiveness and continuity. Adopting this tactic, Hart, Maloney, and Damon (1987) interviewed participants ranging from first-graders to sophomores in high school. They discovered four developmental levels of the basis for the sense of sameness:

1. Physical characteristics remain the same: eye color
2. Psychological features remain the same: intelligence
3. Social recognition: being recognized by friends as the same person
4. Relative sameness: though slightly different, essentially the same

The researchers also discovered four developmental levels of distinctiveness:

1. Physical features: taller than anyone in the class
2. Psychological features: smarter than anyone
3. Unique combination: smart, friendly, short
4. Unique inner world: private thoughts and feelings

These four developmental stages of continuity and distinctiveness have been ordered this way: (1) marks early childhood, (2) marks the rest of childhood, (3) marks early adolescence, and (4) marks late adolescence. Notice that for both continuity and distinctiveness, the first progression is from physical to psychological characteristics. After that, continuity depends on the social environment and finally on being somewhat the same as earlier. The feeling of distinctiveness progresses to a dependence on a unique combination of features and then moves on to a focus on the private self.

Notice also that virtually all these characteristics fall under the heading of personal identity. The sources of social identity are hardly mentioned, perhaps because the participants were interviewed about continuity and distinctiveness simultaneously. When asked how we are different from others, most people will answer with personal characteristics. Another reason may be that youngsters are more preoccupied with personal identity. Attention to the social components of identity may have to await their moving from the relatively cloistered world of family and school to the larger stage of the adult world.

The adolescent must deal with two basic problems of identity. First, puberty initiates rapid changes in size and secondary sex characteristics. In just a few years, the individual's appearance changes from that of a child to that of an adult. The prior continuity of body is shattered, which may lead to the question, "Am I the same person I was before?"

Identity 113

Second, there are many different role models, and the adolescent has difficulty in choosing appropriate ones. Trying out any new role, whether on stage or in everyday life, is not easy. Remember, too, that an adolescent has one foot in childhood and the other in adulthood. Yearning for the past that is now perceived nostalgically as an easier time, the adolescent is expected to move forward into adult roles.

Thus, identity can become embroiled in complexity, rapid change, and multiple expectations. In the past, the solution lay in moving to a stable identity through marriage, career, and a place in the community. For many young people today, this solution is more difficult to attain, leading to a crisis for some adolescents, which brings us to the theory of Erik Erikson (1950). In his developmental theory of identity, the child *identifies* with adults and older peers, imitating them and wanting to be like them. Some of these identities are rejected and some retained as the child matures, as the child and then the adolescent tries on this or that identity as one would clothes:

> The final identity, then, as fixed at the end of adolescence, is superordinated to any single identification with individuals of the past: it includes all significant identifications, but it also alters them in order to make a unique and reasonably coherent whole of them. (Erikson, 1968, p. 161)

Building on this framework, Marcia (1966, 1987, 1994) laid out a sequence of four identity statuses during late adolescence. In his research, participants are interviewed about occupational choice, religious and political beliefs, sex roles, and sexuality. The focus is on how much the participants are *exploring* identity options and to what extent they have made a *commitment*. The outcome is assignment to one of the four identity statuses:

1. *Identity diffusion.* In this immature status, adolescents are not committed to any social roles, vocations, or, generally, to any direction in their lives. In **identity diffusion,** they often feel rejected by their family and have few or no close personal relationships.

2. *Foreclosure.* **Foreclosure** means that there has been no adolescent exploration of options because the adolescent is strongly committed to values acquired during childhood and not subsequently examined. These individuals tend to retain the childhood absolutes of right and wrong, good and bad, and they have trouble in being flexible in their close relationships.

3. *Moratorium.* In a **moratorium,** these adolescents have temporarily given up the struggle to achieve a mature identity because they are still exploring and are not ready to commit themselves to a particular direction. They are the

most conflicted group, inconsistently being anxious, acquiescent, and rebellious by turns.

4. *Identity achievement.* Having explored and resolved the issue of selecting from many options, these individuals have committed themselves to an adult identity. By definition, they represent the most mature and flexible identity status.

Unfortunately, Marcia (1966, 1987, 1994) did not distinguish between the various sources of identity. Consider a young woman who aims for personal achievement and intends to become a physician. Let us say that she fails in her premedical studies and cannot become a physician. Now she reverts to the diffusion stage, as she reconsiders her vocational identity. A second woman wants to be a housewife and mother. She is likely to marry and have children, and she can remain in the identity achievement stage. The point is that an original vocational identity, depending as it does on ability, may not be realized; however, the identity that derives from social roles, which does not depend in any important sense on ability, is more likely to be realized. Furthermore, in people with traditional sex roles, vocational identity will be more an issue for men, and social identity is expected to be more crucial for women. Here, as elsewhere, two issues are basic to understanding identity: (a) sex differences and (b) analyzing identity into its particular personal and social sources.

A different approach has been taken by Berzonsky (1989), who proposed three cognitive styles as the bases of Marcia's (1966, 1987, 1994) four kinds of identity. These styles presumably transcend identity and typify the person's general cognitive tendencies. Adolescents in the diffuse identity status tend to *avoid* dealing with problems, procrastinating until the problems become too pressing. Those who have foreclosed identity use a *normative* orientation, depending on societal norms and the teachings of parents and other socializing agents. Those in the last two identity statuses, moratorium and identity achievement, seek information about themselves in solving personal problems. An attempt to validate these ideas, using a factor analysis of coping strategies, met with mixed results too complex to be discussed here (see Berzonsky, 1992).

What are the contributions of parents versus peers in the development of adolescent identity? Parents, not surprisingly, are interested in continuity in the development of their children's identity, whereas their adolescent children are likely to push for separation.

These various ideas on the development of identity, especially the idea of a stormy adolescence, have been investigated mainly in the context of our own society. Are there cultural differences? Most social scientists agree that in all cultures, adolescence represents transition. But as we have seen, culture plays a crucial role in social identity:

It is the transition of social identity that varies most across cultures, and the modern adolescent's struggle for self must be explained primarily in terms of how society and culture shape that transition. In other cultures, the transition in social identity from child to adult is carried off without anything like the difficulties of identity crisis. (Baumeister & Tice, 1985, p. 196)

Maturity

Marcia (1987) acknowledged that the issue of identity continues throughout adulthood:

Unsuccessful identity resolutions at late adolescence do not necessarily mean that an identity will never be constructed. Even if one has not moved out of Foreclosure during late adolescence, there are plenty of disequilibrating events in a life cycle to elicit identity crises. (p. 165)

Let us assume that individuals achieve an adult identity in their 20s. In Marcia's terms, it is identity achievement; in my terms, it is a stable combination of personal and social sources of identity. Now move the calendar forward 20 to 25 years and consider the social sources of identity. Many married partners have grown apart, and a fair percentage have divorced. The children have left the home or are about to do so, attenuating the parental role. Parents and members of the extended family's older generation are starting to become decrepit or have already died. The limits of one's vocational status have been reached or are about to be, and there are few signs of progress along this line. Significant sources of social identity remain but less than previously, and one's commitment to them tends to wane.

Next, consider the personal sources of identity. The face is becoming lined, hair is turning gray, and the body is sagging with the weight of age. Earlier daydreams have not been realized. The feeling of continuity has been weakened by these changes, which are not for the better. And by the late 40s, one senses that there are fewer years ahead than there are behind. The clock is ticking, and if the personal sources predominate, existential anxiety becomes more salient.

These various developments may cause a problem that has been variously labeled midlife crisis, burnout, or the empty nest syndrome. The response varies: wanting to start another family, getting divorced, marrying again, changing careers, becoming more religious, being "born again" or changing religions, taking up a national or political cause, or entering psychotherapy.

I should not overstate the case, however. Many people, perhaps the majority, do not experience this identity crisis. Perhaps they have foreclosed on an identity and are rigidly sticking to it. Perhaps they have a mature identity that allows them to deal flexibly with the changes wrought by advancing age. Or, in my terms, they have sufficient personal and sources of identity to handle this kind of problem. Then again, perhaps they are part of a collectivist culture or subculture, where there is a place for everyone from birth to death. Safely located in a network of societal structures and familial roles, such people do not have an identity crisis in middle age. But in our **individualist** culture, there may be such a crisis—Erikson (1950) dichotomized it as generativity versus stagnation—which may be one reason why some social commentators have criticized our way of life. We are now in a position to examine differences among cultures.

Individualism and Collectivism

Distinguishing between a personal self and a social self falls within the province of several social sciences. Ralph Turner (1976), a sociologist who reflected on the social upheavals in this country during the 1960s, divided people into *institutionals* and *impulsives*. For institutionals, "The true self is recognized in acts of volition, in the pursuit of institutional goals, and not in the satisfaction of impulses outside institutional frameworks" (p. 991). For impulsives, the true self is recognized by spontaneous behavior that fulfills personal needs and urges: "*Self-as-impulse tends to transform the institutional order into a set of norms, all cramping expression of the true self*" (p. 1009). The two kinds of people overlap the contrast between individualists and collectivists, a distinction that differentiates cultures.

Recall that one of the defining features of self-related behavior is the boundary between self and nonself, a concept familiar to anthropologists. Western cultures such as ours tend implicitly to think of a person in these terms:

> a bounded, unique, more or less integrated motivational and cognitive universe, a dynamic center of awareness, emotion, judgment, and action organized into a distinctive whole and set contrastively both against such wholes and against a social and natural background. (Geertz, 1975, p. 48)

This is a description of an *individualist* culture in which the personal sources of identity predominate. The boundary between self and others is much looser in **collectivist** cultures, in which identity derives mainly from family and other social groups and for whom concept of individuality is foreign.

A social psychologist, Edward Sampson (1988), suggested a similar kind of differentiation—specifically, between two kinds of individualism. One kind is *self-contained individualism,* which has the sharp boundary between self and others just described. The other kind is *ensembled individualism:* "Who I am is defined in and through my relations with others. I am completed by these relations and do not exist apart from them" (p. 20). The second kind appears to be what others have called collectivism.

Within psychology, the leading authority on individualism and collectivism is Harry Triandis (1989, 1995), who has a book by that name. In his description of individualist cultures, personal goals are placed ahead of goals of the group. One personal goal is realizing one's true self by means of self-actualization: discovering the *real you.* There is an emphasis on emotional independence, self-reliance, and achievement, together with a feeling of being inherently a separate person. Others are useful for the social comparison that occurs in self-evaluation (see the last chapter). Children are reared to seek independence and, eventually, self-actualization. Considerable attention is directed toward the private, personal aspects of the self.

In a collectivist culture such as that of Japan, group goals are placed ahead of individual goals. There is a focus on conformity, harmony, reliability, and being nice to other members of the group, as well as on emotional dependence, solidarity with the family or group, duties, obligations, and group harmony. There is little or no distinction between group and personal goals. Parents raise their children to be respectful and to fit in with the group and conform to it. An emphasis on personal goals is regarded as selfish and immature. As a result, identity derives only minimally from personal sources and maximally from social sources: "The self gains meaning by being firmly suspended and supported by a web of mutually binding relationships" (Heine et al., 1999, p. 5).

The individualist-collectivist dichotomy has also been framed in terms of construing the self as *independent* or as *interdependent* by Markus and Kitayama (1991). They proposed that within our own culture, men tend to have an independent self-construal, and women have an interdependent self-construal. This suggestion was confirmed in review of literature on gender differences in the United States (Cross & Madson, 1997).

Meanwhile, a major study compared the self-construals of men and women in Australia, the United States, Hawaii, Japan, and Korea (Kashima et al., 1995). To no one's surprise, self-construals in the United States and Australia were marked by independence and individuality. The unexpected finding was that

> gender and cultural differences do not have a great deal of overlap. Women are not like Asians. Cultural differences are most pronounced on the individualist dimensions of the self.... By contrast, gender differences emerged

most clearly on the relational dimension of the self, the extent to which people regard themselves as emotionally related to others. (Kashima et al., 1995, p. 932)

This research seems to confirm an earlier conception of a sex difference in whether personal or social components prevail in determining identity.

It remained for Brewer and Gardner (1996) to organize these various kinds of self-construal into an analysis based on inclusiveness. The most inclusive level is the *collective* self: a feeling of belonging to large-scale groups such as nationality and religion. The next lower level is the *relational* self: a feeling of being linked to family, close friends, and coworkers. (The collective and relational selves comprise what I have called the *social self.*) The least inclusive level is the *personal* self: a focus on the aspects of the self that are distinctive and individual.

SUMMARY

1. Identity differs from self-esteem: Identity answers, "Who am I?" and the answer lends meaning to life.
2. The two major sources of identity are personal and social.
3. The social sources include interpersonal roles (e.g., mother), gender, organized social groups, ethnicity, religion, nationality, and outcast groups. These sources vary in being innate or voluntary, close or distant in interaction, degree of commitment, and awareness.
4. Personal identity, emphasizing individuality, has these sources: appearance, masculinity or femininity, personality traits, private feelings, and daydreams.
5. Having a unified self and a sense of continuity of self involves both personal and social sources of self.
6. Social identity theories contrast personal identity with social identity, the latter involving self-categorization and depersonalization.
7. Adolescents are faced with changes in personal identity (body) and social identity (novel roles). Some postpone exploring their identity, but others commit early.
8. The Western self tends to be individualist, with a sharp boundary between self and others and an emphasis on independence and personal achievement. The Eastern self is collectivist, with an indistinct

Identity

boundary between self and other and an emphasis on cooperation and group achievement.
9. Gender differences in the self involve relations with others: independence for men and interdependence for women.

DICHOTOMIES

central-peripheral: some sources of identity are crucial, others are less important

continuous-discontinuous: feeling the same now as in the past versus feeling different

direct-vicarious: participant versus spectator on teams or in other groups

individual-group: feeling separate and special versus feeling attached or merged

positive-negative: a socially approved versus socially disapproved identity

private-public: unobservable versus observable aspects of sources of personal identity

unitary-multiple: the feeling of being a single person versus having multiple roles and commitments

GLOSSARY

collectivist   a culture or subculture that emphasizes strong ties to others and groups

foreclosure   commitment to an identity early in development

gender identity   a feeling of maleness or femaleness

identity diffusion   a lack of commitment to any identity

individualist   a culture or subculture that emphasizes strong separation from others

moratorium   delay as a means of dealing with an adolescent identity crisis

multiple personality a psychiatric disorder involving several identities

negative identity a commitment to a group society frowns on

personal identity who you are based on unique, individual sources

social identity who you are based on relationships, roles, and group membership

social roles culturally defined expectations and behaviors, such as parent, doctor

5

Self-Consciousness

Private Self-Focus
Public Self-Consciousness
Private Versus Public Self-Focus
Two Factors of Private Self-Awareness
Theory

Modern research on self-consciousness begins with a book by Duval and Wicklund (1972) in which they discussed their research on the impact of manipulations that induce attention to the self. Two graduate students and I became interested in the topic and started to do research, which will be discussed later. We decided that there might well be individual differences in self-consciousness. There was no extant measure, so we set about devising a questionnaire (Fenigstein et al., 1975).

Self-awareness has been an important issue in several psychological approaches. Increased self-awareness is both a tool and a goal of uncovering therapies such as psychoanalysis, nondirective psychotherapy, transactional analysis, encounter groups, and sensitivity training. With these approaches as background, we constructed a list of topics that would map the domain of self-consciousness:

1. preoccupation with past, present, and future behavior;
2. sensitivity to inner feelings;

3. recognition of one's positive and negative attributes;

4. introspective tendencies;

5. picturing or imagining oneself;

6. awareness of appearance and presentation;

7. concern over the appraisal of others.

We came up with 38 items and administered them to a sample of college men and women. A factor analysis yielded three major factors, which accounted for considerable variance. We then winnowed out items with lower factor loadings or that were endorsed too rarely or frequently and revised items that were ambiguous. The final version survived successive samples amounting to roughly 2,000 participants. There were three factors (see Table 5.1).

The rationale for the names of these factors may be seen in the items. The **private self-consciousness** items involve focusing on the inner aspects of the self that are not open to observation by others. The **public self-consciousness** items deal with attending to one's appearance and behavior, which may be observed by anyone. The *social anxiety* items concern shyness, embarrassment, and related issues involving unease and discomfort about being in social situations, which clearly belong in the next chapter on embarrassment and shyness and therefore will not be further discussed here.

Public self-consciousness generally correlates in the .30s with private self-consciousness, though it varies from the .20s to the .40s. An after-the-fact explanation of this moderate correlation assumes that there are three kinds of people. Some turn inward and examine both the private and public aspects of themselves, which would yield a high positive correlation. Some simply do not examine either aspect of themselves, which again would yield a high positive correlation. And some people attend to one aspect but not the other, which would yield a high negative correlation. When all three kinds of people are combined, the result is a moderate positive correlation between the two kinds of self-consciousness.

Despite the correlation between the two kinds of self-consciousness, they bear different relationships with other traits. People who are very high in public self-consciousness may be so distressed about the observable aspects of themselves that a likely consequence is shyness or low self-esteem. Public self-consciousness correlates in the .30s with shyness and in the negative .20s with self-esteem (Perry & Buss, 1990). Private self-consciousness has no conceptual link to either shyness or self-esteem and does not correlate with them.

Self-Consciousness 123

TABLE 5.1 The Self-Consciousness Questionnaire

Private self-consciousness
1. I'm always trying to figure myself out.
2. Generally, I'm not very aware of myself. (reversed)
3. I reflect about myself a lot.
4. I'm often the subject of my own fantasies.
5. I never scrutinize myself. (reversed)
6. I'm generally attentive to my inner feelings.
7. I'm constantly examining my motives.
8. I sometimes have the feeling that I'm off somewhere watching myself.
9. I'm alert to changes in my mood.
10. I'm aware of the way my mind works when I work through a problem.

Public self-consciousness
1. I'm concerned about my style of doing things.
2. I'm concerned about the way I present myself.
3. I'm self-conscious about the way I look.
4. I usually worry about making a good impression.
5. One of the last things I do before leaving my house is look in the mirror.
6. I'm usually aware of my appearance.

Social anxiety
1. It takes me time to overcome my shyness in new situations.
2. I have trouble working when someone is watching me.
3. I get embarrassed very easily.
4. I don't find it hard to talk to strangers. (reversed)
5. I feel anxious when I speak in front of a large group.
6. Large groups make me nervous.

SOURCE: Fenigstein et al. (1975).

Some of the research to be discussed has used both the private and public self-consciousness scales. In virtually every instance, when one of these traits has had a significant impact, the other has not. Therefore, when one self-consciousness trait is discussed, the other usually will not be mentioned.

Before proceeding, a few words about usage. People vary in the strength of tendency to focus on the private or public aspects of themselves. These enduring dispositions, assessed by the self-consciousness questionnaire, will be called *self-consciousness*. And there are brief periods when we turn attention toward ourselves—when writing a diary or gazing in a mirror, for example. This temporary focus on the self will be called *self-awareness*. Self-awareness refers to the transient state, and self-consciousness refers to the trait.

Private Self-Focus

Self-Consciousness and Self-Awareness

Here I review evidence that a small mirror induces **private self-awareness.**

Let us start with an early investigation of the impact of both a mirror and private self-consciousness on aggression (Scheier, 1976). Participants were angered and then allowed to use electric shock to punish other "participants" (really experimental confederates) in the **aggression machine paradigm** (Buss, 1961). Half of these angered participants aggressed when in front of a small mirror; for the other half, there was no mirror. Cross-cutting these conditions, half the participants were high in private self-consciousness, and the other half were low.

Participants in the mirror condition aggressed more intensely than participants in the no-mirror condition. Participants high in private self-consciousness aggressed more intensely than those low in private self-consciousness. Recall that these participants had been angered. When the mirror turned their focus inward, presumably they became more aware of their anger and therefore aggressed more intensely. Participants high in private self-consciousness, by definition, tend to focus on the private aspects of the self. When they did and became more aware of their anger, they aggressed more intensely. And these effects were additive: The participants who aggressed most intensely were high in private self-consciousness and in front of a small mirror. Parenthetically, there were four comparable groups of participants who were not angered; for them there was no impact of either the mirror or the trait on aggression intensity. And private self-consciousness is uncorrelated with trait aggression.

In other research on the impact of focusing on the private self, college men were shown slides of nude women, and they rated the slides on a scale from extremely unpleasant to extremely pleasant (Scheier & Carver, 1977). Compared to a control group, participants in front of a mirror rated the slides as more attractive. There were parallel findings for private self-consciousness: Highs rated the pictures as more attractive than Lows did. As part of this experiment, Highs and Lows were shown slides of atrocities (e.g., a pile of dead bodies). Highs rated them as more unpleasant than Lows did.

In a follow-up study by the same researchers, positive and negative moods were induced by having participants read lighthearted statements or depressing statements, which were known from previous research to induce positive or negative moods. Participants in front of a mirror reported being more depressed than controls after reading the depressing statements and more elated after reading the positive statements. Similarly, after reading the negative statements, those high in private self-consciousness reported being more depressed than those low in private self-consciousness. After reading the positive statements, the Highs reported being more elated than the Lows did.

There is also research demonstrating that focusing on the private aspects of the self results in a stronger relationship between self-reports and behavior. Consider two studies that used the aggression machine paradigm. Carver (1975) selected men who reported being opposed to the use of electric shock or condoned its use. In the control condition (no mirror), there was no difference between these two groups in the intensity of electric shock. In the mirror condition, those who condoned shock used it more intensely than those who opposed its use. Evidently, the mirror-induced self-focus led to behavior consistent with their attitudes.

In a study that is related conceptually, college students filled out a questionnaire on the trait of aggressiveness, and later their aggression was assessed in the laboratory with the aggression machine (Scheier, Buss, & Buss, 1978). For Highs, the correlation between the self-report of aggressiveness and aggression machine performance was .66; for Lows, the correlation was .09. Clearly, those high in private self-consciousness behaved in a manner consistent with their self-reported personality trait of aggressiveness.

When individuals are pressured directly to change their opinions, they may resist and hold their ground in an attempt to demonstrate that they still have freedom of choice. This phenomenon, called *reactance,* is expected to be stronger in those who have a clear idea of what their original opinion is. Participants in front of a mirror showed more reactance than did a control group (Carver & Scheier, 1981b).

In the same study, Highs displayed more reactance when pressured to change their attitude than did Lows. Focusing on the private aspects of the self appears to induce greater clarity of personal attitudes. These authors also used a counterattitudinal manipulation to induce cognitive dissonance, which is known to alter attitudes. Participants in front of a mirror resisted changing their attitude more than control participants did, and Highs resisted attitude change more than Lows did.

What about private sensations? College women were told that an inert powder would cause increases in heart rate, tightness of the chest, and sweating (Gibbons, Carver, Scheier, & Hormuth, 1979). Control partici-

TABLE 5.2 Parallels Between Private Self-Awareness (mirror) and Private Self-Consciousness (trait)

The State (Mirror)	The Trait
Angry aggression is intensified	Angry aggression is intensified
Nude pictures rated more attractive	Nude pictures rated more attractive
Elation and depression are intensified	Elation and depression are intensified
Self-reported attitude toward electric shock correlates with its use	Self-report of aggression correlates with its use
Original attitude is changed little by cognitive dissonance	Original attitude is changed little by cognitive dissonance
Pressure to conform is resisted	Pressure to conform is resisted
Suggestions about bodily sensations are resisted	Suggestions about the flavor of a drink are resisted

pants reported some of the suggested sensations, but participants in front of a small mirror did not report these sensations, presumably because they focused on their true internal sensations. In an analogous study, participants drank a peppermint-flavored drink, rated it, and then drank a second drink (Scheier, Carver, & Gibbons, 1979). Half the participants were told that the second drink was stronger in flavor and the other half were told it was weaker. Those low in private self-consciousness were swayed considerably by these suggestions, rating the second drink stronger or weaker, respectively. But those high in private self-consciousness, focusing internally on the actual taste, changed their ratings hardly at all. However, an experiment with a small mirror and a bogus drug manipulation found that self-aware participants were not more aware of their body sensations (Levine & McDonald, 1981), a rare negative finding.

These various results are summarized in Table 5.2. In some experiments, the same procedure was used to study both the state and the trait. In other studies, the procedures were closely analogous. Taken together, they demonstrate remarkable parallels between private self-awareness and private self-consciousness: Participants in front of a mirror behave essentially like participants high in private self-consciousness. It follows that a small mirror causes people to focus on the internal, private aspects of the self.

It might seem paradoxical that a mirror would cause private self-awareness rather than public self-awareness. After all, it is the overt, public face that is seen in the mirror. The explanation may lie in habituation. How many times have we seen the image of our head and shoulders in a bathroom mirror? Even if the rate is as little as once a day, the frequency must run into many thousands over the course of life. Eventually, this reflected visage is so familiar that it has no impact on oneself as a social object. If the public aspects of the self have habituated out, what remains as the object of self-focus when a mirror is reflecting one's face? Presumably, the private aspects of the self.

Intensification

Examine the first three entries in Table 5.2, and you will discover that the presence of a small mirror, or being high in private self-consciousness, amplifies ongoing emotional states. Other research on the trait of private self-consciousness has documented this effect on several different behaviors. Participants listened to audiotapes of humorous errors, called bloopers, and their laughter was tape-recorded (Porterfield et al., 1988). The correlation between private self-consciousness and laughter was .34. The authors concluded, "The laughter findings support the affect intensification hypothesis. The amusement induced by bloopers was intensified by dispositional self-consciousness" (p. 416).

Participants were asked to volunteer for an experiment in which they would be given electric shock, ostensibly as an aid to medical research (Scheier, Carver, & Gibbons, 1981). When told that the electric shock would be weak, 100% of those high in private self-consciousness volunteered, compared with 75% of those low in private self-consciousness. When told that the electric shock would be very strong, the percentage of Lows remained about the same, but only 50% of the Highs volunteered, presumably because of their more intensely experienced fear.

One way of minimizing intense negative emotions is to avoid thinking about them. Drinking alcohol may accomplish this end by minimizing self-awareness (Hull, 1981). If so, when people experience negative emotions, those high in private self-consciousness, who by definition are more aware of their private selves, should drink more. Participants, as part of a "taste test," either succeeded or failed in a task and then drank wine (Hull & Young, 1983). The participants could drink as much wine as needed, the real purpose being to discover how much alcohol was consumed. The Highs drank more wine after failure than after success, but the Lows showed no such difference. Evidently, only those high in private self-consciousness felt the need to minimize self-awareness after failure by consuming more alcohol.

Subsequently, alcoholics who had abstained from drinking for at least 3 weeks completed a life events survey that included positive and negative events of the previous year (Hull, Young, & Jouriles, 1986). Three months later, their drinking behavior was evaluated. Among those high in private self-consciousness, the relapse rate for the ones who had experienced mainly negative events the year before was 70%, but for the ones who had experienced mainly positive events, it was only 14%. For those low in private self-consciousness, the relapse rates were 40% and 38%, respectively. Thus, private self-consciousness intensified the impact of both positive and negative events.

Blue-collar workers often toil under conditions of noise, breakdown of machinery, and time pressure. Frone and McFarlin (1989) suggested that those high in private self-consciousness should react more intensely to the stresses of work. They found that workers high in private self-consciousness reported more work stress and more somatic symptoms than did those low in private self-consciousness.

Those high in private self-consciousness may be especially susceptible to low spirits. When participants kept a diary of their moods, Highs reported more instances of negative moods than Lows at work and in the home (Flory, Raikkonen, Matthews, & Owens, 2000). And when specifically negative social interactions occurred, Highs reported greater increases in negative moods.

Self-Knowledge

Accessibility

If you have been reflecting about yourself, the resulting personal knowledge should be more accessible than if you have been ignoring yourself. Participants were asked whether particular trait terms applied to them (Turner, 1978c). Those high in private self-consciousness took less time than did those low in private self-consciousness.

Similarly, Highs made self-descriptive judgments and self-reference decisions faster than Lows (Mueller, 1982). When asked to provide trait adjectives that applied to themselves, Highs listed more terms than the Lows (Turner, 1978b). In a memory task, participants high in private self-consciousness remembered more self-relevant words than did those low in private self-consciousness (Hull, Levinson, Young, & Sher, 1983).

Better access to the private aspects of oneself should also lead to better memory for self-related material. Participants were given words that described either traits or nontraits (Turner, 1980). A surprise memory test later revealed that Highs remembered more trait words than did Lows. Presumably, those high in private self-consciousness are more attuned to issues involving self-reference.

Accessibility means knowing your own attitudes and retaining them. Participants were exposed to persuasive messages with or without a small mirror (Hutton & Baumeister, 1992). In the mirror condition, participants were less likely to go along with the message, especially if it involved an issue they knew about and deemed important.

Scottish college students were selected who believed that stereotyping politicians is appropriate or inappropriate (Macrae, Bodenhausen, & Milne, 1998). They were shown a picture of a balding, fat, middle-aged man in a blue suit and told that he was a member of parliament. They were asked to describe him, and their descriptions were coded for being stereotyped by blind raters. During the descriptions, there was a mirror in front of half the participants and no mirror for the other half (control group). For participants who condoned stereotyping politicians, the mirror *increased* how stereotyped their descriptions were. For participants who opposed such stereotyping, the mirror *decreased* how stereotyped their descriptions were. The fact that the mirror moved behavior in opposite directions helps to solidify the conclusion that private self-awareness makes attitudes more accessible and therefore have a stronger impact on behavior.

Self-Reports and Behavior

Those who score high on the trait of private self-consciousness report on the questionnaire that they regularly try to figure themselves out, reflect about themselves, scrutinize themselves, examine their motives, and generally focus on the personal aspects of themselves. As a result, they are likely to know themselves better than those who are low in private self-consciousness.

Again examine Table 5.2, this time the last four entries. They reveal that people high in private self-consciousness (a) have considerably higher correlations between self reports of traits or attitudes and behavioral tests of these self-reports; (b) retain their original attitudes when confronted with cognitive dissonance; (c) resist pressure to conform, presumably because they have a clear idea of what their original opinion is and thus are not easily swayed; and (d) resist false suggestions about their own sensations.

In another questionnaire study, participants reported on their own altruism and were given the opportunity to offer help (Smith & Shaffer, 1986). For those high in private self-consciousness, the correlation between self-reported altruism and helping behavior was .56; for those low in private self-consciousness, it was .12.

In a variation on this theme, participants wrote stories about how dominant they would be and then were placed in a group situation and told to be as dominant and assertive as possible (Turner, 1978a). For those high in private self-consciousness, story dominance correlated .67 with behavioral dominance; for those low in private self-consciousness, it was .33. An alternative way of checking on self-knowledge is to determine whether others see you as you see yourself. Participants were asked to imagine that a friend had angered them and they were to act out what they would typically do as a consequence (Klesges & McGinley, 1982). Their aggressive behavior with a Bobo doll as the victim was rated. At the same time, a friend was asked how the subject would react. There was much closer agreement between participants' behavior and friends' predictions for Highs than for Lows.

In an analogous behavioral study, participants were asked to write down three words that described themselves without using words referring to appearance (Bernstein & Davis, 1982). Then they were videotaped in a discussion group, and the tape was shown to judges. These judges were to match what they saw on the tape with the three-word descriptions. The matches were considerably closer for participants high in private self-consciousness than for those low in private self-consciousness.

These findings were confirmed by another matching experiment (Franzoi, 1983). Participants completed an adjective checklist on themselves, then friends evaluated them using the same adjective checklist. There was greater agreement between the self-reported adjectives and the friends' adjectives for Highs than for Lows.

The bottom of Table 5.2 also reveals that a small mirror can enhance the relationship between self-reports and behavior. In a study not yet mentioned, participants responded to a questionnaire on the trait of sociability with a mirror present or absent (Pryor, Gibbons, Wicklund, Fazio, & Hood, 1977). A few days later, they were placed in a waiting room with an experimental accomplice who posed as a participant. She rated participants for sociability, and the number of words spoken by the participant were counted; together they formed a composite of sociable behavior. When the self-report was completed without a mirror, the correlation between the trait of sociability and sociable behavior was .03, but with a mirror it was .55. When the experiment was repeated, these correlations were .28 and .73, respectively.

In a complementary experiment, this time the mirror was present or absent not during the administration of the self-report but during the laboratory test of the relevant behavior (Gibbons, 1978). College men filled out a questionnaire on attitudes toward pornography—for example, whether they enjoyed reading magazines such as *Playboy* and *Penthouse*. One month later, they were asked to rate how exciting pictures of nude women were. In the mirror condition, the correlation was .60, but in the no-mirror control, it was –.21.

Public Self-Consciousness

We have seen that people high in private self-consciousness know themselves well, but there is an analogous kind of self-knowledge in those who are high in public self-consciousness. They concentrate on the overt, social aspects of themselves and therefore should know what kind of an impression they make on others. College women were videotaped while talking to a researcher and asked how viewers of the videotape would regard them (Tobey & Tunnell, 1981). Then judges watched the tapes and evaluated the women's personalities. Women high in public self-consciousness were better at predicting the impression they would make than were those low in public self-consciousness.

Gallaher (1992) had observers watch participants moving about and rated them for expressiveness (e.g., lots of gestures) and expansiveness (e.g., broader gestures). The participants also rated themselves for these two stylistic features. For Highs, the correlations between observers' ratings and self-reports were .67 for expressiveness and .55 for expansiveness. For Lows, the correlations were, respectively, .07 and –.05. Evidently, those low in public self-consciousness had paid no attention to an important aspect of their overt behavior, their style of movement.

Clearly, focusing on oneself leads to better self-knowledge. If the focus is on the private aspects, there is better understanding of one's emotions, motives, attitudes, and personality. If the focus is on the public aspects, there should be better understanding of the perspective of others about oneself.

Being observed may sometimes be threatening. Participants were allowed to practice for a forthcoming task in an experiment on self-handicapping (Shepherd & Arkin, 1989). The Highs self-handicapped more than the Lows. A more recent experiment, mentioned in the self-esteem chapter, used a camera to induce public self-awareness (Hirt et al., 2000). Compared with a control group, the male self-aware participants tended to self-handicap, particularly those who felt threatened; there were no effects for women.

Appearance

People who have a keen sense of themselves as a social object are likely to be concerned with their appearance. College women were told in advance that their pictures would be taken in the laboratory (Miller & Cox, 1982). Judges examined the pictures and evaluated how much makeup had been applied. The amount of makeup correlated .32 with public self-consciousness. Public self-consciousness also correlated .40

with participants' belief that makeup enhances appearance and social interactions and .28 with judged attractiveness of the participants.

Other researchers have also reported that women high in public self-consciousness are more attractive than those low in public self-consciousness (Turner, Gilliland, & Klein, 1981). These investigators also found that when asked to express their like or dislike of their physical features (e.g., hair and eyes), Highs reacted faster than Lows.

In our culture at least, women are more concerned about their appearance than men, so it is not surprising that research on appearance and public self-consciousness has tended to use women as participants. Two appearance questionnaires are especially relevant here. One deals with body ideals—specifically, ideals and self-discrepancies from these ideals for hair, face, body proportions, and the importance of these features (Cash & Szymanski, 1995). Public self-consciousness correlated .26 with self-ideal discrepancies and .48 with importance. The somewhat different Appearance Schemas Inventory consists of items that "reflect beliefs about the importance, meaning, and perceived influences of appearance in one's life" (Cash & Labarge, 1996). It correlated .59 with public self-consciousness.

The role of public self-consciousness in self-perception of appearance is not limited to women. As we saw in Chapter 2, men are concerned about losing hair, but this concern is considerably stronger in men high in public self-consciousness, the correlation being .48 (Franzoi et al., 1990).

Attention From Others

College women participated in an experiment with two other ostensible participants who were in reality experimental accomplices (Fenigstein, 1979). These accomplices completely ignored the participant while having a conversation between themselves. All this happened in a "waiting room," after which the participant was given a choice of continuing in the experiment with these two "participants" (accomplices) or obtaining two new partners. Those high in public self-consciousness chose other partners, avoiding those who shunned them to a much greater extent than those low in public self-consciousness. In replies to later questions, Highs liked the accomplices less than did Lows only in the rejection condition; when not rejected, they had no reason for liking the others less. And Highs felt more responsible for the way the others behaved than did Lows. Thus, when Highs were the targets of shunning, they directed some of the blame to themselves, which is exactly what we would expect from people who have an acute sense of themselves as social objects.

In a rare field study, participants were approached in an airport and asked to sample a brand-name peanut butter and a bargain brand peanut butter (Bushman, 1993). There was either an audience, including a companion, or no audience or companion. Public self-consciousness was expected to accentuate a preference for the national brand because "national brand products have more favorable public images than do bargain brand products. Image is very important to public self-conscious individuals" (Bushman, 1993, p. 858). Public self-consciousness did elevate the preference for the brand-name peanut butter, especially when there was an audience.

Small groups of students were told that some of them had been chosen randomly to participate in an experiment, and each student was asked to estimate the probability that he or she had been so selected (Fenigstein, 1984). The estimates of self-as-target correlated .34 with public self-consciousness: Highs exaggerated whether they had been chosen.

Fenigstein (1984) had a new sample of participants fill out a self-as-target questionnaire. A typical statement was, "You are giving a public lecture and before you finish, some people get up and leave." There were two answers to each statement, one involving the self as target—for example, "The people left because the lecture was boring." Again, those high in public self-consciousness answered more of the questions in the direction of self-as-target than did those low in public self-consciousness. Evidently, a focus on the public aspects of the self can make one somewhat self-centered.

Fenigstein and Vanable (1992) carried this idea one step further:

> To see oneself as an object of attention, especially to others, may leave one susceptible to the idea that others are more interested in the self than is the case; the self-referent perceptions of the behavior of others is one of the hallmarks of paranoid thought. (p. 136)

These authors constructed a paranoia scale (typical item: "Someone has it in for me"), and it correlated with public self-consciousness from .37 to .41 over four successive samples of participants. These correlations were confirmed in research by Buss and Perry (1992) on aggression. The correlations between public self-consciousness and **hostility** were .32 for men and .49 for women. Among the items on the hostility scale were several items that tapped suspicion—for example, "I am suspicious of overly friendly strangers."

Paranoia would seem to be the extreme end of a focus on oneself as a social object. Though public self-consciousness correlates with paranoia, a strong sense of oneself as a social object is best regarded as a requisite for paranoia but not as equivalent to it.

Private Versus Public Self-Focus

Self-Consciousness

In the studies reviewed so far, when one kind of self-consciousness has had an impact, the other kind has not. Additional research has demonstrated the *contrasting* effects of private self-consciousness versus public self-consciousness.

An experiment cited earlier used the well-known Asch conformity paradigm (Froming & Carver, 1981). In an auditory perception study, participants' error scores (indicating compliance) were correlated with the two self-consciousness traits. The error scores correlated *negatively* with private self-consciousness: Those higher in private self-consciousness made few errors because, knowing what they heard, they refused to comply with group pressure. The correlation between error scores and public self-consciousness was *positive*: Those higher in this trait, being concerned about themselves as social objects, conformed more to group pressure, resulting in more errors.

Recall that when asked to register like or dislike of their physical features, those high in public self-consciousness reacted faster than did those low in this trait (Turner et al., 1981). Perhaps each kind of self-consciousness causes sensitivity to different kinds of self-reference. Participants were shown a list of words serially and asked to say yes or no for three questions: Is it a long word? Does it describe how you typically feel or think? Does it describe the way people typically see you? (Agatstein & Buchanan 1984). Notice that the questions involve, respectively, no self-reference, private self-reference, and public self-reference. A few minutes later, there was a surprise recall test. Participants high in private self-consciousness and low in public self-consciousness recalled more private self-reference words than the other two kinds. For participants high in public self-consciousness and low in private self-consciousness, recall was best for public self-reference words.

Nasby (1989) confirmed these findings in a recognition task. Participants high in private self-consciousness had more intrusions, called false alarms, of private self-reference words than did those low in private self-consciousness. Participants high in public self-consciousness had more intrusions of public self-reference words. Presumably, such intrusions indicate a more articulated self-schema. On this assumption, Nasby (1989) concluded that his results demonstrated that private self-consciousness (but not public self-consciousness) predicts the extent to which individuals have articulated the private component of the self-schema, whereas public self-consciousness (but not private self-consciousness) predicts the extent to which individuals have articulated the public components of the self-schema. (p. 121)

Follow-up research yielded the same results for private versus public self-consciousness, this time for the ideal self.

In everyday life, personal standards of fairness may conflict with social pressure to be regarded as a nice person, a conflict examined by Greenberg (1983). Participants were asked to divide $10 between a high-output worker who did 75% of the work and a low-output worker who did 25% of the work. Fairness suggests an equitable distribution of the money: $7.50 to the high-output worker and $2.50 to the low-output worker. But all participants were told that they would meet with the low-output worker after the money was allocated. The social pressure of dealing with this person might lead to an equal distribution of money. Those high in *public* self-consciousness tended to offer about the same amount to each worker and reported less concern about doing what seemed fair. Participants high in *private* self-consciousness tended to offer more money to the high-output worker and reported less concern about making an impression on the low-output person.

These findings were conceptually replicated by Kernis and Reis (1984). Evidently, people high in private self-consciousness focus more on personal standards of morality, whereas those high in public self-consciousness focus on themselves as social objects and therefore are concerned with the impression they make on others.

A related study used ratings of behavioral intentions to assess the strength of personal attitudes and social norms for each participant (Davis, Kasmer, & Holtgraves, 1982). In predicting behavioral intentions, *private* self-consciousness correlated positively with the strength of personal attitudes and negatively with social norms. The findings for *public* self-consciousness were more complex, with this trait having an impact on behavioral intentions only when normative influences became stronger.

In an experiment on cognitive dissonance mentioned earlier, participants were induced to write counterattitudinal essays (Scheier & Carver, 1980). This procedure incited a conflict between their original attitude and the one they were induced to write. A focus on the private aspects of the self would make participants attend to their original (private) attitude, rendering the attitude more resistant to change. A focus on the public aspects of the self would make participants attend to their public behavior (writing an essay in the opposite direction), making the attitude more susceptible to change. Participants high in private self-consciousness, focusing on their original attitude, resisted change. Participants high in public self-consciousness, focusing on their public behavior, changed their attitude in the direction of the essays they wrote.

In each of these experiments, participants high in private self-consciousness oriented toward the covert, personal aspects of the self, and participants high in public self-consciousness oriented toward the overt, social aspects of the self. This divergence is especially interesting in light of fact that the two kinds of self-consciousness usually correlate in the .30s and sometimes higher. Clearly, when we know only that a person focuses on the self, this knowledge is too vague. A focus on the internal, private aspects of the self leads to very different behavior than a focus on the external, public aspects of the self.

Self-Awareness

There is substantial evidence that a small mirror induces private self-awareness, but which kind of self-awareness is elicited by an audience? Several experiments compared a mirror and an audience in the same study. In the first of two experiments, college men were allowed to aggress against women in the aggression machine paradigm (Scheier, Fenigstein, & Buss, 1974). The presence of a mirror inhibited the intensity of aggression, presumably because the mirror caused them to become aware of the well-known rule that men treat women gently. The audience, consisting of three people, had little impact. As to why, we suggested it was because the participants simply ignored the audience. To guarantee that participants would attend to the audience, in the second experiment, participants were told to check regularly to see if anyone in the audience had a question. Now the audience had an impact, inhibiting the level of aggression. Perhaps the audience reminded participants of the same injunction to go easy on women, though this hypothesis is after the fact. So the question remains as to which kind of self-awareness is elicited by an audience.

The answer came from two other experiments, again using the aggression machine paradigm, and all the participants were men (Froming, Walker, & Lopyan, 1982). The first experiment used only participants who (a) were opposed to the use of physical punishment but (b) believed that most people favored it. They were given the opportunity to physically punish another man in the aggression machine paradigm. In addition to a control group, one group was in front of a mirror, and one group had an audience.

Compared with the control condition, the mirror caused a *clear drop* in the intensity of aggression. The authors concluded that the mirror caused participants to become more aware of their personal beliefs (oppose the use of physical punishment). An ordinary audience had no effect compared with the control condition, but an evaluative audience caused a *clear increase* in the intensity of aggression. The authors concluded that the audience made participants aware of the attitude of most people (condone using physical punishment).

The second experiment used only men who (a) were in favor of the use of physical punishment but (b) believed that most people were opposed to it. The same paradigm and conditions were used as in the first experiment. In comparison to the control condition, the mirror caused *an increase* in the intensity of aggression, presumably because participants were made aware of their personal attitude (favor physical punishment). This time, the evaluative audience had no effect, but an evaluative audience of experts caused a *clear drop* in aggression intensity, presumably because participants were made aware of the attitude of most people (opposed to physical punishment).

These experiments by Froming et al. (1982) are important in establishing the contrasting effects of a small mirror and an audience, first in one direction and then in the other direction. Experimental conditions that move in opposite directions from a control group (the first experiment) are unusual in psychology, but duplicating this feat in the opposite direction (the second experiment) is truly rare.

The mirror caused these participants to become more aware of their private attitude, which is consistent with what is already known about the mirror: It elicits private self-awareness. The audience caused these participants to become more aware of the attitudes of others, which surely is linked to an awareness of oneself as a social object. It follows that an audience elicits public self-awareness. But not just any audience elicits public self-awareness. In these experiments, it also required evaluation and expertness. In the previously mentioned research (Scheier et al., 1974), it required getting the participants to attend to the audience. The problem may be the artificiality of a very small audience in the laboratory. In everyday life, a larger audience may reasonably be expected to elicit public self-awareness (more of this issue in the next chapter when conspicuousness is discussed).

Two Factors of Private Self-Awareness

I have waited until now to discuss whether private self-consciousness may be subdivided because most of the research with the self-consciousness

TABLE 5.3   Two Factors of Private Self-Consciousness

Self-reflectiveness
1. I'm always trying to figure myself out.
2. I reflect about myself a lot.
3. I'm often the subject of my own fantasies.
4. I'm constantly examining my own motives.
5. I sometimes have the feeling I'm off somewhere watching myself.

Internal state awareness
1. I'm generally attentive to my inner feelings.
2. I'm alert to changes in my mood.
3. I'm aware of the way my mind works when I work through a problem.

NOTE: The two reversed items in the original private self-consciousness factor were dropped in this factor analysis.

questionnaire has used the entire private self-consciousness scale. Almost a decade after the publication of the questionnaire, a new factor analysis of it appeared (Burnkrant & Page, 1984). Instead of the three factors (Fenigstein et al., 1975), they found four. As we did, they found a public self-consciousness factor and a social anxiety factor. But they also distinguished two factors of private self-consciousness, which they named *self-reflectiveness* and *internal state awareness* (see Table 5.3). The two factors correlated strongly: .54, which is not surprising, for in our original research we found a single factor, not two. Correlations tend to bounce, as may be seen in the correlation between self-reflectiveness and internal state awareness across four large samples of participants: .41, .53, .59, and .68 (Hoyle, 1993).

Since 1984, the factor structure of the self-consciousness questionnaire has been investigated a number of times. It has been translated into other languages, but caution suggests limiting the research to those in the English-language version (Anderson, Bohon, & Berrigan, 1996; Bernstein, Teng, & Garbin, 1986; Chang, 1998; Creed & Funder, 1999; Kingaree & Ruback, 1996; Mittal & Balasubramanian, 1987; Reeves, Watson, Ramsey, & Morris, 1995; Trapnell & Campbell, 1999). Most of these studies found two private self-consciousness factors, roughly the same as those in Table 5.3, though the items were not identical; for example, "I reflect about myself a lot" sometimes loaded on both self-reflectiveness and internal state awareness.

Of particular interest is how each of the two factors relates to other personality variables, especially those relating to abnormality. Self-reflectiveness correlates with anxiety, social anxiety, neuroticism, depression, **negative self** and peer descriptions, and low self-esteem—a combination suggesting neurotic behavior. Internal state awareness is unrelated to most of these traits, but it has been linked to the need for cognition (a rough measure of curiosity) and to personal identity, neither of which is related to self-reflectiveness, and to positive self-evaluation. Also, internal state awareness correlates moderately with conscientiousness (one of the superfactors of personality that involves dutifulness, deliberation, and a need for order), but self-reflection is unrelated.

After reviewing research on the two factors, Trapnell and Campbell (1999) suggested that the self-reflectiveness factor should really be called "rumination," and the internal state awareness factor should be called "reflection" (we shall stick to the original names for the two factors of the private self-consciousness scale). Accordingly, they constructed a questionnaire specifically to assess rumination and reflectiveness. It yielded the two factors they expected. Examples of the rumination factor are as follows: "I always seem to be rehashing in my mind recent things I've said or done" and "Sometimes it's hard for me to shut off thoughts about myself." Examples of the reflectiveness factor are as follows: "I often like to look at my life in philosophical ways" and "People often say I'm a 'deep,' introspective type of person." Internal state awareness was found to correlate in the .30s to .40s with their reflectiveness factor but not at all with their rumination factor. Self-reflectiveness was found to correlate about the same—roughly, in the .50s—with *both* their reflectiveness and rumination factors.

I have discussed the psychometric properties of the private self-consciousness scale as though the evidence is overwhelming that there are two distinct factors. Certainly, most studies have reported two factors. However, there are exceptions. Three factors—that is, only one private self-consciousness factor—were reported for a slight revision of the self-consciousness questionnaire (Scheier & Carver, 1985; see also a study by Bernstein et al., 1986). One other investigation requires special attention because it applied a set of criteria, which taken together are more stringent than those used in any other factorial study: approximation to simple structure, relative invariance across communality estimates, and the best fit in confirmatory factor analysis (Britt, 1992). On the basis of these criteria, the three-factor solution turned out to be better than the four-factor solution, the one with two private self-consciousness factors.

Britt's (1992) conclusion that there is only one private self-consciousness factor makes sense in light of the research discussed earlier in the chapter. Of particular importance were the fairly precise parallels between the impact of private self-consciousness and that of a small mirror (private self-awareness). But there are other reasons. The reflectiveness factor of Trapnell and Campbell (1999) correlates with both the internal state awareness and self-reflectiveness factors of the self-consciousness scale. Also, dividing private self-consciousness into two factors yields two scales with a small number of items, which is known to weaken reliability. One outcome is that correlations with these scales vary considerably. For example, in three successive samples of participants, the three-item internal state awareness scale yielded correlations with self-esteem of .66, .37, and .30 (Kingaree & Ruback, 1996).

Consider also that even when the private self-consciousness scale is divided into two factors, the two factors yield the same results. To cite just one example, in an experiment demonstrating that making participants sad leads to a focus on the private aspects of the self, Green and Sedikides (1999) wrote, "The results of the two experiments reported in this article were not different across the two subscales. Therefore we presented overall PSC [private self-consciousness] scores" (p. 117).

These various facts offer reasons to use the entire private self-consciousness scale and not divide it into subfactors. But other facts mentioned earlier suggest that it may also be useful to separate it into two factors. Examine the items in Table 5.3, and you will see that the two factors differ in intensity of focus on the private aspects of the self. The self-reflectiveness items contain the words *always, a lot, often,* and *constantly,* suggesting perhaps an excessive attention to the self, bordering on obsessiveness. The internal state awareness items are much milder, suggesting a more neutral inward focus. The interpretation seems straightforward. Paying attention to yourself in the sense of introspecting and trying to understand yourself is entirely appropriate and may even promote mental health. But being preoccupied with yourself is more problematic and at odds with good mental health. Of course, having problems of living might cause anyone to focus inward.

Theory

Objective Self-Awareness

The earliest theory appeared in the book *A Theory of Objective Self-Awareness* (Duval & Wicklund, 1972). A cousin to the cognitive dissonance theory of Leon Festinger (1954), this theory makes four assumptions:

1. Self-awareness causes self-evaluation.
2. The immediate result is a comparison of current behavior against a standard.

Typically this comparison yields a negative discrepancy: behavior not up to the standard.

3. The negative discrepancy is aversive, motivating behavior to escape being self-aware.
4. If escape is not possible, an attempt is made to reduce the discrepancy between the behavior and the standard.

Under some conditions, participants do attempt to escape from the aversiveness of self-awareness. For example, a female confederate was either friendly or unfriendly to male participants, and later the participants could listen to tape recordings of their own voices (Gibbons & Wicklund, 1976). Rebuffed participants listened less to their own voices than welcomed participants did.

However, subsequent research, reviewed by Carver and Scheier (1981a), has demonstrated that self-awareness is not necessarily aversive. Indeed, aversiveness occurs *only* when it is experimentally induced: when participants are asked about their own emotions when they contemplate their deaths (Arndt, Greenberg, Simon, Pyszczynski, & Solomon, 1998), when participants are failed on a task (Greenberg & Pyszczynski, 1986), or when participants are negatively evaluated or are saddened (Green & Sedikides, 1999; Sedikides, 1992).

Hull and Young (1983) have suggested that alcohol is consumed to reduce self-awareness, which is consistent with the hypothesis that self-awareness is aversive. However, in subsequent research on the trait of private self-consciousness, only those high in private self-consciousness *who failed* in a task consumed more alcohol (Hull et al., 1986). This finding and others discussed earlier in the "Intensification" section mean that self-awareness is aversive only after negative outcomes. And with respect to the trait of self-consciousness, if self-awareness is always aversive, we are puzzled by the behavior of people high in private self-consciousness, who frequently turn their attention to their psychological insides; surely they are not masochists.

Objective self-awareness theory nicely accounts for situations in which there is a clear standard. When men were allowed to aggress against women, the standard was that women are to be treated kindly (Scheier et al., 1974). Accordingly, a mirror had the effect of reducing the intensity of aggression. But often there is no clear standard to guide behavior. In a subsequent experiment on aggression, men were angered and allowed to aggress against other men (Scheier, 1976). A mirror resulted in more intense aggression, but what is the standard for aggression when one is angered? And when participants are exposed to stimuli that lighten or darken mood, a mirror heightens the positive or negative mood (Scheier & Carver, 1977). But what is the standard for how much the mood is intensified?

These are just samples of a body of research bearing on the theory of self-awareness, much of which has already been reviewed. In brief, there is some evidence consistent with the theory of objective self-awareness. However, self-awareness is often not aversive and may indeed be sought after. There are many situations in which there is no clear standard against which to compare present behavior and therefore no basis for assuming a discrepancy. And the theory makes no attempt to account for the personality traits of private and public self-consciousness.

Control Theory

If the theory of objective self-awareness is vague about what a standard is, **control theory** is more explicit: "Standards are simply specifications of qualities, of states, or of actions" (Carver & Scheier, 1981a, p. 120). Also,

> the kinds of standards that are of greatest concern to us here and things that have long been familiar to psychologists under other names. Attitudes, for example, provide behavioral standard. Desires represent standards. So do instructions. And so do the results of our more elaborate reasoning processes. (Carver & Scheier, 1981a, p. 120)

This list is certainly specific enough, but by this definition, what is not a standard? Defined that way, standards are so ubiquitous—qualities, states, actions—that they are involved in most of our behavior. The outcome is a theory that might account for any finding.

Carver and Scheier (1981a) went on to discuss the existence of a standard:

> We presume that behavioral specifications are encoded in memory in the same fashion as is other information. As schemas develop for the recognition of event categories, some schemas . . . include behavior-specifying information. When a schema that includes such information is accessed and used in the classification of a stimulus input, the response-specifying information may also be accessed as part of the schema. That information, then, constitutes the behavioral standard. (p. 121)

I have quoted extensively from the theory in an attempt to show how it predicts behavior when self-awareness is an issue. A key issue is the concept of *standards,* which the theory has expanded to include a wide variety of psychological contents and processes, but some questions remain. Is it appropriate to assume that when you see horrible picture, there is a standard for how bad it is? Is only one standard operating at any given time? The theory should clarify these issues, but they are minor when compared with the large body of research spawned by the theory, as may be seen throughout this chapter.

Self-Relevance

One alternative to the theory of objective self-awareness assumes that "self-awareness corresponds to the encoding of information in terms of its relevance for the self and as such directly entails a greater responsiveness to the self-relevant aspects of the environment" (Hull & Levy, 1979, p. 757). This approach is beguiling in its simplicity, for it states merely that our self-interest makes us attend more to stimuli that affect us than to stimuli that do not. No one would argue with this proposition, but it does not help us explain (a) why private self-awareness and self-consciousness intensify emotions and mood or (b) why the impact of private self-awareness or self-consciousness is so different from the impact of public self-awareness and self-consciousness.

Self-Consciousness Theory

This theory was first proposed in a book, *Self-Consciousness and Social Anxiety* (A. H. Buss, 1980), after some of the earlier research but before much of the subsequent research on self-awareness and self-consciousness. It deals with (a) **inducers** of private and public self-awareness and their impact and (b) a more speculative account of how self-awareness and self-consciousness develop.

Private Self-Awareness

Inducers

One way to activate private self-awareness is to turn away from social stimuli and daydream about yourself. Most people fantasize about romance, ambition, or just getting away from it all. Another way is simply to introspect, examining current moods, motives, or the meaning of one's existence. Writing a diary is a possibility, but it depends on what is written. If the diary is merely a journal of events—classes attended, trips taken, or friends met—there is little attention to the self. But if it recounts secret thoughts and feelings deriving from the innermost self, the diarist is in a state of private self-awareness. Similarly, certain kinds of meditation may instigate private self-awareness—specifically if it allows or encourages a focus on the self. The last inducer, a small mirror, has already been discussed.

Intensification

As we have seen, focusing on the private aspects of the self *intensifies* current feelings and emotions such that elation is heightened, sadness is deepened, and anger is roused. There are many examples in everyday life of such augmentation. Suppose you are to take an exam for which you are not fully prepared. The more you think about your lack of preparation, the more worried you become. Suppose you are scheduled for a root canal. The more you imagine what will happen to you in the dentist's chair, the more upset you become. Suppose you have just fallen deeply in love. The more you think about how you love that person, the more in love you become (and the happier you become).

Such polarization has been demonstrated in research on attitudes. Participants were either asked to think about a liked or disliked partner, or they were distracted in the control condition (Sadler & Tesser, 1973). Compared with the control group, the thinking group liked the likable partner better and disliked the dislikable partner more. In follow-up research on attitudes and on the pleasantness or unpleasantness of slides, the longer the participants thought about the attitudes of the slides, the more polarized were their reactions (Tesser & Conlee, 1975).

More recent research, conducted long after the theory was first published in 1980, lends weight to the assumption that self-focus intensifies emotion (Lyubomirsky, Caldwell, & Nolen-Hoeksema, 1998). Mildly depressed participants were given one of two sets of instructions. In the self-focused condition, they were asked to think about their current level of energy, their feelings, their character, and why they turned out the way they had. Afterward, they reported being more depressed. In the distraction condition, they were asked to think about clouds in the sky, what a well-known painting looks like, and the look of a shiny trumpet. Afterward, they reported being less depressed. The same two conditions were used with nondepressed participants. For them, neither self-focus nor distraction affected mood. Thus, self-focus led to intensification only when there was an emotion that might be intensified.

The point of this research and the earlier everyday examples is that focusing directly on psychological reactions that are affect laden tends to sharpen the affect, making it more positive or more negative. So when we turn the focus inward and there is a current emotion or feeling, it is like looking directly into a flashlight: It seems brighter. And people who chronically turn attention inward—those high in private self-consciousness—tend to experience moods and emotions more deeply.

Clarification

Research on information processing has amply demonstrated that attention and repetition are crucial to memory. When you meet a man, if you do not pay close attention to his name because you are occupied with looking him in the eye and shaking his hand, you are likely to forget his name. Of course, if subsequently his name keeps coming up, you will remember it. Now consider those high in private self-consciousness, who chronically direct their attention inward. The effect of such attention, multiplied over time, is to make them more familiar with themselves, more ready to offer a truer and more complete self-report.

The explanation does not work as well in accounting for the finding that making a self-report in front of a small mirror results in a true self-report. One possibility is that any focus of attention at the time memories are to be retrieved tends to enhance memory—hypnosis, for example. However, self-consciousness theory is on shakier ground here.

Public Self-Awareness

Inducers

Social Attention. One of the most potent inducers of public self-awareness is receiving close attention from others. It may occur in front of an audience or simply because others are staring. This kind of self-awareness is also heightened when people are being filmed or tape-recorded.

Public scrutiny often elicits a feeling of exposure, either that one's clothes are somehow transparent, revealing nakedness, or that one's skin is transparent, revealing thoughts and feelings. For most people, being closely examined elicits at least a faint feeling that there is something wrong with the public self. Why is public self-awareness typically uncomfortable, almost like the feeling motorists have when they see a police car in the rearview mirror? Presumably because of the way we are socialized, a topic soon to be discussed.

But too little attention is also an immediate cause of public self-awareness. Recall that shunning made participants uncomfortable enough to request other partners (Fenigstein, 1979). When people are ignored, they often seek an explanation in their own appearance or behavior, thereby focusing on the self as a social object.

Perceptual Feedback. **Perceptual feedback** is provided through modern technology, which offers us images that tell us how we appear to others. A tape recording of your own voice sounds different from hearing your own voice because bone conduction is missing. What you hear on the tape is what you sound like to others. You hear aspects of your voice that ordinarily escape awareness: pitch, loudness, accent, and inflections.

Videotapes may be more compelling. Now there are views of yourself from the side, displaying facial and body profiles or views from the back that may embarrass you: "Is my nose that funny looking? Am I that fat? Is my hair such a mess? (Alternatively, am I that bald?)" Now add facial expressions and posture that are not pleasing, and it is clear that perceiving yourself as others perceive you is usually a blow to self-esteem. Even physically attractive men and women find fault with what they see, for they tend to focus on their minor imperfections.

Most of the problem stems from the novelty of these views of yourself as others see you. Singers and announcers hear recordings of their voices so often that they habituate to the sounds and are not made aware of themselves as social objects. Similarly, movie actors see themselves on the screen frequently enough to habituate to the sight of themselves from all angles, and eventually the movies do not induce public self-awareness. Presumably, the same kind of habituation occurs to the visage we see in our bathroom mirror every day, the basic assumption (mentioned earlier) of why the presence of a small mirror induces private self-awareness.

Development

At birth, infants possess neither kind of self-awareness, but by school age, they are able to focus on both aspects of the self. The development of self-awareness continues throughout childhood, reaching a peak at adolescence. This section is normative in tracing the sequence of milestones for most children. But some children are precocious and some are laggards in development.

Private Self-Awareness

Private self-awareness starts with a developmental trend toward covertness. Infants are completely uninhibited in expressing emotion, and when distressed, they cry, scream, and thrash about. As children mature, they gradually inhibit expression of their emotions. They may still become frightened or angry, but as the years pass, these emotions are first partially suppressed and later sometimes kept completely covert. In older children and especially in adults, a placid exterior may conceal intense, private feelings and emotions.

The play of infants typically is entirely overt: handling objects and playing such games as peek-a-boo. Gradually, children start using fantasy, and a stick becomes an imaginary horse. Later, all the overt elements may be dropped in place of play that occurs entirely in the imagination. Even more relevant to the private self, wish-fulfilling fantasies occur with the self as hero, and most of us rarely make them known.

When infants first learn speech, they sometimes practice it alone, talking to themselves. As the years pass, the motor elements slowly disappear and the lips no longer move, as self-talking becomes entirely covert. When talking to ourselves, we often focus on the internal aspects of the self that are not open to observation.

Thus, there are three components of the developmental trend toward covertness: emotional inhibition, self-directed fantasy, and talking to oneself. Once children learn to conceal some of their overt behavior and are capable of fantasy that is detached from reality, they are likely to turn attention inward toward the covert self. And their private self-awareness is especially acute when there is a clear discrepancy between inner feelings and behavioral expressions: one's private anger versus a relatively placid exterior.

Private Self-Consciousness (The Trait)

What are the developmental origins of private self-consciousness? The answer is made difficult by the absence of research on this question. The problem is compounded by the fact that the behavior is covert: We do not know when another person is turning attention inward. Still, it may be worthwhile to examine several possibilities, bearing in mind that they are speculative.

One is fantasy, a component of covertness. Some children have vivid imagery, which delights them and reinforces the tendency to daydream. They are likely to develop fantasies about themselves, as are children who are read to and encouraged by books and other media to engage in fantasy. At the opposite pole are children with an impoverished imagination, which is not enhanced by being read to or other media; they are less likely to develop private self-consciousness.

A second possibility is Jung's (1933) personality trait of *introversion*. Introverts, by definition, turn their attention inward onto plans, thoughts, and imagery. Not all these cognitions are self-directed, for they may involve composing music, constructing a theory, or planning a building, which means that not all introverts are necessarily high in private self-consciousness. Nevertheless, any time attention is directed inward, a focus on the self becomes more likely. Other things equal, introverted children are more likely to become high in private self-consciousness than extraverts.

Alternatively, consider the possibility that some children gradually develop the supertrait called *openness*. Adults who score high on this trait have been described by professional observers as being artistic, curious, imaginative, insightful, and original (McCrae & John, 1992). Some of these attributes might lead to an internal focus, so it is not surprising that openness correlates from the .30s to the .40s with private self-consciousness (Trapnell & Campbell, 1999).

The social segment of the environment is crucial. When others are not available, their absence may turn children inward on themselves. Isolated children are likely to develop fantasies, sometimes imaginary playmates, and may therefore start focusing on the inner self. Other things equal, they are likely to become high in private self-consciousness.

Public Self-Awareness

Awareness of oneself as a social object requires assuming the perspective of another person toward yourself so that you can observe yourself as others do. This kind of social **perspective taking** is emphasized by sociologists who use concepts such as *mirror image self* and *generalized other* (Cooley, 1902; Mead, 1934).

How do children learn to take the perspective of another person? It is likely to be acquired through an advanced form of imitation learning. Parents observe children and comment on their behavior, often asking plaintively, "What will people think of you?" After many repetitions, children may imitate their parents by asking the same question about themselves. Such imitation is strengthened by the knowledge that others are looking at them and either approve or disapprove what they see.

Such contingencies raise the issue of instrumental conditioning. Once children can regard themselves as social objects, rewards and punishments not only affect behavior but also signal whether the children perceive themselves as others see them. Rewarded behavior implies that children perceive themselves correctly, that is, in line with the views of others. Punished behavior may reveal a discrepancy between self-views and the views of others. Notice that instrumental conditioning has now shaded over into cognitive learning. And certain kinds of punishment are effective only against someone who is capable of public self-awareness—ridicule, for example.

When children are taught to attend to the observable aspects of themselves, what specifically are they asked to focus on? These components of the public self were mentioned briefly earlier, but here they are described in more detail. The most obvious features involve appearance. Socialization training emphasizes minimal standards of grooming and teaches children and adolescents to be aware of others' scrutiny. And children are taught about body modesty.

The other component of the public self involves behavioral style. Individuals are expected to have a more or less erect posture and not slump. There is a minimal standard for coordination, and those who walk and sit awkwardly or clumsily handle utensils and tools are downgraded or even ridiculed. Behavioral style extends into social behavior in the rule-governed contexts called *formal*. Individuals are expected to be aware of status differences and to greet and leave people with appropriate phrases.

Older children who have undergone the usual socialization are aware of the social regulations governing appearance and stylistic behavior. When these rules are abrogated, there are social penalties: ridicule, scorn, teasing, and rejection by others. When children become aware of a deficiency in appearance or a mistake in style, a frequent reaction is embarrassment, which represents an acute, negative awareness of the public aspects of oneself.

Puberty is marked by rapid body growth and development of secondary sex characteristics. The body of an adolescent feels and looks different, not only to the adolescents but also to everyone else. Parents and siblings comment on the rapid changes, often in a teasing fashion. Keenly aware that they feel different and look different, adolescents are certain that everyone is looking at them, examining them. When strolling down the street, they have something in common with movie or rock stars: a belief that they are the center of attention. For some, the attention is welcome, and they may even show off, perhaps with a female hip swing or a male swagger. For many, the attention is distressing in making them feel naked and exposed. Whether the reaction is positive or negative, public self-awareness reaches its peak during adolescence.

Public Self-Consciousness (The Trait)

Parents vary considerably in how intensely they socialize their children. At one extreme, formal parents, sometimes labeled old-fashioned, lay down strict rules of appearance and deportment. Children's attention is firmly directed toward themselves as social objects. Such children are likely to become high in public self-consciousness.

At the other extreme are parents who are casual about appearance and demeanor. They are more likely to value independence in their children and only minimally direct attention to the externals of self. Such children are expected to become low in public self-consciousness.

TABLE 5.4 Developmental Determinants of Private and Public Self-Consciousness

Private Self-Consciousness	*Public Self-Consciousness*
Covertness	Socialization
Fantasy	Formality
Introversion	Changes in body appearance
Openness	Conspicuous family

Aside from explicit socialization, the social environment of children is relevant here. Consider children of ministers, politicians, and media stars. Family life is something like living in a fishbowl: There is a stream of visitors, and the public is intensely curious about everyone. Unless the children are protected by a wall of privacy, they learn early that others will closely examine them. Most of them will become high in public self-consciousness and retain it beyond adolescence.

One outcome is a person high in public self-consciousness who readily feels conspicuous. There is a keen awareness of being the focus of others' attention, as well as a self-focus on the observable aspects of the self. This description applies especially to the Japanese: "An external frame of reference leads Japanese to have a heightened awareness of their audience. . . . In this way, rather than being seen as participants, they may more aptly be viewed as imagined objects in the eyes of others" (Heine et al., 1999, p. 8). Clearly, Japanese are higher in public self-consciousness than are Americans.

The ostensible developmental determinants of the traits of private and public self-consciousness are summarized in Table 5.4.

SUMMARY

1. Attention may be focused on the private or the public aspects of the self.
2. Private self-consciousness has been found to (a) intensify emotions and motives and (b) enhance self-knowledge. The trait may consist of both a generalized tendency to reflect about the self and a more specific awareness of inner states.

3. Public self-consciousness has been shown to (a) intensify feelings of being observed and (b) enhance knowledge of the observable aspects of the self.
4. Objective self-awareness theory assumes that self-focus means comparison with a standard, which is aversive and leads to attempts to bridge the gap.
5. Control theory also assumes the self-focus means comparison with a standard but distinguishes between private and public self-awareness.
6. Self-consciousness theory (a) assumes the facts stated in numbers 2 and 3 above, (b) lists the inducers of private and public self-awareness, and (c) speculates about their development.

DICHOTOMIES

aware-unaware: knowing yourself versus not knowing yourself

individual-group: focusing on your own feelings versus others' attitudes

private-public: inner self versus outer self

GLOSSARY

aggression machine paradigm   a laboratory procedure for studying physical aggression

control theory   a theory of self-focused attention

hostility   resentment and suspicion of others

inducers   events or manipulations that refer to causing self-attention

negative self   what you do not want to become

objective self-awareness   a consistency theory of self-focused attention

perceptual feedback   photos or movies of you or a tape recording of how you sound

perspective taking seeing yourself as others see you

private self-awareness a temporary state of focusing attention on the inner self

private self-consciousness the personality trait of focusing on the inner self

public self-awareness a temporary state of focusing on yourself as a social object

public self-consciousness the personality trait of focusing on yourself as a social object

6

Embarrassment

Blushing
Other Nonverbal Aspects
Causes
Development
Theories

Blushing

Blushing does not always occur during embarrassment, but it is surely the most distinctive sign of embarrassment. The cheeks redden, giving them a pink or even a red color, which is easiest to observe in light-skinned people. Though harder to spot in those whose skin is dark, it may be discernible as a different shading of the skin. Self-reports of blushing were used in a study by Simon and Shields (1996) of complexion and blushing in Asians, Blacks, Hispanics, and Whites. The lighter the complexion of the face, the more frequently individuals reported a color change when they blushed and the more frequently their blushes influenced others' reactions to their embarrassment.

The extent of the blushing depends partly on individual differences. For most people, only the cheeks become rosy, but in some people, the pattern includes the ears, the chin, and even the neck. It is a reasonable guess that intensity plays a role too. Other things equal, the more extreme the embarrassment, the greater the area of blushing and the deeper the color.

Two kinds of blushes have been observed (Leary, Britt, Cutlip, & Templeton, 1992). The most typical kind occurs suddenly and is as just described. The other is a *creeping blush,* which "occurs slowly, appearing at first as small splotches or streaks that appear much like a rash on the upper chest or neck. Over a period of several minutes, the rash spreads upward to the upper neck, jaw, and cheeks" (Leary et al., 1992, p. 457).

Physiology

Blushing involves filling the capillary bed of the cheeks and sometimes the ears and neck, which suggests activation of the parasympathetic division of the autonomic nervous system. There are data consistent with this hypothesis. College men were divided into fear and embarrassment groups (Buck & Parke, 1972). The fear group was told that they would subsequently receive painful electric shocks. The embarrassment group was told that they would subsequently be asked to suck on a baby bottle, a breast shield, a pacifier, and some rubber nipples. The participants waited 2 minutes while physiological measures were taken, and then the experiment ended without participants enduring shock or sucking on objects.

The level of **skin conductance,** a measure of physiological arousal, rose higher in the fear condition than in the embarrassment condition. Heart rate changed little in the fear condition but dropped significantly in the embarrassment condition. These findings suggest the dominance of parasympathetic activation: weak arousal, cardiac deceleration, and dilation of capillaries.

Subsequently, in unpublished research, I tried to discover whether skin temperature rose during blushing. Participants were asked to recall their most embarrassing memories. Some participants blushed, their skin temperature rose a little, and they reported being embarrassed. Some participants blushed but reported not being embarrassed. And some participants blushed and reported being embarrassed, but their skin temperature did not rise. Thus, skin temperature was not closely linked to blushing (change of color).

This finding raises two questions. First, many people report feeling that their face becomes hot when they are embarrassed. Is it possible that when some people are embarrassed, they feel hot cheeks but do not blush? Second, when blood rushes to the face and causes it to become red, the temperature should rise accordingly. Why does it not in many individuals?

The answers came from an experiment that measured both skin temperature and reddening of the face (Shearn, Bergman, Hill, Abel, & Hinds, 1990). College men and women were asked to stand in front of a television camera and sing the U.S. national anthem with lots of arm movements. The next day they sat in front of an audience of four people, and after baseline recording, they watched a video of their singing the day before (embarrassment manipulation) and a video of the murder scene from the movie *Psycho* (to elicit nonsocial arousal).

A photoelectric cell recorded changes in the color of the cheeks. They reddened strikingly when participants were embarrassed as compared to watching the murder scene. In men but not women, cheek temperature also rose comparably higher when the participants were embarrassed. For both sexes, in the embarrassment condition, however, skin temperature was not at all correlated with blushing. The authors speculated that "skin blood flow and coloration reflect surface capillary behavior, whereas temperature reflects the activity of subpapillary venous plexi and associated deeper vascular structures" (Shearn et al., 1990, p. 690). Whatever the physiological explanation, we now know why in my research blushing occurred without a rise in skin temperature, and skin temperature rose without blushing. We also know that the best measure of blushing is reddening of the cheeks, but embarrassment is also accompanied by a rise in skin temperature, so this measure may also be used to assess the physiological component of embarrassment.

Skin conductance was also recorded, and it rose higher in embarrassment than in nonsocial arousal. This finding tells us that embarrassment is not mediated solely by the parasympathetic division of the autonomic nervous system. This idea connects with a conclusion reached by Cutlip and Leary (1993), who reviewed physiological research on flushing and blushing and suggested that blushing is mediated by both divisions of the autonomic nervous system. In an earlier article, Leary and his colleagues put forth this hypothesis: "Blushing may result from inhibition of normal sympathetic tone" (Leary et al., 1992, p. 449). Perhaps skin temperature and skin conductance may involve only the sympathetic division, but blushing may involve only the parasympathetic division.

Occurrence

Blushing is likely to be more intense when there is an *audience* of several people (Shearn, Bergtman, Hill, Abel, & Hinds, 1992). Again, participants watched a video of themselves singing (experimental) and the murder scene from *Psycho*. There were three conditions: the subject alone, one other person present, or an audience of four people. There was some blushing when the participants were alone or had an audience of one person but considerably more intense blushing when the audience was four people. Evidently, the presence of one person was not sufficient to constitute an audience, but four people did suffice, and this audience enhanced blushing.

Employing the same basic procedure to induce blushing, Shearn and Spellman (1993) investigated *empathic* blushing. Participants watched the video of themselves singing, accompanied by a friend and a stranger. The participants blushed, of course, and so did the friend. The stranger also blushed a little but hardly more than when he or she watched the scene from *Psycho*. However, in a second experiment, the same authors showed that when empathy is induced, strangers do blush vicariously. When strangers had previously been asked to sing, giving them an experience in common with the participants, the strangers blushed considerably more than a control group of strangers.

Asendorpf (1990) had participants proceed through this sequence: wait with a confederate, get to know him, make evaluative statements about the confederate with him present, and talk to the experimenter (baseline). There was a much higher frequency of blushing during the two interaction periods (get to know and evaluate) than in the just waiting and control periods. The confederate, who of course knew which condition was ongoing, judged whether the participant blushed, knowledge that might be a source of contamination in determining whether blushing occurred.

There is also the Blushing Propensity Scale (Leary & Meadows, 1991), constructed by asking participants to rate on a 5-point scale how often they blushed in 14 social situations. Blushing was rated as occurring frequently in these five situations: when I'm embarrassed, when I've been caught doing something improper or shameful, when I look stupid or incompetent in front of others, when others sing happy birthday to me, and when I'm the center of attention.

Other Nonverbal Aspects

Perhaps a more frequent facial expression during embarrassment is smiling. There is little or no mirth involved, rather a silly smile, sometimes accompanied by a nervous giggle or laugh. It has been reported that when embarrassed, women tend to giggle and men tend to guffaw (L. Buss, 1980). Some embarrassed women also covered their mouths, but no men did.

Subsequent research specified in more detail the nature of the embarrassed smile. Keltner (1995) had participants arrange their faces in awkward expressions, with the experimenter closely examining their faces and correcting their many mistakes. Then the participants were told to relax, and the first 12 to 15 seconds of this relaxation period were videotaped and later inspected for smiling, head movements, and gaze (more of the latter two shortly). The participants were asked to identify which emotions they were experiencing, and two groups were selected: embarrassed and amused. Both groups displayed *smile controls* or what I have called a silly smile: partially obscuring the smile or not allowing the muscles of the mouth to pull it up. But smile controls occurred more frequently in embarrassed participants.

In research mentioned earlier, Asendorpf (1990) divided smiles into those judged as embarrassment and those judged as nonembarrassment. On examination of the videotapes, it was found that in embarrassed smiles, gaze aversion peaked a second and a half *before* the smile occurred. In nonembarrassed smiles, the gaze aversion peaked half a second *after* the smile started.

Both experiments found that gaze aversion occurred when participants were embarrassed. Interestingly, Keltner (1995) reported something specific about the gaze aversion: Embarrassed participants looked *down* longer than did amused participants, and embarrassed participants had more downward head movements and touched the face more.

What about the co-occurrence of smiling and gaze aversion? Asendorpf (1990) suggested that they are opposed reactions. Smiling is part of the approach response to others, but gaze aversion seemingly breaks off contact. The presence of both simultaneously would therefore signal ambivalence. However, this particular gaze aversion and downward head movements appear to be components of an abasement reaction, that is, acknowledging a social mistake. Such acknowledgment surely is an attempt to return to good graces and maintain contact, not break it off.

In brief, nonverbal expressions other than blushing occur in embarrassment. However, notice that these other expressions also occur in other emotional reactions. Smiling occurs in amusement, downward head movement and gaze aversion occur in abasement, and the latter two may occur when a person feels merely conspicuous but not embarrassed (more of this issue below). This overlap poses a problem for observational and experimental research on embarrassment, but two solutions are available. One is to turn to a *verbal* aspect of embarrassment. If individuals say that they feel silly or foolish, clearly they are embarrassed. The other solution is to observe awkward, abashed attempts by people to extricate themselves from the social situation.

Across Cultures

In an unusual study, adults in Greece, Italy, Japan, the United Kingdom, and West Germany self-reported the physiological and nonverbal aspects of embarrassment (Edelmann & Iwawaki, 1987). Of particular interest were those aspects mentioned by at least 15% of the participants in each country. Blushing and a rise in facial temperature were prominent, as expected, but so were a fast-beating heart and tense muscles. Whatever the limits of questionnaires and the range of cultures examined, this study appears to verify the symptoms of embarrassment that researchers in this area have specified. Given the aforementioned research of Shearn et al. (1990) and the suggestion of Cutlip and Leary (1993), the physiological symptoms appear to fall into two categories: (a) blushing, representing parasympathetic activation, and (b) a rise in temperature, heart rate, and muscle tension, representing the general arousal of sympathetic activation. The other nonverbal reactions mentioned frequently were smile or grin and averted gaze.

Embarrassment has also been found in Asia (Edelmann & Iwawaki, 1987) and the Middle East (Stattin, Magnusson, Olah, Kassin, & Reddy, 1991), and it has been observed in Africa and several Pacific islands (Eibl-Eibesfelt, 1972). Clearly, this is a universal emotion.

Reported Feelings

Two studies compared embarrassment with other self-conscious emotions in college students. The first contrasted embarrassment with shame (Miller & Tangney, 1994). There was a considerably higher frequency of the following reports for embarrassment than for shame: the feeling hit quickly and was mild and of shorter duration; self-laughter and laughter by others; and feeling awkward, worrying about what others might think, feeling that others were looking at me, and being bothered that others were present.

A follow-up study asked college students to rate three self-conscious emotions for a variety of attributes (Tangney, Miller, Flicker, & Barlow, 1996). Compared with shame and guilt, the following attributes were rated higher for embarrassment: shorter duration, unanticipated, felt less bad, less angry at self, physiological changes, felt less responsible, felt others were looking, was less interested in making amends, believed others were more amused and less angry, and easier to talk about the event now.

These self-reports make sense. Compared with the other two self-conscious emotions, embarrassment is milder, the feeling dissipates faster, and there is greater conspicuousness and more awareness of physiological changes (mainly blushing). Clearly, embarrassment is a less serious emotion than shame and guilt with respect to both the felt experience and the social consequences.

Causes

Researchers of embarrassment have assigned its various elicitors to a few major categories, based mainly on the reports of college students, supplemented by the reports of other adults and of adolescents. Gross and Stone (1964) assembled hundreds of anecdotes into three categories, which they named unsupported identity, loss of poise, and loss of confidence. Examination of the participants' reports reveals that they overlap considerably with the next trio of categories (Sattler, 1965): impropriety, lack of competence, and conspicuousness. Another set of self-reports found that the most embarrassing incidents involved awkwardness, forgetfulness, and violations of privacy (Sharkey & Stafford, 1990). A more recent catalog of self-reports used four categories (Miller, 1992, 1996): individual behavior, interactive behavior, audience provocation, and bystander behavior. Part of bystander behavior is **empathic embarrassment,** an important addition to the list.

Self-reports have also been factor analyzed to yield five factors (Modigliani, 1968): accidental foolishness, inability to respond, being the passive center of attention, watching someone else fail, and inappropriate sexual encounters. Edelmann (1987) reported four factors: embarrassment to others, vicarious embarrassment, others' behavior, and appearing foolish. When Iranian and Japanese children rated the embarrassability of 92 situations, four factors emerged that were common to the two cultures: being stared at, bodily immodesty, being criticized, and proscribed social behavior (Hashimoto & Shimizu, 1988). As a review of embarrassment across cultures concluded, "Regardless of their language, religion, climate, and level of industrialization ... people suffer embarrassment when unwanted events reveal undesirable information about themselves to others" (Miller, 1996, p. 104).

Clearly, there is some overlap among the various categorizations, but by slicing the pie differently, each list offers its own perspective on the causes of embarrassment, thereby adding to our understanding of it (see the reviews by Keltner & Buswell, 1997; Leary et al., 1992). I offer a modification of my earlier list (A. H. Buss, 1980).

Conspicuousness

We feel **conspicuous** when we receive more than the usual attention to ourselves. Attention from others may be regarded as a dimension: from being shunned at the low end, through moderate attention in the middle, to excessive attention at the high end. The high end, a feeling of being in the spotlight, often causes embarrassment. Conspicuousness is an element in most causes of embarrassment.

We may feel especially noticeable because of being suddenly and uniquely different from those around us. Visualize walking into a large elevator filled with a team of very tall basketball players, entering a bar frequented entirely by people of a different sexual persuasion, or appearing in normal dress at a party only to discover that everyone else wears a costume. The resulting feelings of excessive visibility and therefore of embarrassment occur, not because of anyone's behavior but merely because of being an oddity.

The actions of others are a more typical cause of embarrassment. They may stare or closely examine another person, often eliciting a feeling of psychological nakedness: What are they staring at? Are my clothes or hair in disarray? Is dirt on my face? Why am I the center of attention? The scrutiny may be more direct, people pointing out a smudge or an unclosed zipper. Others may say that you are blushing in an attempt (usually successful) to induce a blush. If you are already blushing, the excessive attention to your face tends to make it even redder.

Conspicuousness often occurs in a group of people. Apsler (1975) exploited this knowledge, inducing embarrassment in the laboratory by asking participants to sing, dance, or imitate a 5-year-old throwing a temper tantrum. Some students blush when they are called on in the classroom. Many people are embarrassed when a speaker calls them up on stage. Speakers themselves may become embarrassed when they listen to themselves being introduced and must sit there passively enduring the inspection of the audience. Passivity is also the lot of the birthday celebrant who must endure being sung to ("Happy Birthday").

Ridicule

Ridicule skates thin ice between amusement and hostility. The target often is appearance (face, hair, body, clothes) or ignorance (of a fact such as who is president or of normally expected social behavior such as etiquette). Or the target may harbor feelings best kept hidden, such as a crush on another person. If the teasing is nothing more than twitting or poking fun, the result is likely to be embarrassment. If the actions of others become more serious, as in scoffing, jeering, and deriding, the result is more likely to be shame or perhaps anger. But embarrassment, though acutely uncomfortable for a few moments, is a reaction to an essentially humorous or silly situation.

Teasing also focuses all eyes directly on the target person, causing a feeling of conspicuousness. The target of ridicule consequently suffers from double jeopardy: being laughed at and receiving excessive attention from others. Even if no one is laughing, being forced to engage in silly or undignified behavior tends to cause embarrassment. Recall the Buck and Parke (1972) experiment, in which men were asked to suck on a baby bottle and a rubber nipple, and the Shearn et al. (1990) experiment, in which participants untrained in music were asked to sing before an audience.

Overpraise

It is a rare adult who has escaped becoming embarrassed through **overpraise.** The experience is sufficiently common for us to accept it without comment. There is an inherent paradox: Though a compliment should make us feel good, we blush and suffer mild discomfort. The solution may lie in conspicuousness, for an essential component of overpraise is receiving too much attention. At some time or other, most parents have trotted out their children to friends or relatives and described their recent school or other accomplishments with pride. The ensuing embarrassment might be attributed solely to feeling conspicuous. Or it might be attributed to *any* discrepancy between the achievement and the excessive praise.

These three hypotheses—overpraise, conspicuousness, and any discrepancy—were evaluated in unpublished laboratory research to be described in detail for what it tells us about reactions to evaluation (L. Buss, 1980). Buss (1980) pretested college women, having them rate themselves for attractiveness and sensitivity to others. She selected those who rated themselves near the middle of both dimensions. Weeks later, they were participants in an experiment that ostensibly studied first impressions. A woman experimental accomplice, pretending to be a participant, rated the real participant for attractiveness and sensitivity: higher (overpraise), lower (underpraise), or the same as the participants had earlier rated themselves (accurate). There were 20 participants in each of these three groups. The experimenter, without knowing the original self-ratings, observed blushing, giggling, and gaze avoidance.

Nineteen of the 20 overpraised participants blushed, 7 of the accurate participants, and 3 of the underpraised participants. Giggling was observed in 16 of the overpraised, 5 of the accurate, and none of the underpraised participants.

This experiment was followed up by the running of three more groups to complete the gender combinations: a woman rated by a man, a man rated by a man, and a woman rated by a woman. The findings from these three combinations were highly similar to the findings obtained when a woman rated a woman, with one exception. When men were overpraised, they did not giggle; only women did.

Notice that roughly one third of the participants in the accurate condition blushed. This finding is in accord with observations of everyday life. Some people evidently have never learned to deal with compliments and, even when the compliment is accurate, become embarrassed. But the major determinant of embarrassment was overpraise, which elicited blushing in most of the participants. Thus, the paradox remains unresolved, but perhaps the solution lies in the concept of the private-public distinction.

Breaches of Privacy

Privacy is discussed in detail in Chapter 8, but breaches of privacy are a major cause of embarrassment, so they are discussed here as well. We start with situations involving three major senses: sight, hearing, and touch.

The most frequent and perhaps most intense embarrassment occurs over body modesty. The fear of being seen naked is sufficiently strong to invade nighttime imagery, with many people reporting a dream of wandering the streets unclothed. In everyday life, even being partially unclothed in public is sufficient to evoke a blush, but only one person is embarrassed. But consider a common though thankfully an infrequent event: A man inadvertently enters a room where a woman is not fully dressed. If one enters a bathroom when someone is already there, even if you are both of the same sex, it may cause embarrassment. It is nobody's fault, but having been strongly socialized in body modesty, especially in relation to elimination and washing, both are intensely embarrassed.

Then there are body noises, best not described, which cause embarrassment when heard by others. Here an internal event leads to an external stimulus. But there is another auditory breach of privacy: when a private conversation is overheard. For example, while waiting in line, two people are commenting about a friend's lack of taste in clothes, only to discover that the friend is just behind them and has been listening.

Concerning touch, there are parts of the body that are not to be touched except when two people are intimate. If a stranger or friend accidentally touches these parts—for example, a man brushes against a woman's breast or a woman against a man's genitals—both usually become embarrassed. In our society, some men have been taught that it is unmanly to hug others. So when a man hugs another man, they both become acutely uncomfortable.

Being touched represents the endpoint of personal space, an area around each of us, most noticeably to the front (Hall, 1966).

So far the breaches of privacy have been physical in the sense that we often wish to be unseen, unheard, and untouched, else we may suffer from embarrassment. But there is a *psychological privacy,* which involves keeping things to oneself, even if the motives or impulses are not blameworthy or praiseworthy.

Consider also a crush: the desperate longing for another person who may be unaware of it. Why not reveal this feeling to the object of desire? Because the other person may be a stranger, a casual acquaintance, or a (platonic) friend. If the hidden impulses are revealed by a Freudian slip, the result is acute embarrassment.

We may understand that exposure of a crush causes discomfort, but why does embarrassment occur when a person learns that he or she is the object of another person's crush? There is no obvious answer, but a reasonable guess is that it reveals something too private for the depth of the relationship. For instance, if an acquaintance were to divulge details of his or her marital sex life, it would be too private a revelation for the superficial relationship. Any time a disclosure presumes a closer personal relationship than the one that exists, the recipient is likely to become embarrassed. And romantic partners are expected to share secrets that no one else knows about. Inadvertent disclosure of material that was supposed to be limited to the couple causes embarrassment (Petronio, Olson, & Dollar, 1989).

Mistakes

We laugh when other people stumble, causing them to become embarrassed. A load of dishes crashes to the floor, and the room explodes with amused applause. A guest spills coffee on the host's sofa. A man stumbles and lands on the floor, unhurt. A woman spills the contents of her purse or a man's suitcase pops open to reveal his underwear. I watched a rotund man blush when he rose out of a light cane chair and the chair came up with him. Imagine wearing a hairpiece and it becomes askew or, worse still, falls off.

Probably the most common social error that leads to embarrassment is forgetting another person's name, but others are equally recognizable.

There is also saying the wrong thing to a particular listener or asking the wrong question: "Are you pregnant?" to a woman who is not. There is introducing a person and using the wrong name; asking about the other person's wife, only to be told that he is divorced or widowed; criticizing actors as a group, only to discover that the other person is an actor; and gossiping about a woman, only to discover that the listener is her cousin.

Obvious violations of etiquette also cause embarrassment. For example, at the dinner table, a man starts to eat and suddenly notices that everyone's head is bowed for a premeal prayer. Or a woman is talking loud enough to be heard over numerous other conversations, when she does not hear someone call the group to order, asking for silence, and she is the only one left talking.

A personal experience is relevant. My wife and I, seeking to buy a house, went to inspect a home that presumably was for sale. A Spanish-speaking maid let us in, and we proceeded to examine closets, bathrooms, and bedrooms, discovering a sick child in one bedroom. Then the owner entered the house and asked us politely what we were doing, which is when we learned that it was the wrong house. We were intensely embarrassed, but to our relief, she was a realtor who knew the nearby house we were looking for and was not at all upset. But it is on my list of life's most embarrassing moments.

Vicarious Embarrassment

Recall the experiments by Shearn and Spellman (1993) in which participants' friends or strangers watched a video of the participants singing. Friends displayed vicarious blushing, but strangers did not. However, when strangers had previously been asked to sing and later watched a video of the participants singing, the strangers blushed. Evidently, when friendship or a shared experience results in empathy, this feeling causes vicarious embarrassment.

Another experiment used self-reports of embarrassment (Miller, 1987). In the experimental condition, participants watched other participants dance, laugh for 30 seconds as if a joke had been told, sing, and throw a temper tantrum as a 5-year-old would—all previously used to induce embarrassment in the participants. In the control condition, participants watched other participants listening to music, copying the words to a song, and related nonembarrassing tasks. The experimental participants reported being more embarrassed.

These experiments confirm observations of everyday life. Most of us have at one time or another squirmed uncomfortably while watching friends or family members engage in foolish behavior. And we may even become embarrassed for a stranger who is caught in a compromising situation that we had previously experienced.

Development

First Appearance

Newborn infants do not blush, but older children and adults do. When do children first display embarrassment? The three studies that have tried to answer this question are worth examining in detail.

The first asked parents to recall signs of embarrassment seen in their children during the past 6 months (Buss, Iscoe, & Buss, 1979). Embarrassment was not defined, so it was left up to the parents, mostly mothers, to report signs of this emotion. As a result, we had to screen parental replies (e.g., some reported anger, which of course is not the same as embarrassment). We scored the presence of embarrassment if there was blushing, silliness, a funny smile, giggling, a nervous laugh, hands covering the mouth, or verbal report of embarrassment by the child. All these are indicators of embarrassment in adolescents and adults.

Gender differences were very small and inconsistent across age groups, so the data for the two sexes were combined. Also, there were so few reports about 3- and 4-year-old children that we combined these age groups, as we did also with the 11- and 12-year-old children. There were too few reports of children younger than age 3 and older than age 12 to yield reliable data, so these ages were omitted. The data are shown in Table 6.1.

Embarrassment was reported in a minority of the 3- and 4-year-olds but rose steeply to a majority of the 5-year-olds. It climbed a little further in the 6-year-olds and then leveled off for the older children. Thus, it starts for some children at 3 or 4 years of age, but the norm appears to be 5 years of age.

This interpretation is consistent with other evidence. Children were asked to select gifts for themselves, their parents, and older siblings (Flavell, 1968). Three-year-olds tended to choose the same presents for others as for themselves. Some 4-year-olds picked gifts that would be appropriate for others, half the 5-years olds did, and all of the 6-year-olds did. And White (1965) documented a developmental shift occurring at about 5 years of age, from simple conditioning to more cognitive learning. These two pieces of evidence suggest that at about 5 years of age, children have acquired the advanced cognitions and perspective taking necessary for the development of a sense of social self. I assume that in

TABLE 6.1 Frequency of Reported Embarrassment During Childhood

Age in Years	Embarrassment/Total	%
3 and 4	9/35	26
5	19/32	59
6	32/44	73
7	38/51	75
8	37/57	67
9	36/54	67
10	26/36	72
11 and 12	28/44	64
Sum	225/353	64
Blush/embarrassed	128/225	57

the absence of such a social self, there is nothing to get embarrassed about.

The limitations of the embarrassment study require comment. The reports were made by parents: untrained observers who may not have had sufficient opportunity to observe their children, especially if the parents both worked. And the reports were retrospective, covering the previous 6 months, which means that the ages reported in Table 6.1 are on the high side by 6 months and perhaps longer.

More controlled research clearly was needed. It was supplied by Michael Lewis and his colleagues (Lewis, Sullivan, Stanger, & Weiss, 1989), who had mothers bring their infants into the laboratory. In two experiments, the infants were exposed to procedures designed to induce mild embarrassment. In the first one, the infants were placed in front of a mirror, and several signs of embarrassment were recorded: smiling, gaze aversion, and nervous movements of the hand (blushing rarely occurs in infants). These frequencies of embarrassment were observed:

9 to 12 months, 2 of 9 infants;

15 to 18 months, 3 of 10 infants;

21 to 24 months, 5 of 8 infants.

In the second experiment, infants averaging almost 2 years of age were exposed to the mirror situation, were excessively complimented, and were asked to dance by both the experimenter and the mother. The frequencies of embarrassment, expressed in percentages, were the following:

mirror, 25%;

compliment, 32%;

dance for mother, 23%;

dance for experimenter, 32%.

The only children who displayed signs of embarrassment were those who previously demonstrated mirror image recognition, that is, self-referential behavior.

In a follow-up experiment, many of the same children were observed in the same four situations when they were about 3 years of age (Lewis, Stanger, Sullivan, & Barone, 1991). The percentages of observed embarrassment were the following:

mirror, 35%;

compliment, 27%;

dance for mother, 20%;

dance for experimenter, 50%.

Thus, over a period of 1 year, the frequency of embarrassment rose slightly in response to the mirror and somewhat more to the experimenter's request to dance but not in the other two situations. The researchers counted the number of participants who displayed embarrassment in at least one of these four situations. The percentage rose from 52% of the 2-year-olds to 82% of the 3-year-olds. Lewis et al. (1991) summarized the findings from all three experiments this way: "We find that no or fewer children exhibit embarrassment before 15-18 months, between 18 and 24 months approximately 50 per cent of children show this emotion, and by 3 years more than 80 per cent exhibit embarrassment" (pp. 489-490).

At face value, then, embarrassment may be fully developed at the age of 3 years, a conclusion that relies on the particular way that Lewis and his colleagues measured embarrassment: smiling, followed by gaze aversion and self-touching. But it is a silly smile that indicates embarrassment, not just any smile. In embarrassment, participants partially obscure the smile, sometimes making it lopsided (Keltner, 1995). In embarrassment, gaze aversion does not follow smiling but precedes it (Asendorpf, 1990). As Lewis (1995a) himself wrote,

> In embarrassment, people are more apt to tilt their heads and to engage in gaze avert/look behavior. This is not gaze aversion with the head bowed as in an avoidance response; nor is it immobility of action, as in removing oneself from the situation. Indeed, it is a gaze-avert, gaze-return to the other person (people) present. (p. 204)

Several questions remain: Why did so many children display embarrassment in only one situation? Why was there a higher frequency of embarrassment when the experimenter requested dancing than when the mother did? And why were there sex differences among the 2-year-olds but not in the 3-year-olds? Of course, such questions arise only because of the groundbreaking research of Lewis and his colleagues.

The research of Lewis et al. (1991) was reviewed by a disinterested psychologist, Miller (1996), who concluded,

> Thus when some 2-year-olds appear coy in response to their reflections, I'd not call them embarrassed, at least not in any adult sense of the emotion. They are self-conscious and conspicuous, however, and their sheepish behavior may result from the combined influences of inborn temperaments that make some children shy . . . and the sheer marvelous novelty of self-recognition. (p. 86)

This is a more conservative approach to the data than that of Lewis and his colleagues, who concluded that the 2-year-olds were embarrassed.

Developmental Course

At what age do children understand what embarrassment is? Children of three different age ranges were interviewed, and their responses were coded (Crozier & Burnham, 1990). Children in the 5- to 6-year age range made no mention of embarrassment, only of shyness. Children in the 7- to 8-year and 10- to 11-year age ranges included both embarrassment and shyness in their responses.

In an earlier study, children of varying ages were asked to imagine knocking down cans in a crowded supermarket or singing in front of others (passive audience) and then reported how they felt (Bennett, 1989). The frequencies of embarrassment responses per 16 participants in the age group were as follows:

5 years old: 2/16

8 years old: 7/16

11 years old: 12/16

13 years old: 16/16

Then other participants were told that the audience was displaying ridicule (active audience). Now the frequencies of embarrassment were as follows:

5 years old: 7/16

8 years old: 12/16

11 years old: 14/16

16 years old: 14/16

Clearly, whether the audience was passive or active made a difference. For the passive audience, there was little embarrassment among 5-year-olds, some among 8-year-olds, and a high frequency among the two older groups. Thus, the two youngest groups of children, 5 and 8 years of age, were not sensitive to their own potentially embarrassing behavior, but they were sensitive to being ridiculed by others. These data are consistent with the idea of early and late forms of embarrassment, to be discussed later.

The tendency to become embarrassed is expected to increase throughout childhood. Teasing and ridicule, especially by age mates, occurs more often during the elementary school years, as children perfect verbal cruelty. Children also become ever more aware of the private-public distinction. These trends reach a peak in adolescence, when informal observations reveal that teenagers seem especially prone to blushing. Elementary school, high school, and college students were asked to recall their earliest embarrassing experience (Horowitz, 1962). The highest frequency of embarrassment was reported for the 11- to 15-year period of adolescence.

After adolescence, teasing and ridicule diminish, social situations become familiar, and the pressures of socialization wane. As a result, the frequency of embarrassment is expected to wane as the years of adulthood pass, and blushing is self-reported to decrease in frequency during adulthood (Shields, Mallory, & Simon, 1990). Older people are rarely embarrassed.

Theories

Opinion of Others

Darwin (1873/1955) attempted to account for blushing, which he equated with embarrassment. Though Darwin noted that attention to oneself is important, he went on to suggest, "It is not the simple act of reflecting on our appearance, but the thinking what others think of us, which excites a blush" (p. 325). He mentioned several social mistakes familiar to all of us, such as breaches of etiquette and of modesty, but subsumed them under one principle,

> this principle being a sensitive regard for the opinion, more particularly for the depreciation of others, primarily in relation to our personal appearance, especially our faces; and secondarily through the force of association and habit, in relation to the opinion of others on our conduct. (pp. 336-337)

Darwin was obviously a keen observer of social behavior, and if his theory seems familiar, perhaps it is because it anticipates a modern approach, **self-presentation.**

Appeasement

Charles Darwin (1873/1955) denied that blushing had any adaptive function. Castelfranchi and Poggi (1990) suggested that he was wrong, that blushing is an involuntary appeasement gesture:

> Those who are blushing are somehow saying that they know, care about, and fear others' evaluations and that they share those values deeply; they also communicate their sorrow over any possible faults or inadequacies on their part, thus performing an acknowledgement, a confession, and an apology aimed at inhibiting others' aggression or avoiding social ostracism. (p. 240)

They were aware that blushing is not easily detected in dark-skinned people. They suggested that the blusher would be aware of the embarrassment, an aversive state that would be avoided by not engaging in proscribed behavior. If that seems speculative, consider their second suggestion, that blushing evolved before our species differentiated into different races. I find their arguments less than compelling and conclude that Darwin was correct: Blushing is a sign of embarrassment. However, whether blushing or other signs of embarrassment have an adaptive function is still an open question, one to be discussed at the end of the next chapter.

Self-Presentation

One step beyond being sensitive to the opinion of others is attempting to manage impressions. Goffman (1959) popularized the idea that each person presents a self in a manner analogous to an actor playing a role on stage. We present to others an image consisting of appearance and demeanor, thereby establishing a social identity for others to observe. Especially relevant to embarrassment are any claims we make to advance a particular social agenda. For example, the target of a flatterer may regard the compliment as merely an attempt at ingratiation, which should cause the flatterer to become embarrassed. In brief, embarrassment represents failed self-presentation.

Modigliani (1968) built on Goffman's (1959) approach by adding self-esteem and suggesting a three-step sequence: First, an event undermines the person's self-presentation; second, the person becomes aware that others see that he or she is discredited; and third, this awareness causes at least a temporary drop in self-esteem.

The self-presentation approach has been adopted by several psychologists to explain not only embarrassment but also shyness and, more generally, social anxiety (Arkin, Appelman, & Burger, 1980; Schlenker & Leary, 1982; Semin & Manstead, 1982). The implied reference is to adult behavior. Thus, most adults try to behave maturely and with conduct that is not only acceptable but also pleasing to others. When mistakes are made or social accidents occur, the wished-for image crumbles and embarrassment ensues. The embarrassed reaction serves as a signal to others of awareness and responsibility for the social mistake (Schlenker, 1980). Blushing, then, might be an appeasement reaction (more of this issue in the next chapter).

Only one self-presentation theorist has applied the idea to children. Edelmann (1987) assumed that children in the 4- to 7-year range display an early kind of embarrassment. They are aware

> that certain behaviors provoke ridicule and teasing while others do not. This may well see the emergence of a "primitive" embarrassment which involves being embarrassed by others' reactions without being fully aware of why the reactions occur. From the age of 8 years it is more likely that the child will wish to convey a particular impression of self recognizing the impression that he/she creates for others. As the child's motivation to manage impressions and his/her awareness of how these impressions are viewed by others increases the "mature" embarrassment is a much more likely outcome should unintentional transgression occur. (p. 119)

Edelmann (1987) proceeded to offer a six-step model of embarrassment:

1. People attempt to present images of themselves to others in accord with standards or goals.
2. Any social mistake means that an undesired image is being projected.
3. Awareness of this fact focuses attention on the self.
4. A real or imagined audience focuses attention solely on the public self.
5. This self-focus intensifies embarrassment.

6. The response to the predicament is an impression management strategy.

Self-presentation theory offers a reasonable explanation for the embarrassment that follows a social error, including the mistake of breaching another person's privacy. But it cannot explain other breaches of privacy. If you are in a bathroom and a stranger inadvertently enters, neither one is presenting any particular image, yet you will be as embarrassed as the stranger. This approach cannot account for the embarrassment of a boy being teased for having red hair or being embarrassed as a result of being teased about a girl having a crush on him. And neither conspicuousness nor embarrassment deriving from overpraise can be explained by failed self-presentation. In brief, self-presentation theory offers a reasonable account of many social mistakes but not of a variety of embarrassment-eliciting situations in which no image is being projected to others.

Self-Reference and Evaluation

Lewis et al. (1989) proposed a theory of several self-conscious emotions, including embarrassment. The theory was later elaborated to include two types of embarrassment (Lewis, 1995a, 1995b). The earlier kind, appearing sometime before the age of 2 years, requires only a sense of self, as evidenced by mirror image recognition:

> The ability to have a self in the world that is known to the self is a key maturational device where a life of primary emotions is transformed to a richer set of emotions, the self-conscious emotions. . . . I believe this transition is a species-specific maturational transition that takes place in the last half of the child's second year. (1995, p. 76)

The second type of embarrassment requires internalization of societal standards, rules, and goals, which develop during the third year of life. By age 3, then, children are assumed to be capable of *evaluative embarrassment,* which is essentially a milder form of shame. This advanced kind of embarrassment requires not only self-consciousness but also self-evaluation, which is based on internalized rules and standards.

Acute Public Self-Awareness

What follows is an enlargement of my original theory of embarrassment (A. H. Buss, 1980). The basic assumption remains: Embarrassment is an emotion involving distressing awareness of the self as a social object. In the absence of public self-awareness, there is no reason to become embarrassed, which is why this emotion is absent in animals and human infants. My theory of public self-awareness, discussed in the last chapter, postulates that awareness of oneself as a social object requires first the cognitive ability to focus attention on the observable aspects of oneself and, second, socialization practices that induce this self-focus. The task here is to account for the six causes of embarrassment discussed earlier in this chapter.

All children are taught the ways of their group through various kinds of learning—specifically, instrumental conditioning, imitation, and cognitive learning, especially perspective taking. Because embarrassment is an emotion, it is also shaped by classical conditioning, as particular social events during childhood and adolescence become linked to the blushing, related expressions, and feelings characteristic of embarrassment.

Prosocial behavior by the child is reinforced by goods, status, affection, and so on. Behavior that opposes or ignores the goals of socialization is punished physically or verbally. The most potent verbal punishment consists of laughter, teasing, and ridicule. Once the child acquires public self-awareness, such punishments tend to make the child embarrassed.

During the second year of life, children are initiated into toilet training. By the third year of life, they are often teased for "accidents" involving bladder or bowels.

Laughter and ridicule also start early in the area of modesty. Children are taught to conceal certain body parts in public and to reserve nakedness for certain occasions (bath) and certain rooms (bathroom, bedroom). When children violate taboos involving privacy, they are often made to feel silly or foolish.

Somewhat later in childhood, usually starting with grammar school, children are teased and ridiculed for another kind of immodesty: bragging and conceit. In our society, well-socialized people do not tout their own accomplishments. If they do so, others react with raucous laughter, sarcastic remarks, and caricature—all of which tend to cause embarrassment.

Starting at grammar school age, children are introduced to manners and etiquette. They are taught appropriate social behavior in more formal contexts, and they learn the difference, for example, between eating at home and eating in a restaurant. Again, the penalty for mistakes is often ridicule and teasing, and children become embarrassed when others laugh at them.

Gradually, children learn about two other kinds of privacy. They learn that certain activities must be clandestine: plotting and scheming with others, masturbation, and reading about, talking about, or viewing sexual behavior. The other kind of privacy involves the private self: fantasies, feelings, ambitions, and memories that are known only by oneself. The child learns caution about disclosing them because peers and unsympathetic adults might laugh or ridicule them. Presumably, older children and adolescents are painfully inhibited about expressing affection because of a past history of intense embarrassment when such sentiments are disclosed or simply by watching what happens to others when such disclosure occurs.

So far, four causes of embarrassment have been discussed: ridicule, social mistakes, breaches of privacy, and overpraise. But why does conspicuousness sometimes cause embarrassment? The answer starts with pointing out when children are most conspicuous. They are singled out for attention mainly when they have violated some social taboo: immodesty, lack of manners, clumsiness, or a breach of privacy. Typically, the child is laughed at or ridiculed, causing embarrassment. Thus, during childhood, a link is forged between conspicuousness and embarrassment. After many repetitions, conspicuousness becomes so closely associated with embarrassment that close scrutiny by others may cause embarrassment.

Vicarious embarrassment requires two other cognitive advances fostered through socialization practices—namely, empathy and taking the perspective of another. Those are the necessary conditions. The sufficient condition is suffering embarrassment ourselves. Then, when we observe another person being embarrassed, we share a part of the same feeling. This completes an account of the various causes of embarrassment.

The dichotomy between a primitive self and an advanced self, mentioned earlier, bears directly on the concept of public self-awareness. In my approach, infants can recognize themselves in the mirror (primitive self-awareness) without being aware of themselves as social objects (advanced self-awareness). Thus, a 2-year-old clearly has achieved self-recognition but lacks the advanced cognitions and the extended lessons of socialization that result in public self-awareness. Lacking public self-awareness, a 2-year-old human infant has no more reason to become embarrassed than does a chimpanzee.

This theory implies that the research ostensibly demonstrating embarrassment in 2-year-olds (Lewis et al., 1989) establishes only a *primitive self-awareness.* Two-year-olds, when recognizing themselves in a mirror, clearly are self-aware, but it is not the advanced, public self-awareness that I deem necessary for embarrassment to occur. By 3 years of age, some children have a sufficient sense of themselves as social objects and have undergone sufficient socialization to display embarrassment (Buss et al., 1979). I assume that such children are precocious, have undergone intensive socialization, or both. Most children are unlikely to show embarrassment until 4 years of age. Recall the research of Povinelli et al. (1996), presented in Chapter 1, demonstrating that children do not have a sense of continuing self until 4 years of age. That is the age when they have autobiographical memory and when representative intelligence has developed sufficiently. These are all developmental markers of an advanced, cognitive sense of self, a prerequisite for embarrassment.

The age norms for embarrassment are of course based on an interpretation of conflicting developmental data: Lewis's and mine. Embarrassment might some day be unequivocally demonstrated in 2-year-olds, for example, by blushing. If that were to occur, my requirement of an advanced awareness of oneself as a social object as a necessary condition for embarrassment would be proved incorrect. Two options would then remain. First, abandon self-consciousness theory, a drastic course that would discard elements of the theory that are unchallenged. Second, amend the theory to include two kinds of embarrassment, as Lewis (1995b) suggested. The first kind would be primitive, occurring at 2 years of age and requiring only an elemental sense of self. The second kind would be more advanced, requiring a later sense of oneself as a social object.

Recall, too, Edelmann's (1987) suggestion that at 8 years of age, an even more mature kind of embarrassment develops, involving a clearer sense of the impression made on others. If we put the theories together, the result is a three-stage model of the development of embarrassment. The first stage, occurring at 2 years of age, requires only a primitive sense of self. The second stage, occurring at 4 years of age, requires an advanced sense of self. And the third stage, occurring at 8 years of age, requires self-presentation. But such a theory awaits a conclusive demonstration that embarrassment develops as early as 2 years of age.

SUMMARY

1. Blushing is the most distinctive sign of embarrassment, which may also be accompanied by gaze aversion and a silly smile.
2. Embarrassment may be caused by conspicuousness, breaches of privacy, ridicule, overpraise, and social mistakes.
3. There is controversy over whether embarrassment first occurs in children at 18 months or 4 years of age.
4. Different theories of embarrassment attribute it to (a) failed self-presentation, (b) negative self-evaluation, or (c) acute public self-awareness.

DICHOTOMIES

aware-unaware: blushing and knowing or not knowing you are blushing

dependable–not dependable: blushing is infrequent and controllable versus frequent and not controllable

direct-vicarious: experienced embarrassment versus empathic embarrassment

private-public: violation of this boundary typically causes embarrassment

GLOSSARY

conspicuousness being the center of attention or feeling that you are

empathic embarrassment being embarrassed at the plight of another person

overpraise receiving too much praise in public

prosocial behavior behavior valued by society

self-presentation managing impressions others have of you, presumably by projecting self-image

skin conductance a measure of physiological reactivity

7

Shame and Guilt

Causes of Shame
Shame Versus Embarrassment
Theories of Shame and Guilt
Adult Theories
Developmental Theories
Evolutionary Theories

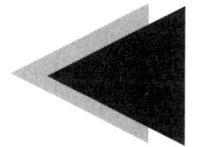

This chapter starts with shame because it is similar to embarrassment in several ways. In both, gaze is averted, and the face may be covered by the hands. Both involve intense awareness of oneself as a social object. In both, the emotional reaction is negative, and there is a strong desire to escape from the social situation. These similarities cause a problem of self-labeling so that when asked to report on an instance of shame, some individuals report being embarrassed (Tangney, 1992). Embarrassment and shame may be regarded as being on a dimension of social wrongdoing, with embarrassment at the low, silly end and shame on the high, serious end.

But they are demonstrably different in their reactions. Unlike embarrassment, in shame there is usually a stricken look, often one of sadness. People verbalize feelings of regret, chagrin, and humiliation, for they are mortified at their own behavior and have a strong desire to escape from the eyes of onlookers or a desperate wish to sink into the earth. There is none of the feeling of foolishness present in embarrassment. Rather, shame involves sorrow, even self-disgust. Consider these quoted reactions to a shameful event reported by college students: wanted to crawl under a rock and die; felt dumb and humiliated because everyone knew; felt hurt, confused, regretting; wanted to cry and try to hide it from others; felt less of a person than others; depressed, mad at myself; felt failure, humiliation, regret; and felt ashamed, stupid, and mad at myself (these self-reports and several to come are from my own unpublished research on almost 300 college students).

Causes of Shame

Sexual Immorality

Unlike embarrassment, shame is often the consequence of immorality. Virtually all societies have rules about sexual behavior and pregnancy. In some cultures, the loss of a woman's virginity before marriage is considered disgraceful. In ours, it was once scandalous for a woman to conceive a child out of wedlock, but today's world is different in this respect than it was 50 years ago, and shame rarely attaches to a single woman's pregnancy. However, we still deplore a married woman's bearing the child resulting from an extramarital affair.

The reaction to rape is especially interesting. Some people conclude that the woman is tainted because "she asked for it." They obviously believe in a just world: Victims must have done something to deserve punishment. But the victims themselves, though knowing they are innocent, still feel degraded by what was done to them, and many are too humiliated to reveal the crime against them.

Homosexuality is more acceptable today than it once was, though admitting to it can still result in dismissal from a job. Most adult homosexuals are not ashamed of their sexual outlet, but many adolescents are. They may have been socialized at home, in school, at church or temple, and in peer interaction to believe that homosexuality is sinful and abnormal. To the extent that these messages are received, adolescent homosexuals are likely to believe that their sexual impulses indicate depravity or, more generally, a character flaw.

Illegality

Minor infractions of the law are not a concern to us. Virtually no one will engage in self-blame if caught sneaking trinkets through customs or fudging on income tax. But except for criminals who make their living outside the law, most of us would be ashamed if caught at more serious crimes—murder, kidnapping, or robbery. Discovery of most thefts, especially of goods belonging to friends and relatives, would also result in humiliation, but shoplifting may be regarded as too trivial to warrant shame. The disgrace following exposure of embezzlement is usually sufficient to elicit a feeling of humiliation, perhaps an inability to face family and friends: How do you tell your children that you have cheated others out of their life savings?

Cheating on school exams has also changed over time. Several generations ago, it was regarded as wrong by most students, but most nowadays find it acceptable, and it is known to be widespread. However, even a student who condones cheating is disgraced when caught, for the action is revealed to other students, faculty, and especially to parents, who do not necessarily share students' loose morality on this matter.

Other Socially Disapproved Actions

There are behaviors that are not illegal or sexually immoral but are still considered reprehensible. Some actions may be viewed out of character, meaning that they would not happen ordinarily, for example, while drunk. Thus, an inebriated man might paw a woman, damage furniture, or wreck a car; a married woman might flirt wantonly or mention private matters best not disclosed. Sober reflection of such actions is likely to result in shame. A student reported being ashamed of being so drunk that he cursed his mother and father.

The remainder of disapproved behavior occurs in more usual circumstances. Most people tell lies occasionally to escape punishment or censure or merely to escape an aversive situation and think nothing more about it. However, some lies cannot be so easily dismissed. A student reported being intensely ashamed of having told a present girlfriend that he had never had sex with his previous girlfriend. A woman holding a statewide office in Texas falsely claimed to have graduated with distinction from a university but was disgraced when it was discovered that she had not even graduated.

The omission of socially expected behavior may also cause shame. Consider this situation: A child may be drowning in a flooded creek, and among several watchers is a man known as a strong swimmer, but he refuses to dive in because of the risk to himself. Imagine an older boy who is challenged to fight but cries and runs away. Among many groups of adolescent and young adult men, there is a set of expectations called **machismo.** These males are supposed to show courage and display a brave front, and they brag about their sexual exploits and sometimes about their illegal activities. If they can be stared down, if their self-presentation falters, they feel humiliated.

Another masculine problem among men of all ages is that of impotence. Physicians and psychologists report that it is a more frequent occurrence than is generally known, and in many cases, the problem is physiological. Nevertheless, almost with exception, when a man is temporarily impotent, he is mortified at this seeming failure of manhood.

A different kind of omission involves the refusal to share goods and especially money when such selfishness harms those who are denied. The most well-known and frequent instance is ex-husbands who owe child support but simply cut off the money. In an occasional egregious case, the ex-husband is living in relative luxury while his children are on welfare. Any man who has undergone the usual socialization will be humiliated when his gross negligence is unearthed.

Public Failure

We are confronted with reasonable goals that we are expected to meet and are trained to feel shame when we fall short. Thus, it is anticipated that virtually all middle-class adolescents will graduate from high school. Those few who do not are humiliated when they see their classmates succeed where they have failed. Even public knowledge of exam scores may be a source of shame. It took just a few students to be upset by the public notice of their poor scores and complain, forcing colleges to substitute codes for students' names when posting the results of exams. The situation worsens when there is a familial history of educational success and a high school graduate, for example, cannot gain entrance to a college with a decent ranking. In Japan, students whose applications to universities are turned down bring disgrace not only to themselves but also to their family, in some instances resulting in the student's suicide.

In the United States, there is intense pressure to succeed at athletics. We can recognize the stress on a basketball player who is shooting two foul shots as time expires in a game. She misses both, and her team loses by one point, resulting in painful humiliation. Similarly, when a team is heavily favored to win and loses the championship game, the entire team hangs its collective head.

Failure in business carries its own opprobrium. The law has given bankruptcy a veneer of respectability these days, but many businesspeople still feel shame when they must declare their failure for all to see. Being fired may also lead to humiliation, and even people who have lost their jobs through *downsizing* may feel degraded because they have lost the role of breadwinner. And many Americans experience shame when impoverishment forces them to seek welfare.

Stigma

Bodily deformities are a source of shame. Consider inborn features such as facial birthmarks, crossed eyes, harelip, complete absence of hair, and dwarfism. Consider also the results of accidents or illness: severely pitted skin, frozen facial muscles, the result of mastectomy, lameness, or a bent back (osteoporosis). Anyone with these features must be aware that strangers stare or turn away to avoid what they perceive as ugly. Some people with these bodily stigmata manage eventually to put aside any negative feelings, but others are all too keenly aware of their blemishes and avoid contact with strangers.

Amputation of body parts because of illness or accidents is usually not a cause of shame, but there are two exceptions. One is the loss of a woman's breasts through surgery to treat cancer. A common reaction is feeling less of a woman and an intense desire to hide the body or even the fact of the mastectomy. The other exception is removal of a man's testes because of cancer or injury. Two reasons men give for feeling ashamed in this situation are: the loss of a body part, which must be hidden, and the inability to procreate, a devastating threat to masculinity.

Stigma may also be psychological, resulting from the revelation of dishonorable behavior. Usually, the vile behavior occurred in the past and is only presently revealed. We also have read that some prostitutes, thieves, cheats, and embezzlers do reform and eventually take their place as upstanding citizens of the community, where they are held to a social standard of socially acceptable behavior. If their past is now uncovered, they are likely to react as would anyone else in the community, with intense humiliation. In addition, we have all read of ministers being caught with prostitutes and of priests having molested altar boys. There is a larger point here: The more exalted or the more public the position in society—clergy, judges, and even teachers and elected officials—the higher is the social standard and therefore the greater is the humiliation at the uncovering of wrongdoing.

Moreover, a stain on one person's honor often spreads to everyone in the family: when the father is discovered to be a criminal or a traitor, when the mother has a past history of child abuse, and, even these days, when a son openly declares homosexuality. A few years ago, the man I hired as an exterminator of insects around my home was found to be a pedophile, a discovery widely disseminated in newspapers and on television. He was so ashamed that while awaiting trial he hanged himself.

Imagine the disgrace of his wife and son, whose predicament became known to almost everyone in the community and who were able to continue the family exterminator business only by changing its name. These last examples may also be regarded as *vicarious shame,* deriving not from one's own defects but from those of family members, even those of previous generations: a skeleton in the family closet.

There was a time in this country when a child born out of wedlock was branded as a bastard, the child being stigmatized by the actions of the mother and father. Such vicarious shame may also occur through broader association—say, one's nationality. After World War II, when German civilians were forced to walk through concentration camps, some of them experienced a deep and abiding sense of shame at being a citizen of a country that would commit such atrocities. Some citizens of our country are ashamed as Americans of the history of genocide against Indian tribes, the slavery of Blacks, or the interning of Japanese Americans during World War II.

Shame Versus Embarrassment

This chapter began with similarities between embarrassment and shame. Now that the reactions involved in shame and its various causes have been discussed, we can proceed to the differences between these two emotions.

Research

Shame and embarrassment have been compared in a few studies. Babcock and Sabini (1990) gave participants shame and embarrassment scenarios and asked the participants to characterize them. Shame was found to be more serious and to involve more intentional behavior. Compared with shame, embarrassment has also been found to involve less surprise and self-disgust (Mosher & White, 1981) and less responsibility (Manstead & Tetlock, 1989).

The most comprehensive comparisons were made in two studies by Tangney and her colleagues. In the first one, every participant was given a stack of cards, each containing a phrase exemplifying shame or embarrassment, and told to sort them into a shame pile or an embarrassment pile (Miller & Tangney, 1994). Here is a sampling of the statements with a higher frequency of being assigned to the shame pile: feeling was strong, feeling lasted longer, caused by a deep-seated flaw, feel like a bad person, blame myself, feel immoral, angry with myself, and others are disgusted with me. These shame attributes make sense, but the authors recognized a problem: "The binary sorting procedure employed here forced participants to make fine distinctions that may have underestimated the similarities between the two emotions" (Miller & Tangney, 1994, p. 284). In addition, in an earlier study, in which participants described shame-inducing and guilt-inducing situations, Tangney (1992) found that embarrassing situations were more likely to elicit shame than guilt, suggesting at least some overlap between shame and embarrassment. And some of the causes of shame that are different from those of embarrassment might be the same causes that elicit guilt, such as immorality.

A subsequent study attempted to deal with some of these issues (Tangney et al., 1996). Participants were presented with items dealing with the phenomenology of embarrassment, shame, and guilt and asked to rate them on 5-point scales to indicate extent of agreement with the items. Embarrassment was found to differ significantly from both shame and guilt in these ways: least negative emotion, least immorality, most temporary feeling, most physiological changes, less anger at oneself, less desire to atone, more surprising, more accidental, and more benign reactions of others.

Keltner and Buswell (1997) had college students recall events that made them embarrassed, ashamed, or guilty; the causes were coded, and the five most frequent ones were examined. More frequently mentioned for embarrassment than for shame or guilt were clumsiness, social error, a problem in appearance, failure of privacy, and conspicuousness. These causes were mentioned more frequently in shame and guilt than for embarrassment: hurt others emotionally, failure to meet others' expectations, and failure at duties.

A Conception

Here I integrate statements from the chapter on embarrassment with those made earlier in this chapter. An essential element of both shame and embarrassment is a strong awareness of oneself as a social object, but the *causes* of this public self-awareness are different. Embarrassment may be caused merely by others staring, by a minor error in manners, or by overpraise; shame, never. Teasing often results in embarrassment; shame, rarely. Accidental body immodesty causes embarrassment, not shame. The disclosure of feelings or urges that might be best kept private may cause embarrassment or shame, but the *content* of the disclosure reveals a difference. In embarrassment, it may be something positive, such as a vaulting ambition, whereas in shame it is always something negative, such as past dishonor or current depraved urges. Public failure and immorality are too serious for mere embarrassment, but they do cause shame. Stigma, whether relating to body or family, tends to cause shame rather than embarrassment.

Several of the *reactions* of the two emotions are different. In research documented in the last chapter, blushing occurred when participants were embarrassed. Castelfranchi and Poggi (1990) offered a different view. They suggested that blushing might occur when a person is both embarrassed and ashamed. If so, they argued, it would be shame that causes the blushing, not embarrassment. However, I was able to elicit blushing merely by asking participants to recall an embarrassing event. Blushing may be induced by having participants sing or watch a videotape of themselves singing (Shearn et al., 1990), as well as by similar means (see the reviews by Keltner & Buswell, 1997; Leary et al., 1992). There is no comparable evidence that shaming people causes them to blush. Therefore, it seems safe to conclude that blushing is frequently seen in embarrassment but rarely (if ever) in shame. Whenever blushing seems to occur in shame, it is because that emotion is accompanied by embarrassment.

Two other reactions differentiate the two emotions. A silly smile or giggle may accompany embarrassment but never shame. In embarrassment, one feels foolish; in shame, humiliated.

The *consequences* of the two emotions are also different. Onlookers typically react to one's embarrassment with laughter and acceptance but to one's shame with scorn and rejection. Embarrassment is of little importance to oneself, and there is minimal and temporary loss of self-esteem. Shame is of great importance to oneself, and there is a major and sometimes enduring loss of self-esteem.

These various differences between embarrassment and shame are summarized in Table 7.1. They should not blind us to the similarities mentioned at the start of the chapter, the most important of which is that both emotions involve acute awareness of oneself as a social object. Also, there are causes that overlap. Thus, if a man or woman is seen masturbating, the reaction will depend on the person's view of sexual behavior. An older, more conservative view of sex would lead to shame; a new, more liberal view would lead to embarrassment. Loss of control of oneself, as in fainting, might cause embarrassment in this country, but in Japan it might cause shame. When President George H. Bush vomited and fainted at a public dinner in Japan, Americans saw it as embarrassing, Japanese as shameful.

Theories of Shame and Guilt

The rest of the chapter deals with theories of shame and guilt, some of which have derived from research and others of which have driven re-

Shame and Guilt

TABLE 7.1 Embarrassment Versus Shame

	Embarrassment	*Shame*
Distinctive causes		
Conspicuousness	Yes	No
Error in manners	Yes	No
Overpraise	Yes	No
Teasing	Yes	Usually not
Accidental immodesty	Yes	No
Leakage/disclosure	Of affection, ambition	Of baseness, infamy
Immorality	Usually not	Yes
Public failure	No	Yes
Stigma	Usually not	Yes
Reactions		
Blushing	Often	Rarely
Grinning, laughing	Often	Never
Feeling	Foolish	Humiliated
Opposite feeling	Poised	Pride
Consequences		
Others' reactions	Laughter, acceptance	Scorn, rejection
Duration	Temporary	May be lasting
Impact on self-esteem	Minor	Major

search. To impose order on these diverse theories, I present them in this sequence: adult theories, developmental theories, and evolutionary theories.

Adult Theories

Interpersonal Theory of Guilt

Baumeister, Stillwell, and Heatherton (1994) acknowledged that guilt is a feeling state but assumed its concerns are strictly interpersonal. They suggested two major sources of guilt: empathy and fear of being excluded by the group: "The affective roots of guilt lie in human relatedness, that is, in the human capacity to feel the suffering and distress of others and in the basic fear of alienating actual or potential relationship partners" (p. 246). They added that humans generalize and so become guilty when a rule has been broken, even when there is no harm to others or public knowledge of the behavior. We must wonder, though, whether empathy is an essential precursor of guilt, for people have felt guilty about, for example, running over an animal or committing a sin against God, events that do not involve empathy.

In their framework, guilt serves to enforce the norms and rules that govern social interaction, influence others by making them feel guilty, and make victims feel better when they become aware of the transgressor's discomfort. These functions would seem to apply equally to shame. Perhaps the authors would agree, for they define guilt as applying only to specific actions, whereas shame applies to the whole self. If shame involves the entire self, it may serve the above functions even better than guilt. Thus, it appears that the functions served by shame and guilt offer no basis for distinguishing between them, nor can fear of exclusion.

Dynamic Theories of Shame Versus Guilt

Shame and guilt have also been the focus of theorizing by psychoanalysts. Early, orthodox psychoanalytic theory dealt only with shame, which was thought to occupy a position during development between a child's anxiety and an adult's conscience. Erik Erikson (1950) linked shame with self-awareness: "Shame supposes that one is completely exposed and conscious of being looked at; in a word, self-conscious. One is visible and not ready to be visible" (p. 252). In contrasting shame with guilt, he wrote, "Visual shame precedes auditory guilt, which is a sense of badness to be had all by oneself when nobody watches and everything is quiet—except the voice of the superego" (p. 253). He saw guilt as occurring at the developmental stage immediately after shame, requiring some internalization of parental injunctions to form a conscience.

The orthodox psychoanalytic position was modified by Piers and Singer (1953). They assumed that shame derives from a gap between the **ego-ideal** (ideal self) and the **ego** (real self). The ego-ideal represents internalized parental standards and goals. When the ego fails to live up to these standards, the ego-ideal is contemptuous of the ego, which fears being abandoned by this internalized parent-surrogate. Guilt also derives from **internalized parental attitudes,** which form the conscience. When the ego transgresses the moral code instilled by the parents, the conscience demands that the ego suffer. Thus, guilt is essentially self-hatred, whereas shame is self-contempt.

Lynd (1958) adopted a similar position but with further modifications. She connected guilt with anxiety and shame with inferiority. In foreshadowing more recent approaches, she saw guilt as involving specific transgressions of the moral code. Shame, in contrast, also involves the realm of achievement and, by implication, the self more generally.

The theme that shame is the more generalized emotion was adopted by another psychoanalyst, Helen Lewis (1971), who also distinguished between the two emotions on the basis of the focus of attention:

> The experience of shame is directly about the *self,* which is the focus of evaluation. In guilt, the self is not the central object of negative evaluation, but rather the *thing* done or undone is the focus. In guilt, the self is negatively evaluated in connection with something but is not itself the focus of the experience. (p. 30)

Like previous psychoanalytic writers, she regarded guilt as a more mature emotion than shame. Unlike them, she regarded immorality as not being exclusive to guilt but also a potential cause of shame.

The assumption that shame differs from guilt mainly along a dimension of generality-specificity now dominates theorizing about the two emotions, especially that of June Price Tangney, who has adopted much of Helen Lewis's theorizing. She views guilt this way:

> So, guilt involves the perception that one has done something "bad." But although the person experiencing guilt may experience it for the moment *as if* he or she is a bad person, his or her self-concept and identity remain essentially intact. (Tangney, 1990, p. 103)

And about shame: "The entire self is painfully scrutinized and negatively evaluated" (Tangney, 1990, p. 103).

Tangney tested these assumptions in two kinds of research. The first kind assessed **shame proneness** and **guilt proneness** through answers to scenarios on the Self-Conscious Affect and Attribution Inventory (SCAAI) (Tangney, 1990). Here is an example of a scenario: "A friend asks you to do him/her a favor. Though you could reasonably go out of your way slightly, you just don't feel like doing it. So you turn him/her down. Later you tell yourself" (p. 106). Participants then rated the likelihood of reacting with shame ("Why am I so selfish?") or guilt ("I'll find a way to make up for this."). There was a third option, externalization ("Some people expect too much of their friends"), which is not relevant to shame or guilt. It is hardly mentioned at all in Tangney's subsequent publications and not relevant here.

Tangney's criteria for selection of items were the following: The response options could be clearly scored by her and three graduate students, the reactions were fairly common, and the items were appropriate for both sexes. She used this measure or one almost identical to it (called TOSCA) in a wide range of studies, and indeed, she has been the most prolific researcher of shame in guilt in the past decade or two. As Tangney, Niedenthal, Covert, and Barlow (1998) concluded about self-discrepancies (a topic to be discussed in Chapter 10), there may be a problem in how self-discrepancies are measured. Similarly, we need to find out precisely what is being measured by Tangney and her colleagues in their research on shame and guilt by examining the responses to the 13 scenarios (SCAAI).

Tangney was kind enough to supply the responses. Close reading of those labeled *shame* reveals three kinds of reactions:

1. embarrassment: three items with the word *embarrassment* and one conspicuous item;

2. escape or avoidance: two items with the word *avoid* plus one item about wishing not to attend a ceremony plus one item about wishing to disappear;

3. berating oneself in broad terms: being a loser, a bad friend, selfish, careless, and dishonest.

Three different clusters of items is not surprising, for there was no factor analysis. Tangney (1990) reported that "most individual shame items correlated more substantially with the Shame subscale than with the Guilt subscale and vice versa" (p. 106), but such item analysis does not preclude the presence of several factors. On the basis of the content of the items, it would appear that Tangney's operational definition of shame includes embarrassment, a desire to escape, and negative self-attributions.

Examination of the responses labeled *guilt* reveals four categories:

1. atoning or remedying: study more, apologize, cancel a date, make up for an act, treat the other well, redo something, apologize, and wonder how to return a favor;

2. concern for the other person: worry that the other has misread one's availability, worry about one's best friend, and concern about offending;

3. behaving better: think before speaking, study harder;

4. negative but circumscribed self-reactions: being annoyed with oneself and feeling bad.

Thus, in Tangney's measure of guilt, attempts to atone for actions or remedy a situation predominate, with concern for the other person and feeling bad as minor components. In this conception, feeling guilty means being more narrowly focused on wrongdoing or a bad situation, feeling empathic, and trying to remediate. In contrast, feeling ashamed includes being acutely aware of oneself as a social object (conspicuous, embarrassed), strong and generalized negative self-reactions, and avoidance of the consequences of wrongdoing.

On the SCAAI scenarios, guilt and shame correlated .43 to .48 over four studies (Tangney, 1990). However, on the TOSCA, guilt and shame correlated a surprisingly high .68 (Keltner & Buswell, 1997), indicating considerable overlap between guilt proneness and shame proneness.

Shame proneness and guilt proneness, as assessed by the SCAAI, were correlated with self-report measures of empathy and distress (Tangney, 1991). Empathy correlated .36 with guilt, and distress correlated .34 with shame: "Empathic responsiveness, the 'good' moral affective category, was generally positively related to the tendency to experience guilt. In contrast, an index of the more self-oriented personal distress was associated with proneness to shame" (Tangney, 1991, p. 605).

Let us examine the results in light of these guilt items: feeling bad for having looked at another's private papers, worrying about one's best friend, and being concerned about having offended someone. These are empathic concerns, which surely account for at least some of the correlation of .34 between guilt and empathy.

Now consider the three embarrassment items mentioned earlier, one of which includes feeling uneasy, as well as several self-deprecating shame items (e.g., being selfish and dishonest). These appear to indicate personal distress, a commonality that may account for some of the correlation of .34 between personal distress and shame.

Shame has also been linked to attributional style. Tangney, Wagner, and Gramzow (1992) reported that shame proneness correlates with negative self-attributions that are stable and global. However, consider these three responses labeled *shame proneness:* being a loser, being selfish, and being a dishonest person. They obviously fit the definition of negative, global self-attributions. Another response, being a bad friend, might fit this category. Thus, at least 3 and perhaps 4 items out of 13 involve stable global attributions, which means that part of the observed relationship between these attributions and shame proneness is built into the way shame proneness was measured.

In the same article, Tangney, Wagner, and Gramzow (1992) reported a relationship between shame proneness and psychopathology, especially with depressive, negative self-statements. The four above-mentioned responses indicating shame proneness—loser, selfish, dishonest, and bad friend—appear to be precisely the kind of items endorsed by depressed people, which makes it difficult to interpret their findings.

Tangney deserves credit for her attempt to assess individual differences in shame and guilt, but in her research, some assessment items overlap the dispositional variables she related to shame and guilt. Is shame but not guilt related to personal distress, to negative and global self-attributions, and to depression? Is guilt but not shame related to empathy? Perhaps, but these relationships are in part *built into* the scenarios of shame and guilt.

In the second kind of research, Tangney (1992) had participants describe shame and guilt experiences to discover the frequency of causes of these emotions. Lying, cheating, and stealing were mentioned more frequently in guilt than in shame. These findings suggest that immoral behavior is more likely to cause guilt than shame. Failure, embarrassment, socially inappropriate behavior or dress, and hurting someone emotionally were mentioned more frequently in shame than in guilt. These data suggest that interpersonal concerns that do not involve morality are more common in shame than in guilt. Tangney (1990) was appropriately cautious in reminding us that "the majority of situations mentioned by respondents appear capable of engendering both emotions" (p. 206).

In another study of causes, mentioned earlier, Keltner and Buswell (1997) reported the frequency of recalled events that led to shame or guilt. On the basis of any difference that had a p value of at least .05, these causes of guilt were mentioned more frequently than shame: failure at duties, lying, cheating, neglecting another, not helping another, failing to reciprocate, and breaking a diet; all except the last two deal with issues of character. However, in other research, most of these causes have also been mentioned in shame.

Tangney et al. (1996) again had participants describe their experiences of shame and guilt, this time asking them to agree or disagree with statements on a 5-point scale. A meaningful difference on a 5-point scale, a difference useful for drawing conclusions, would be half a point. Using this criterion, there are two meaningful differences: greater physiological change and more hiding in shame than in guilt. On the basis of what is known about embarrassment, we may add that there appear to be more physiological changes and more hiding in embarrassment than in guilt. In this study and an unpublished one (Tangney, Marschall, Rosenberg, Barlow, & Wagner, 1994), it was found that not only shame but also guilt occurred in public situations, findings that bear on a theory to be discussed later.

Generalized Versus Specific

Prominent theorists—Baumeister et al. (1994) and Michael Lewis (1995b), for example—have echoed the theories of Helen Lewis and Tangney in positing that shame is a generalized emotion encompassing the entire self, with dire consequences for self-esteem, whereas guilt is specific to a particular action and hardly involves the self at all. It follows that shame is more painful and may give rise to defensiveness or anger, but guilt is less painful and gives rise to attempts to atone for the proscribed actions.

What is the empirical basis of these assumptions? They are not validated by Tangney's studies (Tangney, 1992; Tangney et al., 1996), in which participants freely recalled shame and guilt experiences. The assumptions, as we have seen, are to some extent built into Tangney's (1990) assessment of shame proneness and guilt proneness, but the only independent evidence comes from the aforementioned study by Keltner and Buswell (1997). They reported that when coders rated the causes mentioned by participants, the causes of shame were slightly but significantly more general than those of shame. Even if we accept the findings of this single study as the basis for drawing conclusions, it does not tell us whether shame applies more broadly to the self and is more enduring than guilt.

All this research has used college students as participants whose shame and guilt experiences may be only mild preludes to more intense experiences in more mature adults. And the research, with good reason, sought experiences common enough to obtain (statistically) reliable effects. Therefore, it may be useful to turn to examples that have been reported in everyday life, some of which seldom occur but are striking enough to inform us about these issues.

There are examples of generalized guilt and guilt having an enduring impact on the self:

(a) Women who have had abortions later describe enduring guilt over terminating the pregnancy, including the mother of "Baby Doe" in the Supreme Court decision that legalized abortion.

(b) Some drivers who have maimed victims or caused death, especially when the drivers were drunk, report lasting feelings of guilt.

(c) Parents whose children have turned out bad say they feel guilty about how they raised the children.

(d) Some highly religious people report painful and lasting feelings of guilt about proscribed behavior or even "bad thoughts," which they label as sinful.

(e) Confessions have been made years later, sometimes at the door of death, about previous crimes or other immoral behavior. In 1998, newspapers reported a man's confession to a murder 50 years after the unsolved crime occurred, during which time he was a model citizen. Imagine the corrosive, pervasive effects of guilt on the man's self that made him willing to risk condemnation and jail time for a crime no one else knew about.

(f) Children, on learning that their mothers died while giving birth to them, feel guilty about "causing" the mothers' deaths.

(g) Survivors of the Holocaust report enduring guilt about being one of the few who survived, as though it was somehow their fault that the others died.

And there are examples of specific shame that do not generalize to the entire self:

(a) students who are caught cheating on an exam;

(b) men who have a brief episode of impotence;

(c) people who are caught while masturbating;

(d) professional athletes who are captured on television engaging in childish behavior (e.g., spitting on an opponent);

(e) a child or adolescent who is caught stealing a small item;

(f) men who believe that going to a prostitute is acceptable behavior but who are arrested, and the transient exposure causes temporary and specific shame;

(g) an adolescent male who fails to meet a challenge to fight an opponent in front of peers.

These lists appear sufficient to make the points that (a) shame may be specific to a particular event and have no lasting impact on the self, and (b) guilt may generalize and have a lasting impact on the self. Tangney and others have cited instances of shame being generalized and guilt being specific. When those facts are added to the above two lists, it is clear that both shame and guilt may be generalized or specific, which means that the generality-specificity issue cannot be used as a basis of differentiating them.

Two options remain. One is to abandon attempts to distinguish between the two emotions and assume that they are merely different labels for a single negative self-emotion. There is support for this idea in the confusion most people have in labeling these as separate emotions: When participants are asked about the emotion being experienced, what some call guilt is labeled shame by others. Furthermore, our English words do not necessarily translate into appropriate emotions in other languages. The terms *shame* and *guilt,* respectively, do not match the Italian *vergogna* and *senso de colpe* (Castelfranchi & Poggi, 1990).

The second option is to the keep the distinction because of a difference in the facial expression of the two emotions: a clear pattern in shame but none in guilt (Keltner & Buswell, 1997). But there is another basis for maintaining the distinction.

Private Versus Public Self

In earlier writing (A. H. Buss, 1973, 1980), I suggested that guilt is private and shame is public, but subsequent research revealed that guilt may occur in public and shame may occur in private (Tangney et al., 1994). Research based on participants' reports has revealed that shame may occur in private, which has caused me to rethink my position. All theorists agree that shame and guilt involve a focus on the self. My modified position is that the focus in shame is on the public aspects of the self, and the focus in guilt is on the private aspects of the self. The theory starts by describing the emotions.

Emotions

Guilt is defined in everyday terms as having a *bad conscience,* a feeling of being bad, sinful, or, in some religious contexts, evil. People have reported hearing the voice of a parent or of God, knowing that it is not a true sensory event or, in some instances, believing that the voice is there, which is a hallucination. When we experience guilt, we cannot stop up our ears or hide from the demands of conscience or the voice of God, for initially there is no escape. However, the guilty person may be regarded as a prosecuting attorney, defense lawyer, and jury, which is why guilt may sometimes be rationalized away in a manner analogous to a clever lawyer getting a culpable client off on a technicality.

Shame is a feeling of *humiliation* when something bad about oneself, something best hidden, is revealed to others. In this respect, shame is related to embarrassment, but shame involves more serious social lapses, including immoral behavior. Now the jury is others, who are less likely to be swayed by attempts to evade responsibility. Recall that the emotion opposite to embarrassment is poise, but the emotion opposite to shame is *pride,* especially in accomplishments known to be applauded by others. Opposite to guilt is the quieter *virtue,* especially in the sense of character: being ethical, considerate, and trustworthy.

Self-Awareness

Guilt and shame differ in self-focus. In guilt, the focus is on those aspects of the self that are not open to observation, that is, *private self-awareness*. Recall that when the focus is on the body, it may be on a variety of sensations that are privy only to the experiencing person. In shame, the focus is on those aspects of the self that are open to observation by anyone, that is, *public self-awareness*. Such awareness also occurs when the focus is on the body, that is, on the externals of the body that can be seen by others.

Guilt and shame also differ in a related dichotomy involving the self: personal versus social. Recall that when your achievements are being evaluated as a source of self-esteem, the standard may be individual, such that efforts others deem successful may be deemed unworthy by you. Or the standard may be social, your self-esteem being boosted by a poor performance that wins out over weaker competitors (e.g., having good self-esteem because of being a big frog in a small pond). Consider also the sources of identity, which may be personal or social (see Chapter 4).

The research of Froming et al. (1982) is relevant here (see Chapter 5). One group of participants, who were exposed to a mirror, was influenced by their personal feelings about punishment, not the social expectations of others. The other group of participants, who were observed by an audience, was influenced by the social expectations of others, not their personal feelings about punishment. Analogously, guilt involves the *personal and private self,* which means that the negative self-evaluations of guilt are based on individual standards of conduct. Admittedly, such standards derive from socialization, but the application of such rules and even the rules themselves are modified by the personality and experiences of each person to make them individualized. The clearest and purest case of guilt occurs when a guilty man has harmed another person but no one else knows: guilt without shame.

That guilt involves the private self does not preclude its occurring in the presence of others. Indeed, a major cause of guilt is harming others, so the *actions* that elicit guilt tend to be social. If others in addition to the victim observe the harmful acts, the perpetrator may feel both guilty and ashamed, both conscience stricken and humiliated. But a bad conscience derives not from being seen by others but by a focus on the private self. If the perpetrator believed that the act was not harmful or that it was completely justified, thereby denying personal responsibility, the perpetrator might feel shame if he or she was condemned by others but not necessarily guilt.

Shame involves the *social and public self,* which means that the negative evaluations affect oneself as a social object. If a person is observed engaging in behavior that he or she knows others decry, that person becomes ashamed. No contemplation is necessary, for the feeling is as reflexive as the feeling of embarrassment. Presumably, there are only small individual differences in the standards involved in shame but large group differences, which are based on the experiences of sociologically determined aggregations such as classes and cultures.

Why is shame so prominent in Japan? One reason is that there are so many significant audiences around: "The cycles of on-stage formality constrained by shame and the off-stage informality are ... well patterned in Japanese society" (Lebra, 1983, p. 200). Elsewhere, Lebra (1992) went on to describe two kinds of Japanese selves that are directly analogous to the public self and the private self:

> Japanese do divide self into the outer part and the inner part.... It is the inner self that provides for the fixed core for self-identity and subjectivity, and forms the potential basis of autonomy from the ever-insatiable demands from the social world. The inner self is also identified as the residence (shrine) of a god that each person is endowed with. (p. 112)

The socially circumscribed outer self is oriented to shame; the more autonomous inner self is oriented to guilt.

This description of the Japanese self is consistent with my assumption that shame is primarily social and public. But it is seemingly at odds with the research of Tangney and her colleagues, which has demonstrated that guilt is public as well as private and that shame is private as well as public. Resolving this conflict requires further details of my approach.

Alone Versus With Others

The crucial distinction I am drawing between guilt and shame is that between the private and the public *self,* not between being alone (private) versus having an audience watching one's behavior (public): not the presence or absence of others but the object of the self-focus. When the negative emotion is directed toward the self, is it focused on the private aspects of the self that are not open to observation (private self), or is it directed to those aspects of the self that others can see (public self or self as a social object)? If guilt involves only the private self, as I am postulating, one may feel guilty but not necessarily ashamed when others are around. For example, suppose while driving, a man tries to avoid hitting a dog and swerves into a child, breaking the child's leg. Bystanders do not blame him, so he experiences no shame, but he might feel guilty about harming the child, even though it was accidental. The negative evaluation, though occurring in a social context, is directed toward the private self.

The more typical case, however, is the co-occurrence of guilt and shame, as when bystanders blame a driver for harming a child. Such co-occurrence is one of the reasons that most people confuse guilt with shame. When people feel both guilty and ashamed, they might call it shame or guilt, for any mix of emotions is likely to be labeled as a single dominant emotion. This issue is not specific to guilt and shame. It may occur when people are both happy and sad, scared and angry, or excited and afraid.

The confusion may derive from the words used by parents and other socialization agents when they are chastising children. If an older girl hurts her younger brother, her mother might say, "You should be ashamed of yourself," when the girl clearly has done something to feel guilty about. Furthermore, there is little agreement among psychologists and other social scientists about the definitions of shame and guilt, so we should not be surprised that the two emotions overlap in reports obtained from participants. In my own unpublished research, some college students have reported feeling guilty and others reported feeling ashamed as a result of unseemly behavior after heavy drinking (cursing a parent or having sex with a friend's partner). In published research cited earlier, many of the causes of shame were also causes of guilt.

Imagery and Memory

As a species with advanced cognitions, we use imagery or language to recall prior events or to anticipate future ones. Consider the common fear of delivering a speech to an audience, a public fear. We may reflect about previous bad experiences when speaking in public, or we may anxiously anticipate performing poorly the next time. There may be a real audience or an internalized, private audience: "Behavior is often performed for both types of audiences, as when an actress tries both to earn her public audience's applause and to meet the demands of her internalized drama coach" (Baldwin & Holmes, 1987, p. 1096).

When we are alone, the memory of being insulted may cause some anger, or the memory of a sexual encounter may cause mild lust. As Leary et al. (1992) wrote about embarrassment, "We would expect to find that people occasionally blush in private when they imagine being the focus of others' undesired attention. For example, a solitary person recalling a public embarrassment might, in fact, blush" (p. 456). In shame as well as in embarrassment, the emotion *evoked* in social contexts may also be *experienced* in private but only because the event is **re**presented in memory. Such recall accounts for shame being experienced in private, when the internalized "audience" is an image or other cognitive evocation of a real audience. Whether shame occurs when others are around or in seclusion, its focus is assumed to be on the self as a social object.

Self-Cognitions

The major cause of guilt is harming others, so in this respect, guilt may be regarded as a social emotion. But the fact that the proscribed acts are social does not mean that the focus is on the self as a social object. Rather, it is directed to the private self, which, by definition, is not open to observation. Consequently, harming someone does not automatically elicit guilt, which requires the cognitive act of focusing on the private aspects of oneself and only then making the negative self-evaluation or not feeling guilty. Consider how to induce guilt in another person, and I shall use the stereotype of what has been called Jewish guilt (it is not limited to Jews). The son says that he intends to marry a Catholic woman. The mother replies, "Marry anyone you want, but I'm going to take to my bed and die." She is trying to make him believe that he is harming her. If anyone else tried to harm his mother, he would attack that person. If he accepts responsibility for hurting her, he will attack himself verbally but silently, that is, experience guilt. Guilt requires such self-cognitions, but shame occurs automatically when a person is observed in proscribed behavior.

Religion

Religion plays little or no role in the origin of shame, which is acquired largely in secular settings through the actions of parents and other socialization agents. Some religions in our society, however, play a major role in the origin of guilt. Jews have a day of atonement, when they read, fast, pray, and contemplate prior actions that might be sinful. Catholics are more specific and detailed in having a weekly confessional. It is true that parishioners are disclosing to another person, a priest, but the priest is there representing God. As such, he must not reveal what he has heard, and his duty is to assign appropriate penance, which varies with the seriousness of the proscribed behavior or even proscribed impulses or thoughts. After carrying out the penance, the sinner is forgiven.

Catholic guilt clearly involves the private self. Only God (or his representative) knows what has been confessed, and it is assumed that God knows even if the sinner has not confessed: "His eye is on the sparrow." It follows that for religious Catholics, there is no escape from guilt. When such a person becomes guilty, there is no place to hide. For the religious, there is no escaping an omniscient God. Aside from religion, for guilt may also originate in secular settings, those who are religious cannot escape a private, knowledgeable self.

In contrast, when a religious person becomes ashamed, he or she tries to hide from those observing him or her in an attempt to alleviate the exposure of the social self to negative evaluation. If the shameful behavior is serious enough, he or she may be forced to abandon old friends or even move to another town and then try to restore his or her good name. Thus, one can escape from shame and reduce the negative public self-awareness. But it is more difficult to escape from a bad conscience, from one's private self.

Expiation

A religious person expiates first by confessing to God (or his representative). The next step depends on the particular religion or culture. If it emphasizes "an eye for an eye," the next step is self-denial or self-punishment "to cleanse the soul." The last step is somehow making amends by performing good deeds, especially for the victim, if there is one. If the person is not religious, there is no formal confession, though the guilty person may unburden himself or herself to a confidant. But typically, making amends is crucial in attempting to *convince oneself* that the scale is now balanced, that self-respect is restored.

Freeing oneself of shame also requires doing good deeds and in that way reestablishing one's good name. We have the example of Richard Nixon, who, after the disgrace of having to resign from the presidency for crimes against the Constitution, attempted to expiate by being statesmanlike for the rest of his life. He was successful and was lauded at his funeral; however, later disclosures of even more perfidy on taped conversations in the White House permanently besmirched his honor.

Expiation also depends on the actions that caused the shame. If the cause is public cowardice, especially by men, the shame cannot be removed merely by making amends. Instead, it is necessary to confront a subsequent dangerous situation and display unusual courage, behavior that cancels out the previous humiliation. Whether it is a show of courage or making amends, the goal is to *convince others,* that is, to repair damage to one's social self.

Distinctive Causes

Some of the causes of shame do not elicit guilt. Having been discussed earlier, they will receive only brief mention. One distinctive cause of shame is *exposure* of forbidden behavior, including some kinds of sexual behavior—sadism and masochism, for example—and illegal acts that do not physically harm others. Middle-class embezzlers are ashamed when their crime comes to light, but typically they do not experience guilt. Public failure, whether it involves letting down the group or the team or cowardice, elicits shame, not guilt. Then there is stigma. It may be body disfigurement or the shameful actions of one member of the family, whose dishonor spreads to the entire family (vicarious shame).

Harm to another person may result in shame or guilt. But there is a subcategory that applies only to guilt: harm in which there is no perpetrator or, at least, the person experiencing guilt is not the perpetrator: the **survivor guilt** mentioned earlier. What are the cognitive processes underlying such guilt? My guess is this sequence:

1. Why am I one of the rare ones still alive when all else died?
2. I could have been one of them.
3. If I had not been saved, one of the others would have made it.
4. So in a sense, I am responsible for their death.

If this sequence appears not quite rational, neither is feeling guilty when you have caused no harm to anyone. As for children who learn that their mothers died during their births, presumably the cognitive sequence would be the same, except for the added "If I had never been born, she would still be alive." Survivor guilt is paradoxical in that innocent people feel guilty. But they do not experience shame.

The other distinctive cause of guilt occurs only among people of certain religions, as discussed earlier. It is sins against God, involving proscribed behavior that no one is aware of. If only God knows, the person has nothing to be ashamed of but is aware of sin (guilt).

The distinctions between these two emotions are summarized in Table 7.2. There are other causes of guilt and shame. For example, the exposure of sexual misconduct by a man usually evokes shame, but if the exposure also harms his wife or child, he is likely to experience guilt as well. Table 7.2, however, contains only the *distinctive* causes of guilt and shame. When *all* the causes of these emotions are considered, there are more causes of shame than of guilt. The reason is that shame is elicited not just by immorality but also by forbidden behavior that is not necessarily immoral, by stigma, and by public failure. That shame has more causes does not mean that it has a more generalized impact on the self, whereas guilt is specific to the action. Rather, it means that shame is likely to be elicited more frequently than guilt.

For purposes of exposition, the contrast between guilt and shame has been emphasized. Bear in mind that they are both negative self-

TABLE 7.2 Guilt Versus Shame

	Guilt	Shame
Emotion	Bad conscience	Humiliation
Self-awareness	Private	Public
Role of religion	Major	Minor, if at all
Escape	None	Hide
Expiation	Restore self-respect	Restore good name
Distinctive causes	Sole survivor	Exposure of forbidden behavior
	Sin against God	Failure in public
		Stigma

attributions, share some causes, and are easily confused by most people, who tend to use the two terms almost interchangeably. If we did not distinguish between guilt and shame, what would be lost?

My theory suggests several answers. First, because it is based on the differentiation of the self into private and public aspects, it is linked to other realms of the self for which this differentiation is important and informative: body image, identity, self-esteem, and self-disclosure. Notice that only the public aspect of body image is involved in shame, the example being facial or bodily awareness.

The linkage with self-consciousness offers a second advantage—specifically, in the way embarrassment is placed on a dimension of public self-consciousness with shame, thus accounting for the overlap between them. Recall the reports of participants in several studies and in Tangney's (1990) assessment of shame proneness. The focus in guilt is on the private self, which distinguishes it from both embarrassment and shame. Thus, shame is viewed as intermediate between embarrassment and guilt, sharing some features with each of them: public self-consciousness in both embarrassment and shame, and forbidden behavior and serious consequences in both shame and guilt.

Third, the impact of culture on shame and guilt has been well established. Japan is known as a shame culture because of its extreme emphasis on the public aspects of the self, as revealed in the concept of **face**:

> Efforts are made to appease an audience, or an internalized awareness of an audience, as this is the immediate source of self-evaluation. In contrast, the

behavior and attitudes of North Americans are relatively more determined by internal attributes, which, although influenced by others, are understood to be relatively free from ongoing influence. (Heine et al., 1999, p. 8)

The contrasting individualism of North American culture allows for an increased role in society of a more individual, personal self-emotion—namely, guilt.

Fourth, the theory makes contact with the stages of moral development (Kohlberg, 1969). The cardinal rule in the next to last stage, Stage 5, is that social rules govern our behavior, and we must conform to these rules. Presumably, exposure of violations of such rules results in shame. In the last stage of moral development, Stage 6, the cardinal rule is that of personal conscience. Each person judges his or her own actions according to individual scruples, and violations result in guilt whether or not any one else knows.

Developmental Theories

Attributions and Self-Consciousness

Already mentioned in the last chapter, the theory of Michael Lewis (1992, 1995a, 1995b) starts with the development of self-consciousness and embarrassment at roughly 2 years of age. Recall that he posited an evaluative kind of embarrassment similar to shame but less serious. Such evaluation requires an internalized set of standards, rules, and goals, which are acquired through socialization during the third year of life. This set, together with self-referential behavior, enables the child to make negative self-attributions—that is, shame or guilt—when he or she fails or in some way breaks a rule. An example was offered in which a child is told to play with a toy that is rigged to break. Some children act blameless, but "some children try to repair the toy. This is suggestive of guilt. Finally, some children simply collapse in a response indicative of shame" (Lewis, 1995b, p. 77).

There is research bearing on this theory: failure in children. In one study, children were videotaped while failing (Stipek, Recchia, & McClintic, 1992). Coders rated the videos for evidence of negative self-evaluation: gaze aversion, avoidant postures (e.g., head down or back to experimenter), and closed posture. These expressions were observed only in children older than the age of 32 months, leading these authors to infer that roughly 32 months mark the appearance of shame: "While facial expressions might reflect mere disappointment, an attempt to shield the self from the experimenter's gaze is considered evidence of shame by most theorists" (Stipek et al., 1992, p. 50).

A similar study also measured shame as a reaction to failure, which was defined as "body collapsed, corners of the mouth are downward/lower lip tucked between the teeth, eyes lowered, gaze downward or askance, withdrawal from the task situation, and negative self-evaluation (i.e., 'I'm no good at this')" (Lewis, Alessandri, & Sullivan, 1992, p. 632). Shame was scored if three of these five responses occurred.

Might this behavior be merely a discouraged reaction to having failed, that is, sadness? The authors answered this question by suggesting that in contrast to sadness, shame is marked by a lowered head and a stooped body posture. However, shame was scored even if two of the five responses were missing, and the missing two surely were lowered head and stooped body posture for at least some of the children. Furthermore, these two features may not be exclusive to shame but overlap sadness, embarrassment, and shyness, a position endorsed by Michael Lewis (1992): "Over one hundred years of research make it quite clear that there is no single measure, or set of measures, that is likely to bear a strong one-to-one correspondence with the experience of shame" (p. 26).

Now consider the ostensible cause of shame in both studies: failure on a task. Such failure has been widely used to study frustration, the blocking of motivated behavior. If we follow the logic of these two sets of researchers, frustration leads to shame. However, decades of research have shown that when participants fail, they respond with anger, discouragement, sadness, denial, or combinations of these reactions. Thus, whether the children's reactions were shame or merely disappointment or sadness remains open to question.

Primitive and Advanced Self-Awareness

Michael Lewis's theory captures some of the essential developments required for the appearance of shame and guilt: socialization involving standards and rules, cognitive ability to understand these rules, and self-awareness. It differs from my approach mainly with respect to the underpinnings of self-awareness.

Recall the distinction between a primitive sense of self, observed in animals and human infants, and an advanced sense of self, observed only in older human children. This advanced sense of self may appear at roughly 4 years of age—in a minority of precocious children, perhaps 3 years of age—marked by the first signs of embarrassment and shame. The emotions involve the self as a social object, the public self, a product of socialization.

Guilt is also a product of socialization, but it is based on awareness of the private self. How do we train children to be guilty? Partly by modeling guilt but more typically by trying to get them to assume responsibility for harming others and feel bad about it. A mother might tell her child, for example, that the child is hurting her feelings or making her sick. Or the child might undergo religious training that teaches that God is omniscient and therefore aware of all the child's sins. Such training, religious or secular, may start early in childhood, but feelings of guilt await the additional development of awareness of the private aspects of oneself. Private self-awareness, the tendency to introspect, simply takes longer to develop than public self-awareness. I suggest that it takes about 2 years longer, which delays guilt until the age of 6 or even 7 years.

In brief, I assume that the advanced cognitions, the socialization practices, and the time needed to socialize children, which are necessary for embarrassment and shame, lead to the appearance of these emotions by 4 years of age or so. But guilt, which involves the private self, requires an additional 2 years or so. The empirical bases for the first appearance of shame and embarrassment were discussed in the last chapter. The age landmark suggested for guilt is speculative.

There is evidence consistent with my theory. Children were presented with pictorial vignettes in which parents forbid a child to take money from a jar in the parents' bedroom, and then the child in the vignette does take a few coins (Harter, 1999). The child participants were asked to describe how the pictorial child would feel. The predominant emotion described by the 4- to 6-year-olds was that of fear. For 6- to 7-year-olds, it was being ashamed at being caught. For the 7- to 8-year-olds, it was so-called shame even when not being caught, which in my framework is guilt.

Evolutionary Theories

Appeasement

One kind of evolutionary approach emphasizes how our species is like other animals. Castelfranchi and Poggi (1990) saw shame as "an alarm system for face saving, and its function is to protect our goal of esteem and self-esteem" (p. 233). This statement presents us with a paradox, for shame, by most accounts, does not maintain self-esteem but lowers it.

As we saw earlier, these authors viewed blushing as a hallmark of shame, an uncontrollable facial expression meant to appease others:

> Those who are blushing are somehow saying that they know, care about, and fear others' evaluations and that they share those values deeply; they also communicate their sorrow over any possible faults or inadequacies on their part, thus performing an acknowledgement, a confession, and an apology aimed at inhibiting others' aggression or avoiding social ostracism. (Castelfranchi & Poggi, 1990, p. 240)

They added that the abasing head posture and averted gaze of shame also serve an appeasement function.

This functional approach to embarrassment also was adopted by Leary and his colleagues (Leary & Meadows, 1991; Leary et al., 1992): "Blushing, then may be a social attention diversion or distraction mechanism comparable to nonhuman appeasement displays. Besides their shared functions of remediation or appeasement, both are elicited by undesired attention from conspecifics and typically deflect it" (Leary et al., 1992, p. 455). They scrupulously added possible objections to blushing as **appeasement**: It may increase conspicuousness, and it is hard to perceive in dark-skinned people.

Subsequently, Keltner and his colleagues (Keltner, 1995; Keltner & Buswell, 1997; Keltner, Young, & Buswell, 1997) theorized about appeasement:

> Reactive forms of appeasement follow actual, discrete events, such as transgressions of morals or conventions, that disrupt social relations and require immediate response. Reactive forms of appeasement, therefore, are likely to be discrete and state-like in nature and engage humans in brief emotional exchanges. Embarrassment and shame are two forms of reactive appeasement that redress different kinds of transgressions. (Keltner et al., 1997, p. 362)

They mentioned research demonstrating that people who display signs of embarrassment or shame are treated better or at least not as harshly as those who do not. There is no dispute over this fact, but there is another interpretation (Goffman, 1959; Leary et al., 1992). We expect people to be embarrassed when minor mistakes are made but to be ashamed when serious transgressions have been exposed, and we view them as unsocialized or amoral if they do not express these emotions. So the fact that embarrassed or ashamed reactions lead to less censure may reflect nothing more than others' disappointment that the anticipated reactions of a socialized person did not appear.

Embarrassment may serve an appeasement function for minor social mistakes, but people also become embarrassed when they have not erred and have nothing to apologize for. The last chapter mentioned situations in which innocents tend to blush: the woman who is in the bathroom when a man inadvertently enters, the speaker who is overpraised, or the adolescent whose crush on another person is disclosed. The victims have not transgressed—only the private-public barrier has been breached—so there is no need for appeasement. In brief, embarrassment may serve a social function in some situations but not in others.

As for shame, consider the basic assumption that a display of shame will make observers more tolerant of the transgressor, thereby leading to better social relations. This assumption seems reasonable when the cause of shame is letting the group down, as when a group endeavor fails because of inadequacies of the leader, and the leader's display of shame induces sympathy. But many of the behaviors that elicit shame involve immorality or a character defect such as cowardice. Would the ashamed mien of an exposed child molester or the thief of others' life savings cause observers to forget or forgive the immoral behavior? Surely not. If shame has functional value, it may lie not in appeasement but in its role as an unpleasant emotion to be avoided. If the negative emotional state and the opprobrium of the group are sufficiently aversive, transgressors might refrain from the shame-eliciting behavior in the future. Whatever the function of shame, there remains the question of the necessary and sufficient conditions for it to occur in our species.

Necessary and Sufficient Conditions

My evolutionary approach adopts a different perspective, focusing on both how our species is similar to other animals and how we are different. It starts with an account of shame, but what follows applies to a lesser extent to the milder emotion of embarrassment.

First, there must be a *highly social species* in which there is regular or continuous contact with others of the species. Second, there must be close *bonds of attachment,* not limited to mother and offspring during infancy but continuing until maturity. For evidence of such attachment, consider jealousy, which involves an unwillingness to share a close attachment, or an abundance of touching one another on the body and the face, which indicates empathy. Third, there must be *at least minimal socialization* of offspring to prepare them for social life as adults. Fourth, there must be a relatively *long childhood,* enabling the second and third conditions to occur. These four conditions appear to be met by wolf packs, gorillas, and especially by the species closest to us, chimpanzees.

These are *necessary* conditions, but do they suffice? Consider a pack of wolves. A beta wolf attempts to get at food or a female belonging to the alpha wolf, who discovers it. The beta wolf knows it will be punished when discovered, so it adopts a submissive posture to mitigate punishment. This posture and its impact on the more dominant animal are innate; the same innate behavior may be seen in our pet dogs, for whom the human master is the alpha animal. The submissive posture is of course an appeasement gesture. The alpha animal's muted responses to it are adaptive in minimizing the probability of severe injury and maximizing a restoration of peaceful relations. No shame is involved unless one is willing to anthropomorphize and impute human emotions to animals without further evidence. If so, what are the *sufficient* conditions for shame?

First, there must be the extensive and *deep socialization,* well documented in our species, which goes beyond anything seen in other social species. Second, there must be the cognitive ability to make *attributions of causality,* such as assigning blame to others or to oneself or to assign causality to the situation or the person. Third, there must be the cognitive ability to *focus attention on the self,* so that the emotions and attributions we direct toward others—anger, disgust, or even amusement, for example—may be directed toward ourselves. Fourth, there must be the cognitive ability to *understand complex social rules* and standards. The rules and standards vary from one society to the next, but they all have the goal of establishing appropriate behavior by members of the community.

As a consequence of the earlier sufficient conditions, breaking of rules or not living up to social standards usually leads to a negative self-evaluation and the emotion of shame when there is an audience present. But shame may also occur in the absence of others, which means there must be an additional condition: the *ability to* re*present* prior social situations so vividly that the emotion that occurred earlier is again experienced when the person is alone.

As far as we know, ours is the only species that meets the second set of requirements and therefore the only species in which shame appears. Other animals simply do not possess the advanced cognitions and childhood socialization required for awareness of the self as a social object, let alone shame or guilt. When a dog hangs its head and tucks its tail between its legs after soiling the living room carpet and being discovered, it is merely displaying innate body postures adopted to lessen or avoid potential punishment by a higher-ranking, more powerful other (the owner).

If social animals can lessen punishment by being submissive and if it tends to restore peace in the community, does shame add anything to our species' adaptation? Yes, in two ways. First, it adds a new kind of social censure, delivered by an audience that attacks the miscreant's *social self* and therefore his or her self-esteem and social identity. We are more likely to inhibit selfish motives because we foresee damage to our social self and are less likely to repeat forbidden behavior. Second, the social punishment is likely to last longer and even occur in private through the mechanism of cognitive *re*presentation.

The necessary and sufficient conditions for the evolution of shame also apply to guilt, but the development of guilt requires more than an audience reacting to forbidden behavior. Unlike shame, it requires an evaluation of the self by oneself (or God) based on rules and standards that, though acquired through socialization, are now part of the personal and private self. As Lebra (1983) noted about guilt in Japan, it occurs only after reflection, whereas shame tends to be reflexive.

The shame reaction, which includes a downcast mien and attempts to hide, may be observed by others, so we know when another person experiences shame. Guilt is not as open to observation. Typically, we know it is being experienced only if the guilty person discloses it (remediation occurs in shame as well as guilt, so the fact of expiation is an insufficient basis for inferring guilt). If a person commits an act that society believes should induce guilt, does the person feel guilty? Because it is hard to tell, socializing guilt is more laborious, especially when the more abstract religious guilt is involved. One outcome is likely to be a lower frequency of guilt in the population. Both the lower frequency and the difficulty of observing guilt suggest that it is less useful to the community as a means of suppressing unwanted behavior. It follows that guilt is less universal than shame and is generally less functional as a means of social control.

Finally, it is not clear whether shame, guilt, or embarrassment evolved as adaptations for social control within the group. They may well be by-products of the advanced cognitions uniquely present in our species, adaptations whose functional value has already been established (see Buss, Haselton, Shackelford, Bleske, & Wakefield, 1998). It would not be the only example of an adaptation that evolved for one function in establishing a potential for another function via socialization.

SUMMARY

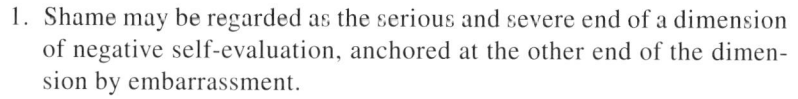

1. Shame may be regarded as the serious and severe end of a dimension of negative self-evaluation, anchored at the other end of the dimension by embarrassment.
2. The causes of shame are discovered immorality, illegality, public failure, and personal stigma.
3. Both shame and guilt involve negative self-labeling, sadness, and lowered self-esteem.
4. One theory of shame and guilt distinguishes between them this way: Guilt is a reaction to a specific breach of conduct, followed by a need

to atone, whereas shame is a generalized self-reaction, accompanied by a strong desire to escape.
5. Another theory of shame and guilt assumes that guilt involves a bad conscience, a focus on the private aspects of the self, and an inability to escape, whereas shame involves a feeling of humiliation, a focus on the public aspects of the self, and the possibility of escape by hiding.
6. A developmental theory of shame and guilt assumes that they occur only after rules and standards have been internalized and then a child breaks a rule or fails on a task, starting at 3 years of age.
7. There are several evolutionary theories of shame. One regards it as an appeasement signal, which makes others more tolerant of the transgressor. Another regards shame as a reaction to being socially excluded. A third specifies the necessary and sufficient conditions for shame to evolve.

DICHOTOMIES

central-peripheral: in one theory, the distinction between guilt (central) and shame (peripheral)

direct-vicarious: shame caused by your own actions versus related others' actions

private-public: feeling guilty but no one else knows versus feeling ashamed and everyone knows

GLOSSARY

appeasement the idea that expressions of embarrassment or shame minimize punishment

ego the psychoanalytic equivalent of the real self

ego-ideal the psychoanalytic equivalent of the ideal self

expiation confessing to bad behavior and making amends

face prominent in Japan, maintaining social standards in public

guilt proneness a traitlike measure derived from responses to scenarios

internalized parental attitudes   in one theory, the source of conscience

machismo   the extreme of masculinity

*re***presenting**   recalling earlier situations and experiencing again the linked emotions

shame proneness   a traitlike measure derived from responses to scenarios

stigma   typically, a body defect that causes shame

survivor guilt   feeling bad about being the rare or only survivor of a catastrophe

8

Boundaries I

Privacy

Self-Disclosure
Motivation to Self-Disclose
Personality Traits
Sex Differences
Personal Space
Privacy Components

The boundary between persons was mentioned earlier when the self in Western cultures was contrasted with the self in Eastern cultures and when empathy and altruism were discussed. In the present chapter, the boundary of the self concerns *privacy*:

> Privacy mechanisms define the limits and boundaries of the self. When the permeability of those boundaries is under the control of a person, a sense of individuality develops.... If I can control what is me and not me, if I can define what is me and not me, and if I can observe the limits and scope of my control, then I have taken major steps toward understanding and defining what I am. Thus privacy mechanisms help me to define me. Furthermore, the peripheral functions toward which control is directed—regulation of per-

sonal interaction and self/other interface processes—ultimately serve the goal of self-identity. (Altman, 1975, p. 50)

The boundary may be tightly wound around the self, others being shut out or kept away. Or the boundary may be extensive, admitting others into the region of the self. One kind of boundary involves the private self. Do you freely share your thoughts and feelings or keep them bottled up and unavailable to others? Several other boundaries involve the public self. Are you willing to be seen and heard by others or do you insist on screening them out? Do you let others (literally) come close to you, or do you keep them at a distance? Can you work and concentrate with others close by, or must you go off by yourself?

These various boundaries define the contents of this chapter. The chapter starts with the boundary around the private self: *self-disclosure.* Then the chapter deals with boundaries around the public self, the sequence being *concealment, personal space,* and *seclusiveness.*

Self-Disclosure

You may choose to keep secrets to yourself or reveal them to others. Several questions immediately come to mind. *What* might you disclose or keep secret? To *whom* do you disclose? *Why* do you disclose? Why do you *not* disclose?

Content

Questionnaires about the content of self-disclosure typically contain a mixture of contents. Consider some of the items under the heading of *body* listed by Jourard and Lasakow (1958): feelings about facial appearance, worries about appearance, past record of illness, and present physical measurements. The first two items deal with the private self and the last two with the public self.

The Public Self

Past social behavior has to be known to one or more people, by definition, but it may not be easily accessible to those presently around. If exposure of the behavior to the general public would cause shame or fear of punishment, there would be strong motivation to conceal it. To make the point, I shall cite examples of immoral and perhaps even criminal behaviors. There is stealing, causing injury when driving while intoxicated, child abuse, murder, and rape. In addition to these aggressive behaviors, there is a list of sexual behaviors that one would not want exposed: adultery, child molestation, sadism, masochism, and incest. President Bill Clinton was so bent on concealing his affair with a White House intern right in the White House that he lied about it in a legal deposition, laying the groundwork for an impeachment trial.

Anyone committing any of these acts would be loath to admit it, but *victims* of sexual acts also tend to keep quiet. There is shame connected with having been raped, molested, or seduced into incest, perhaps because many people regard the victims as being psychologically or morally degraded. Worse still, many victims blame themselves, a feeling that often is encouraged by the perpetrators and sometimes by others. After all, there is a widespread belief in a just world: "People get what is coming to them."

Though these sexual and aggressive acts are reported daily in the media, most of the population has neither committed such acts nor been the victim of them. For most of us, the negative social behavior we do not want revealed is minor, consisting mainly of lying and cheating. For a minority, homosexuality must not be admitted because of the realistic fear of social censure and even the loss of a job. In the military, the rule has been formalized to "Don't ask, don't tell."

Information also can be discovered by a thorough search of documents. You may not wish to divulge your income, debts, or educational level, even though these facts are not necessarily negative. But they are available to a diligent searcher, which means that they are essentially *public*.

The Private Self

Let us assume that you have never engaged in any of the aggressive, sexual, or immoral behavior just mentioned. But surely you have had antisocial or immoral *impulses*. Who has not become so enraged as to wish harm, perhaps even death, to another person? Who has not been tempted to cheat or steal? Who has not wondered about the excitement of illicit sex? These impulses or feelings are of course entirely covert, part of the private self. To admit them would result in shame, so only a deeply religious person might confess to them: Before he was president, Jimmy Carter admitted in a *Playboy* interview that he had lusted in his heart, though the inner impulses did not prompt outer behavior.

Not all sexual impulses are negative, however, and ordinary sexual arousal may indeed be considered as a positive impulse. Consider also a *crush*: the desperate longing you may have for another person who may be entirely unaware of it. Why not reveal this feeling to the object of your desire? Because the other person may be a stranger or just a casual acquaintance, or the other person (or you) may be married or attached to another. In such situations, disclosure of your romantic feelings would cause you to blush, so you would not reveal your feelings. But someone else might guess them, and as we saw in Chapter 7, disclosure of such feelings typically causes embarrassment. Thus, when the private-public boundary is breached, the resulting negative emotions depend on what is uncovered. If positive impulses or feelings, the consequence is embarrassment; if negative impulses or feelings, the consequence is shame.

In addition to positive and negative private impulses and feelings, there are also neutral ones. Many people have an occasional dream of glory, vaulting ambition to win political office, the Olympics, or a beauty contest. Some want to be the first to explore Mars, to win a Nobel Prize, or to become a movie star. They realize that admitting such a grandiose ambition would lead to teasing or ridicule, so they keep it to themselves.

Another part of the private self that is neither positive nor negative consists of religious thoughts and feelings. In their solitude, some people pray quietly, talk to God, or listen to God. Some have epiphanies, mystical experiences that may lead to religious conversion. Others meditate, seeking alternative states of consciousness that offer a sense of wonder beyond everyday experience. These various products of meditation and religious contemplation are socially acceptable and therefore may be communicated to others. But some people regard religious experiences as solely between them and God. Thus, aspects of the private self would not be greeted with ridicule or punishment but nevertheless may be kept hidden.

In brief, several dichotomies about the content of self-disclosure may have negative consequences. These are summarized in Table 8.1. If the information concerns prior bad behavior, it makes a difference whether you did it or you were the victim. The information may be private or public, potentially eliciting guilt or shame. And if the information is private, it may be positive, eliciting embarrassment, or negative, eliciting shame.

Recipient

Perhaps you know someone who is completely closed, never revealing anything personal to anyone. Such a person is rare. So is someone who is completely open, talking about the most intimate details about the self to virtually anyone. Most of us are at neither extreme and thus are willing to disclose personal matters to some people but not to just anyone.

TABLE 8.1 Dichotomies of Taboo Topics

Perpetrator-victim: you committed the act versus it was done to you

Private-public: thoughts, feelings, impulses versus actions

Guilt-shame: your harmful acts are known only to you versus perhaps known to others

Embarrassment-shame: disclosure of positive versus negative secrets

Positive-negative: secret crush versus secret impulse to harm someone

The most intimate aspects of the self tend to be revealed to only a select few. You might talk freely to a psychotherapist, who needs to know everything about you if the therapy is to progress. You might bare your soul to a member of the clergy. Religious Catholics regularly enter the confessional booth, where they are expected to reveal any sinful behavior, for the priest who hears this confession is sworn to secrecy. Whether the listener is a member of the clergy or a therapist, you would be expected to reveal both personal and social secrets.

There is another professional person who also requires that you unburden yourself. Your lawyer needs to know the full details of any immoral or illegal behavior, and if you hold back anything, he or she cannot defend you adequately. Like the two professional people mentioned above, lawyers can be trusted not to divulge what you tell them. However, unlike the above professionals, lawyers do not need you to disclose aspects of your private self: thoughts, feelings, impulses, and daydreams that only you know.

If you reveal damaging information about yourself to a professional person who is there to offer help or comfort, you will be neither judged nor punished. But similar disclosures to those close to you are a different matter. Your spouse may condone an illegal act but not extramarital sexual behavior or an extramarital love affair. Actually, there is a sex difference on this issue (Buss, Larsen, Westen, & Semmelroth, 1992). The question was, "What would upset or distress you more: (a) imagining your mate having sexual intercourse with someone else, or (b) imagining your mate forming a deep emotional attachment to someone else?" Most men answered that they would be more upset at sexual infidelity, but most women would be more upset by romantic infidelity.

In professional contexts, a tape recorder is often used. Is the taping of self-disclosure beneficial? Two experiments supplied an answer (Pennebaker, Hughes, & O'Heeron, 1987). In the first one, participants were asked to talk about experiences that were stressful, painful, or guilt inducing. Judges rated the tapes, dividing the participants into high versus low self-disclosers. Skin conductance levels—a measure of arousal—of the high disclosers were lower than those of the low disclosers.

In the second experiment, one group of participants again talked into a tape recorder, and the other group talked to a "confessor" hidden behind a curtain. In a subsequent summary of the results, Pennebaker (1997) wrote,

> When alone, students let go and disclosed highly intimate parts of themselves. Indeed, their physiological measures, such as skin conductance levels, indicated that the highly disclosing students were not inhibiting what they said. Among students talking to the anonymous father confessor, however, their physiological levels were constantly elevated. They remained on guard the entire time. (p. 111)

Evidently, disclosing intimate or painful experiences into a tape recorder is beneficial.

There is little disclosure to casual acquaintances and strangers, with one exception: People sitting next to one another on an airplane or train may relate personal experiences. Ordinarily, the private self is not uncovered, nor are negative aspects of the social self. Of course, you would not reveal central aspects of the self, only peripheral ones. But many autobiographical memories may be revealed, as well as future plans. Why would you reveal your past, ambitions, or current problems to a total stranger? Perhaps because the two of you are thrown together for only a few hours but will never see each other again, so there are unlikely to be negative consequences. Or perhaps you may respond to the other person's revelations with some of your own (more of this later).

In more formal situations, the self-disclosure of a stranger may be annoying. A male confederate self-disclosed either superficial or intimate information to male participants (Ashworth, Furman, Chaikin, & Derlega, 1976). The intimate self-disclosure caused participants to have greater skin conductance and heart rate increase—both measures of arousal—and greater reported discomfort than the superficial self-disclosure.

Motivation to Self-Disclose

Why do people self-disclose? Derlega and Grzelak (1979) answered by offering five functions of self-disclosure: social validation, expression, relationship development, self-clarification, and social control. What follows is a modification and elaboration of their list.

Social Comparison

Suppose you have an emotional reaction or you are unsure how to interpret the behavior of others. You need to check on whether your feelings and attitudes are sensible or idiosyncratic, so you might tell them to someone else. That person's reactions to your disclosure inform you whether you are off base or on the mark. Thus, one reason for self-disclosure is social comparison (Festinger, 1954).

There is a downside to social comparison, however. In attempting to evaluate the social reality of your emotions and attitudes, you might discover how negative and unrealistic your feelings are. After repeatedly learning that others do not validate your ideas, you would probably start keeping them to yourself. Thus, social comparison may also be a reason not to disclose.

Confession

Suppose you are under considerable stress or facing an intense crisis. You might be ambivalent over whether to marry immediately or wait. You might have disturbing thoughts or impulses, or you might have committed an immoral or criminal act. One solution is to seek out a member of the clergy and confess your sins, or you might seek help from a therapist or a close friend with whom you can share your psychological burdens.

Research demonstrates that self-disclosure is a good idea. Spouses who lost a loved one through accidental death or suicide and were willing to confide in others had less illness subsequently than those who remained silent (Pennebaker & O'Heeron, 1984). College students who wrote about their most traumatic experiences eventually had better functioning of their immune system and fewer visits to the health center than those who wrote about specific neutral topics (Pennebaker, Kiecolt-Glaser, & Glaser, 1988). These findings have been fleshed out with numerous case histories (Pennebaker, 1997).

Internal Pressure

Of course, your problems may not be so acute. Perhaps you have been obsessing about an important issue in your life and need to talk it over with a close friend. Alternatively, you might be carrying a grudge against someone close to you and need to get it off your chest. Or the crush you have on someone becomes so intense that you must blurt it out. In elaborating a fever model of self-disclosure, Stiles (1987) wrote,

> Upsetting or stressful events generate a subjective sense of pressure, of something being bottled up. Often the pressure incorporates emotions—usually anger, despair, fear, remorse, or some others negative feeling, though great joy and happiness can also impel people to disclose. Although the pressure is probably greatest immediately or shortly afterward, powerful or psychologically important events can leave a need to talk that lasts for months or years. (p. 261)

Getting things off your chest may be costly, though. When others hear about your grudges, they may judge you as hostile or perhaps even paranoid. The result might be lost friendships. If you have a secret desire for another person, expressing this affection to its object may have an unwanted outcome: Your affection is not returned. Being spurned is so painful that people tend to keep a crush to themselves.

There may be an even more humiliating consequence. Monica Lewinsky, under pressure and seeking advice, repeatedly telephoned a close friend to tell her about the sexual relationship with Bill Clinton. The "friend" tape-recorded several conversations and turned them over to the special prosecutor who was investigating the president. Monica Lewinsky lost all privacy. Her sexual behavior was reported to the entire world, and she became the butt of countless jokes on radio and television.

Relationship

One reason to reveal information about yourself is to develop a relationship (Derlega, Metts, Petronio, & Margulis, 1993, chap. 2). If people are to become friends or develop an intimate relationship, they need to find out about each other. Saying something personal about yourself signals your interest in the other person. Beyond that, you also indicate trust in the other person, for your revelations are not made to just anyone. Such trust, which involves something of an extension of self, means that you are opening yourself up to the other person, extending yourself.

But you may not want to develop a deeper relationship. To keep the relationship superficial, you are better off not disclosing much about yourself. Indeed, when a stranger or casual acquaintance starts relating intimate details, you are usually taken aback, for it is too early in the interaction to open up so much. So you keep your distance by refusing to reciprocate.

People are likely to differ in whether they actually want close relationships, and there is a questionnaire that assesses avoidance of intimacy (Pilkington & Richardson, 1988). Typical questions involve the danger of getting too close to others, fear of being hurt, not sharing personal information, and a preference for keeping people at a distance.

Of course, people may already be in a relationship in which some self-disclosure is expected. One study compared the self-disclosure of spouses with that of strangers (Morton, 1978) on two dimensions of intimacy. The first was *descriptive*: "One can be intimate solely by presenting very private, otherwise unavailable facts about oneself (e.g., a detailed account of one's sex life or a suicide attempt" (Morton, 1978, p. 73). The other dimension was *evaluation*: personal feelings and judgments, such as what one hates about another person. Spouses self-disclosed more intimately than strangers on the description dimension but not on the evaluation dimension.

The extent of disclosure may be an important issue for marriage partners, and an oft-heard complaint from wives is that their husbands will not open up. The nature of the relationship is especially important during adolescence, when disclosing to peers versus parents becomes an important issue. Adolescents may refrain from disclosing to their parents to create a sense of privacy and to diminish the potential for parental interference (Burhmester & Prager, 1995). A number of studies reviewed by these authors revealed that over the course of childhood through adolescence, self-disclosure to peers rises steeply, but self-disclosure to parents does not rise.

Reciprocity

There is strong pressure to reciprocate self-disclosure, a phenomenon first discovered by Jourard (1964). If the other person reveals something, there is an implicit norm that requires you to say something personal about yourself. One of the earliest studies illustrates the typical experimental setup (Worthy, Gary, & Kahn, 1969). The women participants were scheduled in groups of four and given 10 minutes to get acquainted. Subsequently, they were separated by partitions, and they communicated by sending notes. On each of 10 trials, each subject was provided with a set of seven questions that varied in intimacy and were numbered in order of increasing intimacy. The participant chose which question to answer, wrote down its number, and answered it. Then the note was passed to another participant, and the same procedure was repeated. The more intimate the disclosure by a participant, the more intimate was the reply. This was an especially strong relationship: Initial intimacy of disclosures correlated .77 with disclosures made in reply.

Subsequent research has confirmed the fact of **reciprocity** as one of the most stable findings in the self-disclosure literature (Cappella, 1981; Cozby, 1973). But there are important exceptions. Davis (1976) asked same-sex participants to get to know each other and provided them with a set of topics they might discuss. He found no *mutual* reciprocity. Instead, "the less disclosing partner tended to assume the following, reciprocating role, whereas the more disclosing partner assumed the leading role; there was in fact no firm evidence that the more disclosing members engaged in any reciprocity at all" (p. 791).

This finding makes sense, for in most interactions, one member tends to take the lead, the other following. Along this line, there are individual differences in self-disclosure. At one extreme are people who may reveal a lot about themselves, even when the other person does not. At the other extreme are people who are close-mouthed about themselves, even when the other person self-discloses (more about this issue below).

The degree of acquaintance is also important. Most of the studies have used strangers as participants. In one study, both strangers and friends were used as participants (Derlega, Wilson, & Chaiken, 1976). The strangers tended to reciprocate self-disclosure, but the friends did not. Presumably, the strangers were just being polite and knew that they would never again meet. Friends knew they would see each other again and so did not have to match the level of disclosure during the single encounter.

Reciprocity does not necessarily extend to the most intimate topics. When one person self-discloses a topic of moderate intimacy, the other person usually reciprocates. But when original disclosure is extremely intimate, only a small percentage of people reciprocate with the same degree of intimacy (Cappella, 1981).

Self-Clarification

Saying something out loud often illuminates murky ideas or feelings. So, for example, if you cannot decide whether to go for a career as a lawyer, you might tell a friend all the pros and cons of being in the legal profession. After hearing yourself talk, you might realize that you really do want to be a lawyer.

Alternatively, writing down your thoughts and emotions often helps shed light on them. Once they are externalized, you can examine them in the pages of your diary and see yourself more clearly. Also, memory may be faulty, especially after months or years, and a written account compensates for any memory lapses.

The contents of a diary fall into two categories. The first kind consists of the events of everyday life: what you did and with whom, what you bought, the trip you took, the movie you saw, the job you took, and so on. This kind of diary approximates a journal, a record of daily events. As an account of events that would not bring about shame or punishment, it might be shown to almost anyone.

The second category consists of aspects of the private self: feelings, hurts, grievances, romantic daydreams, ambitions, questions about religion or the meaning of life, comments about your body or self-esteem, and the fruits of meditation. Such a diary is ordinarily kept locked to minimize the risk of exposure. A family member or someone who happens to be in your home may come across the diary and read it. A brother, for example, might torment his sister with quotations from her diary.

Even more serious, the diary might contain evidence of wrongdoing, for some people are self-centered enough to write actions for which they may be culpable.

Perhaps the best-known example occurred a few years ago when U.S. Senator Bob Packwood maintained a diary with extensive accounts of his and others' sexual affairs and potentially criminal wrongdoing. To his considerable discomfort, he was ordered by the Senate to turn over his complete diary to the Ethics Committee. When the contents of the diary were made public, he eventually ended his political career and wound up as a lobbyist.

These various reasons for disclosing or not disclosing are summarized in Table 8.2. Notice that every motive for opening up about yourself is accompanied by an equally valid reason for not doing so. As a result, consciously or unconsciously, most people engage in a cost-benefit analysis, and only if the benefits outweigh the costs do they self-disclose. One potential cost when telling another person a secret is the possibility that the listener will reveal it to someone else. So a crucial issue is *trust* in the other person, for suspicion inhibits any desire to self-disclose.

Personality Traits

Individual differences in self-disclosure have been assessed by several questionnaires. The earliest one, containing 60 items, asked about six different areas that might be disclosed (Jourard & Lasakow, 1958):

1. attitudes and opinions (e.g., my personal views on drinking),
2. tastes and interests (e.g., my favorite reading matter),

TABLE 8.2 Motives and Risks of Self-Disclosing

Motive	Risk
Social comparison	Discover problems
Need to confess	Fear of being judged
Get it off your chest	Rejection
Intensify a relationship	Relationship gets too deep
Reciprocity	Other does not reciprocate
Clarify	Fear of what is revealed

3. work or studies (e.g., what I enjoy most in work),

4. money (e.g., whether or not I have savings and the amount),

5. personality (e.g., what it takes to hurt my feelings deeply),

6. body (e.g., my past record of illness and treatment).

The authors suggested that there were two clusters here, the first three areas being disclosed more readily and the last three less readily. For all 60 items, participants reported disclosing most to their mothers and less so to fathers and friends.

The next questionnaire inquired about disclosing to four different kinds of people, with each set of items varying in degree of intimacy (Chelune, 1976). Two kinds of information were sought: the target of self-disclosure and how much self-disclosure. This approach was followed by Miller, Berg, and Archer (1983), who had 10 items and asked participants how much they would disclose to a same-sex stranger versus a same-sex friend.

We can appreciate these attempts to assess individual differences in self-disclosure as first steps, at the same time regretting that they did not include factor analysis of the items. Such analysis would offer an empirical basis for dividing items into clusters. Furthermore, the items on these questionnaires deal with specific contents of what might be disclosed, such as *my personal habits* or *my worst fears,* rather than items about the general tendency to disclose, such as *it's hard to talk about myself* or *I am a private person.* More about these issues later, but for now let us examine how individual differences in self-disclosure relate to other personality dispositions.

Disclosers and "Openers"

In addition to their self-disclosure questionnaire, Miller et al. (1983) also constructed an *opener* scale, which assesses the ability to get others to self-disclose: being a good listener, being trusted, being sympathetic, and getting others to relax. Participants who scored high on the opener scale (**openers**) were successful in getting low disclosers to reveal themselves. But openers had no impact on high disclosers, perhaps because the latter were already disclosing freely (a ceiling effect). In a subsequent experiment, high or low openers interviewed others who were high or low openers (Shaffer, Ruammake, & Pegalis, 1990). Again, openers were better able to obtain self-disclosures than low openers only when the discloser was a low opener.

It has been shown that lonely people have difficulty in self-disclosing to others, especially in an opposite-sex interaction (Solano, Batten, & Parish, 1982). Given the items on the opener scale—getting others to relax, for example—is it possible that lonely people are poor at getting others to disclose? Evidently they are, the correlation between degree of loneliness and the opener scale being –.57 (Berg & Peplau, 1983).

Self-Consciousness

People who are high in private self-consciousness, by definition, chronically attend to the private aspects of themselves. As a result, they have more private information *available* for disclosure, and, other things equal, they might be higher in the trait of self-disclosing. There is moderate supporting evidence for this suggestion. The self-disclosure questionnaire of Miller et al. (1983) correlated .25 with private self-consciousness when the designated recipient of the self-disclosure would be a same-sex stranger; public self-consciousness correlated a nonsignificant .11.

The relationship between private self-consciousness and self-disclosure may be a little stronger for males. Franzoi and Davis (1985) selected four items from the Miller et al. (1983) scale and the correlated self-disclosure (to peers) with private self-consciousness. For their high school participants, the correlations were .36 for males and .27 for females. In a follow-up study, this time with college students who were in a relationship, private self-consciousness correlated with self-disclosure to peers .34 for men but only .16 for women (Franzoi, Davis, & Young, 1985).

We know that people high in private self-consciousness have more and better knowledge of themselves (see Chapter 5). It follows that because the content of this self-awareness (emotions, thoughts, aspirations and doubts) is typical material for intimate self-disclosure, persons possessing such detailed and accurate self-knowledge would seem better equipped to self-disclose, whereas persons lacking such elaborate self-knowledge would be less able to share personal information with others. (Davis & Franzoi, 1987, p. 66)

In the research just discussed, self-disclosure was measured by self-reports of participants. What happens when the *recipient* of self-disclosure assesses how much disclosure occurred? Unacquainted women interacted in pairs for roughly 10 minutes, and then each rated how much the other disclosed (Reno & Kenny, 1992). The extent of self-disclosure was unrelated to either private or public self-consciousness. When participants rated their own self-disclosure, as in the earlier research, it did correlate significantly with private self-consciousness. There are two possibilities here: (a) participants high in private self-consciousness think that they disclose more (self-rating) but in reality do not (partner's rating), or (b) the partners used (other college students) may not be the best persons to evaluate the extent of self-disclosure during a brief interaction with a stranger. So the relationship between self-consciousness and self-disclosure is still an open question.

Is there is a relationship between self-consciousness and *reciprocity* of self-disclosure, that is, a person's reaction to another's self-disclosure? Recall the experiment by Shaffer and Tomarelli (1989), mentioned in Chapter 5. They asked a subject and a confederate to become acquainted by taking turns talking about themselves. The confederate always spoke first, offering disclosures that were high or low in intimacy, first to determine how intimate the subject's reply would be, *as assessed by independent judges* who were unaware of the details of the experiment. The researchers were concerned with the known correlation between private and public self-consciousness. Therefore, they split their college student participants (of both sexes) into four groups, only two of which concern us here: high private, low public self-consciousness and low private, high public self-consciousness. When the confederate disclosed information low in intimacy, both groups responded with low-intimacy disclosures. And when the confederate disclosed information high in intimacy, both groups responded with information high in intimacy. Thus, both private and public self-consciousness led to reciprocity of self-disclosure, leading the authors to theorize that

> there are at least two paths to disclosure reciprocity: one that is paved by self-presentational concerns or the desire to present a positive public image, and one that is mediated by internalized norms or values that specify that a

person should respond in kind to the self-disclosures of a new acquaintance. (Shaffer & Tomarelli, 1989, p. 775)

The conclusion linking public self-consciousness to self-presentation is supported by earlier research on self-disclosure reciprocity (Shaffer, Smith, & Tomarelli, 1982). The measure of self-presentation was the Self-Monitoring Questionnaire (Snyder, 1974), which will be discussed further in Chapter 10. Participants high in self-monitoring reciprocated self-disclosure, whereas those low in self-monitoring did not. Evidently, participants who are either self-presenters (self-monitors) or high in public self-consciousness want to appear in the best light and please the other person, so they willingly reciprocate self-disclosure.

Attachment

Building on earlier work on young children, Main, Kaplan, and Cassidy (1985) and Hazan and Shaver (1987) categorized three styles of close attachment to others: secure, ambivalent, and avoidant. It is reasonable to expect that secure people willingly disclose to others, avoidant people are reluctant to do so, and ambivalent people are between these two extremes. These hypotheses were tested in three studies (Mikulincer & Nachson, 1991). In the first study, college students completed questionnaires on self-disclosure and **attachment style.** Secure participants reported the greatest amount of disclosure, ambivalent participants were next, and avoidant participants reported the least disclosure.

In the second study, participants were told that they would interact with a stranger who was described as liking or not liking to speak about himself or herself. The participants then indicated in advance their willingness to self-disclose and their liking for the stranger. Secure and ambivalent participants were more willing to reciprocate the amount of self-disclosure, and they liked the stranger more than did avoidant participants.

The third study was an experiment in which first a confederate and then the subject self-disclosed. For half the participants, the confederate's disclosure was intimate, and for the other half, it was not intimate. The results were summarized this way: "Reciprocity disclosure and liking for a high discloser existed among secure and ambivalent persons, but not among avoidant persons. In addition, secure persons were more responsive to partner's conversation than both avoidant and ambivalent subjects" (Mikulincer & Nachson, 1991, p. 327).

This research is important in that it combines questionnaire research with experimental manipulations, yielding convergent findings. Secure people tend to trust others, seek at least a minimal relationship with them, and therefore are willing to self-disclose and reciprocate intimacy of disclosure. Avoidant people, as their label suggests, want to keep their distance from others, are distrustful, and therefore are reluctant to self-disclose or to reciprocate intimacy of self-disclosure. Ambivalent people share tendencies of the other two attachment groups. Like secure people, they want to get to know others, but like avoidant people, they do not trust others. Therefore, they vacillate between disclosing and not disclosing, between reciprocating disclosure and not reciprocating.

It seems reasonable to assume that avoidant people are lonely, and research on lonely people is consistent with this assumption. Lonely people disclose less to opposite-sex acquaintances than do people who are not lonely (Jones, Hobbs, & Hockenberry, 1982). Strangely enough, at the start of a relationship, lonely people are likely to disclose more intimate information to a same-sex peer than do people who are not lonely, and lonely people believe that they do not sufficiently self-disclose to significant others (Solano et al., 1982).

Sex Differences

Men and women tend to talk about different topics (Caldwell & Peplau, 1982). Women talk about their relationships with family members and their own feelings, fears, and weakness. In one study, regardless of whether the interaction was with a spouse or a stranger, women disclosed more about love, misery, or shame than men did (Morton, 1978). In general, men talk about cars, sports, work, politics, money, and their strengths. Compare these sets of topics, and you will readily see that the women's topics are more intimate than the men's. So it is no surprise that a quantitative review of gender differences found that women generally disclose more intimately than men do (Dindia & Allen, 1992).

The thrust of most research is that the sex difference occurs mainly in same-sex interaction: woman-woman or man-man. In a male-female conversation, the sex difference tends to be small and inconsistent across studies. One possibility is that when women disclose more, men reciprocate by disclosing more than they ordinarily would, thereby reducing the sex difference (Rubin, Hill, Peplau, & Dunkel-Schletter, 1980). However, these psychologists were studying dating couples, and in an ongoing relationship, both parties are expected to open up.

What about friends? College students kept a record of every contact with friends that lasted at least 10 minutes (Wheeler, Reis, & Nezlek, 1983). Women disclosed with more intimacy than men in same-sex interactions but not in opposite-sex interactions. Similarly, a romantic pairing eliminates any sex difference: "Our data suggested one strong situational factor that encouraged intimacy in males: interactions with opposite-sex romantic partners, which yielded no sex differences herein" (Reis, Senchak, & Solomon, 1985, p. 1215).

There is also research with English participants showing that in opposite-sex interaction, men disclose more than women (Davis, 1978). Men took the lead in selecting more intimate topics, and women followed reluctantly with less intimate topics, reporting that they enjoyed the interaction less than men did. These findings are consistent with the earlier research with same-sex partners (Davis, 1976), which found that one partner took the lead, disclosing more, and the other followed, reciprocating disclosure. When the partners are of the opposite sex, men often take the lead, which may be why women disclose less.

These findings are not specific to England, for they have been duplicated in the United States (Derlega, Winstead, Wong, & Hunter, 1985). But there is a complication. Another study conducted in the United States used opposite-sex confederates who disclosed a lot or a little (Shaffer & Ogden, 1986). One group was told that they would not see the other person again; the other group was told that they would see the other person again. With no prospect of future interaction, women disclosed more than men did. But the prospect of future interaction caused men to disclose more and women to disclose less, the result being no sex difference.

A follow-up experiment revealed that (psychologically) masculine men—but not nonmasculine men—disclosed more to women and less to men when there would be future interaction (Shaffer, Pegalis, & Bazzini, 1996). These authors suggested that highly masculine men were using self-disclosure to cultivate a relationship with a woman but would avoid the appearance of wanting to be close to a man for fear that it would question their masculinity.

What about children? Several studies converge on a set of sex differences (Burhmester & Prager, 1995). Both boys and girls self-disclose more to mothers than to fathers. Girls tend to disclose more than boys do. Concerning self-disclosure to same-sex friends, there is no sex difference in the 6- to 8-year range. Girls self-disclose slightly more in the 9- to 11-year range, and this sex difference increases during the 12- to 20-year range. Children report that they disclose more to a sister than to a brother but more to a sibling of the same sex than to a sibling of the opposite sex (Howe, Acquan-Assee, & Bukowski, 1995). In brief, despite the complications just mentioned, I can discern that there appear to be two generalizations: (a) females self-disclose more than males, and (b) females tend to be the more frequent recipients of self-disclosure.

Personal Space

The physical border between self and nonself is the skin, but there is a *psychological boundary* that extends beyond the skin and into the space around the body. This bubble of space was first described by anthropologist Edward Hall (1966) in his book *The Hidden Dimension*. He distinguished four zones of space, two of which are relevant here. The distances are approximate and limited to North Americans and Northern Europeans.

The *intimate* zone starts with touching and extends to a foot and a half. The near phase is about half a foot; if a stranger or even a friend comes closer, it is experienced as an intrusion on the self. We will extend this part of our personal space only to lovers, close family members, or those offering sympathy and soothing when we are emotionally distraught. There are exceptions, of course, such as shaking hands or even occasional hugging and being touched by professionals such as physicians, dentists, and chiropractors.

The far phase of the **intimate zone** extends from half a foot to a foot and a half. Good friends are allowed this close; so is your lawyer. Casual acquaintances and certainly strangers are not allowed this close. Observe a crowded elevator, where people are squeezed together and are uncomfortable at this invasion of the bubble of space around them.

What Hall (1966) calls the **personal zone** starts at one and a half feet and extends out about a foot. Casual friends and acquaintances are allowed this close but not strangers. Observe people waiting for an elevator, and they typically will stay at least two and a half feet away if there is room. Hall has identified the major reason that we dislike crowding: It forces others to encroach on others' personal space and forces them to encroach on ours. So we resort to social playacting and pretend that they are not there, for example, by avoiding any eye contact.

In research on personal space, one procedure is to advance on the subject, invading his or her personal space. In a typical experiment, the experimenter briefly stopped moving, obtained the subject's report of discomfort, and moved a little closer (Hayduk, 1981). Participants felt slightly uncomfortable when approached to about two and a half feet, moderately uncomfortable at a foot and a half, and very uncomfortable at about a foot. Comparable results were obtained with blind participants, so visual nearness is not crucial.

There are also nonverbal signs of stress when personal space is invaded: twitching, darting eyes, body movement, and speech errors (Kanaga & Flynn, 1981). Stress level rose as an interviewer moved from 4 feet to $2\frac{1}{2}$ feet away from participants. These two experiments, samples of a larger group of studies, are consistent with the zones suggested by

Hall (1966). Clearly, each of us has a bubble of space that marks off a psychological boundary of the self.

Variations

Northern Europeans and North Americans have been found to have a larger personal space than do Mediterraneans and Mexicans (Evans & Howard, 1973). Arabs, whether friends or strangers, approach each other much closer than do Americans (Watson, 1970). Thus, when Americans travel to countries closer to the equator, they are likely to feel that these natives of such countries are invading their personal space.

In America, there are both developmental trends and gender differences. The preferred distance of children is small, commensurate with their smaller body size, but it increases with age (Tennis & Dabbs, 1975). Girls will allow others to come closer than will boys (Evans & Howard, 1973). As girls develop, their preferred opposite gender distance diminishes, but that of boys does not (Wagner, 1975). This gender difference evidently is maintained throughout life: "The literature indicates that males and females of all ages have different preferences for interpersonal distance: males set larger distances toward others than females do" (Hall, 1983, p. 104). In addition, others approach females more than males. Given the differences in personal space among cultures, it seems likely that the gender differences may be attributed to socialization practices, a position endorsed by Hayduk (1983): "It is the cognitive and social carriers of sex effects, and not biological sex per se, that allow the expansion of female spaces, or the shrinking of male spaces" (p. 308).

Privacy Components

At the start of the chapter, there were several questions about privacy. Two of them have been discussed: self-disclosure and personal space. Another question involves body modesty. The last question concerns not wanting to be seen or heard by others, which is a combination of modesty and personal space. This way of approaching privacy derives from an attempt to assess individual differences in privacy (Buss & Prince, 1992).

The participants were 973 college men and women (almost evenly divided) whose data were combined when we saw that there were only trivial and random sex differences. The items were designed to measure reluctance to disclose about oneself, concealment, and personal space. The three factors or scales that emerged are presented in Table 8.3. The table presents only the factor loadings for the scale the item was assigned

TABLE 8.3 Factors of the Privacy Questionnaire (factor loadings after each item)

Self-disclosure
1. It is hard for me to talk about myself. (.67)
2. I prefer that people know only a little bit about me. (.42)
3. If I kept a diary, I would never show it to anyone. (.34)
4. I sometimes find myself telling casual acquaintances things about myself. (reversed) (.70)[a]
5. There are many things about myself that I would rather not talk about with other people. (.52)
6. I will not talk about personal matters unless someone else does so first. (.67)

Concealment
1. When at home, I prefer to keep the window shades closed so that passersby cannot see in, even when I am dressed. (.57)
2. I feel very uncomfortable when using public restrooms. (.60)
3. I would much prefer a car with tinted windows so that other people could not see me. (.58)
4. I hate being in a room when the people next door can overhear you. (.56)
5. I strongly object to a bystander listening when I am on the telephone. (.51)
6. I do not like getting undressed in locker rooms. (.56)

Personal space
1. I would rather study alone than have others around. (.54)
2. It is difficult to really concentrate on a problem when other people are around. (.54)
3. I need lots of room around me. (.55)
4. It is a lot easier to do many things if you just tune people out. (.58)
5. I only way I can really unwind is to get away from everybody. (.45)
6. I need time away from others so that I can get in touch with myself. (.63)
7. When working or studying, I need lots of elbow room. (.64)

SOURCE: Adapted from Buss and Prince (1992).
a. This item also loaded .30 on the concealment factor.

to. The factor loadings of the items on the other two scales were uniformly low, with the single exception noted in the table.

There should be no surprise that such factors emerged when items were written with them in mind. But the factors were not foreordained, for the items still had to survive an empirical test: being administered to a large sample of participants and then being factor analyzed. And a number of items, especially several involving personal space, did not survive the factor analysis.

The *self-disclosure* factor consists of items about *not* divulging information about oneself. People who endorse these items maintain a sharp psychological boundary between themselves and others. They are protecting the *private* self (diary) and, to some extent, the public self (hard to talk about self). They prefer to be self-contained, and those at the extreme end of the dimension might be described as secretive.

The second factor, *concealment,* deals only with the *public* self. People who endorse these items do not want to be seen or heard in what they consider private situations. Knowing that others may see or hear them, they want to prevent such observation. It is not just body modesty (undressing, public restrooms) but, more generally, keeping out of the sight or hearing of others (tinted windows, telephone).

The third factor, *personal space,* combines two parts of the dimension of personal space and of course involves the public self. The first part consists of how far or near people are when they are in the same room, the preference being for greater distance (elbowroom). The extreme of this dimension is people being so far away that they are not even present (study alone, get away from everybody), the preference being for seclusion.

With one exception, the items are written in the direction of wanting privacy. People who do not especially need privacy tend not to endorse these items. Such people find it easy to talk about themselves. Their personality may be described as open, for there is hardly any psychological barrier between themselves and others. They do not mind using public restrooms or being overheard on the telephone. And they do not mind others being around and do not require solitude.

How do these three factors of privacy relate to other personality traits? The answer is contained in Table 8.4, with correlations based on a sample of 973 participants (Buss & Prince, 1992).

As we saw in Chapter 6, shy people tend to back off from others, so as might be expected, shyness correlates strongly with concealment. And shy people tend to be inhibited and more cautious about revealing themselves, so as might be expected, shyness also is moderately related to not self-disclosing and (weaker still) to personal space. Self-esteem is negatively correlated with all three privacy factors, especially so with concealment and less so with self-disclosure and personal space. Emotional loneliness, it will be recalled, involves a feeling that close relationships are absent. This trait correlated modestly with personal space and more strongly with not self-disclosing and concealment.

TABLE 8.4 Relationship of Privacy to Other Personality Traits (correlation coefficients)

	Self-Disclosure	Concealment	Personal Space
Shyness	.38	.48	.29
Self-esteem	−.24	−.35	−.15
Emotional loneliness	.33	.34	.24
Private self-consciousness	.06	.16	.30
Public self-consciousness	.08	.21	.21

The .06 correlation between private self-consciousness and self-disclosure requires explanation. Recall that previous self-disclosure questionnaires inquired about the *content* of the potential disclosure and that one of them correlated in the 20s to 30s with private self-consciousness. But our questionnaire inquired about the *broad tendency* to self-disclose (e.g., "hard to talk about myself"), and it is unrelated to private self-consciousness. Evidently, people high in private self-consciousness are neither generally open nor closed persons, though they do have more (potentially) to reveal about their private selves. As for the other correlations involving private self-consciousness, it is moderately related to personal space and less so to concealment.

In brief, the factor analysis and the correlations in Table 8.4 demonstrate the importance of distinguishing among three components of privacy: self-disclosure, concealment, and personal space. Whether to self-disclose involves the boundary between the private self and the public self. Concealment and personal space involve only the public self, either a psychological boundary of exposure to observation (concealment) or how far out the self extends (personal space), that is, a spatial boundary.

SUMMARY

1. Whether self-disclosure will occur depends on the intimacy of the topic and the relationship with the recipient.
2. People are motivated to self-disclose because of a need for social comparison, to achieve self-clarification, to get it off their chest, or to

deepen a relationship. The boundary here is between the private and the public self.
3. A second kind of boundary consists of the *personal space* around a person, which may be tight or expansive. This boundary involves only the public self.
4. A third kind of boundary involves *concealment*: allowing others to see or hear you. This boundary involves only the public self.

DICHOTOMIES

central-peripheral: intimate versus nonintimate topics

inner-outer: feelings not disclosed versus feelings disclosed

open-closed: self-disclosing versus secretive

personal-social: the privacy of a single person versus the privacy of couples

public-private: information available to others versus available only to oneself

GLOSSARY

attachment style   secure, ambivalent, or avoidant with others

intimate zone   lovers and families members are allowed this close

openers   people who can get others to self-disclose

personal zone   friends are allowed this close

reciprocity   self-disclosure in response to another's disclosure

9

Boundaries II

Empathy and Altruism

Empathy
Determinants of Empathy
Altruism
Cost and Benefit
Development
Evolution
Sex Differences

> *How selfish soever man may be supposed there are evidently some principles in his nature which interest him in the fortunes of others, and render their happiness necessary to him, although he derives nothing from it except the pleasure of seeing it.*
> —Adam Smith (1759/1876, p. 47)

This quotation includes elements of both **altruism** and **empathy.** The alternative to selfishness (your own happiness) is altruism (the happiness of others). And the sole reward is pleasure derived from others' happiness, which involves empathy, one of Adam Smith's moral sentiments.

The happiness and pleasure in the quotation draw focus on the positive consequences that befall another person, for example, winning a lottery: delight at the other's good fortune. Indeed, if there is any association with the recipient, you might bask in reflected glory. If you were in any way responsible for the other's success, you might reasonably share the good feeling. And if your efforts involved sacrifice for the other person, others might admire you for your altruism.

So when good things happen to people, others may share the joy empathically and perhaps even gain personal reward. However, empathy and altruism more typically occur in response to another's suffering or need, and the hoped for outcome is nothing more positive than relief from suffering or the other's need being met. Consequently, the focus of most research and theory is on negative situations, when prominent reactions to the other's suffering are compassion and altruistic behavior. Both reactions may be regarded as an extension of self to others.

Empathy

Empathy and Perspective Taking

The term *empathy* was coined at the turn of the 20th century as an English translation of a German word; before that, philosophers and psychologists used the term *sympathy* (Wispe, 1986). Citing the need for precision of language, Wispe (1986) wanted to keep the two concepts distinct: "In empathy, the empathizer 'reaches out' for the other person. In sympathy, the sympathizer is 'moved by' the other person. In empathy, we substitute ourselves for others. In sympathy, we substitute others for ourselves" (p. 318).

Some researchers and theorists in this area have adopted Wispe's (1986) usage. Thus, Eisenberg and Fabes (1990) link sympathy with compassion and empathy with **perspective taking.** Most psychologists, however, link sympathy with empathy and contrast it with perspective taking.

Nevertheless, Wispe (1986) was correct in calling attention to differences between two types of reactions to the suffering of others. In accord with present usage, I shall call them *perspective taking* and *empathy*. Their attributes are summarized in Table 9.1. Perspective taking emphasizes the cognitive reaction to another's suffering: using imagination to put yourself in the other's shoes. Empathy emphasizes the emotional reaction to another's suffering, signified by the terms *sympathy* and *compassion*.

TABLE 9.1 Perspective Taking Versus Empathy

Perspective Taking	Empathy
Understanding	Sympathy
Implicit goal is accuracy	Implicit goal is communion
Act as if you are the other person	Feel that you are the other person
Reach out for the other person	Moved by the other person

This conceptual distinction has been validated by a factor analysis of items of an empathy questionnaire (Davis, 1983). One factor, called emotional empathy, contains items such as, "I am often quite touched by the things I see happen" and "I have tender, concerned feelings for people less fortunate than me." A second factor, called perspective taking, contains items such as, "When I'm upset with someone, I usually try to put myself in his shoes for a while" and "I try to understand my friends better by imagining how things look from their perspective."

In a subsequent experiment on perspective taking, college students watched a video of an interview with a college student who was having a little trouble adjusting to college (Davis, Conklin, Smith, & Luce, 1996). One group was told to imagine themselves in the same situation (perspective taking), and another group was told to closely observe the interview (control). Then all participants were asked to use adjectives to describe the person being interviewed. Previously, the participants had used adjectives to describe themselves. The perspective-taking condition led to more common adjectives being used for both self and other than did the observing condition, leading the authors to conclude that "at the level of mental representation, the effect of active perspective taking will be to create a merging of self and other" (Davis et al., 1996, p. 714). More of merging later.

Sex Difference

The large literature on the sex difference in empathy—females are more empathic than males—has been reviewed exhaustively (Eisenberg & Lennon, 1983). As for the origins of this sex difference, we know that women are expected to be more nurturing than men, perhaps because of their greater role in reproduction (more of this later, when altruism is discussed). Girls are socialized to be more empathic, especially when expressing grief or sadness at the plight of others. But the sex difference shows up early in infancy, when girls respond to a tape recording of an infant crying with more reflexive crying than boys (Simner, 1971).

Empathy and Distress

The most primitive reaction to another's suffering is **motor mimicry.** Adult participants watched as an experimental accomplice "accidentally" dropped a large television set on an already (seemingly) injured finger that was in a splint (Bavelas, Black, Lemery, & Mullett, 1986). Most participants winced and showed other reflexive signs (open mouth, grimace) of mimicking the other's pain. Motor mimicry occurs as early as the first week of life (Simner, 1971).

Later in childhood, we may expect the reflexive reaction to suffering to be replaced by emotional reactions such as distress and empathy. In one experiment, preschoolers and second graders were shown one of three videos: a boy and girl frightened in a thunderstorm (distress), a young girl sad because her pet died (sadness), and a girl with spina bifida, having trouble walking (empathy) (Eisenberg & Fabes, 1990). Heart rate accelerated during the distress video but decelerated during the videos of sadness and empathy.

Aside from videos, participants might recall empathy-arousing situations. Schoolchildren and adults were asked to recall when a friend was going through a bad time (empathy), when they were worried (distress), or what the route to school was (neutral) (Eisenberg et al., 1988). There were no particular heart changes during recall of neutral memories, but heart rate accelerated during distress and decelerated during empathy. In addition, the self-report of distress was highest in distress, and the self-reports of sadness and empathy were highest during empathy.

The reactions of participants have also been assessed through the use of adjectives. Participants watched what they thought was closed-circuit television—actually a video—of a woman being given random electric shocks that seemed to hurt her (Batson, O'Quinn, Fultz, & Vanderplas, 1983). The adjectives they checked were factor analyzed, yielding these two factors:

Distress: alarmed, grieved, upset, worried, disturbed, perturbed

Empathy: sympathetic, moved, compassionate

Subsequent research added more adjectives to the empathy factor: tender, warm, and softhearted (Batson, Fultz, & Schoenrade, 1987). But another set of researchers discovered that the situation was more complex.

Again, participants listened to a tape of a woman in distress and checked the adjectives that described their emotional reactions (Fultz, Schaller, & Cialdini, 1988). This time, a factor analysis yielded *three* factors:

Empathy: *sympathetic, touched,* softhearted, and confused

Sadness: *sympathetic, touched,* low-spirited, heavy hearted, sad, *feeling low*

Distress: *feeling low,* distressed, disturbed, troubled, uneasy

The italics identify descriptions that were common to any two factors. Notice that being sympathetic and being touched occur in both the empathy and sadness factors and that feeling low occurs in both the sadness and distress factors. Such overlap is not surprising, for our emotions are seldom entirely distinct. But the remaining adjectives demarcate three different emotional reactions to another's suffering, separating distress from both empathy and sadness.

Just watching someone suffer may cause physiological distress. College students watched as an experimental accomplice, in the role of a subject, played a roulette game (Krebs, 1975). He was rewarded with money on some trials and punished by receiving electric shock on others. The punishment trials elicited increased heart rate and skin conduction (more sweating). These reactions were especially strong for the observers who believed that they were similar to the accomplice receiving the shock.

Both laboratory evidence and casual observations in everyday life agree that when we see another person severely hurt or in excruciating pain, our reaction may be not only empathy but also personal distress. We are both sympathetic and upset. Suppose that we help the other person at some cost to ourselves, but by doing so, we reduce our own distress. Obviously, reducing personal distress is rewarding.

When we empathize, do we share the *same emotion* as the other person, or is the emotion what we *would feel* if we were in the situation? The answer depends on the relationship to the other person and whether there are prior shared experiences. Said another way, the answer depends on whether there is at least a partial merging of self with other versus an extension of self to the other, a distinction emphasized by Wispe (1986). An example is empathic embarrassment, which was discussed in Chapter 6. If you are watching someone make a fool of himself, the embarrassment you experience might be based on how you would feel in that situation. Or the embarrassment you feel might be the same emotion experienced by the man doing something foolish.

The concept of *merging* is part of an approach that assumes the underlying presence of self-centeredness in all behavior. Thus, empathy is assumed to arise from a confusion between self and other (Wegner, 1980), and close relationships may be assessed by overlapping circles between self and other (Aron, Aron, & Smollan, 1992). Whether it is merging, blurring of the line between self and other, or a sense of **oneness** with another that accounts for empathy and, as we shall see later, altruism, the underlying assumption is that at bottom we are all selfish.

Batson et al. (1997) disagree sharply: "One must recognize the uniqueness of the other and his or her experience, distinct from oneself and one's own experience, to appreciate the plight of and to feel for another" (p. 497). In this view, we are capable of putting aside the tendency to be self-centered and reach out emotionally to those we know are different from us.

Determinants of Empathy

Empathy Enhancers

Clearly, we would feel strong empathy for a clone, and nature has provided a tiny minority of the population with an equivalent: an identical twin. Not surprisingly, identical twins report strong empathy toward each other. Of course, the blood relationship may be considerably weaker and still promote empathy, as with siblings who share roughly 50% of their genes. Fraternal twins, because they are reared together, are expected to have an even closer bond. And parents share precisely 50% of their genes with their children, which surely promotes empathy.

What happens within families may also determine whether empathy occurs. For example, participants watched a sympathy film and then reported on family cohesiveness (Eisenberg et al., 1991). Family cohesiveness correlated modestly with sympathetic and sad reactions to the film.

Parental practices should be important in the development of empathy, but there have been few studies. College students were asked how their parents behaved toward them during the students' middle childhood (Barnett, Howard, King, & Dino, 1980). The students were divided into high- and low-empathy groups on the basis of an empathy questionnaire. High empathizers reported that their parents had been more affectionate and spent more time with them.

Such retrospective reports provide some evidence, but obviously a longitudinal study would be better. It was supplied by Koestner, Franz, and Weinberger (1990), who compared the empathic concern of 31-year-olds with the reports of parental practices made 26 years earlier. The level of empathy in the 31-year-olds was assessed with self-reported adjectives. Only two relationships were significant for both sexes: Empathy at 30 years correlated .38 with parents' involvement with child care and .23 with the mother's tolerance for dependency. For women only, empathy correlated .44 with maternal strictness and .46 with maternal inhibition of aggression.

Prime examples of *nongenetic* relationships are close friends and spouses, especially those who have been married for a long time. Of course, the bond may cut across species. A movie of the chimpanzee Washoe, who was taught sign language, shows her reacting with distress and rushing to soothe her human "mother" when the latter feigned crying. The chimpanzee Lucy lived with two humans, and when they became ill, Lucy would run over and groom and soothe them and then become upset if they did not quickly recover (Temerlin, 1975).

As mentioned in Chapter 4, feeling that you are part of a broader social group contributes to identity. Such social identity is especially strong in collectivist cultures or subcultures. As a result, there is an extension of self to others in the close-knit group, especially those social entities that involve face-to-face interaction, such as fraternities and sororities. To the extent that you identify with others in such groups, you are likely to sympathize intensely when they suffer.

In most societies, children learn either by direct tuition or by imitation to sympathize with the suffering of others. Most children learn this lesson and, by adolescence at least, are prepared to sympathize with the plight of others.

Last, there are some experiences, especially those that stand out over the course of life, that we share with others. Consider pregnancy for women and childbirth for both parents. Or consider negative life events: two soldiers fighting in the same battle or the profound loss of a husband after many years of marriage. The emotions induced by these common events bind us experientially to others, allowing (perhaps) for a partial merging of self with other or at least an extension of self to the other.

These enhancers of empathy are summarized in Table 9.2. The left column lists the enhancers (determinants). The right column lists the ostensible feelings: whether they are the same as those of the other person or the feeling that would occur if you were in the same situation. For some spouses and friends, it would be the same emotion, but for other spouses and friends, it would be "as if." Notice that merging is believed to occur mainly when there are significant common life experiences. And the reason for the question mark for a spouse or best friend is that the feeling might be either the same emotion or an as-if emotion.

TABLE 9.2 Enhancers of Empathy

Determinants	Feeling
Genes	
Identical twins	Same emotion
Siblings	Would feel
Parents	Would feel
Interpersonal bonds	
Spouse	?
Best friend	?
Collectives	
Group identity	Would feel
Socialization	
Teaching by society	Would feel
Common experiences	
Childbirth	Same emotion
Battle	Same emotion
Widowhood	Same emotion

Reducers of Empathy

Just as there are people who sympathize with the suffering of others, there are people who are completely uncaring or, worse still, cruel. The determinants of *lack* of empathy are the mirror images of the enhancers of empathy. Thus, when there is no genetic overlap, competition for resources might make people less empathic. The opposite of an interpersonal bond is hostility, which is likely to engender an uncaring attitude toward the other person. Instead of group identity with other members of the collective, there is either neutrality (uncommon) or competitiveness and hostility (common) toward members of out-groups. Thus, prejudice toward Blacks has in the past led to lynchings, and racial violence is still evident today. Nazis went still further by regarding Jews as less than human, thereby denying any possible basis for empathy.

Last, young children tend to be cruel toward others because the process of socialization is just beginning. For a minority of children, the lessons of society are simply not being taught, and some of them are willing to kill another human being as casually as they would swat a fly. And for a still smaller minority (psychopaths), the lessons of society have been taught but not absorbed. In the absence of any extension of self to others, they regard people as objects and therefore as potential victims to be exploited.

Altruism

Empathy Versus Egoistic Emotions

Earlier, we saw that another's misfortune might cause both empathy and distress. Presumably, if you help another person because of empathy, that is altruistic and therefore an extension of self. But if you help solely to relieve your own distress, that is self-centered or egoistic. If true altruism represents a wide boundary around the self, including others, then egocentric behavior represents a tight boundary around the self, excluding others.

The possibility that relieving your own emotional arousal underlies seemingly altruistic behavior has been the theme of psychologists who deny that there is purely altruistic behavior. A leading proponent of this stance—a tight boundary around the self—has been Robert Cialdini, who has contributed several experiments with colleagues. Cialdini, Darby, and Vincent (1973) suggested that when another's suffering leads to the observer feeling *sad,* such sadness could be remedied by an act of helping, which enhances mood. They elevated participants' mood by praise or unexpected money, which diminished helping behavior. In a later study, inducing sadness in high school students led to increased helping (Cialdini & Kenrick, 1976). Still later, Cialdini, Schaller, Houlihan, Arps, and Fulz (1987) produced evidence that led them to conclude that only sadness leads to helping behavior. We help others to get over being sad at their plight. The title of their paper was "Empathy-Based Helping: Is It Selflessly or Selfishly Motivated?" Their answer was that it is selfishly motivated.

If so, can there be truly altruistic motivation? A theorist long ago answered yes (MacDougall, 1908). When another person is suffering, we might react with two different vicarious emotions. One, which he called sympathetic pain, is essentially distress; it presumably leads to self-centered motivation (reducing our own distress). The other, which he called the tender emotion, is essentially compassion or empathy: It presumably leads to altruistic motivation (reducing the other person's distress).

Many decades later, Batson et al. (1989) also answered yes, but they backed up their ideas with data. After observing a person in need, participants reported their own emotional reaction, yielding two groups: those experiencing personal distress or sadness and those experiencing empathy. Empathic participants helped more than distressed participants, which means that empathy may lead to helping victims for their own sake.

Other experiments strengthened this conclusion. Reacting to another's need with facial distress was negatively related to intentions to help (Eisenberg et al., 1988). Facial concern, presumably empathy, was positively related to intentions to help. Dovidio, Allen, and Schroeder (1990) showed that empathy led to helping behavior over and above the helping behavior that originated in sadness.

There is another possibility, however. It has been suggested that a crucial aspect of empathy is "an enhanced sensitivity to vicarious joy and relief at the resolution of the help recipient's needs" (Smith, Keating, & Stotland, 1989, p. 642). Participants watched a video of a woman freshman considering leaving college because of feeling isolated and experiencing stress. Some participants were asked to imagine how she felt (empathy), and others were asked merely to observe (nonempathy). The empathy participants offered more advice than did the nonempathy participants. In addition, some participants were told they would receive feedback about what happened to the woman; they offered more advice than those who would not receive feedback, which confirms the value of **empathic joy,** presumably an egoistic motive.

These findings did not sit well with Dan Batson, who rejects the idea that all altruism is egoistic. So first the vicarious joy experiment was repeated, and the same results were found (Batson et al., 1991). In their subsequent experiments, participants were allowed to choose whether to hear an update on the woman's condition. One group was told that the probability of her improvement was 20%, a second group 50%, and a third group 80%. Presumably, the greater the probability of her improvement, the greater the empathic joy and therefore the higher the number of participants choosing to hear an update. But there was no increase in choosing to hear the update as improvement went from 20% to 50% to 80%, suggesting that there are limits to the impact of empathic joy.

There is other evidence that empathic joy is linked with altruism. Participants were asked to volunteer to offer help to the terminally ill, families of people with AIDS, abused children, or women who need to escape from bad marriages (Davis et al., 1999). Trait empathy was a major determinant of such volunteering. In a follow-up, trait empathy was closely linked to the satisfaction of actual help (empathic joy) in those situations.

These issues relate to the personal-social dichotomy. When others are in need, people may react with distress, sadness, or subsequently with empathic joy, which is *egocentric* (personal), or with empathy, which is *sociocentric* (social). Said another way, helping behavior may be *self-directed*—to relieve a negative state, to achieve empathic joy, or, as we saw earlier, to achieve a reward—all of which represent a narrow boundary around the self. Or the helping behavior may be altruistic, that is, *other-directed*—directed only to relieve the other person's distress—which represents a broad boundary around the self.

Altruistic Motives

Why help another person when there is a cost to yourself? One answer is that there is always a selfish motive for seemingly altruistic behavior: Even if another person benefits, the donor does also, though the benefit may be disguised or distant in time. The other answer is that truly altruistic behavior does occur, motivated by a concern for the plight of another person: Either there is no benefit to the donor, or any benefit is an unintended consequence of the altruistic act.

Social Bonds

Attachment. Parents quickly establish an intense emotional bond with their infants. Parents put up with considerable discomfort to nurture their young. They rise in the middle of the night to feed or comfort their infants, they stay up all night, if necessary, with a sick child; they change diapers; and they tolerate the aversive sound of an infant crying.

In their role of caretakers, parents feed, clothe, and nurture their young, often at cost to themselves. Many women postpone having a career or just surrender the goal. Some fathers have lost their jobs to stay with a seriously ill child. Parent-child attachment is altruistically a one-way street, from parent to child.

Romantic love is altruistically a two-way street. The attachment bond is so strong that each lover is willing to make sacrifices for the other. This bond continues in a committed relationship long after the infatuation phase has waned. In both kinds of relationship, though, gift giving and sacrifice are usually not purely altruistic, for the recipient is likely to reciprocate and to be especially loving.

Siblings are often at odds with each other, but in most families, they still maintain close social bonds and are capable of extremely altruistic behavior. They are likely to give blood to other siblings, and because of the genetic overlap, they are prime candidates for donating organs. Several years ago, a basketball player on the San Antonio Spurs suffered from kidney failure and needed a transplant. A matched kidney was required, and a brother gladly gave up one of his own. This would seem to be an act of pure altruism, but as we shall see, the genetic overlap provides an escape clause for those who argue against pure altruism.

The best examples of altruism in relationships occur in everyday life, but there is an exception, a laboratory study (Cialdini, Brown, Lewis, Luce, & Neuberg, 1997). College students were asked to describe one of four persons of the same sex: a stranger they saw on campus, a casual acquaintance, a good friend, or a close family member (preferably a brother or sister). In the first experiment, they were asked to imagine that this person had just been evicted from an apartment and then to indicate the level of help they would offer. It ranged from none, to helping find a place to live, to offering to share one's own place to live. The participants rated their empathic concern through adjectives such as *sympathetic* and *compassionate*. They also completed a *oneness* index: the extent to which one's self overlapped the other's self. As in research mentioned earlier in the chapter, empathy concern was linked to the extent of helping; so was a feeling of oneness. However, when the feeling of oneness was controlled statistically, the impact of empathic concern disappeared.

The second experiment was similar, but this time the stranger, acquaintance, good friend, or sibling had died, leaving two children without a home. The options ranged from donating money to a fund for the children all the way to raising the children as one's own. Again, oneness and empathic concern were linked to the extent of helping, and again, controlling for oneness wiped out the effect of empathic concern. As the authors wrote,

> Close attachments may elevate benevolence not because individuals feel more empathic concern for the close other but because they feel more *at one with* the other.... If people locate more of themselves in the others to whom they are closely attached, then the helping that takes place among such individuals may not be selfless. (Cialdini et al., 1997, p. 483)

Oneness represents an extension of self to another, widening the boundary around the self. In my framework, the presence of such inclusiveness denies egoism and makes the case for true altruism.

Social Identity

Nationality is a potent source of social identity, with most people being patriotic. In an experiment mentioned in Chapter 4, college men were told that Russian men tolerated more pain from electric shock than did American men (Buss & Portnoy, 1967). The men immediately tolerated higher levels of pain to demonstrate that American men can take it at least as well as Russians. They were willing to endure pain for the sake of patriotism. Examples from everyday life are more poignant. During wartime, American men have volunteered for high-risk missions. The ultimate sacrifice is of course a suicide mission. Toward the end of World War II, when the Japanese faced defeat, some of their aviators volunteered to bomb American aircraft carriers by crashing into them. Some time later, Jim Jones, the charismatic leader of a fringe religious group, led his followers out of the country. When the group was investigated by federal authorities, he saw this as a threat and ordered everyone to commit suicide after killing those who would not obey. A significant minority were willing to commit suicide in the name of their religious identity.

At a more personal level, identities involve fraternities and even colleges. In a follow-up to the Cialdini et al. (1997) experiments on oneness, empathy, and helping behavior, this time the person needing help was a woman in the same college (Batson et al., 1997). Imagining her plight and her feelings led to more empathy and more helping but little merging, and whatever merging did occur had no influence on helping. Thus, merging is likely to occur and have an impact on helping behavior mainly with those with whom we have a close interpersonal bond, but merging does not extend to social identity. This conclusion, however, does not deny the possibility of altruistic behavior being motivated by a strong social identity—patriotism, for example—only that such altruism would not be due to merging.

Religion

Are religious persons more altruistic? The answer requires that we distinguish the various ways in which people are religious. We start with a distinction drawn by Allport and Ross (1967). At one pole are those for whom religion is a means to an end, which is an *extrinsic* orientation: "Persons with this orientation may find religion useful in a variety of ways—to provide security and solace, sociability and distraction, status and self-justification" (p. 434). At the other pole are those for whom religion is an end in itself, which is an *intrinsic* orientation: "Persons with this orientation find their master motive in religion. Other needs, strong as they may be, are regarded as of less ultimate significance, and they are ... brought into harmony with the religious beliefs and prescriptions" (p. 434).

A meta-analysis of six studies revealed that, as expected, those with an intrinsic orientation tended to be altruistic (Trimble, 1993). What was not expected was a *negative* relationship between an extrinsic orientation and altruism. Batson (1976) added a third kind of religiosity, called the *quest*. Those with this orientation view religion as the examining and questioning of basic values and beliefs.

How do these three kinds of religiosity relate to altruism? To answer this question, Batson and Gray (1981) confronted college women with the case of a woman who was desperately lonely. In one experimental condition, she wanted help in the form of companionship; in the other condition, she wanted no help. Those with an extrinsic means orientation did not offer help when it was asked for. Those with an intrinsic end orientation offered some help not only when it was wanted but also when it was not wanted. Presumably, they were driven by an inner (selfish?) need to help, not by altruism, for they insisted on helping whether the other person needed it or not. Only those with a quest orientation abided by her wishes, offering help when it was asked for and not offering help when she did not want it, which suggests that they were altruistically motivated.

There followed two similar experiments (Batson, Olesin, et al., 1989). The first one again revealed that those with an extrinsic means orientation and those with an intrinsic end orientation were not altruistic, but neither were those with a quest orientation, a failure to confirm. The second experiment confirmed this pattern, except this time the quest orientation participants behaved altruistically (confirmation).

Summary

The various motives for altruism are summarized in Table 9.3. Though distress is not listed as an altruistic motive because it has been regarded as an egocentric motive, it has also been interpreted as other-centered:

> Aside from its egoistic element, empathic distress has certain dimensions that clearly mark it as an altruistic motive. First, it is aroused by another's misfortune, not just one's own; second, a major goal of the ensuing action is to help the other, not just the self; and third, the potential for gratification for the actor is contingent on the actor's doing something to reduce the other's distress. (Hoffman, 1981, p. 134)

TABLE 9.3 Altruistic Motives for Helping Others

Motive	Example or Elaboration
Empathy	Helping another is its own reward
Attachment	Relieving a loved one's suffering is its own reward
Oneness	Feeling at one with the other
Social identity	Patriotism (e.g., risking your life for your country)
Religion	Your beliefs require "good works"

But both Batson and Cialdini, however much they disagree about the role of empathy in altruism, do agree that it is self-centered to help another person *solely* to relieve your own distress. True altruism cannot be self-centered but must be other-centered.

The motives listed in Table 9.3 all involve the ultimate goal of helping others. These motives are strongly socialized. The motives of empathy and social bonds have been interpreted as involving a merging between the self and the other (oneness), an issue that is still being debated. Another debate concerns whether all these motives are truly altruistic. Thus, Batson and Shaw (1991) would include only empathy as altruistic and the remaining motives as egoistic.

Cost and Benefit

Only saints are completely altruistic, with no consideration ever given to selfish motives. But for the rest of us, self-interest is ever present, though it may be overcome by a more powerful altruistic motive. Thus, there is always an explicit or implicit cost-benefit analysis, at least in our species.

First, consider when the potential cost is severe. The other person may need to be saved from raging waters, but the rescue effort is too dangerous. The other person may need so much money that the expense to the donor would lead to virtual bankruptcy. The other person may be so ill physically as to cause excessive personal stress. Among nurses who deal with terminally ill patients, some experience considerable psychological and physical discomfort (Stotland, Mathews, Sherman, Hanson, & Richardson, 1979). Now consider when the benefits are too modest. If the other person is at risk of drowning, your efforts at rescue might be unlikely to succeed. Or the other person may seek charity though possessing the essentials of everyday life. A reporter discovered that many of the people in a line for free food had color television sets, and some had telephone voice mail. Are they needy enough to warrant our altruism?

In these various examples, altruistic behavior would be unlikely because the cost is too high or the benefit too low. What determines the cost-benefit ratio that leads to altruism? Presumably, not only the egocentric and sociocentric variables listed in Table 9.3 but also two issues to be discussed shortly: evolution and personality.

Development

We know that infants are completely self-centered, but at some time during childhood, they become capable of altruism. Observations of 2-year-olds revealed that they became upset at another's distress but did nothing about it (Bridges, 1932). Children in the 3- to 4-year age range also became upset but tried to help. Of course, the fact that some children at this age occasionally behave altruistically does not mean that most children do. Pairs of children of different ages were asked to divide nuts between themselves (Ugurel-Semin, 1952). Most children in the 4- to 6-year age range were selfish, but this tendency dropped sharply thereafter and disappeared by 10 years of age. There was little equality or generosity at the early ages, but by age 8, generosity reached a peak that was maintained subsequently, and equality occurred in 12-year-olds.

Recall that the relief of sadness can motivate altruistic behavior in adults, but there is evidence that this effect does not occur in children (see Cialdini & Kenrick, 1976, for a review). These researchers, noting the possibility of a developmental sequence, experimented on children in three age ranges: 6 to 9 years, 11 to 14 years, and 15 to 18 years. They participated in a bogus task and were rewarded with coupons that could be exchanged later in the week for a prize. They were told that some children would not receive any coupons but that the participants might share some of their coupons with those less fortunate. Meanwhile, half the participants were asked to imagine and reminisce about sad experiences; the other half, neutral experiences. The youngest children contributed virtually no coupons in either condition. Children in the middle range contributed slightly more coupons when sad than when in a neutral mood. And in the oldest group, sadness resulted in considerable altruism and the neutral mood almost none.

These data provided a springboard for a developmental model of altruism as hedonism (Cialdini, Baumann, & Kenrick, 1981). The first stage occurs in young children who have not yet been socialized and therefore do not possess a norm for sharing material goods. Any time they give away something, they deprive themselves, so they do not share with the needy. In the second stage, children have been socialized and know that they are expected to share. But they have not yet learned that altruistic behavior is intrinsically rewarding. In the third stage, late adolescence, "Helping has been so frequently paired with direct reinforcement that it has become a reinforcing event in itself. Under these circumstances, altruism . . . will appear under the same conditions that produce other forms of gratification" (Cialdini et al., 1981, p. 221). One limitation of this model is that it applies principally to the sharing of resources. Its application to helping behavior that costs time or risks danger is doubtful. And it completely omits empathy, which can be a motive for altruism.

As a counterpoint, there is a developmental theory of empathy (Hoffman, 1987). The first year of life is marked by motor mimicry, for the infant is in the process of distinguishing between self and other. Such differentiation is complete by the second year of life, when the child is capable of going beyond mimicry to becoming distressed at another's suffering. During the rest of childhood, there is an increasing ability to adopt the perspective of the other person, so that by adolescence, the more advanced empathy of adults comes to the fore.

Evolution

Evolutionary theory assumes that each individual attempts to survive and reproduce. Those that are better adapted leave behind more offspring, who in turn leave behind more offspring. Each individual competes for resources and mates and therefore has a built-in selfishness, which obviously is adaptive. It follows that altruism must be maladaptive. But altruism does occur, for example, when parents defend their offspring even at the risk of their own lives. Thus, evolutionary theory was confronted with the paradox of seemingly maladaptive behavior: altruism.

This paradox led to the modern evolutionary thesis that focuses on genes as well as individuals. The basic assumption is *inclusive fitness*: that individuals act to sustain not only themselves but also their blood relatives. It is the genes that are selfish, not the individual. The closer the genetic relationship, the more altruistic behavior will occur. A sister is more likely to sacrifice for a brother than for a cousin; a parent is more likely to sacrifice for a child than for a niece or nephew. Precise predictions can be made on the basis of the degree of genetic overlap.

When we use the individual and not the gene as the basic unit, however, the evolutionary approach assumes that selfishness is innate. Notice that such innate selfishness directly opposes one sociological approach, mentioned earlier, which assumes that selfishness may derive from cultural norms.

Reciprocal Altruism

Recall that one selfish motive for helping another person is the anticipation of distant reward. Such anticipation means that it is adaptive to help another individual, even at temporary cost to oneself, a hypothesis called *reciprocal altruism* (Trivers, 1971). If each seemingly altruistic act were repaid later so that the altruist eventually benefited, both donor and recipient would benefit. Thus, there would be an adaptive payoff for reciprocal altruism, resulting in those who participated leaving behind more offspring. If this tendency were to continue generation after generation, it would eventually become part of the biological heritage of the species. Notice that such reciprocal altruism is innate, in contrast to the kind of reciprocal altruism that can be learned through socialization or through learning that today's altruism by others will be repaid some time in the future.

Several conditions would foster an altruistic tendency being built into the genes (Trivers, 1971). There must be repeated social interaction, so that earlier altruism is reciprocated later. Such enduring interaction will occur only if the group is relatively small and stable over time. When these conditions are met, cooperation pays off, for *inter*dependence is more adaptive than independence.

Reciprocal altruism assumes no necessary blood relationship between the donor and the recipient. Donors are altruistic toward others not because they share genes but because cooperation is adaptive. This perspective is of course different from that of inclusive fitness, which assumes that we are altruistic only toward those with whom we share genes. Wilson (1978) attempted to reconcile these different views:

> The altruistic impulse can be irrational and unilaterally directed at others; the bestower expresses no desire for equal return.... I have called this form of behavior "hard-core" altruism. Where such behavior exists, it is likely to have evolved through kin selection or natural selection, operating on the entire, competing family or tribal units. We would expect hard-core altruism to serve the altruist's closest relatives and to decline steeply in frequency and intensity as the relationship becomes more distant. "Soft-core" altruism, in contrast, is ultimately selfish. The "altruist" expects reciprocation from society for himself or his closest relatives.... The capacity for soft-core altruism can be expected to have evolved primarily by selection of individuals and to be deeply influenced by the vagaries of cultural evolution. (pp. 155-156)

Sex Differences

Mammalian mothers carry a disproportionate burden of biological investment in their offspring. They not only bear the young through many months of pregnancy—at least in humans and related species—but also breast-feed and otherwise do the major share or all of other nurturing efforts. Such an enduring investment establishes a clear biological basis for females being more altruistic toward their offspring than males.

But altruistic behavior requires that parents must recognize who their children are. Mothers know but fathers cannot be as certain. And for other blood relatives such as siblings, recognition of genetic overlap may be a problem. Hoffman (1981), suggesting that another mechanism is needed, wrote, "What therefore must have been acquired through natural selection is a predisposition or motive that, although biologically based, is nevertheless amenable to control by perceptual and cognitive processes" (p. 128). The mechanism he offered is empathy. Presumably, individuals are more empathic toward closer relatives than those with less genetic overlap. But how general is this explanation? The parents of many animals are altruistic toward their young, but how many of them are empathic: bees, whales? Empathy may be a biologically based mediator of altruism, but if so, it may be restricted to humans and animals close to our species.

The research literature on sex differences in altruism toward *strangers* is mixed. Men are more likely to help a stranger in distress, especially if the victim is a woman and especially when there are onlookers. Eagly and Crowley (1986) suggested that male altruism is stereotypically heroic, consisting of rescuing others from risky situations, especially women and children. I selected one study to illustrate this sex difference because adolescents were observed in mixed-sex groups in an everyday life situation during an extended bicycle trip (Zeldin, Small, & Savin-Williams, 1982). Girls were more likely to help when someone needed comforting and boys when someone needed physical assistance: "The observed sex differences in verbal support and physical assistance may thus reflect the adolescent's response to the cultural expectation that girls express comfort or empathy and that boys react in a nonemotional, instrumental manner" (Zeldin et al., 1982, p. 1497).

These findings are consistent with those found in women in seven different cultures, where it is almost exclusively women who occupy the nurturing roles in which altruism is likely to occur (Whiting & Edwards, 1973). And in our society,

> Women are expected to care for the personal and emotional needs of others, to deliver routine forms of personal service, and, more generally, to facili-

tate the progress of others toward their goals. The demand for women to serve others is especially strong within the family and applies to some extent in other close relationships, such as friendship. (Eagly & Crowley, 1986, p. 284)

Thus, women appear to have a wider extension of self to others than men do.

SUMMARY

1. Empathy involves shared feelings, whereas perspective taking is cognitive, consisting of putting yourself in another's shoes.
2. Empathy has been interpreted as a merging or sense of oneness with another.
3. Empathy is more likely when there is a relationship, a feeling of group identity, or strong socialization for shared feelings.
4. Some psychologists believe that all seemingly altruistic behavior is really selfish. One theory suggests that we are altruistic toward those with whom we share genes. There is evidence, however, that true altruism does occur with nonrelatives, especially in the context of empathy.
5. Without necessarily being aware of it, most individuals are likely to engage in a cost-benefit analysis before they behave altruistically.
6. Women tend to be more empathic and altruistic than men.

DICHOTOMIES

direct-vicarious: being distressed by another's misfortune versus being empathic

individual-group: altruism toward one person versus toward a group (patriotism)

open-closed: a wide boundary around the self versus a tight boundary

personal-social: self-centered versus extending the self to others

positive-negative: delight at others' good fortune versus sympathy for others' loss

GLOSSARY

altruism self-sacrifice for the benefit of another person

empathic joy elation when you relieve another's suffering

empathy vicariously sharing another's emotion

motor mimicry a reflexive facial or bodily reaction to another's emotion

oneness a feeling of identity with another person

perspective taking seeing the world from another's point of view

10

Self-Concepts

Empirical Self-Concept
Self-Schemas
Self-Discrepancies
Possible Selves
Self-Presentation

A century ago, the self was regarded as a crucial aspect of personality. Interest in it was buried by the advent of behaviorism, but it was resurrected by the adoption of psychoanalytic ideas in the United States just before and after World War II. A major player was a nonpsychoanalyst, Gordon Allport (1937, 1943), who provided the impetus for theory and research on the self.

One of the immediate consequences was the assumption that *consistency* is the hallmark of the **self-concept.** Thus, Lecky (1945) regarded the self-concept as central to personality and assumed that the prime motive in personality is a striving for unity and consistency. He foreshadowed later ideas about self-schemas (soon to be discussed) by suggesting that concepts about the self are organized to determine which incoming information is accepted. Shortly afterward, Snygg and Combs (1949) gave the self-concept a central place in their theory of personality. Carl Rogers (1951) also saw the self-concept as crucial to successful adjustment to the demands of the world. In his definition, the self-concept consists of features that we are aware of and can control. Again, consistency was paramount, as the self attempts to maintain and enhance itself.

These theories prompted an outpouring of research and theory on the self-concept, reviewed twice by Ruth Wylie. In her second book, she concluded,

> While constructs concerning the self may seem to be needed . . . these constructs have been stretched to cover so many inferred cognitive and motivational processes that their utility for analytic and predictive purposes has been greatly diminished. . . . One possible implication of this dilemma is that theories which depend heavily on overgeneralized self-referent constructs should be abandoned as potentially scientific tools. (Wylie, 1974, p. 319)

Her critique of extant research, however, led to more careful empirical work on the self-concept.

Empirical Self-Concept

To discover the self-concept, investigators merely ask participants about themselves. Perhaps because such research is so easy and certainly because of considerable interest in the self, the literature on the self-concept is enormous. So I selected two examples of work that demonstrate a *hierarchical* self-concept.

An early attempt proposed a general self-concept at the top of the hierarchy (Shavelson, Hubner, & Stanton, 1976). One step below are two broad sub-self-concepts. The first is the *academic* self-concept, which includes the school subjects of English, history, mathematics, and science; clearly, the participants were public school students. The other major sub-self-concept consists of *nonacademic* issues. These are (a) social, which includes peers and significant others; (b) emotional, which includes specific emotional states; and (c) physical, which includes ability and appearance. And each of these three may be further divided into specific behaviors.

This classification was cast in a form analogous to hierarchical models of intelligence. A series of studies, summarized by Marsh, Byrne, and Shavelson (1992), initially validated this hierarchical model. However, subsequent research cast doubt on the model, using structural equation modeling and related numerical techniques of data analysis too complex for this book (Marsh & Yeung, 1998).

Also in the 1970s, Rene L'Ecuyer, writing in the French language, offered another classification of the self-concept. More recently, he summarized his conception in English (L'Ecuyer, 1992). At the top of the hierarchy, partially reflecting the ideas of William James, are the following *structures* of the self: material, personal, adaptive, social, and self/nonself. The substructures are somatic, possessive, self-image, identity, and activities. The lowest level of the hierarchy are the following: social attitudes, references to sexuality, references to others, and opinions of others.

Even this brief account reveals that these classifications of the self-concept overlap personality. Try replacing the term *self* with the term *person,* and it becomes clear that these versions of the self-concept are dealing with each person's account of his or her own personality. The exception is the school subjects of Marsh et al. (1992), though we are left to wonder why school subjects should be considered part of anyone's self-concept. The basic problem is that the way the self-concept is measured, it may consist of anything that people might say about themselves, ranging from something as central as their core identity to something as trivial as whether they like rock music.

To cite one more example, adolescents in 10 different countries were given 99 short descriptions and asked how well each described them (Offer, Ostrow, Howard, & Atkinson, 1988). It was concluded that the differences among cultures were small and that there is something like a universal self-concept. This conclusion flies in the face of marked differences in the self between individualistic cultures and collective cultures, as we saw in the identity chapter. As such, it offers another reason for questioning the value of research on a *generalized* self-concept.

Self-Schemas

Schema, a term widely used in cognitive psychology, unfortunately has several meanings. However, for present purposes, a schema will be defined as *organized* understanding or ideas that attempt to make sense out of experience. In this sense, a schema is something like a theory people develop in dealing with the everyday world.

Perhaps the earliest attempt to deal with the self as a schema was that of Theodore Sarbin (1952), who wrote that the self "is seen as an *inference,* a high-order inference or cognitive structure, which develops as a result of and consists of lower-order inferences (or reference-schemata)" (p. 19).

Self-Schemata

Markus (1977) came up with the idea of *self-schemata* (*schemata* is the Latin plural for *schema,* but these days the term has been Anglicized, so the plural is currently *self-schemas*): "*Self-schemata are cognitive generalizations about the self, derived from past experience, that organize and guide processing of self-related information contained in the individual's social experiences*" (p. 64). Said another way, self-schemas represent attempts to extract meaning from the events that befall the self by using ideas gleaned from prior behavior.

In her research, Markus (1977) focused on the personality trait of independence and selected three groups of participants: (a) schematic independents, who rated themselves at the upper range of the trait of independence and said that this trait was important for them; (b) schematic dependents, who rated themselves at the lower range of the trait of independence and said that this trait was important for them; and (c) aschematics, who rated themselves in the middle range of the trait of independence and said that this trait was unimportant for them.

There are two problems here. First, in the selection of these groups, being schematic is confounded with being extreme on the trait, that is, being high or low in independence. We do not know if any differences between schematics and aschematics are due to having or not having a schema or to being extreme on a trait dimension. Second, if participants say a trait is important, that is taken as evidence that they have a schema. But importance is not part of the definition of a schema (see above). A trait might be important to a person without the cognitive organization that defines a schema. Nevertheless, Markus has come up with an interesting idea about the self, one that helps inform us about the self-concept.

Self-Knowledge

Neisser (1988) was more specific in outlining five kinds of self-knowledge. The first four consist of the ecological self, interpersonal self, extended self, and private self. How, then, do we experience a sense of unity in the self? The answer is the conceptual self, which

> helps to hold all the others together. It does so by providing a roughly coherent account of ourselves as persons in interaction with our neighbors; an account that is almost always similar in structure, though different in detail, from the one that our neighbors would give us. (Neisser, 1988, p. 55)

In this approach, the conceptual self is a more closely specified version of a self-concept, one that has particular cognitive properties.

Sarbin's and Neisser's conceptions, however, are best regarded as introductions to the idea of a **self-schema.** Others have pinned down the self-schema in greater detail and have spelled out the cognitive processes assumed to be involved.

Self-Concept as Theory

At roughly the same time that researchers were investigating the self-concept, others were exploring the self as a schema. Epstein (1973) proposed that the self-concept "is a theory that the individual has unwittingly constructed about himself" (p. 407). He saw each person's theory of the self as having the same properties as any scientific theory. It is extensive, having concepts available for a variety of topics, which can be differentiated. It is internally consistent, which appears to echo Lecky's (1945) idea that the self is consistent and strives for unity. And the theory of self is assumed to be useful in seeking pleasure, avoiding pain, maintaining self-esteem, and organizing experience. This last property, *organizing experience,* is central to subsequent theorizing about the self as a schema.

Egocentricity and Self-Reference

Greenwald (1980) viewed the self as fabricating and revising personal history in a manner analogous to a totalitarian political system. In his view, the self is **egocentric** in attributing causation to the self when often the causation lies elsewhere. The self is self-serving in taking credit for success but avoiding blame for failure. It tends to interpret events as confirming these self-serving biases, and it resists any change. In a sense, this approach adopts the idea of the self as a theory but a theory that is badly skewed toward enhancing and protecting the self.

Evidence on how we process information has sustained this view (Greenwald & Pratkanis, 1984). Material that you produce is remembered better than material presented to you. Virtually any experience that happens to you is remembered better than any event in which you are not involved. In general, anything that relates to you or even your familiar surroundings is better remembered than other material. Presumably, this impact of self-reference on memory is part of your self-schema, which biases the way you organize experience.

Self-Complexity

Earlier chapters in this book have included various aspects of the self, such as body focus, self-esteem, and identity, to name a few. And as we saw in this chapter, the empirical self-concept has been divided into particular elements. If there are different elements of the self, are there individual differences in the number of such elements as well as in their distinctiveness? The answer is yes; people do vary in what has been called **self-complexity** (Linville, 1985). Participants are asked to describe themselves by grouping traits into categories; having many categories that do not overlap defines self-complexity. Initially, it was found to act as a buffer against the stresses of everyday life; for example, people high in self-complexity were less likely to suffer from headaches and depression (Linville, 1987). Subsequently, self-complexity was linked with being under *more* stress (Showers, Abramson, & Hogan, 1998), which means that self-complexity has its downside.

Self-Clarity

As might be expected from individual differences in self-consciousness (see Chapter 5), some people have a clear idea of who they are, and others are unclear about who they are. To assess **self-clarity,** Campbell et al. (1996) devised a 12-item questionnaire. There were only 2 positive items, one of which was as follows: "In general, I have a clear sense of who I am." The remaining 10 items were all worded negatively, that is, in the direction of an absence of clarity. Based on their content, there are four kinds of items:

Conflicted: "My beliefs about myself often conflict with one another."

Changeable: "My beliefs about myself seem to change very frequently."

Inconsistent: "On one day I might have one opinion about myself, and on another day I might have a different opinion."

Self-ignorant: "Sometimes I think I know other people better than I know myself."

Because 10 of the 12 items are negatively worded, perhaps the questionnaire should be labeled self-*un*clarity. Participants who endorse these 10 items would be admitting to a good deal of conflict and ignorance about themselves. So it is not at all surprising that the questionnaire strongly correlates with neuroticism, depression, and (low) self-esteem.

Self-Discrepancies

William James (1890), who touched on several aspects of the self, was the first to discuss the discrepancy between people's aspirations and their present position. More than a half century later, this kind of discrepancy became the focus of client-centered therapy (Rogers, 1951). The details needed for research were spelled out in an edited volume by Rogers and Diamond (1954). Presumably, there is a dimension of ideals that ranges from what people would most like to be to what people would least like to be. There is a comparable dimension of the real self, that is, the way people see themselves now. An **ideal self** that is much poorer than the real self indicates a lack of self-value. One goal of client-centered therapy is to reduce this gap, especially by focusing on the unreality of an excessively high ideal self.

The Undesired Self

The ideal self typically has been contrasted with the real self, but Ogilvie (1987) suggested a problem: "To pit the real self in opposition to the ideal self may rob the ideal self of its more logical rival, the un-ideal self, an aspect of the self system we will refer to as the undesired self" (p. 380). This **undesired self** consists of memories of embarrassing or shameful behavior and negative emotions such as anger and hostility. Participants selected traits that were ideal, traits suggesting "how I hope never to be" (undesired self), traits as they were currently (real self), and their life satisfaction. As expected, the *smaller* the distance between the real self and the ideal self, the better was life satisfaction. And, as might be expected, the *greater* the distance between the real self and the undesired self, the better was life satisfaction, but this relationship was considerably stronger than that for the real-self/ideal-self discrepancy. Said another way, life satisfaction seems to depend more on distancing oneself from negatives than getting closer to positives.

Ideal and Ought Selves

The earlier ideas of James and Rogers were developed in further detail as part of *self-discrepancy theory* (Higgins, 1987). Again, the *actual* self is defined as what you presently believe about yourself, and the *ideal* self is defined in terms of your hopes and aspirations. The novel addition is the **ought self,** which is defined by your obligations, duties, and responsibilities. Thus, three domains of the self are postulated: actual, ideal, and ought selves.

Next, two perspectives of the self are distinguished: your own versus that of others who know you. These two perspectives are crosscut with the three selves to yield six of what Higgins (1987) calls self-state representations:

your own actual self,

our actual self as seen by another,

your own ideal self,

your ideal self as seen by another,

your own ought self,

your ought self as seen by another.

Finally, four kinds of **self-discrepancies** are outlined, together with a prediction of the emotional outcome of each one. The first discrepancy is between *actual/own* and *ideal/own*. This, of course, is the familiar idea of self versus ideal first formulated by James (1890) and further developed by Rogers (1951). Higgins (1987) predicted that awareness of unfulfilled aspirations leads to disappointment and dissatisfaction with the self. The second discrepancy is between *actual/own* and *ideal/other*. The disappointment here derives from failing to achieve the aspirations established by others. The predicted emotion is shame or its weaker sister emotion, embarrassment. Higgins pointed out that the emotions deriving from these first two self-discrepancies involve the absence of positive outcomes, that is, failure to achieve what is expected either by yourself or by others.

The third discrepancy is between *actual/own* and *ought/other*. At issue is awareness of having violated rules set down by others. The predicted emotion is fear of punishment from others. Higgins (1987) was drawing a fine line between ideal and ought. The distinction resides in the difference between failing to engage in positive behavior (not meeting others' ideals), which leads to shame, versus engaging in negative behavior (violating others' rules), which leads to fear of rejection. The last discrepancy is between *actual/own* and *ought/own*. The emphasis here is not so much on obligations as on rules that prohibit behaviors deemed by yourself as unworthy. The emotional outcomes are feelings of guilt and self-contempt: "Guilt involves feeling that one has broken one's own rules concerning how one ought to conduct one's life" (Higgins, 1987, p. 323).

An early study attempted to confirm these hypotheses by linking the four kinds of discrepancies to statements about the self (Higgins, Klein, & Strauman, 1985). The actual/own versus ideal/own discrepancy was associated with feeling disappointed in self, blameworthy, and not living up to one's own standards. The actual/own versus ideal/other was related to feeling unworthy and sensitive to signs of rejection, especially when not meeting expectations of others. The actual/own versus ought/other discrepancy was linked to experiencing shame and a lack of pride. The shame link is consistent with Higgins's hypothesis, but the lack of pride is not because it refers to a failure to act, whereas the hypothesis assumed that the shame would derive from violation of rules. The actual/own versus ought/own, hypothesized to be paired with guilt, was indeed correlated with guilt and anxiety about violating rules, but the correlations were negative, that is, opposite to the prediction.

In brief, the hypotheses about the actual/own versus ideal/own discrepancy (feeling blameworthy) and the actual/own versus ideal/other discrepancy (not living up to expectations) were supported. The hypothesis about the actual/own versus ought/other discrepancy was partially supported, but the prediction about the actual/own versus ought/own discrepancy was not supported. And a subsequent study found no relationship between the ought/own discrepancy and guilt (Tangney et al., 1998).

Although not specific to guilt, the discrepancy between actual and ought can lead to self-criticism, as revealed in a study of prejudice (Devine, Monteith, Zuverink, & Elliot, 1991). Participants high and low in prejudice were asked how they should act toward Blacks and toward homosexuals (ought) and how they do act toward them (actual). Among the low-prejudiced participants only, those who had large actual/ought discrepancies were highly self-critical; they checked adjectives such as *embarrassed, shamed,* and *guilty.*

Meanwhile, Higgins and his colleagues, bowing to empirical findings, abandoned the idea that the actual/own versus ought/own discrepancy would be linked to guilt. Instead, the focus shifted to the distinction between feelings of fear and restlessness versus feelings of disappointment and dissatisfaction: "According to self-discrepancy theory, the actual/own:ideal/own discrepancy should be related to the disappointment/dissatisfaction cluster, whereas the actual/own:ought/other discrepancy should be related to the fear/restlessness cluster" (Higgins, 1987, p. 327). Analyses using partial correlations confirmed these predictions (Strauman & Higgins, 1987b). This study also employed questionnaires on social anxiety and depression. Social anxiety, which involves public and social relationships, appropriately correlated with the actual/own versus ought/other discrepancy. Depression, which is more private and personal, appropriately correlated with the actual/own versus ideal/own discrepancy.

These findings were initially confirmed by two studies. One had participants imagine a negative event and then assessed their mood (Higgins, Bond, Klein, & Strauman, 1986). Participants with an actual/self versus ideal/self discrepancy felt more dejected, and participants with an actual/self versus ought/other discrepancy felt more agitated. The second study had participants rate how much they actually, ideally, or ought to possess a set of personal attributes (Strauman & Higgins, 1987a). When a mismatch was activated between actual and ideal selves, the outcome was temporary sadness, but when a mismatch was activated between actual and ought selves, the outcome was momentary anxiety and agitation.

The difference between the ideal self and the ought self was further demonstrated in research on interpersonal strategies that the participants might opt to use (Higgins, Roney, Crowe, & Hymes, 1994). The approach strategy involved being a good friend, and the avoidance strategy involved trying not to be a poor friend. Participants with a self/ideal discrepancy tended to select the approach strategy, but participants with a self/ought discrepancy tended to choose the avoidance strategy.

Subsequent research demonstrated that the ideal self and the ought self are more stable than the actual self and that the actual versus ideal self-discrepancy and the actual versus ought discrepancy are fairly stable over a 3-year period (Strauman, 1996). However, there are limits to how broadly self-discrepancy theory may be applied (Newman, Higgins, & Vookles, 1992). Consistent with predictions, a discrepancy between actual and ideal selves correlated with dejection, and a discrepancy between actual and ought selves correlated with agitation but only for firstborns. There were no comparable relationships for later-borns, who comprise most of the population.

As a further complication, a more recent study found that depression is associated not with a self/ideal discrepancy but with a self/ought discrepancy (Carver, Lawrence, & Scheier, 1999). This study asked participants directly about the discrepancy among four selves. When the discrepancy between real and feared selves was large, the real versus ought discrepancy was correlated with guilt. But when the real self was close to the feared self, the real versus ought self-discrepancy did not correlate with guilt. The authors concluded that being near to the feared self triggers avoidance mechanisms.

These various findings suggest greater complexity than Higgins's (1987) original theory, as well as limits to its generality. As Higgins (1999) has commented, the theory may apply only when discrepancies are important and of considerable magnitude. This comment is especially apt in light of the theory's disappointing application to satisfaction about one's body. Ideal and ought discrepancies are of course related to body dissatisfaction; no theory is needed to explain that fact, but these two discrepancies are not differentially related, respectively, to dejection and agitation about one's body (Strauman & Glenberg, 1994; Szymanski & Cash, 1995).

There are further complications (Boldero & Francis, 2000). First, the connections between the actual/ideal and dejection and between the actual/ought discrepancy and agitation depend on whether the reference is to participants as students or family members (social role), whether the issues are central or peripheral (importance), and whether the questionnaires were administered at school or at home (location). Second, there is a strong correlation between the actual/ideal and the ought/ideal discrepancies. Third, actual, ideal, and ought selves vary with respect to the particular factors of personality represented by the five-factor model of surgency, agreeableness, conscientiousness, emotional stability, and intellect. For example, agreeableness best describes the ought self, and emotional stability offers the worst description of the actual self (Hafdahl, Panter, Gramzow, Sedikides, & Insko, 2000).

Regardless of these complexities with North American participants, Higgins's approach has proved of value in studying the Japanese (Heine & Lehman, 1999). The Japanese had a larger discrepancy between self and ideal than either European Canadians or Asian Canadians. Nevertheless, the self/ideal discrepancy of the Japanese was only weakly related to depression. As the authors wrote, "Japanese culture places more emphasis on viewing oneself as inadequate (e.g., as further away from one's ideal). With this as a backdrop, it makes sense to reason that the actual-ideal discrepancies would not bring them as much of a threatening sting" (Heine & Lehman, 1999, p. 922). This research is another reminder of the impact of culture on the self.

Possible Selves

As we saw earlier in the chapter, Hazel Markus (1977) developed the idea of self-schemata. Almost a decade later, she developed the idea of possible selves (Markus & Nurius, 1986). Several possible subselves are specified. Thus, there are *ideal selves,* consisting of what you would like to become, versus *negative selves,* consisting of what you are afraid you might become and may stifle attempts to change. There are also *past selves*: what you might have been. However, the central idea of possible selves is that of **future selves**: what you might become.

Possible selves presumably are not as closely tied to everyday experience as is the present self, which renders them more susceptible to change:

> The construction of possible selves allows one to experience a contingency between one's now self and one's imagined or felt *future self*. The better one is at constructing these possible selves, the more vivid and specific they become, the more one's current state can be made similar to the desired state.
> (Markus & Ruvolo, 1989, p. 228)

This suggestion assumes the primacy of cognitions in determining changes in the self, whereas habits and noncognitive motives are given a subordinate role. If there is any doubt, consider this quotation: "By focusing on possible selves, we believe that we are phenomenologically very close to the actual thoughts and feelings that individuals experience as they are in the process of motivated behavior and instrumental action" (Markus & Ruvolo, 1989, p. 217). We are left to wonder, though, whether most people focus as much on their self-cognitions as is assumed by cognitive psychologists. Recall that people vary considerably in private self-consciousness, the tendency to examine one's psychological insides (see Chapter 5).

The Can Self

The **can self**: Your capabilities and potential define the can self. The can self represents goals that you strive for, in contrast to the future self, which derives from what you are, and only time is needed for it to develop.

These two selves were combined with actual and ideal selves to yield several patterns of discrepancies and equivalences. Two are of particular interest in that they were checked out empirically. Both involve a discrepancy between the actual self and the ideal self. In the first, the *actual* self is discrepant from the *can* self, and the *can* self is roughly equivalent to the ideal self. In this pattern, there is chronic failure to live up to one's potential (can and ideal selves). Participants with this pattern reported feeling like a failure and being listless and helpless.

In the second pattern, the *actual* self is discrepant with the *future* self, and the future self is equivalent to the ideal self. In this pattern, there are chronically unrealized hopes (future and ideal selves). Participants with this pattern reported being discouraged and hopeless. Notice that both patterns result in feeling dejected, but there are different nuances of this negative mood: weakness being linked to problems with the *can* self and hopelessness being linked to problems with the *future* self.

This section on discrepancies has discussed different selves and exposition sufficiently complex to warrant a summary (see Table 10.1).

Higgins (1996) went on to a grander theory, called the *self-digest,* which

Self-Concepts 269

TABLE 10.1 Selves That Might Be Discrepant With Each Other

Actual self: what you are now

Ideal self: your hopes and aspirations

Ought self: your obligations and duties

Past self: what you have been

Future self: what you might become or what you will become

Can self: your capabilities or potential

> represents knowledge of oneself as an object in the world because . . . such knowledge facilitates adaptation to one's environment. . . . It is a handy sourcebook for people about their person-environment fit that helps them fulfill their needs when interacting with their world. (p. 1078)

Clearly, this theory goes well beyond the domain of the self, encompassing a large chunk of the field of psychology.

An even more ambitious theory, called the *symbolic self* (Sedikides & Skowronski, 1997), placed the self within an evolutionary context. The symbolic self consists of cognitive representations of your own attributes (the actual self) but also includes ought, ideal, and future selves, as well as memories of previous achievements and plans for the future. It "often participates in processes that result in efficient cognition, effective behavior, better adjustment, and improved health. These critical and positive consequences suggest the possibility that the symbolic self is an adaptation" (Sedikides & Skowronski, 1997, p. 85). It may be used in the service of impression management, in which you must improvise an overt personality to present to others.

These ideas about adaptation imply a social function for the self-concept. Once you are aware of your self-concept, you may want to validate it with others. Alternatively, you may want to project a possible self or a can self, that is, improvise a personality to present to others. Such self-presentation may be regarded as the *process* aspect of the self-concept, as opposed to the *content* aspects that have been the focus of most of this chapter.

Self-Presentation

In his book, *The Presentation of Self in Everyday Life,* Erving Goffman (1959) drew an analogy between stage behavior and social interaction in real life. His sociological perspective was clear:

> I assume that the proper study of interaction is not the individual and his psychology, but rather the syntactical relations among the acts of different persons mutually present to one another.... A psychology is necessarily involved but one stripped and cramped to suit the sociological study of conversation, track meets, banquets, jury trials, and street loitering. (pp. 2-3)

Despite this "cramped psychology," the approach has been widely adopted by social psychologists, most of whom equate **self-presentation** with impression management. Sometimes the terminology of the stage is used: "Assertive impression management refers to those behaviors initiated by the actor to establish particular identities or attributes in the eyes of another" (Tedeschi & Norman, 1985, p. 295).

When people do self-present, their self-concept is assumed to be central to the process: "The self-concept is the primary determinant of the impressions people try to project.... Claimed images often mirror people's self-concepts" (Leary & Kowalski, 1990, p. 40), and "Impression management often involves an attempt to put the best parts of oneself onto public view. In fact, some people may impression-manage to ensure that others *accurately* perceive them" (p. 40). However, even when the goal is accuracy, distortions are assumed to be inevitable, for most social interaction involves "people's attempts to communicate what they regard as the 'truth' about themselves, with 'truth' defined in terms of desirable images" (Schlenker & Wiegold, 1989, p. 289). Self-presentation may be assertive or defensive (Arkin, 1981).

In brief, self-images are assumed to be the origin of social behavior in which the concern is not only with others' perceptions but also with one's own identity. When the self-presentation is *active,* the self-image is assumed to be filtered and edited to achieve a specific kind of impression (Schlenker & Wiegold, 1989). But when the self-presentation is *passive,* the self-image occurs automatically and without any particular processing.

The self-images presented to others are not necessarily the way the people see themselves but may also be a production of the imagination: "Self-presentations are affected not only by how people think they are but how they would like to be and not be" (Leary & Kowalski, 1990, p. 40). This possibility harks back to the idea of possible selves (Markus & Nurius, 1986).

These quotations point out the variety among theories of self-presentation. Some of them see it as embracing all or most of social behavior; others see self-presentation as reflecting one's identity (e.g., Baumeister, 1982). For many social psychologists, self-presentation or impression management is a crucial aspect not only of the self but of virtually all social behavior. Other social psychologists see less overlap between self-presentation and social behavior. Thus, Jones and Pittman (1982) suggested that self-presentation does not occur when the "behavior in question is task-centered, spontaneously expressive, normatively ritualized, or deliberately self-matching" (p. 234). The term *self-matching* refers to being oneself when in psychotherapy or when in intimate relationships.

Each approach draws on the **drama metaphor,** which I believe is even richer in its implications for everyday life (Buss & Briggs, 1984).

Drama and the Self in Social Interaction

Stage actors present to the audience characters based on a script provided by the playwright and supplemented by the director. They use makeup, costumes, facial expressions, and speech to convey a particular image. By analogy to everyday life, a man might have an image of himself that he wishes to portray, but he is not only the actor but also the director and the scriptwriter. As discussed earlier, this metaphor is appropriate for dealing with certain social situations, especially on a date or a job interview, when people are so eager for acceptance that they attempt to manage impressions. Whether people still attempt to project self-images in most everyday situations is the gray area where theorists differ.

One reason for the disputes among theorists may be that they are examining different kinds of people, for individual differences in self-presentation have been well established (Lennox & Wolfe, 1984; Snyder, 1974). Evidently, some people frequently project their self-images in social contexts, and others rarely do so. The stage metaphor is apt here. When actors leave the stage, they remove their makeup, take off their costumes, and resume normal dress, speech, and facial expressions. They behave like people low in the trait of self-presentation, their social behavior deriving from momentary impulses and emotions and enduring personality dispositions.

But some actors metaphorically seem never to leave the stage in the sense of continuing to present a variety of roles. They persistently present their self-images to others while inhibiting or concealing their momentary impulses and enduring dispositions. They behave like people high in the trait of self-presentation and are good exemplars of the self-presentation theories that see the projection of self-images as the dominant force in social behavior.

Social context is also important. Experimenters typically study strangers who will interact briefly, perhaps an hour or so, in situations sufficiently novel to engage the tendency to self-present. In many everyday situations, perhaps most situations, people are likely to be with friends, relatives, or fellow workers of longstanding, where they are more likely to engage in off-stage behavior: little self-presentation and lots of habitual, dispositionally driven tendencies. If we are to assume that self-images are constructed and projected to others, we should specify the social area in which self-presentation is likely to occur, as well as which people are likely to engage in it frequently.

Beyond self-presentation, the drama metaphor may inform us about identity. Again suppose that a male actor cannot leave the stage behind him but this time in the sense of being stuck in the stage role and continuing it while off stage. If he played Othello, for example, when he left the stage, he would continue to be arrogant and murderously jealous. The roles played on stage are analogous to the social roles adopted in everyday life, where a prominent social role may predominate in contexts when it is no longer appropriate. Thus, a professor might lecture to her family over the dinner table, or a navy man might run a tight ship at home. In these examples, an important social role carries over inappropriately, just as the leading role in a stage play would be unsuitable off stage, back in the dressing room. For such people, a large part of their identity is determined by a crucial social role.

Other people do not carry over a crucial social role into unconnected contexts. A psychiatrist does not attempt to diagnose his friends; a politician does not make speeches to her family. Like the actor who shucks his stage role when he leaves the stage, they adopt different roles in relation to different people. A crucial social role may represent a piece of their identity but not the major share, for there are other important sources, both personal and social (see Chapter 4).

SUMMARY

1. The self-concept emerging from empirical studies depends heavily on the particular questions that are asked.
2. The things that we remember and say about ourselves tend to be egocentric.
3. Early theory and research on self-discrepancies focused on the real self versus the ideal self.
4. Later self-discrepancy theory and research added ought, future, past, undesirable, can, and possible selves.

Self-Concepts

5. Self-presentation in everyday life may be understood in relation to the drama metaphor from which the theory originated.

DICHOTOMIES

aware-unaware: self-clarity versus self-ignorance
central-peripheral: self-concepts high versus low in importance
positive-negative: future self as good versus bad
unitary-multiple: overall self-concept versus different selves

GLOSSARY

can self   what you think your potential is

drama metaphor   on-stage and off-stage behavior analogous to everyday life

egocentric   self-centered

future self   what you think you are likely to become

ideal self   the best self you think is possible though not likely

ought self   what you think your obligations and duties are

self-clarity   how aware you are of exactly who you are

self-complexity   the number of categories you apply to yourself

self-concept   what you say about yourself

self-discrepancy   a gap between two parts of the self

self-presentation   managing impressions others have of you, presumably by projecting self-images

self-schema   an organized, structured set of ideas about yourself

undesired self   what you do not want to become

Glossary

advanced self   the self observed in older children and adults (e.g., identity)

aggression machine paradigm   a laboratory procedure for studying physical aggression

altruism   self-sacrifice for the benefit of another person

anorexia   abnormal dieting to excessive thinness

appeasement   the idea that expressions of embarrassment or shame minimize punishment

attachment style   secure, ambivalent, or avoidant with others

attribution   a guess about the cause of behavior or who caused it

barrier scores   Rorschach indicators of an external body focus

body boundary   me versus not-me

body dissatisfaction   wanting the body to be better looking

body dysmorphic disorder   an abnormally distorted, negative body image

body image   a mental picture of the body

can self   what you think your potential is

collectivist a culture or subculture that emphasizes strong ties to others and groups

confidence the belief that you will succeed

consistency the urge to logically square divergent cognitions

contingent self-esteem self-esteem that depends on comparing yourself with others

conspicuousness being the center of attention or feeling that you are

control theory a theory of self-focused attention

core-periphery theory a developmental explanation of humility and conceit

double stimulation you are both the perceiver and the object of perception

drama metaphor on-stage and off-stage behavior analogous to everyday life

ego the psychoanalytic equivalent of the real self

egocentric self-centered

ego-ideal the psychoanalytic equivalent of the ideal self

empathic embarrassment being embarrassed at the plight of another person

empathic joy elation when you relieve another's suffering

empathy vicariously sharing another's emotion

entity theorist one who seeks evidence of being able, competent

expiation confessing to bad behavior and making amends

face prominent in Japan, maintaining social standards in public

foreclosure commitment to an identity early in development

future self what you think you are likely to become

gender identity a feeling of maleness or femaleness

guilt proneness a traitlike measure derived from responses to scenarios

hostility resentment and suspicion of others

ideal self the best self you think is possible though not likely

identity diffusion a lack of commitment to any identity

incremental theorist one who seeks evidence of improvement or mastery

individualist a culture or subculture that emphasizes strong separation from others

inducers events or manipulations that refer to causing self-attention

internalized parental attitudes in one theory, the source of conscience

interpersonal theory the idea that guilt serves to enforce social rules

intimate zone lovers and families members are allowed this close

looking-glass self the idea that the self is based on others' reactions to you

machismo the extreme of masculinity

mastectomy the removal of a woman's breast

material self the self extended to one's possessions

mirror image recognition of self part of the primitive self

moratorium delay as a means of dealing with an adolescent identity crisis

motor mimicry a reflexive facial or bodily reaction to another's emotion

multiple personality a psychiatric disorder involving several identities

negative identity a commitment to a group society frowns on

negative self what you do not want to become

novelty unfamiliar people or settings

objective self-awareness a consistency theory of self-focused attention

oneness a feeling of identity with another person

openers people who can get others to self-disclose

other-directed   a predominantly social identity—go along to get along

ought self   what you think your obligations and duties are

overpraise   receiving too much praise in public

perceptual feedback   photos or movies of you or a tape recording of how you sound

personal identity   who you are based on unique, individual sources

personal zone   friends are allowed this close

perspective taking   seeing the world from another's point of view

private body awareness   attention to body sensations

private self-awareness   a temporary state of focusing attention on the inner self

private self-consciousness   the personality trait of focusing on the inner self

propriate striving   seeking a central theme of life

prosocial behavior   behavior valued by society

public self-awareness   a temporary state of focusing on yourself as a social object

public self-consciousness   the personality trait of focusing on yourself as social object

reciprocity   self-disclosure in response to another's disclosure

***re*presenting**   recalling earlier situations and experiencing again the linked emotions

Rorschach   A set of ink blots that have been used in research or body focus

self-clarification   self-disclosure to illuminate aspects of oneself

self-clarity   how aware you are of exactly who you are

self-complexity   the number of categories you apply to yourself

self-concept   what you say about yourself

self-discrepancy   a gap between two parts of the self

self-efficacy   confidence that you can perform a specific task

self-enhancement the attempt to boost self-esteem

self-evaluation maintenance a theory about when to bask in reflected glory

self-handicapping using an advance excuse for potential failure

self-image the self that you might be

self-presentation managing impressions others have of you, presumably by projecting self-images

self-protection trying to keep self-esteem from slipping

self-schema an organized, structured set of ideas about yourself

self-verification trying to confirm your own views about yourself

self-worth an intrinsic feeling that you are of value

sensory self the primitive self seen in animals and human infants

shame proneness a traitlike measure derived from responses to scenarios

skin conductance a measure of physiological reactivity

social identity who you are based on relationships, roles, and group membership

social loneliness the feeling of insufficient contact with others

social roles culturally defined expectations and behaviors, such as parent, doctor

socialization preparing the young for adult social life

sociometer hypothesis the assumption that self-esteem equals a feeling that others include you

stigma typically, a body defect that causes shame

survivor guilt feeling bad about being the rare or only survivor of a catastrophe

terror management theory the idea that self-esteem protects against the fear of dying

transsexuals people who feel trapped in a body of the wrong sex

undesired self what you do not want to become

vicarious self-esteem basking in reflected glory

References

Abrams, D. (1994). Social self-regulation. *Personality and Social Psychology Bulletin, 20,* 473-483.

Agatstein, F. C., & Buchanan, D. B. (1984). Public and private self-consciousness and the recall of self-relevant information. *Personality and Social Psychology Bulletin, 10,* 314-325.

Alicke, M. D., LoSchiavo, F. M., Zerbst, J., & Zhang, S. (1997). The person who outperforms me is a genius: Maintaining perceived competence in upward social comparison. *Journal of Personality and Social Psychology, 73,* 781-789.

Allport, G. W. (1937). *Personality: A psychological interpretation.* New York: Holt, Rinehart & Winston.

Allport, G. W. (1943). The ego in contemporary psychology. *Psychological Review, 50,* 451-478.

Allport, G. W. (1961). *Pattern and growth in personality.* New York: Holt, Rinehart & Winston.

Allport, G. W., & Ross, J. M. (1967). Personal religious orientation and prejudice. *Journal of Personality and Social Psychology, 5,* 432-443.

Altman, I. (1975). *The environment and social behavior.* Belmont, CA: Brooks/Cole.

Amsterdam, B. (1972). Mirror self-image reactions before the age of two. *Developmental Psychology, 5,* 297-305.

Anderson, E. M., Bohon, L. M., & Berrigan, L. P. (1996). Factor structure of the private self-consciousness scale. *Journal of Personality Assessment, 66,* 144-152.

Andrews, B. (1995). Bodily shame as a mediator between abusive experiences and depression. *Journal of Abnormal Psychology, 104,* 277-285.

Andrews, B. (1997a). Bodily shame in relation to abuse in childhood and bulimia. *British Journal of Clinical Psychology, 36,* 41-49.

Andrews, B. (1997b). Shame, early abuse, and the course of depression in a clinical sample: A preliminary study. *Cognition and Emotion, 11,* 373-381.

Angyal, A. (1951). A theoretical model for personality study. *Journal of Personality, 20,* 131-142.

Apsler, R. (1975). Effects of embarrassment on behavior toward others. *Journal of Personality and Social Psychology, 32,* 145-153.

Arkin, R. M. (1981). Self-presentational styles. In J. T. Tedeschi (Ed.), *Impression management theory and social psychological research* (pp. 311-333). New York: Academic Press.

Arkin, R. M., Appelman, A. J., & Burger, J. M. (1980). Social anxiety, self-presentation, and the self-serving bias in causal attribution. *Journal of Personality and Social Psychology, 38,* 23-35.

Arndt, J., Greenberg, J., Simon, L., Pyszczynsky, T., & Solomon, S. (1998). Terror management and self-awareness: Evidence that mortality salience provokes avoidance of the self-focused state. *Personality and Social Psychology Bulletin, 24,* 1216-1227.

Aron, A., Aron, E. N., & Smollan, D. (1992). Inclusion of the Other Self Scale and the structure of interpersonal closeness. *Journal of Personality and Social Psychology, 63,* 596-612.

Aronson, E., & Mills, J. (1959). The effect of severity of initiation on liking for a group. *Journal of Abnormal and Social Psychology, 59,* 177-181.

Asendorpf, J. B. (1990). The expression of shyness and embarrassment. In W. R. Crozier (Ed.), *Shyness and embarrassment* (pp. 87-118). New York: Cambridge University Press.

Asendorpf, J. B., & Baudonniere, P.-M. (1993). Self-awareness and other-awareness: Mirror self-recognition and synchronic imitation among unfamiliar peers. *Developmental Psychology, 29,* 88-95.

Ashworth, C., Furman, G., Chaikin, A. L., & Derlega, V. J. (1976). Physiological responses to self-disclosure. *Journal of Humanistic Psychology, 16,* 71-80.

Aspinwall, L. G., & Taylor, S. E. (1993). Effects of social comparison direction, threat, and self-esteem on affect, self-evaluation, and expected success. *Journal of Personality and Social Psychology, 64,* 708-722.

Babcock, M. K., & Sabini, J. (1990). On differentiating embarrassment from shame. *European Journal of Social Psychology, 20,* 151-169.

Bakan, D. (1966). *The duality of human existence.* Boston: Beacon.

Baldwin, M. W., & Holmes, J. G. (1987). Salient private audiences and awareness of the self. *Journal of Personality and Social Psychology, 52,* 1087-1098.

Bandura, A. (1986). *Social foundations of thought and action.* Englewood Cliffs, NJ: Prentice Hall.

Baradell, J. G., & Klein, K. (1993). Relationship of life stress and body consciousness to hypervigilant decision making. *Journal of Personality and Social Psychology, 64,* 267-273.

Barkow, J. H. (1975). Prestige and culture: A biosocial interpretation. *Current Anthropology, 16,* 553-572.

Barlow, D. H. (1988). *Anxiety and its disorders.* New York: Guilford.

References

Barnett, M. A., Howard, J. A., King, L. M., & Dino, G. A. (1980). Antecedents of empathy: Retrospective accounts of early socialization. *Personality and Social Psychology Bulletin, 6,* 361-365.

Barnlund, D. C. (1975). *Public and private self in Japan and the United States.* Tokyo: Simul.

Barsky, A. J., & Klerman, G. L. (1983). Overview: Hypochondriasis, bodily complaints, and somatic styles. *American Journal of Psychiatry, 140,* 273-283.

Batson, C. D. (1976). Religion as prosocial: Agent or double agent? *Journal for the Scientific Study of Religion, 15,* 29-45.

Batson, C. D., Batson, J. G., Griffitt, C. A., Barrientos, S., Brandt, J. R., Sprengelmeyer, P., & Bayley, M. G. (1989). Negative state relief and the empathy-altruism hypothesis. *Journal of Personality and Social Psychology, 56,* 922-933.

Batson, C. D., Batson, J. G., Slingsby, J. K., Harrell, K. L., Peekna, H. M., & Todd, M. (1991). Empathic joy and the empathy-altruism hypothesis. *Journal of Personality and Social Psychology, 61,* 413-426.

Batson, C. D., Fultz, J., & Schoenrade, P. A. (1987). Distress and empathy: Two qualitatively distinct vicarious emotions with different motivational consequences. *Journal of Personality, 55,* 19-39.

Batson, C. D., & Gray, R. A. (1981). Religious orientation and helping behavior: Responding to one's own or to the victim's needs? *Journal of Personality and Social Psychology, 40,* 19-39.

Batson, C. D., Olesin, K. C., Weeks, J. L., Healy, S. P., Reeves, P. J., Jennings, P., & Brown, T. (1989). Religious prosocial motivation: Is it altruistic or egoistic? *Journal of Personality and Social Psychology, 57,* 873-884.

Batson, C. D., O'Quinn, K., Fultz, J., & Vanderplas, M. (1983). Influence of self-reported distress versus altruistic motivation on egoistic versus altruistic motivation to help. *Journal of Personality and Social Psychology, 45,* 706-718.

Batson, C. D., Sager, K., Garst, E., Kang, M., Rubchinsky, K., & Dawson, K. (1997). Is empathy-induced helping due to self-other merging? *Journal of Personality and Social Psychology, 73,* 495-509.

Batson, C. D., & Shaw, L. L. (1991). Evidence for altruism: Toward a pluralism of prosocial motives. *Psychological Inquiry, 2,* 107-122.

Baumeister, R. F. (1982). Self-esteem, self-presentation, and future interaction: A dilemma of reputation. *Journal of Personality, 50,* 29-46.

Baumeister, R. F. (1986). *Identity.* New York: Oxford University Press.

Baumeister, R. F. (1987). How the self became a problem: A psychological review of historical research. *Journal of Personality and Social Psychology, 52,* 163-176.

Baumeister, R. F. (1997). The self and society. In R. D. Ashmore & L. Jussim (Eds.), *Self and identity* (pp. 191-217). New York: Oxford University Press.

Baumeister, R. F., Heatherton, T. F., & Tice, D. M. (1993). When ego threats lead to self-regulation failure: Negative consequences of high self-esteem. *Journal of Personality and Social Psychology, 64,* 141-156.

Baumeister, R. F., Stillwell, A. M., & Heatherton, T. F. (1994). Guilt: An interpersonal approach. *Psychological Bulletin, 115,* 243-267.

Baumeister, R. F., & Tice, D. M. (1985). Self-esteem and responses to success and failure: Subsequent performance and intrinsic motivation. *Journal of Personality, 53,* 450-467.

Baumeister, R. F., Tice, D. M., & Hutton, D. G. (1989). Self-presentational motivations and personality differences in self-esteem. *Journal of Personality, 57,* 547-579.

Baumgardner, A. H. (1990). To know oneself is to like oneself. *Journal of Personality and Social Psychology, 58,* 1062-1072.

Bavelas, J. B., Black, A., Lemery, C. R., & Mullett, J. (1986). I *show* how you feel: Motor mimicry as a communicative act. *Journal of Personality and Social Psychology, 50,* 322-329.

Beach, R. H., Tesser, A., Finch, F. D., Mendolia, M., Anderson, P., Crelia, R., & Whitaker, D. (1998). Self-evaluation maintenance in marriage: Toward a performance ecology of the marital relationship. *Journal of Family Psychology, 10,* 379-396.

Bennett, M. (1989). Children's self-attribution of embarrassment. *British Journal of Developmental Psychology, 7,* 207-217.

Berg, J. H., & Peplau, L. A. (1983). Loneliness: The relationship of loneliness and self-disclosure. *Personality and Social Psychology Bulletin, 8,* 624-630.

Bernstein, L., Teng, G., & Garbin, C. (1986). A confirmatory factoring of the self-consciousness scale. *Multivariate Personality Research, 21,* 459-475.

Bernstein, W. M., & Davis, M. H. (1982). Perspective-taking, self-consciousness, and accuracy in person perception. *Basic and Applied Social Psychology, 3,* 1-19.

Berscheid, E., & Walster, E. (1978). *Interpersonal attraction* (2nd ed.). Reading, MA: Addison-Wesley.

Berscheid, E., Walster, E., & Bohrnstedt, G. (1973). The happy American body. *Psychology Today, 7,* 119-131.

Bertenthal, B. I., & Fischer, K. W. (1978). Development of self-recognition in the infant. *Developmental Psychology, 14,* 44-50.

Berzonsky, M. D. (1989). Identity style: Conceptualization and measurement. *Journal of Adolescent Research, 4,* 267-281.

Berzonsky, M. D. (1992). Identity style and coping strategies. *Journal of Personality, 60,* 771-788.

Block, J., & Robins, R. W. (1993). A longitudinal study of consistency and change in self-esteem from early adolescence to early adulthood. *Child Development, 64,* 909-923.

Boldero, J., & Francis, J. (2000). The relation between self-discrepancies and emotion: The moderating roles of self-guide importance, location relevance, and social self-domain centrality. *Journal of Personality and Social Psychology, 78,* 38-52.

Brewer, M. B. (1991). The social self: On being the same and different at the same time. *Personality and Social Psychology Bulletin, 17,* 475-482.

Brewer, M. B., & Gardner, W. (1996). Who is this "we"? Levels of collective identity and self representations. *Journal of Personality and Social Psychology, 71,* 83-93.

Brewer, M. B., & Pickett, C. L. (1999). Distinctiveness motives as a source of the social self. In T. R. Tyler, R. M. Kramer, & O. P. John (Eds.), *The psychology of the social self* (pp. 71-87). Mahwah, NJ: Lawrence Erlbaum.

Bridges, K. M. B. (1932). Emotional development in early infancy. *Child Development, 2,* 324-341.
Britt, T. W. (1992). The self-consciousness scale: On the stability of the three-factor solution. *Personality and Social Behavior, 18,* 748-755.
Brockner, J., Derr, W. R., & Laing, W. N. (1987). Self-esteem and reactions to negative feedback: Toward greater generality. *Journal of Research in Personality, 21,* 318-333.
Brockner, J., & Lloyd, K. (1986). Self-esteem and likability: Separating fact from fantasy. *Journal of Research in Personality, 20,* 496-508.
Brockner, J., & Swap, W. C. (1983). Resolving the relationship between placebos, misattribution, and insomnia: An individual differences approach. *Journal of Personality and Social Psychology, 45,* 32-42.
Brown, J. D. (1993). Motivational conflict and the self: The double bind of low self-esteem. In R. F. Baumeister (Ed.), *Self-esteem: The puzzle of low self-regard* (pp. 117-130). New York: Plenum.
Brown, J. D. (1998). *The self.* New York: McGraw-Hill.
Brown, J. D., & Dutton, K. A. (1995). The thrill of victory, the complexity of defeat: Self-esteem and people's emotional reactions to success and failure. *Journal of Personality and Social Psychology, 68,* 712-722.
Brown, J. D., & Gallagher, F. M. (1992). Coming to terms with failure: Private self-enhancement and public self-effacement. *Journal of Experimental Social Psychology, 55,* 445-453.
Brown, J. D., & Smart, S. A. (1991). The self and social conduct: Linking self-presentations to social conduct. *Journal of Personality and Social Psychology, 60,* 368-375.
Brown, T. A., Cash, T. F., & Mikulka, P. J. (1990). Attitudinal body-image assessment: Factor analysis of the Body-Self Relations Questionnaire. *Journal of Personality Assessment, 55,* 135-144.
Buck, R. W., & Parke, R. D. (1972). Behavioral and physiological responses to the presence of a friendly or neutral person in two types of stressful situations. *Journal of Personality and Social Psychology, 24,* 143-153.
Burhmester, D., & Prager, K. (1995). Patterns and functions of self-disclosure during childhood and adolescence. In K. J. Rotenberg (Ed.), *Disclosure processes in children and adolescents* (pp. 10-56). New York: Cambridge University Press.
Burnkrant, R. R., & Page, T. (1984). A modification of the Fenigstein, Scheier, and Buss Self-Consciousness Scale. *Journal of Personality Assessment, 48,* 629-637.
Bushman, B. J. (1993). What's in a name? The moderating role of public self-consciousness on the relation between brand label and brand preference. *Journal of Applied Psychology, 78,* 857-861.
Buss, A. H. (1961). *The psychology of aggression.* New York: John Wiley.
Buss, A. H. (1973). *Psychology—Man in perspective.* New York: John Wiley.
Buss, A. H. (1980). *Self-consciousness and social anxiety.* San Francisco: Freeman.
Buss, A. H. (1992). *Ranking of group identification.* Unpublished data, University of Texas, Austin.
Buss, A. H. (1995). *Personality: Temperament, social behavior, and the self.* Needham, MA: Allyn & Bacon.

Buss, A. H., & Briggs, S. R. (1984). Drama and the self in social interaction. *Journal of Personality and Social Psychology, 47,* 1310-1324.

Buss, A. H., Iscoe, I., & Buss, E. H. (1979). The development of embarrassment. *Journal of Psychology, 103,* 227-230.

Buss, A. H., & Perry, M. (1991). *Sources of self-esteem in men and women.* Unpublished data, University of Texas, Austin.

Buss, A. H., & Perry, M. (1992). The Aggression Questionnaire. *Journal of Personality and Social Psychology, 63,* 452-459.

Buss, A. H., & Plomin, R. (1984). *Temperament: Early developing personality traits.* Hillsdale, NJ: Lawrence Erlbaum.

Buss, A. H., & Portnoy, N. W. (1967). Pain tolerance and group identification. *Journal of Personality and Social Psychology, 6,* 106-108.

Buss, A. H., & Prince, D. (1992). *A privacy questionnaire.* Unpublished manuscript, University of Texas, Austin.

Buss, D. M. (1994). *The evolution of desire.* New York: Basic Books.

Buss, D. M., Haselton, M. G., Shackelford, T. K., Bleske, A. L., & Wakefield, J. C. (1998). Adaptations, expectations, and spandrels. *American Psychologist, 53,* 533-548.

Buss, D. M., Larsen, R. J., Westen, D., & Semmelroth, J. (1992). Sex differences in jealousy: Evolution, physiology, and psychology. *Psychological Science, 3,* 251-255.

Buss, L. (1980). *Does overpraise cause embarrassment?* Unpublished research, University of Texas, Austin.

Caldwell, M. A., & Peplau, L. A. (1982). Sex differences in same-sex friendship. *Sex Roles, 8,* 721-732.

Cameron, P. A., & Gallup, G. G., Jr. (1988). Shadow self-recognition in human infants. *Infant Behavior and Development, 11,* 465-471.

Campbell, J. D. (1990). Self-esteem and the clarity of the self-concept. *Journal of Personality and Social Psychology, 59,* 538-549.

Campbell, J. D., Chew, B., & Scratchley, L. S. (1991). Cognitive and emotional reactions to daily events: The effects of self-esteem and self-complexity. *Journal of Personality, 59,* 473-505.

Campbell, J. D., & Fairey, P. J. (1985). Effects of self-esteem, hypothetical explanations, and verbalizations of future performance. *Journal of Personality and Social Psychology, 48,* 1097-1111.

Campbell, J. D., & Fehr, B. (1990). Self-esteem and perceptions of conveyed impressions: Is negative affectivity associated with greater realism? *Journal of Personality and Social Psychology, 58,* 122-133.

Campbell, J. D., Trapnell, P. D., Heine, S. J., Katz, I. M., Lavallee, L. F., & Lehman, D. (1996). Self-concept clarity: Measurement, personality correlates, and cultural boundaries. *Journal of Personality and Social Psychology, 70,* 141-156.

Cannon, W. B. (1929). *Bodily changes in pain, hunger, fear, and rage.* New York: Appleton.

Cappella, J. N. (1981). Mutual influences in expressive behavior: Adult-adult and infant-adult dyadic interaction. *Psychological Bulletin, 89,* 101-132.

References

Carver, C. S. (1975). Physical aggression as a function of objective self-awareness and attitudes toward punishment. *Journal of Experimental Social Psychology, 11*, 410-419.

Carver, C. S., Lawrence, J. W., & Scheier, M. F. (1999). Self-discrepancies and affect: Incorporating the role of feared selves. *Personality and Social Psychology Bulletin, 25*, 783-792.

Carver, C. S., & Scheier, M. F. (1981a). *Attention and self-regulation: A control theory approach to human behavior.* New York: Springer-Verlag.

Carver, C. S., & Scheier, M. F. (1981b). Self-consciousness and reactance. *Journal of Research in Personality, 15*, 16-29.

Cash, T. F. (1989). The psychosocial effects of male pattern balding. *Patient Care, 1*, 18-23.

Cash, T. F. (1990). Losing hair, losing points? The effect of male pattern baldness on social impression formation. *Journal of Applied Social Psychology, 20*, 154-167.

Cash, T. F., & Henry, P. E. (1995). Women's body images: The results of a national survey in the USA. *Sex Roles, 33*, 19-28.

Cash, T. F., & Labarge, A. S. (1996). The psychology of cosmetic surgery. *Cognitive Therapy and Research, 20*, 37-50.

Cash, T. F., & Pruzinsky, T. (Eds.). (1990). *Body images: Development, deviance, and change.* New York: Guilford.

Cash, T. F., & Szymanski, M. L. (1995). The development and validation of the Body-Image Ideals Questionnaire. *Journal of Personality Assessment, 64*, 466-477.

Cash, T. F., Winstead, B. A., & Janda, L. H. (1986). The great American shape-up: Body image survey report. *Psychology Today, 20*(4), 30-37.

Castelfranchi, C., & Poggi, I. (1990). Blushing as discourse: Was Darwin wrong? In W. R. Crozier (Ed.), *Shyness and embarrassment: Perspectives from social psychology* (pp. 230-251). Cambridge, UK: Cambridge University Press.

Cattarin, J., & Thompson, J. K. (1994). A three-year longitudinal study of body image and eating disturbance in adolescent females. *Eating Disorders: The Journal of Treatment and Prevention, 2*, 114-125.

Chang, L. (1998). Factor interpretations of the self-consciousness scale. *Personality and Individual Differences, 24*, 635-640.

Cheek, J. M., & Buss, A. H. (1981). Shyness and sociability. *Journal of Personality and Social Psychology, 41*, 330-339.

Chelune, G. J. (1976). The self-disclosure situation survey: A new approach to measuring self-disclosure. *JSAS Catalogue of Selected Documents in Psychology, 6*, 111-112.

Cialdini, R. B., Baumann, D. J., & Kenrick, D. T. (1981). Insights from sadness: A thee-step model of the development of altruism as hedonism. *Developmental Review, 1*, 207-223.

Cialdini, R. B., Borden, R. J., Thorne, A., Walker, M. R., Freeman, S., & Sloan, L. R. (1976). Basking in reflected glory: Three (football) field studies. *Journal of Personality and Social Psychology, 34*, 366-375.

Cialdini, R. B., Brown, S. L., Lewis, B. P., Luce, C., & Neuberg, C. (1997). Reinterpreting the empathy-altruism, relationship: When one into one equals oneness. *Journal of Personality and Social Psychology, 73,* 481-494.

Cialdini, R. B., Darby, B. K., & Vincent, J. E. (1973). Transgression and altruism: A case for hedonism. *Journal of Experimental Social Psychology, 9,* 502-516.

Cialdini, R. B., & Kenrick, D. T. (1976). Altruism as hedonism: A social development perspective on the relationship of negative mood state and helping. *Journal of Personality and Social Psychology, 34,* 907-914.

Cialdini, R. B., Schaller, M., Houlihan, D., Arps, K., & Fultz, J. (1987). Empathy-based helping: Is it selflessly or selfishly motivated? *Journal of Personality and Social Psychology, 52,* 749-758.

Collins, E. M. (1991). Body figure perceptions and preferences among preadolescent children. *International Journal of Eating Disorders, 10,* 199-208.

Collins, J. K. (1987). Methodology for the objective measurement of body image. *International Journal of Eating Disorders, 6,* 393-399.

Collins, R. L. (1996). For better or worse: The impact of upward comparison on self-evaluations. *Psychological Bulletin, 119,* 51-69.

Colman, N. M., & Oliver, K. R. (1978). Reactions to flattery as a function of self-esteem: Self-enhancement and cognitive consistency theories. *British Journal of Social and Clinical Psychology, 17,* 25-29.

Cooley, C. H. (1902). *Human nature and the social order.* New York: Scribner's.

Coopersmith, S. (1967). *The antecedents of self-esteem.* San Francisco: Freeman.

Cozby, P. C. (1973). Self-disclosure: A literature review. *Psychological Bulletin, 79,* 73-91.

Creed, A., & Funder, D. C. (1999). The two faces of private self-consciousness: Self-report, peer report, and behavioral correlates. *European Journal of Personality, 12,* 411-431.

Crocker, J., & Gallo, L. (1995, August). *The self-enhancing effect of downward comparison.* Paper presented at the 93rd Annual Convention of the American Psychological Association, Los Angeles.

Crocker, J., & Major, B. (1989). Social stigma and self-esteem: The self-protective properties of stigma. *Psychological Review, 96,* 608-630.

Cross, S. E., & Madson, L. (1997). Models of the self: Self-construals and gender. *Psychological Bulletin, 122,* 5-37.

Crozier, W. R., & Burnham, M. (1990). Age-related differences in children's understanding of shyness. *British Journal of Developmental Psychology, 8,* 179-185.

Cutlip, W. D., II, & Leary, M. R. (1993). Anatomic and physiological bases of social blushing: Speculations from neurology and psychology. *Behavioral Neurology, 6,* 181-185.

Darwin, C. R. (1955). *The expression of emotions in man and animals.* New York: Philosophical Library. (Original work published 1873)

Davis, A. D. (1960). Some physiological correlates of Rorschach body image productions. *Journal of Abnormal and Social Psychology, 60,* 432-436.

Davis, D., Kasmer, J., & Holtgraves, T. (1982). *The relationship of private and public self-consciousness to the weights of attitudes and subjective norms as predictors of behavioral intentions.* Unpublished manuscript, University of Nevada, Reno.

Davis, J. D. (1976). Self-disclosure in an acquaintance exercise: Responsibility for the level of intimacy. *Journal of Personality and Social Psychology, 33,* 787-792.

Davis, J. D. (1978). When boy meets girl: Sex roles and the negotiation of intimacy in an acquaintance exercise. *Journal of Personality and Social Psychology, 36,* 684-692.

Davis, M. H. (1983). The effects of dispositional empathy on emotional reactions and helping: A multidimensional approach. *Journal of Personality, 51,* 167-184.

Davis, M. H., Conklin, L., Smith, A., & Luce, C. (1996). The effect of perspective taking on cognitive representation of persons: A merging of self and other. *Journal of Personality and Social Psychology, 70,* 713-726.

Davis, M. H., & Franzoi, S. L. (1987). Private self-consciousness and self-disclosure. In V. J. Derlega & J. H. Berg (Eds.), *Self-disclosure: Theory, research, and therapy* (pp. 59-79). New York: Plenum.

Davis, M. H., Mitchell, K. V., Hall, J. A., Lothart, J., Snapp, T., & Mayer, M. (1999). Empathy, expectations, and situational preferences: Personality influences on the decision to participate in voluntary helping behaviors. *Journal of Personality, 67,* 469-503.

Deaux, K., Reid, A., Mizrahi, K., & Ethier, K. A. (1995). Parameters of social identity. *Journal of Personality and Social Psychology, 68,* 280-291.

Deci, E. L., & Ryan, R. M. (1995). Human autonomy: The basis for true self-esteem. In M. H. Kernis (Ed.), *Efficacy, agency, and self-esteem.* New York: Plenum.

Derlega, V. J., & Grzelak, J. (1979). Appropriateness of self-disclosure. In G. J. Chelune (Ed.), *Self-disclosure: Origins, patterns, and implications of openness in interpersonal relationships* (pp. 151-176). San Francisco: Jossey-Bass.

Derlega, V. J., Metts, S., Petronio, S., & Margulis, S. T. (1993). *Self-disclosure.* Newbury Park, CA: Sage.

Derlega, V. J., Wilson, J., & Chaiken, A. L. (1976). Friendship and disclosure reciprocity. *Journal of Personality and Social Psychology, 34,* 578-582.

Derlega, V. J., Winstead, B. A., Wong, P. T. P., & Hunter, S. (1985). Gender effects in an initial encounter: A case where men exceed women in self-disclosure. *Journal of Social and Personal Relationships, 2,* 25-44.

Devine, P. G., Monteith, M. J., Zuverink, J. R., & Elliot, A. J. (1991). Prejudice with and without compunction. *Journal of Personality and Social Psychology, 60,* 817-830.

Diggory, J. C. (1966). *Self-evaluation: Concepts and studies.* New York: John Wiley.

Dindia, K., & Allen, M. (1992). Sex differences in self-disclosure: A meta-analysis. *Psychological Bulletin, 112,* 106-124.

Donahue, E. M., Robins, R. W., Roberts, B. W., & John, O. P. (1993). The divided self: Concurrent and longitudinal effects of psychological adjustment and social roles on self-concept differentiation. *Journal of Personality and Social Psychology, 64,* 834-846.

Dovidio, J. F., Allen, J. L., & Schroeder, D. A. (1990). The specificity of empathy-induced helping: Evidence of altruistic motivation. *Journal of Personality and Social Psychology, 59,* 249-260.

Dubois, D. L., Bull, C. A., Sherman, M. D., & Roberts, M. (1998). Self-esteem and adjustment in early adolescence. *Journal of Youth and Adolescence, 27,* 557-583.

Dunning, D. (1999). A newer look: Motivated social cognition and the schematic representation of social concepts. *Psychological Inquiry, 10,* 1-11.

Dutton, K. A., & Brown, J. D. (1997). Global self-esteem and specific self-views as determinants of people's reactions to success and failure. *Journal of Personality and Social Psychology, 73,* 139-148.

Duval, S., & Wicklund, R. A. (1972). *A theory of objective self-awareness.* New York: Academic Press.

Dweck, C. S., Davidson, W., Nelson, S., & Enna, B. (1978). Sex differences in learned helplessness: II. The contingencies of evaluative feedback in the classroom and III. An experimental analysis. *Developmental Psychology, 14,* 268-276.

Dweck, C. S., & Leggett, E. L. (1988). A social-cognitive approach to motivation and personality. *Psychological Review, 95,* 256-273.

Eagly, A. H., & Crowley, M. (1986). Gender and helping behavior: A meta-analytic review. *Psychological Bulletin, 100,* 283-208.

Edelmann, R. J. (1987). *The psychology of embarrassment.* Chichester, UK: Wiley.

Edelmann, R. J., & Iwawaki, S. (1987). Self-reported expression and consequences of embarrassment in the United Kingdom and Japan. *Psychologia, 30,* 205-216.

Eibl-Eibesfelt, I. (1972). Similarities and differences between cultures in expressive movements. In R. A. Hinde (Ed.), *Nonverbal communication* (pp. 297-315). Cambridge, UK: Cambridge University Press.

Eisenberg, N., & Fabes, R. A. (1990). Empathy: Conceptualization, measurement, and relation to prosocial behavior. *Motivation and Emotion, 14,* 131-149.

Eisenberg, N., Fabes, R. A., Schaller, M., Miller, P., Carlo, G., Poulin, R., Shea, C., & Shell, R. (1991). Personality and socialization: Correlates of vicarious emotional responding. *Journal of Personality and Social Psychology, 61,* 459-470.

Eisenberg, N., & Lennon, R. (1983). Sex differences in empathy and related capacities. *Psychological Bulletin, 94,* 100-131.

Eisenberg, N., Schaller, M., Fabes, R. A., Bustamente, D., Mathy, R. M., Shell, R., & Rhodes, K. (1988). Differentiation of personal distress and sympathy in children and adults. *Developmental Psychology, 24,* 766-775.

Elliott, E. S., & Dweck, C. S. (1988). Goals: An approach to motivation and achievement. *Journal of Personality and Social Psychology, 54,* 5-12.

Epstein, S. (1973). The self-concept revisited: Or a theory of a theory. *American Psychologist, 28,* 404-416.

Epstein, S. (1980). The self-concept: A review and a proposal of an integrated theory of personality. In E. Staub (Ed.), *Personality: Basic aspects and current research* (pp. 83-131). Englewood Cliffs, NJ: Prentice Hall.

Erikson, E. (1950). *Childhood and society.* New York: Norton.

Erikson, E. (1968). *Identity: Youth and crisis.* New York: Norton.

Evans, G. W., & Howard, R. B. (1973). Personal space. *Psychological Bulletin, 80,* 334-344.

Federn, P. (1926). Some variations on the ego feeling. *International Journal of Psychoanalysis, 7,* 434-444.

Feingold, A. (1992). Good-looking people are not what we think. *Psychological Bulletin, 111,* 304-341.

Fenigstein, A. (1979). Self-consciousness, self-attention, and social interaction. *Journal of Personality and Social Psychology, 37,* 75-86.

Fenigstein, A. (1984). Self-consciousness and the overperception of the self as a target. *Journal of Personality and Social Psychology, 47,* 860-870.

Fenigstein, A., Scheier, M. F., & Buss, A. H. (1975). Private and public self-consciousness: Assessment and theory. *Journal of Consulting and Clinical Psychology, 43,* 522-527.

Fenigstein, A., & Vanable, P. A. (1992). Paranoia and self-consciousness. *Journal of Personality and Social Psychology, 62,* 129-138.

Festinger, L. (1954). A theory of social comparison processes. *Human Relations, 7,* 117-140.

Finn, S. (1988). *The structure of masculinity-femininity self-ratings.* Unpublished research, University of Texas, Austin.

Fisher, S. (1970). *Body experience in fantasy and behavior.* New York: Appleton-Century-Crofts.

Fisher, S. (1986). *Development and structure of the body image* (2 vols.). Hillsdale, NJ: Lawrence Erlbaum.

Fisher, S., & Fisher, R. L. (1964). Body image boundaries and patterns of body perception. *Journal of Abnormal and Social Psychology, 68,* 255-262.

Flavell, J. (1968). *The development of role-taking and communications skills in children.* New York: John Wiley.

Fleming, J. S., & Courtney, H. E. (1984). Dimensionality of self-esteem: II. Hierarchical facet model for revised measurement scales. *Journal of Personality and Social Psychology, 46,* 404-421.

Fleming, J. S., & Watts, W. A. (1980). The dimensionality of self-esteem: Some results for a college sample. *Journal of Personality and Social Psychology, 39,* 921-929.

Flory, J. D., Raikkonen, K., Matthews, K. A., & Owens, J. F. (2000). Self-focused attention and mood during everyday social interactions. *Personality and Psychology Bulletin, 26,* 875-883.

Frable, D. E. S., Platt, L., & Hoey, S. (1998). Concealable stigmas and positive self-perceptions: Feeling better around similar others. *Journal of Personality and Social Psychology, 74,* 909-922.

Franzoi, S. L. (1983). Self-concept differences as a function of private self-consciousness and social anxiety. *Journal of Research in Personality, 48,* 768-780.

Franzoi, S. L., Anderson, J., & Frommelt, S. (1990). Individual differences in men's perception of and reactions to thinning hair. *Journal of Social Psychology, 130,* 209-218.

Franzoi, S. L., & Davis, M. H. (1985). Adolescent self-disclosure and loneliness: Private self-consciousness and parental influences. *Journal of Personality and Social Psychology, 48,* 768-780.

Franzoi, S. L., Davis, M. H., & Young, R. D. (1985). The effects of private self-consciousness and perspective taking on satisfaction in close relationships. *Journal of Personality and Social Psychology, 48,* 1584-1594.

Franzoi, S. L., & Koehler, V. (1998). Age and gender differences in body attitudes: A comparison of young and elderly adults. *International Journal of Aging and Human Development, 47,* 1-10.

Franzoi, S. L., & Shields, S. A. (1984). The Body Esteem Scale: A convergent and discriminant validity study. *Journal of Personality Assessment, 48,* 173-178.

French, S. A., Story, M., Remafedi, G., Resnick, M. D., & Blum, R. W. (1996). Sexual orientation and prevalence of body dissatisfaction and eating disordered behaviors: A population-based study of adolescents. *International Journal of Eating Disorders, 19,* 119-126.

Friedman, M. A., & Brownell, K. D. (1995). Psychological correlates of obesity: Moving to the next research generation. *Psychological Bulletin, 117,* 3-20.

Froming, W. J., & Carver, C. S. (1981). Divergent influences of private and public self-consciousness in a compliance paradigm. *Journal of Research in Personality, 15,* 159-171.

Froming, W. J., Walker, G. R., & Lopyan, K. J. (1982). Private and public self-awareness: When personal attitudes conflict with societal expectations. *Journal of Experimental Social Psychology, 18,* 476-487.

Frone, M. R., & McFarlin, D. B. (1989). Chronic occupational stressors, self-focused attention, and well-being: Testing a cybernetic model. *Journal of Applied Psychology, 74,* 876-883.

Fultz, J., Schaller, M., & Cialdini, R. B. (1988). Three related but distinct vicarious affective responses to another's suffering. *Personality and Social Psychology Bulletin, 14,* 312-325.

Gallaher, P. (1992). Individual differences in nonverbal behavior: Dimensions of style. *Journal of Personality and Social Psychology, 63,* 133-145.

Gallup, G. G., Jr. (1970). Chimpanzees: Self-recognition. *Science, 167,* 86-87.

Gallup, C. G., Jr. (1977). Self-recognition in primates: A comparative approach to the bidirectional properties of consciousness. *American Psychologist, 32,* 329-338.

Garner, D. M. (1997, January/February). The body image survey. *Psychology Today,* pp. 32-84.

Geertz, C. (1975). On the nature of anthropological understanding. *American Scientist, 63,* 47-53.

Gentleman, T. E., & Thompson, J. K. (1993). Actual differences and stereotypical perceptions in body image and eating disturbance: A comparison of male and female heterosexual and homosexual samples. *Sex Roles, 29,* 545-562.

Gibbons, E. J., & Wicklund, R. A. (1976). Selective exposure to the self. *Journal of Research in Personality, 10,* 98-106.

Gibbons, F. X. (1978). Sexual standards and reactions to pornography: Enhancing behavioral consistency through self-focused attention. *Journal of Personality and Social Psychology, 36,* 976-987.

Gibbons, F. X., Carver, C. S., Scheier, M. F., & Hormuth, S. E. (1979). Self-focused attention and the placebo effect: Fooling some of the people some of the time. *Journal of Experimental Social Psychology, 10,* 98-106.

Gibbons, F. X., & Gerrard, M. (1989). Effects of upward and downward social comparison on mood states. *Journal of Social and Clinical Psychology, 8,* 14-31.

Gibbons, F. X., & McCoy, S. B. (1991). Self-esteem, similarity, and reactions to active versus passive downward comparison. *Journal of Personality and Social Psychology, 60,* 414-424.

Goffman, E. (1959). *The presentation of self in everyday life.* New York, NY: Doubleday.

Goldenberg, J. L., McCoy, S. K., Pyszczynski, T., Greenberg, J., & Solomon, S. (2000). The body as a source of self-esteem: The effect of mortality salience on identification with one's own body, interest in sex, and appearance monitoring. *Journal of Personality and Social Psychology, 79,* 118-130.

Green, J. D., & Sedikides, C. (1999). Affect and self-focused attention revisited: The role of affect orientation. *Personality and Social Psychology Bulletin, 25,* 104-119.

Greenberg, J. (1983). Self-image versus impression management in adhering to distributive justice standards. *Journal of Personality and Social Psychology, 44,* 5-19.

Greenberg, J., & Pyszczynski, T. (1986). Persistent high self-focus after failure and low focus after success. *Journal of Personality and Social Psychology, 50,* 1039-1044.

Greenberg, J., Pyszczynski, T., & Solomon, S. (1982). The self-serving attributional bias: Beyond self-presentation. *Journal of Experimental Social Psychology, 18,* 56-67.

Greenberg, J., Solomon, S., & Pyszczynski, T. (1997). Terror management theory of self-esteem and cultural world views: Empirical assessments and conceptual refinements. *Advances in Experimental Social Psychology, 29,* 61-136.

Greenberg, J., Solomon, S., Pyszczynski, T., Rosenblatt, A., Burling, J., Lyon, D., Simon, L., & Pinel, E. (1992). Why do people need self-esteem? Converging evidence that self-esteem serves an anxiety-buffering function. *Journal of Personality and Social Psychology, 63,* 913-922.

Greenwald, A. G. (1980). The totalitarian ego: Fabrication and revision of personal history. *American Psychologist, 35,* 603-618.

Greenwald, A. G., & Pratkanis, A. R. (1984). The self. In R. S. Wyer & T. K. Srull (Eds.), *Handbook of social cognition* (Vol. 3, pp. 129-178). Hillsdale, NJ: Lawrence Erlbaum.

Gross, E., & Stone, G. P. (1964). Embarrassment and the analysis of role requirements. *American Journal of Sociology, 70,* 1-15.

Guardo, C. J. (1971). Development of a sense of self-identity in children. *Child Development, 42,* 1909-1921.

Hafdahl, A. R., Panter, A. T., Gramzow, R. H., Sedikides, C., & Insko, C. A. (2000) Free-response self-discrepancies across, among, and within FF personality dimensions. *Journal of Personality, 68,* 112-151.

Haimes, E. (1987). "Now I know who I really am": Identity change and redefinitions of the self in adoption. In T. Honess & K. Yardley (Eds.), *Self and identity* (pp. 359-371). London: Routledge & Kegan Paul.

Hall, C. C. I. (1995). Asian eyes: Body image and eating disorders of Asian and Asian American women. *Eating Disorders: Journal of Treatment and Prevention, 3,* 8-19.

Hall, E. T. (1966). *The hidden dimension.* New York: Doubleday.

Hall, J. A. (1983). *Nonverbal sex differences*. Baltimore: Johns Hopkins University Press.

Harmon-Jones, E., Simon, L., Greenberg, J., Pyszczynski, T., Solomon, S., & McGregor, H. (1997). Terror-management theory and self-esteem: Evidence that increased self-esteem reduces mortality salience effects. *Journal of Personality and Social Psychology, 72,* 24-36.

Harré, R. (1998). *The singular self.* Thousand Oaks, CA: Sage.

Hart, D., Maloney, J., & Damon, W. (1987). The meaning and development of identity. In T. Honess & K. Yardley (Eds.), *Self and identity* (pp. 121-133). London: Routledge & Kegan Paul.

Harter, S. (1982). The Perceived Competence Scale for Children. *Child Development, 53,* 87-97.

Harter, S. (1986). Processes underlying the construction, maintenance, and enhancement of the self-concept in children. In J. Suls & A. G. Greenwald (Eds.), *Psychological perspectives on the self* (Vol. 3, pp. 136-181). Hillsdale, NJ: Lawrence Erlbaum.

Harter, S. (1988). The construction and conservation of the self: James and Cooley revisited. In D. K. Lapsley & F. C. Power (Eds.), *Self, ego, and identity* (pp. 43-70). New York: Springer-Verlag.

Harter, S. (1993). Causes and consequences of low self-esteem. In R. F. Baumeister (Ed.), *Self-esteem: The puzzle of low self-regard* (pp. 88-116). New York: Plenum.

Harter, S. (1999). *The construction of the self: A developmental perspective.* New York: Guilford.

Hashimoto, E., & Shimizu, T. (1988). A cross-cultural study of the emotion of shame/embarrassment: Iranian and Japanese children. *Psychologia, 31,* 1-6.

Hayduk, L. A. (1981). The permeability of personal space. *Canadian Journal of Behavioural Science, 13,* 274-287.

Hayduk, L. A. (1983). Personal space: Where we stand now. *Psychological Bulletin, 94,* 293-335.

Hazan, C., & Shaver, P. (1987). Romantic love conceptualized as an attachment process. *Journal of Personality and Social Psychology, 52,* 511-524.

Heatherton, T. F., & Vohs, K. D. (2000). Interpersonal evaluations following threats to self: Role of self-esteem. *Journal of Personality and Social Psychology, 78,* 725-736.

Heinberg, L. J., & Thompson, J. K. (1995). Body image and televised images of thinness and attractiveness: A controlled laboratory investigation. *Journal of Social and Clinical Psychology, 7,* 335-344.

Heine, S. J., Kitayama, S., & Lehman, D. R. (in press). Cultural differences in self-evaluation: Japanese readily accept negative self-relevant information. *Journal of Cross-Cultural Psychology.*

Heine, S. J., Kitayama, S., Lehman, D. R., Takata, T., & Ide, E. (2000). *Divergent motivational consequences of success and failure in Japan and North America.* Unpublished manuscript, University of Pennsylvania, Philadelphia.

Heine, S. J., & Lehman, D. R. (1999). Culture, self-discrepancies, and self-satisfaction. *Personality and Social Psychology Bulletin, 25,* 915-925.

Heine, S. J., Lehman, D. R., Markus, H. R., & Kitayama, S. (1999). Is there a universal need for self-regard? *Psychological Review, 106,* 1-29.

Heine, S. J., Takata, T., & Lehman, D. R. (2000). Beyond self-presentation: Evidence for self-criticism among Japanese. *Personality and Social Psychology Bulletin, 26,* 71-78.

Higgins, E. T. (1987). Self-discrepancy: A theory relating self and affect. *Psychological Review, 94,* 319-340.

Higgins, E. T. (1996). The "self digest": Self-knowledge serving self-regulatory functions. *Journal of Personality and Social Psychology, 71,* 1062-1083.

Higgins, E. T. (1999). When do self-discrepancies have specific relations to emotions? The second generation question of Tangney, Niedenthal, Covert, and Barlow (1998). *Journal of Personality and Social Psychology, 77,* 1313-1317.

Higgins, E. T., Bond, R. N., Klein, R., & Strauman, T. J. (1986). Self-discrepancies and emotional vulnerability: How magnitude, accessibility, and type of discrepancy influence affect. *Journal of Personality and Social Psychology, 51,* 5-15.

Higgins, E. T., Klein, R., & Strauman, J. T. (1985). Self-concept discrepancy theory: A psychological model for distinguishing among different aspects of depression and anxiety. *Social Cognition, 3,* 51-76.

Higgins, E. T., Roney, C. J. R., Crowe, E., & Hymes, C. (1994). Ideal versus ought predilections for approach and avoidance: Distinct self-regulatory systems. *Journal of Personality and Social Psychology, 66,* 276-286.

Hirt, E. R., McCrea, S. M., & Kimble, C. (2000). Public self-focus and sex differences and behavioral self-handicapping: Does increasing self-threat still make it "just a man's game"? *Personality and Social Psychology Bulletin, 26,* 1131-1141.

Hirt, E. R., Zillman, D., Erickson, G. A., & Kennedy, C. (1992). Costs and benefits of allegiance: Changes in fans' self-ascribed competencies and team victory versus defeat. *Journal of Personality and Social Psychology, 63,* 724-738.

Hoffman, M. L. (1981). Is altruism part of human nature? *Journal of Personality and Social Psychology, 40,* 121-137.

Hoffman, M. L. (1987). The contribution of empathy to justice and moral judgement. In N. Eisenberg & J. Strayer (Eds.), *Empathy and its development* (pp. 47-80). Cambridge, UK: Cambridge University Press.

Hoge, D. R., & McCarthy, J. D. (1984). Influence of individual and group identity salience in the global self-esteem of youth. *Journal of Personality and Social Psychology, 47,* 403-414.

Hong, Y.-Y., Chiu, C.-Y., & Dweck, C. S. (1993). Reconsidering the role of confidence in achievement motivation. In M. L. Kernis (Ed.), *Efficacy, agency, and self-esteem* (pp. 197-216). New York: Plenum.

Horowitz, E. (1962). Reported embarrassment memories of elementary school, high school, and college students. *Journal of Social Psychology, 56,* 317-325.

Howe, N., Acquan-Assee, J., & Bukowski, W. M. (1995). Self-disclosure and the sibling relationships: What did Romulus tell Remus? In K. J. Rotenberg (Ed.), *Disclosure processes in children and adolescents* (pp. 78-99). New York: Cambridge University Press.

Hoyle, R. (1993). [Raw data]. University of Kentucky.

Hull, J. G. (1981). A self-awareness model of the causes and effects of alcohol consumption. *Journal of Abnormal Psychology, 90,* 586-600.

Hull, J. G., Levinson, R. W., Young, R. D., & Sher, K. J. (1983). Self-awareness-reducing effects of alcohol consumption. *Journal of Personality and Social Psychology, 44,* 461-473.

Hull, J. G., & Levy, A. S. (1979). The organizational functions of the self: An alternative to the Duval and Wicklund model of self-awareness. *Journal of Personality and Social Psychology, 37,* 756-768.

Hull, J. G., & Young, R. D. (1983). Self-consciousness, self-esteem, success-failure as determinants of alcohol consumption in male social drinkers. *Journal of Personality and Social Psychology, 4,* 1097-1109.

Hull, J. G., Young, R. D., & Jouriles, E. (1986). Applications of the self-awareness model of alcohol consumption: Predicting patterns of use and abuse. *Journal of Personality and Social Psychology, 51,* 790-796.

Hume, D. (1949). *An enquiry concerning human understanding.* La Salle, IL: Open Court. (Original work published 1777)

Hutton, D. G., & Baumeister, R. F. (1992). Self-awareness and attitude change: Seeing oneself on the central route to persuasion. *Personality and Social Psychology Bulletin, 18,* 68-75.

Jackson, S. E. (1981). Measurement of commitment to role identities. *Journal of Personality and Social Psychology, 40,* 138-146.

Jacobi, L., & Cash, T. (1994). In pursuit of the perfect appearance: Discrepancies among self-ideal percepts of multiple physical attributes. *Journal of Applied Social Psychology, 24,* 379-396.

James, W. (1890). *Principles of psychology* (Vol. 1). New York: Holt, Rinehart & Winston.

Jones, E. E., & Berglas, S. C. (1978). Control of attributions about the self through self-handicapping strategies: The appeal of alcohol and the role of underachievement. *Journal of Personality and Social Psychology, 4,* 200-206.

Jones, E. E., & Pittman, T. S. (1982). Toward a general theory of strategic self-presentation. In J. Suls (Ed.), *Psychological aspects on the self* (Vol. 1, pp. 231-262). Hillsdale, NJ: Lawrence Erlbaum.

Jones, W. H., Hobbs, S., & Hockenberry, D. (1982). Loneliness and social skill deficits. *Journal of Personality and Social Psychology, 42,* 682-689.

Josephs, R. A., Larrick, R. P., Steele, C. M., & Nisbett, R. E. (1992). Protecting the self from the negative consequences of risky decisions. *Journal of Personality and Social Psychology, 62,* 26-37.

Josephs, R. A., Markus, H. R., & Tafarodi, R. W. (1992). Gender and self-esteem. *Journal of Personality and Social Psychology, 63,* 391-402.

Josselson, R. (1988). The embedded self: I and thou. In D. K. Lapsley & F. C. Power (Eds.), *Self, ego, and identity* (pp. 91-106). New York: Springer-Verlag.

Jourard, S. M. (1964). *The transparent self.* Princeton, NJ: Van Nostrand.

Jourard, S. M., & Lasakow, P. (1958). Some factors in self-disclosure. *Journal of Abnormal and Social Psychology, 56,* 91-98.

Jung, C. G. (1933). *Psychological types.* New York: Harcourt Brace.

Kanaga, K. R., & Flynn, M. (1981). The relationship between invasion of personal space and stress. *Human Relations, 34,* 239-248.

Kashima, Y., Yamaguchi, S., Kim, U., Choi, S.-G., Gelfand, M. J., & Yuki, M. (1995). Culture, gender, and the self: A perspective from individualism-collectivism research. *Journal of Personality and Social Psychology, 69,* 925-937.

Kaslow, F., & Becker, H. (1992). Breast augmentation: Psychological and plastic surgery considerations. *Psychotherapy, 29,* 467-474.

Keltner, D. (1995). Signs of appeasement: Evidence for the distinct displays of embarrassment, amusement, and shame. *Journal of Personality and Social Psychology, 68,* 441-454.

Keltner, D., & Buswell, B. N. (1997). Evidence for the distinctiveness of embarrassment, shame, and guilt: A study of recalled antecedents and facial expressions of emotion. *Cognition and Emotion, 10,* 155-171.

Keltner, D., Young, R. C., & Buswell, B. N. (1997). Appeasement in human emotion, social practice, and personality. *Aggressive Behavior, 23,* 359-374.

Kernis, M. H., Brockner, J., & Frankel, B. S. (1989). Self-esteem and reactions to failure: The mediating role of overgeneralization. *Journal of Personality and Social Psychology, 57,* 707-714.

Kernis, M. H., Cornell, D. P., Sun, C.-R., Berry, A., & Harlow, T. (1993). There's more to self-esteem than whether it is high or low: The importance of stability of self-esteem. *Journal of Personality and Social Psychology, 65,* 1190-1204.

Kernis, M. H., & Reis, H. T. (1984). Self-consciousness, self-awareness, and justice in reward allocation. *Journal of Personality, 52,* 58-70.

Kingaree, J. B., & Ruback, R. B. (1996). Reconceptualizing the private self-consciousness subscale. *Social Behavior and Personality, 24,* 1-8.

Kitayama, S., Markus, H. R., Matsumoto, H., & Norasakkunkit, V. (1997). Individual and collective processes of self-esteem management: Self-enhancement in the United States and self-depreciation in Japan. *Journal of Personality and Social Psychology, 72,* 1245-1267.

Kitzinger, C. (1992). The individuated self-concept: A critical analysis of social-constructionist writing on individualism. In G. M. Breakwell (Ed.), *Social psychology of identity and the self-concept* (pp. 221-250). Guildford, UK: Surrey University Press.

Klesges, R. C., & McGinley, H. (1982). The interactive effects of typical and maximal measures on private and public self-consciousness. *Journal of Personality Assessment, 46,* 44-49.

Koestner, R., Franz, C., & Weinberger, J. (1990). The family origins of empathic concern: A 26-year longitudinal study. *Journal of Personality and Social Psychology, 58,* 709-717.

Kohlberg, L. (1969). Stage and sequence: The cognitive-developmental approach to socialization. In D. A. Goslin (Ed.), *Handbook of socialization theory and research* (pp. 347-380). Chicago: Rand-McNally.

Kostanski, M., & Gullone, E. (1998). Adolescent body image dissatisfaction: Relationships with self-esteem, anxiety, and depression controlling for body mass. *Journal of Child Psychology and Psychiatry and Related Disciplines, 39,* 255-262.

Krebs, D. (1975). Empathy and altruism. *Journal of Personality and Social Psychology, 32,* 1134-1146.

Kruger, J., & Dunning, D. (1999). Unskilled and unaware of it: How difficulties in recognizing one's own incompetence lead to inflated self-assessments. *Journal of Personality and Social Psychology, 77,* 1121-1134.

Lamb, C. S., Jackson, L. A., Cassiday, P. B., & Priest, D. J. (1993). Body figure preferences of men and women: A comparison of two generations. *Sex Roles, 28,* 245-359.

Langlois, J. H., & Downs, A. C. (1979). Peer relations as a function of physical attractiveness: The eye of the holder or behavioral reality? *Child Development, 50,* 409-418.

Langlois, J. H., Roggman, L. A., Casey, R. J., Reiser-Danner, L. A., & Jenkins, V. Y. (1987). Infant preferences for attractive faces: Remnants of a stereotype. *Developmental Psychology, 23,* 363-369.

Leary, M. R., Britt, T. W., Cutlip, W. D., II, & Templeton, J. L. (1992). Social blushing. *Psychological Bulletin, 112,* 446-460.

Leary, M. R., Haupt, A. L., Strausser, K. S., & Chokel, J. T. (1998). Calibrating the sociometer: The relationship between interpersonal appraisals and state self-esteem. *Journal of Personality and Social Psychology, 74,* 1290-1299.

Leary, M. R., & Kowalski, R. M. (1990). Impression management: A literature review and two-component model. *Psychological Bulletin, 107,* 34-47.

Leary, M. R., & Meadows, S. (1991). Predictors, elicitors, and concomitants of social blushing. *Journal of Personality and Social Psychology, 60,* 254-262.

Leary, M. R., Tambor, E. S., Terdal, S. K., & Downs, D. L. (1995). Self-esteem as an interpersonal monitor: The sociometer hypothesis. *Journal of Personality and Social Psychology, 68,* 518-530.

Lebra, T. S. (1983). Shame and guilt: A psychocultural view of the Japanese self. *Ethos, 11,* 192-209.

Lebra, T. S. (1992). Self in Japanese culture. In N. R. Rosenberger (Ed.), *Japanese sense of self* (pp. 105-120). Cambridge, UK: Cambridge University Press.

Lecky, P. (1945). *Self-consistency: A theory of personality.* Long Island, NY: Island.

L'Ecuyer, R. (1992). An experiential-developmental framework and methodology to study the transformations of the self-concept from infancy to old age. In T. M. Brinthaupt & R. P. Lipka (Eds.), *The self: Definitional and methodological issues* (pp. 96-134). Albany, NY: SUNY.

Lennox, R. D., & Wolfe, R. N. (1984). Revision of the Self-Monitoring Scale. *Journal of Personality and Social Psychology, 46,* 1349-1364.

Levine, D. W., & McDonald, P. J. (1981). Self-awareness and the veracity hypothesis. *Personality and Social Psychology Bulletin, 7,* 655-660.

Levine, M. P., Smolak, L., & Hayden, H. (1994). The relation of sociocultural factors to eating attitudes and behaviors among middle school girls. *Journal of Early Adolescence, 15,* 11-20.

Lewis, H. B. (1971). *Shame and guilt in neurosis.* New York: International Universities Press.

Lewis, M. (1992). *Shame, the exposed self.* New York: Free Press.

Lewis, M. (1995a). Embarrassment: The emotion of self-exposure and evaluation. In J. P. Tangney & K. W. Fischer (Eds.), *Self-conscious emotions* (pp. 198-218). New York: Guilford.

Lewis, M. (1995b). Self-conscious emotions. *American Scientist, 83,* 68-78.

Lewis, M., Alessandri, S., & Sullivan, M. W. (1992). Differences in shame and pride as a function of children's gender and task difficulty. *Child Development, 63,* 630-638.

Lewis, M., & Brooks-Gunn, J. (1979). *Social cognition and the acquisition of self.* New York: Plenum.

Lewis, M., Stanger, C., Sullivan, M. W., & Barone, P. (1991). Changes in embarrassment as a function of age, sex and situation. *British Journal of Developmental Psychology, 9,* 485-492.

Lewis, M., Sullivan, M. W., Stanger, C., & Weiss, M. (1989). Self-development and self-conscious emotions. *Child Development, 60,* 146-156.

Lindgren, T. W., & Pauly, I. B. (1975). A body image scale for evaluating transsexuals. *Archives of Sexual Behavior, 4,* 639-656.

Linville, P. W. (1985). Self-complexity and affective extremity: Don't put all your eggs in one basket. *Social Cognition, 3,* 94-120.

Linville, P. W. (1987). Self-complexity as a cognitive buffer against stress-related illness and depression. *Journal of Personality and Social Psychology, 53,* 663-676.

Lyman, R. (2000, October 6). Interview with Janusz Kaminsky. *The New York Times,* p. B26.

Lynd, H. M. (1958). *On shame and the search for identity.* New York: Harcourt Brace.

Lyubomirsky, S., Caldwell, N. D., & Nolen-Hoeksema, S. (1998). Effects of ruminative and distracting responses to depressed mood on retrieval of autobiographical memories. *Journal of Personality and Social Psychology, 75,* 166-177.

MacDougall, W. (1908). *Introduction to social psychology.* London: Methuen.

Macrae, C. N., Bodenhausen, G. V., & Milne, A. B. (1998). Saying no to unwanted thoughts: Self-focus and the regulation of mental life. *Journal of Personality and Social Psychology, 74,* 578-589.

Main, M., Kaplan, N., & Cassidy, J. (1985). Security in infancy, childhood, and adulthood: A move toward the level of representation. *Monographs of the Society for Research on Child Development, 50,* 66-106.

Major, B., Carrington, P. L., & Carnevale, P. J. D. (1984). Physical attractiveness and self-esteem: Attributions for praise from an other-sex evaluator. *Personality and Social Psychology Bulletin, 10,* 43-50.

Manstead, A. S. R., & Tetlock, P. E. (1989). Cognitive appraisals of emotional experience. *Cognition and Emotion, 3,* 225-240.

Marcia, J. (1966). Development and validation of ego-identity status. *Journal of Personality and Social Psychology, 3,* 551-558.

Marcia, J. (1987). The identity status approach to the study of ego development. In T. Honess & K. Yardley (Eds.), *Self and identity* (pp. 161-171). London: Routledge & Kegan Paul.

Marcia, J. (1994). The empirical study of ego identity. In H. A. Bosma, T. L. G. Graafsma, H. D. Grotevant, & D. J. de Levita (Eds.), *Identity and development* (pp. 67-80). Thousand Oaks, CA: Sage.

Markus, H. (1977). Self-schemata and processing information about the self. *Journal of Personality and Social Psychology, 35,* 63-78.

Markus, H., & Kitayama, S. (1991). Culture and the self: Implications for cognition, emotion, and motivation. *Psychological Review, 98,* 224-253.

Markus, H., & Nurius, P. (1986). Possible selves. *American Psychologist, 41,* 954-969.

Markus, H., & Ruvolo, A. (1989). Possible selves: Personalized representations of goals. In L. A. Pervin (Ed.), *Goal concepts in personality and social psychology* (pp. 211-241). Hillsdale, NJ: Lawrence Erlbaum.

Marsh, H. W. (1988). Global self-esteem: Its relation to specific facets self-concept and their importance. *Journal of Personality and Social Psychology, 51,* 1224-1236.

Marsh, H. W., Byrne, B. M., & Shavelson, R. J. (1992). A multidimensional, hierarchical self-concept. In T. M. Brinthaupt & R. P. Lipka (Eds.), *The self: Definitional and methodological issues* (pp. 44-95). Albany, NY: SUNY.

Marsh, H. W., & Yeung, A. S. (1998). Top-down, bottom-up, and horizontal models: The direction of causality in multidimensional, hierarchical self-concept models. *Journal of Personality and Social Psychology, 75,* 519-527.

Mathes, E. W., & Kahn, A. (1975). Physical attractiveness, happiness, neuroticism, and self-esteem. *Journal of Psychology, 90,* 27-30.

Mayhew, K. P., & Lempers, J. D. (1998). The relations among financial strain, parenting, parental self-esteem, and adolescent self-esteem. *Journal of Early Adolescence, 18,* 145-182.

McAdams, D. P. (1997). The case for unity in the (post)modern self. In R. D. Ashmore & L. Jussim (Eds.), *Self and identity* (pp. 46-78). New York: Oxford University Press.

McCrae, R. R., & John, O. P. (1992). An introduction to the five-factor model and its applications. *Journal of Personality, 60,* 175-215.

McGuire, W. J., & McGuire, C. V. (1986). Differences in conceptualizing self versus conceptualizing other people as manifested in contrasting verb types used in natural speech. *Journal of Personality and Social Psychology, 51,* 1135-1143.

McGuire, W. J., McGuire, C. W., Child, P., & Fujioka, T. (1978). Salience of ethnicity in the spontaneous self-concept as a function of one's own ethnic distinctiveness in the social environment. *Journal of Personality and Social Psychology, 36,* 511-520.

Mead, G. H. (1934). *Mind, self and society.* Chicago: University of Chicago Press.

Mendolia, M., Beach, R. H., & Tesser, A. (1996). The relationship between marital interaction behaviors and affective reactions to one's own and one's spouse's self-evaluation needs. *Personal Relationships, 3,* 279-292.

Mikulincer, M., & Nachson, O. (1991). Attachment styles and patterns of self-disclosure. *Journal of Personality and Social Psychology, 61,* 321-331.

Miller, L. C., Berg, J. H., & Archer, R. L. (1983). Openers: Individuals who elicit intimate self-disclosure. *Journal of Personality and Social Psychology, 44,* 1234-1244.

Miller, L. C., & Cox, C. L. (1982). For appearances' sake: Public self-consciousness and makeup use. *Personality and Social Psychology Bulletin, 8,* 748-751.

Miller, L. C., Murphy, R., & Buss, A. H. (1981). Consciousness of body: Private and public. *Journal of Personality and Social Psychology, 41,* 397-406.

Miller, R. S. (1987). Empathic embarrassment: Situational and personal determinants of reactions to the embarrassment of another. *Journal of Personality and Social Psychology, 53,* 1061-1969.

Miller, R. S. (1992). The nature and severity of self-reported embarrassing circumstances. *Personality and Social Psychology Bulletin, 18,* 190-198.

Miller, R. S. (1996). *Embarrassment.* New York: Guilford.

Miller, R. S., & Tangney, J. P. (1994). Differentiating embarrassment from shame. *Journal of Social and Clinical Psychology, 13,* 273-287.

Mitchell, R. W. (1994). Multiplicities of self. In S. T. Parker, R. W. Mitchell, & M. L. Boccia (Eds.), *Self-awareness in animals and humans* (pp. 81-107). New York: Cambridge University Press.

Mittal, B., & Balasubramanian, S. (1987). Testing the dimensionality of the self-consciousness scales. *Journal of Personality Assessment, 51,* 53-68.

Modell, A. H. (1993). *The private self.* Cambridge, MA: Harvard University Press.

Modigliani, A. (1968). Embarrassment and embarrassability. *Sociometry, 31,* 313-326.

Morton, T. (1978). Intimacy and reciprocity of exchange: A comparison of spouses and strangers. *Journal of Personality and Social Psychology, 36,* 72-81.

Mosher, D. L., & White, B. B. (1981). On differentiating shame and shyness. *Motivation and Emotion, 1,* 61-74.

Moyer, A. (1997). Psychosocial outcomes of breast-conserving surgery versus mastectomy: A meta-analytic review. *Health Psychology, 16,* 284-298.

Mruk, C. J. (1999). *Self-esteem* (2nd ed.). New York: Springer.

Mueller, J. H. (1982). Self-awareness and access to material rated as self-descriptive or nondescriptive. *Bulletin of the Psychonomic Society, 19,* 323-326.

Murray, S. L., Holmes, J. G., & Griffin, D. W. (2000). Self-esteem and the quest for security: How perceived regard regulates attachment processes. *Journal of Personality and Social Psychology, 78,* 478-498.

Nasby, W. (1989). Private and public self-consciousness and articulation of the self-schema. *Journal of Personality and Social Psychology, 56,* 117-123.

Neisser, U. (1988). Five kinds of self knowledge. *Philosophical Psychology, 1,* 35-59.

Nelson, K. (1993). The psychological origins of autobiographical memory. *Psychological Science, 4,* 1-8.

Newman, L. S., Higgins, E. T., & Vookles, J. (1992). Self-guide strength and emotional vulnerability. Birth order as a moderator of self-affect relations. *Personality and Social Psychology Bulletin, 18,* 402-411.

Offer, D., Ostrow, E., Howard, K., & Atkinson, R. (1988). *The teenage world: Adolescents' self image in ten countries.* New York: Plenum.

Ogilvie, D. M. (1987). The undesired self: A neglected variable in personality research. *Journal of Personality and Social Psychology, 52,* 379-385.

Orbach, J., Traub, A. C., & Olsen, R. (1965). Psychophysical studies of body image: II. Normative data on the adjustable body-distorting mirror. *Archives of General Psychiatry, 12,* 126-135.

Parker, S. T., Mitchell, R. W., & Boccia, M. L. (Eds.). (1994). *Self-awareness in animals and humans.* New York: Cambridge University Press.

Paxton, S. J., Schutz, H. K., Wertheim, E. H., & Muir, S. L. (1999). Friendship clique and peer influences on body image concerns, dietary restraint, extreme weight loss behaviors, and binge eating in adolescent girls. *Journal of Abnormal Psychology, 108,* 255-266.

Peevers, B. H. (1987). The self as observer of the self: A developmental analysis of the subjective self. In T. Honess & K. Yardley (Eds.), *Self and identity* (pp. 147-158). London: Routledge & Kegan Paul.

Pelham, B. W., & Swann, W. B., Jr. (1989). From self-conceptions to self-worth: On the sources and structure of global self-esteem. *Journal of Personality and Social Psychology, 57,* 672-680.

Pennebaker, J. W. (1997). *Opening up: The healing power of expressing emotions.* New York: Guilford.

Pennebaker, J. W., Hughes, C. F., & O'Heeron, R. C. (1987). The psychophysiology of confession: Linking inhibitory and psychosomatic processes. *Journal of Personality and Social Psychology, 52,* 781-793.

Pennebaker, J. W., Kiecolt-Glaser, J. K., & Glaser, R. (1988). Disclosure of traumas and immune function: Health implications for psychotherapy. *Journal of Consulting and Clinical Psychology, 56,* 239-245.

Pennebaker, J. W., & O'Heeron, R. C. (1984). Confiding in others and illness rate among spouses of suicide and accidental death. *Journal of Abnormal Psychology, 93,* 473-476.

Perry, M., & Buss, A. H. (1990). *Trait and situational aspects of shyness.* Unpublished research, University of Texas, Austin.

Petronio, S., Olson, C., & Dollar, N. (1989). Privacy issues in relational embarrassment: Impact on relational quality and communication satisfaction. *Communication Research Reports, 6,* 21-27.

Phillips, K. A., McElroy, S. L., Keck, P. E., Pope, H. G., & Hudson, J. I. (1993). Body dysmorphic disorder: 30 cases of imagined ugliness. *American Journal of Psychiatry, 150,* 302-308.

Phinney, J. S. (1990). Ethnic identity in adolescents and adults: A review of research. *Psychological Bulletin, 108,* 499-514.

Piaget, J. (1950). *The origins of intelligence.* New Haven, CT: Yale University Press.

Piers, G., & Singer, M. (1953). *Shame and guilt.* New York: Norton.

Pilkington, C. J., & Richardson, D. R. (1988). Perception of risk of intimacy. *Journal of Social and Personal Relationships, 5,* 505-508.

Pilkington, C. J., Tesser, A., & Stephens, D. (1991). Complementarity in romantic relationships: A self-evaluation maintenance perspective. *Journal of Social and Personal Relationships, 8,* 481-504.

Pope, H. G., Gruber, A. J., Choi, P., Olivardia, R., & Phillips, K. A. (1997). "Muscle dysmorphia": An underrecognized form of body dysmorphic disorder? *Psychosomatics, 38,* 548-557.

Porterfield, A. L., Mayer, F. S., Dougherty, K. G., Kredich, K. E., Kronberg, M. M., Marsee, K. M., & Okazaki, Y. (1988). Private self-consciousness, canned laughter, and responses to humorous stimuli. *Journal of Research in Personality, 22,* 409-423.

Posavac, H. D., Posavac, S. S., & Posavac, E. J. (1998). Exposure to media images of female attractiveness and concern with body weight. *Sex Roles, 38,* 187-201.

Povinelli, D. J., Landau, K. R., & Perilloux, H. K. (1996). Self-recognition in young children using delayed versus live feedback: Evidence of a developmental asynchrony. *Child Development, 67,* 1540-1554.

Prentice, D. A. (1990). Familiarity and differences in self- and other-representations. *Journal of Personality and Social Psychology, 59,* 369-383.

Pryor, J. B., Gibbons, F. X., Wicklund, R. A., Fazio, R. H., & Hood, R. (1977). Self-focused attention and self-report validity. *Journal of Personality, 45,* 513-527.

Reeves, A. L., Watson, P. J., Ramsey, A., & Morris, R. J. (1995). Private self-consciousness factors, need for cognition, and depression. *Journal of Social Behavior and Personality, 10,* 431-443.

Rehman, J., Lazer, S., Benet, A. E., Schaefer, L. C., & Melman, A. (1999). The reported sex and surgery satisfactions of 28 post-operative male-to-female transsexual patients. *Archives of Sexual Behavior, 28,* 71-89.

Reis, H. T., Senchak, M., & Solomon, B. (1985). Sex differences in intimacy of social interaction: Further examination of potential explanations. *Journal of Personality and Social Psychology, 48,* 1204-1217.

Reno, R. R., & Kenny, D. A. (1992). Effects of self-consciousness and social anxiety on self-disclosure among unacquainted individuals: Application of the social relations model. *Journal of Personality, 60,* 79-94.

Rhodewalt, F., Saltzman, A. T., & Wittmer, J. (1984). Self-handicapping among competitive athletes: The role of practice in self-esteem protection. *Basic and Applied Social Psychology, 5,* 197-209.

Riesman, D. (1950). *The lonely crowd.* New Haven, CT: Yale University Press.

Roese, N. J., & Olsen, J. M. (1993). Self-esteem and counter-factual thinking. *Journal of Personality and Social Psychology, 65,* 1313-1321.

Rogers, C. R. (1951). *Client-centered therapy.* Boston: Houghton-Mifflin.

Rogers, C. R., & Diamond, R. F. (Eds.). (1954). *Psychotherapy and personality change.* Chicago: University of Chicago Press.

Rosen, J. C. (1996). Body dysmorphic disorder: Assessment and treatment. In J. K. Thompson (Ed.), *Body image, eating disorders, and obesity* (pp. 149-170). Washington, DC: American Psychological Association.

Rosenberg, M. (1965). *Society and the adolescent self-Image.* Princeton, NJ: Princeton University Press.

Rosenblum, G. D., & Lewis, M. (1999). The relations among body image, physical attractiveness, and body mass in adolescence. *Child Development, 70,* 50-64.

Rubin, Z., Hill, C. T., Peplau, L. A., & Dunkel-Schletter, C. (1980). Self-disclosure in dating couples: Sex roles and the ethics of openness. *Journal of Marriage and the Family, 42,* 305-317.

Russell, D., Cutrona, C. E., Rose, J., & Yurko, K. (1984). Social and emotional loneliness: An examination of Weiss's typology of loneliness. *Journal of Personality and Social Psychology, 46,* 1313-1314.

Sadler, O., & Tesser, A. (1973). Some effects of salience and time upon interpersonal hostility and attraction during social isolation. *Sociometry, 36,* 99-112.

Sampson, E. E. (1988). The debate on individualism: Indigenous psychologies of the individual and their role in personal and social functioning. *American Psychologist, 43,* 15-22.

Sarbin, T. R. (1952). A preface to a psychological analysis of the self. *Psychological Review, 59,* 11-22.

Sarwer, D., Wadden, T., Pertschuck M. J., & Whitaker, L. A. (1998). The psychology of cosmetic surgery: A review and new conceptualization. *Clinical Psychology Review, 18,* 1-22.

Sattler, J. M. (1965). A theoretical, developmental, and clinical investigation of embarrassment. *Genetic Psychology Monographs, 71,* 19-59.

Scheier, M. F. (1976). Self-awareness, self-consciousness, and angry aggression. *Journal of Personality, 44,* 627-644.

Scheier, M. F., Buss, A. H., & Buss, D. M. (1978). Self-consciousness, self-report of aggressiveness, and aggression. *Journal of Research in Personality, 12,* 133-140.

Scheier, M. F., & Carver, C. S. (1977). Self-focused attention and the experience of emotion: Attraction, repulsion, elation, and depression. *Journal of Personality and Social Psychology, 35,* 624-636.

Scheier, M. F., & Carver, C. S. (1980). Public and private self-attention, resistance to change, and dissonance reduction. *Journal of Personality and Social Psychology, 39,* 390-405.

Scheier, M. F., & Carver, C. S. (1985). Optimism, coping, and health: Assessment and implications of generalized outcome expectancies. *Health Psychology, 4,* 219-247.

Scheier, M. F., Carver, C. S., & Gibbons, F. X. (1979). Self-directed attention, awareness of bodily states, and suggestibility. *Journal of Personality and Social Psychology, 37,* 1576-1588.

Scheier, M. F., Carver, C. S., & Gibbons, F. X. (1981). Self-focused attention and reactions to fear. *Journal of Research in Personality, 15,* 1-15.

Scheier, M. F., Fenigstein, A., & Buss, A. H. (1974). Self-awareness and physical aggression. *Journal of Experimental Social Psychology, 10,* 264-282.

Schilder, P. (1950). *The image and appearance of the human body.* New York: International Universities Press.

Schlenker, B. R. (1980). *Impression management: The self-concept, social identity, and interpersonal relations.* Monterey, CA: Brooks/Cole.

Schlenker, B. R., & Leary, M. R. (1982). Social anxiety and self-presentation. *Psychological Bulletin, 92,* 641-649.

Schlenker, B. R., & Wiegold, M. F. (1989). Goals and self-identification process: Constructing desired identities. In L. A. Pervin (Ed.), *Goal concepts in personality and social psychology* (pp. 243-290). Hillsdale, NJ: Lawrence Erlbaum.

Schlenker, B. R., Wiegold, M. F., & Hallam, J. R. (1990). Self-serving attributions in social contexts: Effects of self-esteem and social pressure. *Journal of Personality and Social Psychology, 58,* 855-863.

Schneiderman, L. (1956). The estimation of one's own bodily traits. *Journal of Social Psychology, 44,* 89-99.

Schwartz, D. J., Phares, V., Tantleff-Dunn, S., & Thompson, J. K. (1999). Body image, psychological functioning, and parental feedback regarding physical appearance. *Eating Disorders: The Journal of Treatment and Prevention, 7,* 339-348.

Secord, P. F., & Jourard, S. M. (1953). The appraisal of body-cathexis: Body-cathexis and the self. *Journal of Consulting Psychology, 17,* 343-347.

Sedikides, C. (1992). Mood as a determinant of attentional focus. *Cognition and Emotion, 6,* 129-148.

Sedikides, C. (1993). Assessment, enhancement, and verification determinants of the self-evaluation process. *Journal of Personality and Social Psychology, 65,* 317-338.

Sedikides, C., & Skowronski, J. J. (1997). The symbolic self in evolutionary context. *Personality and Social Psychology Review, 1,* 80-102.

Semin, G. R., & Manstead, A. S. R. (1982). The social implications of embarrassment displays and restitution behaviour. *European Journal of Social Psychology, 12,* 367-377.

Shaffer, D. R., & Ogden, J. K. (1986). On sex differences in self-disclosure during the acquaintance process: The role of anticipated future interaction. *Journal of Personality and Social Psychology, 51,* 92-101.

Shaffer, D. R., Pegalis, L. J., & Bazzini, D. G. (1996). When boy meets girl (revisited): Gender, gender-role orientation, and prospect of future interaction as determinants of self-disclosure among same- and opposite-sex acquaintances. *Personality and Social Psychology Bulletin, 22,* 495-506.

Shaffer, D. H., Ruammake, C., & Pegalis, L. J. (1990). The "opener": Highly skilled as interviewer or interviewee. *Personality and Social Psychology Bulletin, 16,* 511-520.

Shaffer, D. R., Smith, J. E., & Tomarelli, M. (1982). Self-monitoring as a determinant of self-disclosure reciprocity during the acquaintance process. *Journal of Personality and Social Psychology, 43,* 163-173.

Shaffer, D. R., & Tomarelli, M. M. (1989). When public and private self-foci clash: Self-consciousness and self-disclosure reciprocity during the acquaintance process. *Journal of Personality and Social Psychology, 56,* 765-776.

Sharkey, W. F., & Stafford, L. (1990). Responses to embarrassment. *Human Communication Research, 17,* 315-342.

Shavelson, R. J., Hubner, J. J., & Stanton, G. C. (1976). Self-concept: Validation of construct interpretations. *Review of Educational Research, 46,* 407-441.

Shearn, D., Bergman, E., Hill, K., Abel, A., & Hinds, L. (1990). Facial coloration and temperature responses to blushing. *Psychophysiology, 27,* 687-693.

Shearn, D., Bergman, E., Hill, K., Abel, A., & Hinds, L. (1992). Blushing as a function of audience size. *Psychophysiology, 29,* 431-436.

Shearn, D., & Spellman, L. (1993). *Empathic blushing in friends and strangers.* Unpublished research, Colorado College, Colorado Springs, Colorado.

Shepherd, J. A., & Arkin, R. M. (1989). Determinants of self-handicapping: The moderating role of public self-consciousness and task importance. *Personality and Social Psychology Bulletin, 15,* 252-265.

Shields, S. A., Mallory, M. E., & Simon, A. (1990). The Body Awareness Questionnaire: Reliability and validity. *Journal of Personality Assessment, 53,* 802-815.

Showers, C. J., Abramson, L. Y., & Hogan, M. E. (1998). The dynamic self: How the content and structure of the self-concept change with mood. *Journal of Personality and Social Psychology, 75,* 478-493.

Shrauger, J. S. (1975). Responses to evaluation as a function of initial self-perceptions. *Psychological Bulletin, 82,* 581-596.

Shrauger, J. S., & Rosenberg, J. E. (1970). Self-esteem and the effects of success and failure feedback on performance. *Journal of Personality, 38,* 404-417.

Simmons, R. G. (1987). Self-esteem in adolescence. In T. Honess & K. Yardley (Eds.), *Self and identity* (pp. 172-192). London: Routledge & Kegan Paul.

Simner, M. I. (1971). Newborn's response to the cry of another infant. *Developmental Psychology, 5,* 136-150.

Simon, A., & Shields, S. A. (1996). Does complexion color affect the experience of blushing? *Journal of Social Behavior and Personality, 11,* 177-178.

Singh, D. (1994). Ideal female body shape: Role of body weight and waist-to-hip ratio. *International Journal of Eating Disorders, 16,* 283-288.

Singh, D. (1995). Female judgment of male attractiveness and desirability for relationships: Role of waist-to-hip ratio and financial status. *Journal of Personality and Social Psychology, 69,* 1089-1101.

Smeets, M.A.M. (1999). Body size categorization in anorexia nervosa using a morphing instrument. *International Journal of Eating Disorders, 25,* 451-461.

Smith, A. (1976). *The theory of moral sentiments.* Indianapolis, IN: Liberty Classics. (Original work published 1759)

Smith, J. D., & Shaffer, D. R. (1986). Self-consciousness, self-reported altruism, and helping behavior. *Social Behavior and Personality, 14,* 215-220.

Smith, K. D., Keating, J. P., & Stotland, E. (1989). Altruism reconsidered: The effect of denying feedback on a victim's status to empathic witnesses. *Journal of Personality and Social Psychology, 57,* 641-650.

Smith, M. B. (1978). Perspectives on selfhood. *American Psychologist, 33,* 1053-1063.

Snyder, M. (1974). The self-monitoring of expressive behavior. *Journal of Personality and Social Psychology, 30,* 526-537.

Snygg, D., & Combs, A. W. (1949). *Individual behavior.* New York: Harper & Row.

Solano, C., Batten, P., & Parish, E. (1982). Loneliness and patterns of self-disclosure. *Journal of Personality and Social Psychology, 43,* 524-531.

Spencer, S. T., Josephs, R. A., & Steele, C. M. (1993). Low self-esteem: The uphill struggle for self-integrity. In R. F. Baumeister (Ed.), *Self-esteem: The puzzle of low self-regard* (pp. 21-36). New York: Plenum.

Stattin, H., Magnusson, D., Olah, A., Kassin, H., & Reddy, N. Y. (1991). Perception of threatening consequences of anxiety-provoking situations. *Anxiety Research, 4,* 141-146.

Steele, C. M. (1988). The psychology of self-affirmation. In L. Berkowitz (Ed.), *Advances in experimental social psychology* (Vol. 21, pp. 261-302). New York: Academic Press.

Stice, E., Spangler, D., & Agras, W. S. (1999). *Effects of exposure to media-portrayed thin-ideal images on adolescent girls: A longitudinal experiment.* Unpublished research, University of Texas, Austin.

Stiles, W. B. (1987). "I have to talk to somebody": A fever model of disclosure. In V. J. Derlega & J. H. Berg (Eds.), *Self-disclosure: Theory, research, and therapy* (pp. 258-282). New York: Plenum.

Stipek, D. J., Recchia, S., & McClintic, S. (1992). Self-evaluation in young children. *Monographs of the Society for Research in Child Development, 57*(Serial No. 226).

Stormer, S. M. (1998). *The cross-gender effects of an experimental media-focused psychoeducational program.* Unpublished doctoral dissertation, University of South Florida, Tampa.

Story, A. (1998). Self-esteem and memory for favorable and unfavorable personality feedback. *Personality and Social Psychology Bulletin, 24,* 51-64.

Stotland, E., Mathews, K. E., Sherman, S. E., Hanson, R., & Richardson, B. Z. (1979). *Empathy, fantasy and helping.* Thousand Oaks, CA: Sage.

Strauman, T. J. (1996). Stability within the self: A longitudinal study of the structural implications of self-discrepancy theory. *Journal of Personality and Social Psychology, 71,* 1142-1153.

Strauman, T. J., & Glenberg, A. M. (1994). Self-concept and body image disturbance: Which self-beliefs predict body size overestimation? *Cognitive Research and Therapy, 18,* 105-125.

Strauman, T. J., & Higgins, E. T. (1987a). Automatic activation of self-discrepancies and emotional syndromes: When cognitive structures influence affect. *Journal of Personality and Social Psychology, 53,* 1004-1014.

Strauman, T. J., & Higgins, E. T. (1987b). *Vulnerability to specific kinds of chronic emotional problems as a function of self-discrepancies.* Unpublished manuscript, New York University.

Strong, S. M., Singh, D., & Randall, P. K. (1999). *Childhood gender nonconformity and body dissatisfaction in gay and heterosexual men.* Unpublished research, University of Texas, Austin.

Swann, W. B., Jr. (1984). Quest for accuracy in person perception: A matter of pragmatics. *Psychological Review, 91,* 457-477.

Swann, W. B., Jr., Griffin, J. J., Jr., Predmore, S. C., & Gaines, B. (1987). The cognitive-affective crossfire: When self-consistency confronts self-enhancement. *Journal of Personality and Social Psychology, 52,* 881-889.

Swann, W. B., Jr., Stein-Seroussi, A., & Gieseler, R. (1992). Why people self-verify. *Journal of Personality and Social Psychology, 62,* 392 401.

Szymanski, M. L., & Cash, T. F. (1995). Body image disturbance and self-discrepancy theory: Expansion of the Body-Image Ideals Questionnaire. *Journal of Social and Clinical Psychology, 14,* 134-136.

Tafarodi, R. W. (1998). Paradoxical self-esteem and selectivity in the processing of social information. *Journal of Personality and Social Psychology, 74,* 1181-1196.

Tafarodi, R. W., & Vu, C. (1997). Two-dimensional self-esteem and reactions to success and failure. *Personality and Social Psychology Bulletin, 23,* 626-635.

Tajfel, H. (1981). *Human groups and social categories.* Cambridge, UK: Cambridge University Press.

Tangney, J. P. (1990). Assessing individual differences in proneness to shame and guilt: Development of the Self-Conscious Affect and Attribution Inventory. *Journal of Personality and Social Psychology, 59,* 102-111.

Tangney, J. P. (1991). Moral affect: The good, the bad, and the ugly. *Journal of Personality and Social Psychology, 61,* 598-607.

Tangney, J. P. (1992). Situational determinants of shame and guilt in young adulthood. *Personality and Social Psychology Bulletin, 18,* 199-206.

Tangney, J. P., Marschall, D. E., Rosenberg, K., Barlow, D. H., & Wagner, P. E. (1994). *Children's and adults' autobiographical accounts of shame, guilt, and pride experiences: An analysis of situational determinants and interpersonal concerns.* Unpublished manuscript, George Mason University, Fairfax, VA.

Tangney, J. P., Miller, R. S., Flicker, L., & Barlow, D. H. (1996). Are shame, guilt, and embarrassment distinct emotions? *Journal of Personality and Social Psychology, 70,* 1256-1269.

Tangney, J. P., Niedenthal, P. M., Covert, M. V., & Barlow, D. H. (1998). Are shame and guilt related to distinct self-discrepancies? A test of Higgins' (1987) hypotheses. *Journal of Personality and Social Psychology, 75,* 256-268.

Tangney, J. P., Wagner, P. E., & Gramzow, R. (1992). Proneness to shame, proneness to guilt, and psychopathology. *Journal of Abnormal Psychology, 103,* 469-478.

Tantleff-Dunn, S., & Thompson, J. K. (1999). *Breast and chest size satisfaction: Relation to overall body image and self-esteem.* Unpublished research, University of South Florida, Tampa.

Taylor, C. (1989). *Sources of self.* Cambridge, MA: Harvard University Press.

Taylor, S. E., & Brown, J. (1988). Illusion and well-being: A social psychological perspective on mental health. *Psychological Bulletin, 103,* 193-210.

Tedeschi, J. T., & Norman, N. (1985). Social power, self-presentation, and the self. In B. R. Schlenker (Ed.), *The self in social life* (pp. 293-322). New York: McGraw-Hill.

Telch, M. J., Lucas, J. A., Schmidt, N. B., Hanna, H. H., Jaimez, T. L., & Lucas, R. A. (1993). Group cognitive-behavioral treatment of panic disorder. *Behaviour Research and Therapy, 31,* 279-287.

Temerlin, M. K. (1975). *Lcu: Growing up Human.* Palo Alto, CA: Science and Behavior Books.

Tennis, G. H., & Dabbs, J. M., Jr. (1975). Sex, setting, and personal space: First grade through college. *Sociometry, 38,* 385-394.

Tesser, A. (1980). Self-esteem and family dynamics. *Journal of Personality and Social Psychology, 39,* 77-91.

Tesser, A. (1991). Emotion in social comparison and reflection processes. In J. Suls & T. A. Wills (Eds.), *Social comparison: Contemporary theory and research* (pp. 115-145). Hillsdale, NJ: Lawrence Erlbaum.

Tesser, A., & Campbell, J. (1983). Self-evaluation maintenance and the perception of friends and strangers. *Journal of Personality, 50,* 261-279.

Tesser, A., & Conlee, M. C. (1975). Some effects of time and thought on attitude polarization. *Journal of Personality and Social Psychology, 31,* 262-270.

Tesser, A., Miller, M., & Moore, J. (1988). Some affective consequences of social comparison and reflection processes: The pain and pleasure of being close. *Journal of Personality and Social Psychology, 54,* 49-61.

Thigpen, C. H., & Cleckley, H. (1954). A case of multiple personality. *Journal of Abnormal and Social psychology, 49,* 135-151.

Thompson, J. K., Heinberg, L. J., Altabe, M., & Tantleff-Dunn, S. (1999). *Exacting beauty: Theory, assessment, and treatment of body image disturbance.* Washington, DC: American Psychological Association.

Thompson, J. K., Penner, L. A., & Altabe, M. N. (1990). Procedures, problems, and the assessment of body images. In T. F. Cash & T. Pruzinsky (Eds.), *Body images: Development, deviance, and change* (pp. 21-48). New York: Guilford.

Thompson, J. K., & Tantleff, S. T. (1992). Female and male ratings of upper torso: Actual, ideal and stereotypical conceptions. *Journal of Social Behavior and Personality, 7,* 345-354.

Thompson, J. K., & Tantleff-Dunn, S. T. (1998). Assessment of body image disturbance in obesity. *Obesity Research, 6,* 375-377.

Thompson, M. A., & Gray, J. J. (1995). Development and validation of a new body assessment tool. *Journal of Personality Assessment, 64,* 258-269.

Tice, D. M. (1991). Esteem protection or enhancement? Self-handicapping motives and attributions differ by trait self-esteem. *Journal of Personality and Social Psychology, 60,* 711-725.

Tiggerman, M., & Pickering, A. S. (1996). Role of television in adolescent women's body dissatisfaction and drive for thinness. *International Journal of Eating Disorders, 20,* 193-203.

Tobey, E. L., & Tunnell, G. (1981). Predicting our impressions on others: Effects of public self-consciousness and acting, a Self-Monitoring Scale. *Personality and Social Psychology Bulletin, 7,* 661-669.

Toulmin, S. (1986). The ambiguities of self-understanding. *Journal for the Theory of Social Behavior, 16,* 41-55.

Trapnell, P. D., & Campbell, J. D. (1999). Private self-consciousness and the five-factor model of personality. *Journal of Personality and Social Psychology, 76,* 284-304.

Triandis, H. C. (1989). The self and social behavior in differing cultural contexts. *Psychological Review, 96,* 506-520.

Triandis, H. C. (1995). *Individualism and collectivism.* Boulder, CO: Westview.

Trimble, D. E. (1993, April). *Meta-analysis of altruism and intrinsic and extrinsic religiousness.* Paper presented at the meetings of the Eastern Psychological Association, Arlington, VA.

Trivers, R. L. (1971). The evolution of reciprocal altruism. *Quarterly Review of Biology, 46,* 35-57.

Turner, J. C. (1982). Towards a cognitive redefinition of the social group. In H. Tajfel (Ed.), *Social identity and intergroup relations* (pp. 15-40). Cambridge, UK: Cambridge University Press.

Turner, J. C., Hogg, M. A., Oakes, P. J., Reicher, S. D., & Wetherell, M. S. (1987). *Rediscovering the social group: A self-categorization theory.* Oxford, England: Blackwell.

Turner, J. C., & Onorato, R. S. (1999). Social identity, personality, and the self-concept. In T. R. Tyler, R. M. Kramer, & O. P. John (Eds.), *The psychology of the social self* (pp. 11-46). Mahwah, NJ: Lawrence Erlbaum.

Turner, R. G. (1978a). Consistency, self-consciousness, and the predictive validity of typical and maximal measures. *Journal of Research in Personality, 12,* 117-132.

Turner, R. G. (1978b). Effects of differential request procedures and self-consciousness on trait attributions. *Journal of Research in Personality, 12,* 431-438.

Turner, R. G. (1978c). Self-consciousness and speed of processing self-relevant information. *Personality and Social Psychology Bulletin, 4,* 456-460.

Turner, R. G. (1980). Self-consciousness and memory for trait names. *Personality and Social Psychology Bulletin, 6,* 273-277.

Turner, R. G., Gilliland, L., & Klein, H. M. (1981). Self-consciousness, evaluation of physical characteristics, and physical attractiveness. *Journal of Research in Personality, 15,* 182-190.

Turner, R. H. (1975). Is there a quest for identity? *The Sociological Quarterly, 16,* 148-161.

Turner, R. H. (1976). The real self: From institution to impulse. *American Journal of Sociology, 81,* 989-1016.

Ugurel-Semin, R. (1952). Moral behavior and the moral judgment of children. *Journal of Abnormal and Social Psychology, 47,* 463-474.

Vallone, R. P., Griffin, D. W., Lin, S., & Ross, L. (1990). Overconfident prediction of future actions and outcomes by self and others. *Journal of Personality and Social Psychology, 58,* 582-592.

Van de Mark, S., & Neuringer, C. (1969). Effect of physical and cognitive somatic arousal on Rorschach responses: An experimental test of the assumption that body image influences the perceptual organization of unstructured stimuli. *Journal of Consulting and Clinical Psychology, 33,* 458-465.

Wagner, P. J. (1975). The development of space and personal time perspective. *Dissertation Abstracts, 36,* 2431-2532.

Watson, J. B. (1970). *Proxemic behavior: A cross-cultural study.* The Hague, The Netherlands: Mouton.

Wegner, D. (1980). The self in prosocial action. In D. M. Wegner & R. R. Vallacher (Eds.), *The self in social psychology* (pp. 131-157). New York: Oxford University Press.

Weiner, B., & Kukla, A. (1970). An attributional analysis of achievement motivation. *Journal of Personality and Social Psychology, 15,* 1-20.

Weiss, R. S. (1973). *Loneliness: The experience of emotional and social isolation.* Cambridge: MIT Press.

Wells, L. E., & Marwell, G. (1976). *Self-esteem: Its conceptualization and measurement.* Beverly Hills, CA: Sage.

Wheeler, L., Reis, H., & Nezlek, J. (1983). Loneliness, social interaction, and sex roles. *Journal of Personality and Social Psychology, 45,* 943-953.

Wheelis, A. (1958). *The quest for identity.* New York: Norton.

White, S. H. (1965). Evidence for a hierarchical arrangement of learning processes. In L. P. Lipsitt & C. C. Spiker (Eds.), *Advances in child behavior and development* (Vol. 2). New York: Academic Press.

Whiting, B., & Edwards, C. P. (1973). A cross-cultural analysis of sex differences in the behavior of children aged 3 through 11. *Journal of Social Psychology, 91,* 171-188.

Wills, T. A. (1981). Downward comparison principles in social psychology. *Psychological Bulletin, 90,* 245-271.

Wilson, E. O. (1978). *On human nature.* Cambridge, MA: Harvard University Press.

Wispe, L. (1986). The distinction between sympathy and empathy: To call forth a concept, a word is needed. *Journal of Personality and Social Psychology, 50,* 314-321.

Wood, J. V., Giordana-Beech, M., Taylor, K. L., Michela, J. L., & Gaus, V. (1994). Strategies of social comparison among people with low self-esteem: Self-protection and self-enhancement. *Journal of Personality and Social Psychology, 67,* 713-731.

Wood, K., Becker, J. A., & Thompson, J. K. (1996). Body image dissatisfaction in preadolescent children. *Journal of Applied Developmental Psychology, 17,* 85-100.

Worthy, M., Gary, A. L., and Kahn, G. M. (1969). Self-disclosure as an exchange process. *Journal of Personality and Social Psychology, 13,* 59-63.

Wright, M. R. (1989). Body image dissatisfaction in adolescent girls and boys. *Journal of Youth and Adolescence, 18,* 71-83.

Wylie, R. C. (1974). *The self-concept* (Rev. ed., Vol. 1). Lincoln: University of Nebraska Press.

Yager, J., Kurtzman, F., Landsverk, J., & Weismeier, E. (1988). Behaviors and attitudes related to eating disorders in homosexual male students. *American Journal of Psychiatry, 145,* 495-497.

Yap, P. M. (1965). Koro—A culture bound depersonalization syndrome. *British Journal of Psychiatry, 111,* 43-50.

Zakin, D. F. (1989). Eating disturbance, emotional separation, and body image. *International Journal of Eating Disorders, 8,* 411-416.

Zeldin, R. S., Small, S. A., & Savin-Williams, R. C. (1982). Prosocial interactions in two mixed-sex adolescent groups. *Child Development, 53,* 1192-1198.

Author Index

Abel, A., 155, 158, 161, 184
Abrams, D., 108
Abramson, L. Y., 262
Acquan-Assee, J., 227
Agatstein, F. C., 134
Agras, W. S., 41
Alessandri, S., 202
Alicke, M. D., 68
Allen, J. L., 244
Allen, M., 226
Allport, G. W., 2, 4, 5, 12, 247, 257
Altabe, M., 34, 35, 39, 41
Altman, I., 212
Amsterdam, B., 16
Anderson, E. M., 138
Anderson, J., 37, 132
Anderson, P., 68
Andrews, B., 43
Angyal, A., 89
Appelman, A. J., 171
Apsler, R., 160
Archer, R. L., 222, 223
Arkin, R. M., 70, 131, 171, 270
Arndt, J., 141
Aron, A., 240
Aron, E. N., 240
Aronson, E., 93

Arps, K., 243
Asendorpf, J., 17, 156, 157, 167
Ashworth, C., 216
Aspinwall, L. G., 69
Atkinson, R., 259

Babcock, M. K., 182
Bakan, D., 57
Balasubramanian, S., 138
Baldwin, M. W., 196
Bandura, A., 50
Baradell, J. G., 28
Barkow, J. H., 81
Barlow, D. H., 29, 158, 183, 190, 191, 193
Barnett, M. A., 240
Barnlund, D. C., 10
Barone, P., 167, 168
Barrientos, S., 244
Barsky, A. J., 28
Batson, C. D., 238, 240, 244, 247, 248, 249
Batson, J. G., 244
Batten, P., 223, 226
Baudonniere, P. M., 17
Baumann, D. J., 250, 251

313

Baumeister, R. F., 2, 59, 70, 110, 111, 115, 129, 185, 190, 279
Baumgardner, A. H., 62
Bavelas, J. B., 238
Bayley, M. G., 244
Bazzini, D. G., 227
Beach, R. H., 68
Becker, H., 38
Becker, J. A., 38
Benet, A. E., 32
Bennett, M., 168
Berg, J. H., 222, 223
Berglas, S. C., 70
Bergman, E., 155, 158, 161, 184
Bernstein, L., 138, 139
Bernstein, W. M., 130
Berrigan, L. P., 138
Berry, A., 63
Berscheid, E., 35, 41, 49
Bertenthal, B. I., 17
Berzonsky, M. D., 114
Black, A., 238
Bleske, A. L., 207
Block, J., 77
Blum, R. W., 39, 40
Boccia, M. L., 16
Bodenhausen, G. V., 129
Bohon, L. M., 138
Bohrnstedt, G., 35, 41
Boldero, J., 267
Bond, R. N., 265
Borden, R. J., 55
Brandt, J. R., 244
Brewer, M. B., 108, 109, 118
Bridges, K. M. B., 250
Briggs, S. R., 271
Britt, T. W., 139, 154, 155, 159, 184, 196, 204
Brockner, J., 27, 63, 65
Brooks-Gunn, J., 17
Brown, J., 47
Brown, J. D., 5, 63, 64, 66, 72
Brown, S. L., 246, 247
Brown, T., 248
Brown, T. A., 34
Brownell, K. D., 42
Buchanan, D. B., 134
Buck, R. W., 154, 161
Bukowski, W. M., 227
Bull, C. A., 77
Burger, J. M., 171

Burhmester, D., 219, 227
Burling, J., 81, 82
Burnham, M., 168
Burnkrant, R. R., 138
Bushman, B. J., 133
Buss, A. H., 19, 26, 27, 28, 34, 37, 54, 56, 57, 59, 60, 61, 62, 95, 97, 121, 123, 124, 125, 133, 136, 137, 138, 141, 143, 159, 165, 172, 174, 179, 193, 229, 230, 231, 247, 271
Buss, D. M., 49, 125, 207, 215
Buss, E. H., 165, 174
Buss, L., 156, 161
Bustamente, D., 238, 244
Buswell, B. N., 159, 183, 184, 189, 190, 191, 193, 204
Byrne, B. M., 258, 259

Caldwell, M. A., 226
Caldwell, N. D., 144
Cameron, P. A., 17
Campbell, J. D., 63, 66, 68, 138, 139, 148, 262
Cannon, W. B., 28
Cappella, J. N., 220
Carlo, G., 240
Carnevale, P. J. D., 49
Carrington, P. L., 49
Carver, C. S., 60, 124, 125, 126, 127, 134, 135, 139, 141, 142, 266
Casey, R. J., 49
Cash, T. F., 34, 35, 37, 38, 132, 267
Cassiday, P. B., 35
Cassidy, J., 225
Castelfranchi, C., 170, 184, 193, 203, 204
Cattarin, J., 42
Chaiken, A. L., 216, 220
Chang, L., 138
Cheek, J. M., 59
Chelune, G. J., 222
Chew, B., 63
Child, P., 94
Chiu, C.-Y., 52
Choi, P., 38
Choi, S.-G., 117, 118
Chokel, J. T., 82
Cialdini, R. B., 55, 239, 243, 246, 247, 249, 250, 251
Cleckley, H., 108
Collins, E. M., 38

Author Index

Collins, J. K., 42
Collins, R. L., 69
Colman, N. M., 71
Combs, A. W., 257
Conlee, M. C., 144
Cooley, C. H., 3, 148
Coopersmith, S., 48
Cornell, D. P., 63
Courtney, H. E., 48
Covert, M. V., 188, 265
Cox, C. L., 132
Cozby, P. C., 220
Creed, A., 138
Crelia, R., 68
Crocker, J., 58, 69
Cross, S. E., 117
Crowe, E., 266
Crowley, M., 253, 254
Crozier, W. R., 168
Cutlip, W. D., II, 154, 155, 158, 159, 184, 196, 204
Cutrona, C. E., 61

Dabbs, J. M., Jr., 229
Damon, W., 111
Darby, B. K., 243
Darwin, C. R., 169, 170
Davidson, W., 52
Davis, A. D., 25
Davis, D., 135
Davis, J. D., 220, 227
Davis, M. H., 130, 223, 224, 244
Dawson, K., 240, 247
Deaux, K., 100
Deci, E. L., 78
Derlega, V. J., 216, 218, 220, 227
Derr, W. R., 65
Devine, P. G., 265
Diamond, R. F., 263
Diggory, J. C., 49
Dindia, K., 226
Dino, G. A., 240
Dollar, N., 163
Donahue, E. M., 107
Dougherty, K. G., 127
Dovidio, J. F., 244
Downs, A. C., 49
Downs, D. L., 82
Dubois, D. L., 77
Dunkel-Schletter, C., 226

Dunning, D., 47, 48
Dutton, K. A., 66
Duval, S., 121, 140
Dweck, C. S., 51, 52

Eagly, A. H., 253, 254
Edelmann, R. J., 158, 159, 171, 175
Edwards, C. P., 253
Eibl-Eibesfelt, I., 158
Eisenberg, N., 236, 238, 240, 244
Elliot, A. J., 265
Elliott, E. S., 51
Enna, B., 52
Epstein, S., 81, 261
Erickson, G. A., 55, 93
Erikson, E., 111, 113, 116, 186
Ethier, K. A., 100
Evans, G. W., 229

Fabes, R. A., 236, 238, 240, 244
Fairey, P. J., 66
Fazio, R. H., 130
Federn, P., 24
Fehr, B., 63
Feingold, A., 36
Fenigstein, A., 34, 37, 121, 132, 133, 136, 137, 138, 141, 145
Festinger, L., 67, 140, 217
Finch, F. D., 68
Finn, S., 103, 104
Fischer, K. W., 17
Fisher, R. L., 24
Fisher, S., 24, 32
Flavell, J., 165
Fleming, J. S., 48
Flicker, L., 158, 183, 190, 191
Flory, J. D., 128
Flynn, M., 228
Frable, D. E. S., 58
Francis, J., 267
Frankel, B. S., 65
Franz, C., 240
Franzoi, S. L., 34, 37, 40, 130, 132, 223, 224
Freeman, S., 55
French, S. A., 39, 40
Friedman, M. A., 42
Froming, W. J., 134, 136, 137, 194
Frommelt, S., 37, 132

Frone, M. R., 128
Fujioka, T., 94
Fultz, J., 238, 239, 243
Funder, D. C., 138
Furman, G., 216

Gaines, B., 72
Gallagher, F. M., 64
Gallaher, P., 131
Gallo, L., 69
Gallup, G. G., Jr., 15, 16, 17
Garbin, C., 138, 139
Gardner, W., 118
Garner, D. M., 40, 41
Garst, E., 240, 247
Gary, A. L., 219
Gaus, V., 69
Geertz, C., 116
Gelfand, M. J., 117, 118
Gentleman, T. E., 40
Gerrard, M., 69
Gibbons, E. J., 141
Gibbons, F. X., 69, 126, 127, 130
Gieseler, R., 74
Gilliland, L., 132, 134
Giordana-Beech, M., 69
Glaser, R., 217
Glenberg, A. M., 267
Goffman, E., 3, 170, 171, 204, 269
Goldenberg, J. L., 82
Gramzow, R., 189, 267
Gray, J. J., 34
Gray, R. A., 248
Green, J. D., 140, 141
Greenberg, J., 48, 81, 82, 135, 141
Greenwald, A. G., 80, 261
Griffin, D. W., 48, 64
Griffin, J. J., Jr., 72
Griffitt, C. A., 244
Gross, E., 159
Gruber, A. J., 38
Grzelak, J., 216
Guardo, C. J., 104
Gullone, E., 39

Hafdahl, A. R., 267
Haimes, E., 91, 106
Hall, C. C. I., 36
Hall, E. T., 5, 163, 228, 229

Hall, J. A., 229, 244
Hallam, J. R., 71
Hanna, H. H., 29
Hanson, R., 249
Harlow, T., 63
Harmon-Jones, E., 81
Harre, R., 1
Harrell, K. L., 244
Hart, D., 111
Harter, S., 4, 49, 50, 76, 77, 78, 203
Haselton, M. G., 207
Hashimoto, E., 159
Haupt, A. L., 82
Hayden, H., 41
Hayduk, L. A., 228, 229
Hazan, C., 225
Healy, S. P., 248
Heatherton, T. F., 70, 71, 185, 190
Heinberg, L. J., 35, 39, 40, 41
Heine, S. J., 82, 83, 117, 150, 201, 262, 267
Henry, P. E., 35
Higgins, E. T., 263, 264, 265, 266, 267, 268
Hill, C. T., 226
Hill, K., 155, 158, 161, 184
Hinds, L., 155, 158, 161, 184
Hirt, E. R., 55, 71, 93, 131
Hobbs, S., 226
Hoey, S., 58
Hoffman, M. L., 248, 251, 253
Hogan, M. E., 262
Hoge, D. R., 48
Hogg, M. A., 108
Holmes, J. G., 64, 196
Holtgraves, T., 135
Hong, Y.-Y., 52
Hood, R., 130
Hormuth, S. E., 126
Horowitz, E., 169
Houlihan, D., 243
Howard, J. A., 240
Howard, K., 259
Howard, R. B., 229
Howe, N., 227
Hoyle, R., 138
Hubner, J. J., 258
Hudson, J. I., 43
Hughes, C. F., 215
Hull, J. G., 127, 128, 141, 143
Hume, D., 106

Author Index

Hunter, S., 227
Hutton, D. G., 59, 70, 129
Hymes, C., 266

Ide, E., 83
Insko, C. A., 267
Iscoe, I., 165, 174
Iwawaki, S., 158

Jackson, L. A., 35
Jackson, S. E., 100
Jacobi, L., 38
Jaimez, T. L., 29
James, W., 3, 4, 12, 13, 263, 264
Janda, L. H., 35
Jenkins, V. Y., 49
Jennings, P., 248
John, O. P., 107, 148
Jones, E. E., 70, 271
Jones, W. H., 226
Josephs, R. A., 57, 65, 70, 72, 73
Josselson, R., 105, 106
Jourard, S. M., 33, 212, 219, 221
Jouriles, E., 128, 141
Jung, C. G., 147

Kahn, A., 49
Kahn, G. M., 219
Kanaga, K. R., 228
Kang, M., 240, 247
Kaplan, N., 225
Kashima, Y., 117, 118
Kaslow, F., 38
Kasmer, J., 135
Kassin, H., 158
Katz, I. M., 262
Keating, J. P., 244
Keck, P. F., 43
Keltner, D., 157, 159, 167, 183, 184, 189, 190, 191, 193, 204
Kennedy, C., 55, 93
Kenny, D. A., 224
Kenrick, D. T., 243, 250, 251
Kernis, M. H., 63, 65, 135
Kiecolt-Glaser, J. K., 217
Kim, U., 117, 118
Kimble, C., 71, 131
King, L. M., 240

Kingaree, J. B., 138, 140
Kitayama, S., 82, 83, 117, 150, 201
Kitzinger, C., 5, 89
Klein, H. M., 132, 134
Klein, K., 28
Klein, R., 264, 265
Klerman, G. L., 28
Klesges, R. C., 130
Koehler, V., 40
Koestner, R., 240
Kohlberg, L., 201
Kostanski, M., 39
Kowalski, R. M., 270
Krebs, D., 239
Kredich, K. E., 127
Kronberg, M. M., 127
Kruger, J., 48
Kukla, A., 51
Kurtzman, F., 40

Labarge, A. S., 34, 132
Laing, W. N., 65
Lamb, C. S., 35
Landau, K. R., 19, 20, 175
Landsverk, J., 40
Langlois, J. H., 49
Larrick, R. P., 70
Larsen, R. J., 215
Lasakow, P., 212, 221
Lavallee, L. F., 262
Lawrence, J. W., 266
Lazar, S., 32
Leary, M. R., 82, 154, 155, 156, 158, 159, 171, 184, 196, 204, 270
Lebra, T. S., 195, 207
Lecky, P., 257, 261
L'Ecuyer, R., 259
Leggett, E. L., 51
Lehman, D. R., 82, 83, 117, 150, 201, 262, 267
Lemery, C. R., 238
Lempers, J. D., 76
Lennox, R. D., 271
Levine, D. W., 126
Levine, M. P., 41
Levinson, R. W., 128
Levy, A. S., 143
Lewis, B. P., 246, 247
Lewis, H. B., 187, 190

Lewis, M., 17, 39, 166, 167, 168, 172, 174, 175, 190, 201, 202
Lin, S., 48
Lindgren, T. W., 32
Linville, P. W., 107, 262
Lloyd, K., 63
Lopyan, K. J., 136, 137, 194
LoSchiavo, F. M., 68
Lothart, J., 244
Lucas, J. A., 29
Lucas, R. A., 29
Luce, C., 246, 247
Lyman, R., 107
Lynd, H. M., 186
Lyon, D., 81, 82
Lyubomirsky, S., 144

MacDougall, W., 243
Macrae, C. N., 129
Madson, L., 117
Magnusson, D., 158
Main, M., 225
Major, B., 49, 58
Mallory, M. E., 169
Maloney, J., 111
Manstead, A. S. R., 171, 182
Marcia, J., 113, 114, 115
Margulis, S. T., 218
Markus, H. R., 57, 72, 73, 82, 83, 117, 150, 201, 260, 267, 268, 270
Marschall, D. E., 190, 193
Marsee, K. M., 127
Marsh, H. W., 48, 258, 259
Marwell, G., 48
Mathes, E. W., 49
Mathews, K. E., 249
Mathy, R. M., 238, 244
Matsumoto, H., 83
Matthews, K. A., 128
Mayer, F. S., 127
Mayer, M., 244
Mayhew, K. P., 76
McAdams, D. P., 13
McCarthy, J. D., 48
McClintic, S., 201, 202
McCoy, S. B., 69
McCoy, S. K., 82
McCrae, R. R., 148
McCrea, S. M., 71, 13
McDonald, P. J., 126

McElroy, S. L., 43
McFarlin, D. B., 128
McGinley, H., 130
McGregor, H., 81
McGuire, C. V., 6
McGuire, C. W., 94
McGuire, W. J., 6, 94
Mead, G. H., 3, 79, 148
Meadows, S., 156, 204
Melman, A., 32
Mendolia, M., 68
Metts, S., 218
Michela, J. L., 69
Mikulincer, M., 225
Mikulka, P. J., 34
Miller, L. C., 26, 27, 28, 131, 222, 223
Miller, M., 68
Miller, P., 240
Miller, R. S., 158, 159, 164, 168, 182, 183, 190, 191
Mills, J., 93
Milne, A. B., 129
Mitchell, K. V., 244
Mitchell, R. W., 16
Mittal, B., 138
Mizrahi, K., 100
Modell, A. H., 13
Modigliani, A., 159, 171
Monteith, M. J., 265
Moore, J., 68
Morris, R. J., 138
Morton, T., 219, 226
Mosher, D. L., 182
Moyer, A., 33
Mruk, C. J., 49
Mueller, J. H., 128
Muir, S. L., 41
Mullett, J., 238
Murphy, R., 26, 27, 28
Murray, S. L., 64

Nachson, O., 225
Nasby, W., 134
Neisser, U., 260, 261
Nelson, K., 20
Nelson, S., 52
Neuberg, C., 246, 247
Neuringer, C., 25
Newman, L. S., 266
Nezlek, J., 226

Niedenthal, P. M., 188, 265
Nisbett, R. E., 70
Nolen-Hoeksema, S., 144
Norasakkunkit, V., 83
Norman, N., 270
Nurius, P., 267, 270

Oakes, P. J., 108
Ockenberry, D., 226
Offer, D., 259
Ogden, J. K., 227
Ogilvie, D. M., 263
O'Heeron, R. C., 215, 217
Okazaki, Y., 127
Olah, A., 158
Olesin, K. C., 248
Olivardia, R., 38
Oliver, K. R., 71
Olsen, J. M., 64
Olsen, R., 31
Olson, C., 163
Onorato, R. S., 108
O'Quinn, K., 238
Orbach, J., 31
Ostrow, E., 259
Owens, J. F., 128

Page, T., 138
Panter, A. T., 267
Parish, E., 223, 226
Parke, R. D., 154, 161
Parker, S. T., 16
Pauly, I. B., 32
Paxton, S. J., 41
Peekna, H. M., 244
Peevers, B. H., 111
Pegalis, L. J., 223, 227
Pelham, B. W., 78
Pennebaker, J. W., 215, 216, 217
Penner, L. A., 34, 223, 226
Perilloux, H. K., 19, 20, 175
Perry, M., 56, 57, 60, 61, 123, 133
Pertschuck, M. J., 36
Petronio, S., 163, 218
Phares, V., 41
Phillips, K. A., 38, 43
Phinney, J. S., 94
Piaget, J., 20
Pickering, A. S., 40

Pickett, C. L., 109
Piers, G., 186
Pilkington, C. J., 68, 219
Pinel, E., 81, 82
Pittman, T. S., 271
Platt, L., 58
Plomin, R., 62
Poggi, I., 170, 184, 193, 203, 204
Pope, H. G., 38, 43
Porterfield, A. L., 127
Portnoy, N. W., 95, 97, 247
Posavac, E. J., 41
Posavac, H. D., 41
Posavac, S. S., 41
Poulin, R., 240
Povinelli, D. J., 19, 20, 175
Prager, K., 219, 227
Pratkanis, A. R., 261
Predmore, S. C., 72
Prentice, D. A., 6
Priest, D. J., 35
Prince, D., 229, 230, 231
Pruzinsky, T., 35
Pryor, J. B., 130
Pyszczynski, T., 48, 81, 82, 141

Raikkonen, K., 128
Ramsey, A., 138
Randall, P. K., 40
Recchia, S., 201, 202
Reddy, N. Y., 158
Reeves, A. L., 138
Reeves, P. J., 248
Rehman, J., 32
Reicher, S. D., 108
Reid, A., 100
Reis, H. T., 135, 226, 227
Reiser-Danner, L. A., 49
Remafedi, G., 39, 40
Reno, R. R., 224
Resnick, M. D., 39, 40
Rhodes, K., 238, 244
Rhodewalt, F., 70
Richardson, B. Z., 249
Richardson, D. R., 219
Riesman, D., 2, 109
Roberts, B. W., 107
Roberts, M., 77
Robins, R. W., 77, 107
Roese, N. J., 64

Rogers, C. R., 79, 257, 263, 264
Roggman, L. A., 49
Roney, C. J. R., 266
Rose, J., 61
Rosen, J. C., 44
Rosenberg, J. E., 64
Rosenberg, K., 190, 193
Rosenberg, M., 59, 62
Rosenblatt, A., 81, 82
Rosenblum, G. D., 39
Ross, J. M., 247
Ross, L., 48
Ruammake, C., 223
Ruback, R. B., 138, 140
Rubchinsky, K., 240, 247
Rubin, Z., 226
Russell, D., 61
Ruvolo, A., 268
Ryan, R. M., 78

Sabini, J., 182
Sadler, O., 144
Sager, K., 240, 247
Saltzman, A. T., 70
Sampson, E. E., 116
Sarbin, T. R., 259, 261
Sarwer, D., 36
Sattler, J. M., 159
Savin-Williams, R. C., 253
Schaefer, L. C., 32
Schaller, M., 238, 239, 240, 243, 244
Scheier, M. F., 34, 37, 60, 121, 124, 125, 126, 127, 135, 136, 137, 138, 139, 141, 142, 266
Schilder, P., 23
Schlenker, B. R., 71, 171, 270
Schmidt, N. B., 29
Schneiderman, L., 31
Schoenrade, P. A., 238
Schroeder, D. A., 244
Schutz, H. K., 41
Schwartz, D. J., 41
Scratchley, L. S., 63
Secord, P. F., 33
Sedikides, C., 74, 140, 141, 267, 269
Semin, G. R., 171
Semmelroth, J., 215
Senchak, M., 227
Shackelford, T. K., 207
Shaffer, D. H., 223

Shaffer, D. R., 129, 224, 225, 227
Sharkey, W. F., 159
Shavelson, R. J., 258, 259
Shaver, P., 225
Shaw, L. L., 249
Shea, C., 240
Shearn, D., 155, 156, 158, 161, 164, 184
Shell, R., 238, 240, 244
Shepherd, J. A., 131
Sher, K. J., 128
Sherman, M. D., 77
Sherman, S. E., 249
Shields, S. A., 34, 153, 169
Shimizu, T., 159
Showers, C. J., 262
Shrauger, J. S., 64, 72
Simmons, R. G., 76
Simner, M. I., 238
Simon, A., 153, 169
Simon, L., 81, 82, 141
Singer, M., 186
Singh, D., 34, 38, 40
Skowronski, J. J., 269
Slingsby, J. K., 244
Sloan, L. R., 55
Small, S. A., 253
Smart, S. A., 64, 72
Smeets, M. A. M., 42
Smith, A., 235
Smith, J. D., 129
Smith, J. E., 225
Smith, K. D., 244
Smith, M. B., 1
Smolak, L., 41
Smollan, D., 240
Snapp, T., 244
Snyder, M., 225, 271
Snygg, D., 257
Solano, C., 223, 226
Solomon, B., 227
Solomon, S., 48, 81, 82, 141
Spangler, D., 41
Spellman, L., 156, 164
Spencer, S. T., 65
Sprengelmeyer, P., 244
Stafford, L., 159
Stanger, C., 166, 167, 168, 172, 174
Stanton, G. C., 258
Stattin, H., 158
Steele, C. M., 64, 65, 70, 72
Stein-Seroussi, A., 74

Author Index

Stephens, D., 68
Stice, E., 41
Stiles, W. B., 218
Stillwell, A. M., 185, 190
Stipek, D. J., 201, 202
Stone, G. P., 159
Stormer, S. M., 41
Story, A., 72
Story, M., 39, 40
Stotland, E., 244, 249
Strauman, J. T., 264, 266
Strauman, T. J., 265, 266, 267
Strausser, K. S., 82
Strong, S. M., 40
Sullivan, M. W., 166, 167, 168, 172, 174, 202
Sun, C.-R., 63
Swann, W. B., Jr., 72, 73, 74, 78
Swap, W. C., 27
Szymanski, M. L., 34, 132, 267

Tafarodi, R. W., 57, 66, 72, 73, 79
Tajfel, H., 89, 108
Takata, T., 83
Tambor, E. S., 82
Tangney, J. P., 158, 177, 182, 183, 187, 188, 189, 190, 191, 192, 193, 200, 265
Tantleff, S. T., 37
Tantleff-Dunn, S. T., 35, 37, 38, 39, 41
Taylor, C., 2
Taylor, K. L., 69
Taylor, S. E., 47, 69
Tedeschi, J. T., 270
Telch, M. J., 29
Temerlin, M. K., 241
Templeton, J. L., 154, 155, 159, 184, 196, 204
Teng, G., 138, 139
Tennis, G. H., 229
Terdal, S. K., 82
Tesser, A., 67, 68, 144
Tetlock, P. E., 182
Thigpen, C. H., 108
Thompson, J. K., 34, 35, 37, 38, 39, 40, 41, 42
Thompson, M. A., 34
Thorne, A., 55
Tice, D. M., 59, 70, 115
Tiggerman, M., 40
Tobey, E. L., 131
Todd, M., 244

Tomarelli, M. M., 224, 225
Toulmin, S., 12
Trapnell, P. D., 138, 139, 148, 262
Traub, A. C., 31
Triandis, H. C., 117
Trimble, D. E., 248
Trivers, R. L., 252
Tunnell, G., 131
Turner, J. C., 108
Turner, R. G., 128, 130, 132, 134
Turner, R. H., 97, 116

Ugurel-Semin, R., 250

Vallone, R. P., 48
Vanable, P. A., 133
Van de Mark, S., 25
Vanderplas, M., 238
Varlow, D. H., 188, 265
Vincent, J. E., 243
Vohs, K. D., 71
Vookles, J., 266
Vu, C., 66, 79

Wadden, T., 36
Wagner, P. E., 189, 190, 193
Wagner, P. J., 229
Wakefield, J. C., 207
Walker, G. R., 136, 137, 194
Walker, M. R., 55
Walster, E., 35, 41, 49
Watson, J. B., 229
Watson, P. J., 138
Watts, W. A., 48
Weeks, J. L., 248
Wegner, D., 240
Weinberger, J., 240
Weiner, B., 51
Weismeier, E., 40
Weiss, M., 166, 172, 174
Weiss, R. S., 61
Wells, L. E., 48
Wertheim, E. H., 41
Westen, D., 215
Wetherell, M. S., 108
Wheeler, L., 226
Wheelis, A., 7
Whitaker, D., 68

Whitaker, L. A., 36
White, B. B., 182
White, S. H., 165
Whiting, B., 253
Wicklund, R. A., 121, 130, 140, 141
Wiegold, M. F., 71, 270
Wills, T. A., 69
Wilson, E. O., 252
Wilson, J., 220
Winstead, B. A., 35, 227
Wispe, L., 236, 239
Wittmer, J., 70
Wolfe, R. N., 271
Wong, P. T. P., 227
Wood, J. V., 69
Wood, K., 38
Worthy, M., 219
Wright, M. R., 39
Wylie, R. C., 50, 258

Yager, J., 40
Yamaguchi, S., 117, 118
Yap, P. M., 43
Yeung, A. S., 258
Young, R. C., 204
Young, R. D., 127, 128, 141, 223
Yuki, M., 117, 118
Yurko, K., 61

Zakin, D. F., 25
Zeldin, R. S., 253
Zerbst, J., 68
Zhang, S., 68
Zillman, D., 55, 93
Zuverink, J. R., 265

Subject Index

Actual self, 263, 264, 268, 269
   seen by another, 264
Adaptiveness, self-esteem and, 80
Adolescent identity crisis, 111, 118
Advanced self, 17-19, 21, 275
   versus primitive self, 18, 19-20
   See also Covertness; Identity; Self-evaluation
Advanced self-awareness, 202
Affiliations, 88
Aggression machine paradigm, 124, 125, 136, 151, 275
Allport's view of self, Gordon, 4, 21. *See also* Bodily self; Extension of self; Identity; Propriate striving; Self-esteem; Self-image
Altruism, 9, 211, 235, 243-248, 255, 275
   another's suffering and, 236
   cost-benefit analysis, 249-250, 254
   developmental theory of, 250-251
   egoistic view of, 244, 276
   gender differences, 253-254
   self-esteem and, 54
   See also Altruistic motives; Empathy; Reciprocal altruism
Altruistic motives, 245-248, 249, 254
   attachment, 245-246, 249, 275

   oneness, 246, 249, 254, 255, 277
   religion, 247-248, 249
   social bonds, 245-246
   social identity, 247, 249
   See also Empathy
American self, 10. *See also* Individualistic culture
Annihilation anxiety, 13
Anorexia, 42, 45, 275
Anxiety, 29. *See also* Panic attacks
Appearance questionnaires, 132
   Appearance Schemas Inventory, 132
   body ideals questionnaire, 132
Asch conformity paradigm, 134
Aspiration/achievement ratio, 4
Attributions, 51, 84, 275
   gender differences, 52
   self-descriptions and, 62-65
Autobiographical memory, 20
Awareness, 97
   body boundary and, 15, 275
   body focus and, 44
   of identity source, 97, 118

"Bask in reflected glory" (BIRG), 55
Blush:

creeping, 154
sudden, 154
See also Blushing
Blushing, 30, 153-156, 169, 196, 203-204, 214
  across cultures, 158
  as appeasement gesture, 170, 171, 204, 208, 275
  conspicuousness and, 160, 176, 276
  embarrassment and, 153, 170, 175, 184
  empathic, 156
  gaze aversion and, 175
  individual differences and, 153-154
  occurrence of, 155-156
  overpraise and, 161, 162, 176, 278
  physiology of, 154-155
  silly smile and, 175, 184
  skin conductance and, 154-155, 176, 279
  See also Blush; Vicarious blushing
Blushing Propensity Scale, 156
Bodily self, 4, 14, 21
Body boundary, 15, 17, 18, 19, 21, 275. *See also* Awareness
Body builders, 38
Body competence, measuring, 26
Body consciousness questionnaire, 26
Body dissatisfaction, causes of, 40-42, 45, 275
  magazines, 40
  teasing about body, 41
  television, 40
Body dysmorphic disorder, 43-44, 45, 275
  consequences to self-esteem, 43-44
Body focus, 7, 11, 14. *See also* Body dissatisfaction, causes of; Body focus development; Body focus disorders; Body image; Private body self; Public self
Body focus development, 38-40
  in adolescence, 39-40
  in adulthood, 40
  in childhood, 38-39
Body focus disorders, 42-44. *See also* Anorexia; Body dysmorphic disorder; Shame
Body identity, 32
Body image, 23, 30-35, 44, 45, 275
  assessing, 33-35
  cultural ideals and, 39
  dependability, 30-33, 44
  everyday functioning and, 30-31
  gender differences, 39

identity and, 31-32
negative, 35, 38, 39
private-public barrier, 30, 44
See also Body integrity; Homosexuals; Transsexuals
Body image questionnaires, 33-35
  Appearance Schemas Inventory, 34
  Body-Cathexis Scale, 33-34
  Body Esteem Scale, 34
  Body-Image Ideals Questionnaire, 34
  Breast-Chest Rating Scale, 37
  Multidimensional Body-Self Relations Questionnaire, 34
Body integrity, 32-33, 44
  limb removal and, 33
  organ removal and, 33
  See also Castration/penis removal; Mastectomy
Body modesty, 162
  privacy and, 229
Body schema, 23
Boundaries of self, 5-6. *See also* Altruism; Boundaries of selfhood; Empathy; Privacy
Boundaries of selfhood, 1, 211-212, 233. *See also* Boundaries of self; Concealment; Personal space; Seclusiveness; Self-disclosure
Burnout, 115

Can self, 268-269, 272, 273, 275
Cash, Thomas, 34
Castration:
  body image and, 33
  shame and, 181
Client-centered therapy, 263
Cognitive dissonance, 135
Coifence, 60
Collective self, 2, 118
Collectivism, individualism and, 116-118
Collectivist culture, 116, 117, 119, 276
  in Japan, 82, 83, 84
  versus individualist culture, 82-83
Concealment, 230, 231, 232, 233
Confidence, 84, 276
  self-worth versus, 80
Consistency, 71-74, 84, 276
  self-concept and, 257, 258
Contingent self-esteem, 78-79, 84, 276
Continuity of identity, 1, 105, 106, 111, 118

Subject Index

developmental levels of basis for, 112, 114
Control theory, 142-143, 151, 276
Core-periphery theory of self-esteem, 78-80, 81, 84, 85, 276
  core of self-esteem, 78
  periphery of self-esteem, 78, 80
Covertness, 17-18
  understanding, 21
Cross-dressing, 32
Culture:
  identity and, 109-111, 119
  shame and, 200-201
  social identity and, 114
  See also Collectivist culture; Individualist culture; Western self, history of

Depersonalization, 108, 118
Destabilization of identity, 110, 111
Dichotomies of self, 21
  aware-unaware, 13, 14, 21, 44, 151, 176, 273
  body focus, 26, 30, 31, 32, 33, 35, 44
  central-peripheral, 13, 14, 21, 33, 44, 84, 119, 208, 233, 273
  continuity-discontinuity, 13, 14, 21, 106-107, 119
  dependable-undependable, 13-14, 21, 31, 44, 84, 176
  direct-vicarious, 11, 21, 84, 93, 119, 176, 208, 254
  embarrassment, 162, 169, 176
  empathy/altruism, 254
  fixed ability-mastery of challenge, 53
  general, 12-14
  identity, 87, 93, 97, 104-108, 117, 119
  individual-group, 10-11, 21, 53, 117, 119, 151, 254
  innate versus voluntary, 53, 97, 118
  inner-outer, 11, 21, 26, 44, 233
  open-closed, 11, 21, 233, 254
  personal-social, 10-12, 21, 52, 53, 57-58, 84, 87, 100, 105-106, 194, 233, 245, 254
  positive-negative, 14, 21, 35, 44, 84, 119, 254, 273
  private-public, 10, 11, 21, 30, 44, 100, 104-105, 119, 151, 162, 169, 176, 205, 208, 214, 233
  self-concept, 273
  self-consciousness, 151
  self-esteem, 52, 53, 57-58, 84, 87
  shame/guilt, 194, 205, 208
  skill versus luck, 52, 53
  temporary versus enduring, 52
  unitary-multiple, 12, 14, 21, 32, 44, 84, 107-108, 119, 273
Dichotomies of taboo topics, 215
Discontinuity of identity, 106-107
Distinctiveness of identity, 111
  developmental levels of basis for, 112
Dominance, self-esteem and, 54
Double awareness, 30
Double stimulation, 15, 17, 18, 19, 21, 22, 276
Drama metaphor, 269-272, 273, 276

Egocentricity, self-reference and, 261, 272, 273, 276
Embarrassment, 8, 30, 196, 204
  appeasement function, 204, 208, 275
  body modesty and, 162
  body noises and, 162
  consequences of, 184, 185
  cross-cultural aspects of, 158
  developmental course, 168-169, 175
  facial expressions and, 156
  first appearance of, 165-168
  gaze aversion and, 157, 158, 161
  giggling and, 156, 161, 184
  guilt and, 158, 159
  nonverbal aspects of, 156-159
  reactions to, 184, 185
  reported feelings of, 158-159
  romantic crush and, 163, 213-214
  shame and, 158, 159, 177
  smiling and, 157, 158, 184
  social function, 205
  touching and, 162-163
  universality of, 158
  versus shame, 177-178, 182-184, 185
  See also Blushing; Embarrassment, causes of; Embarrassment, theories of
Embarrassment, causes of, 159-165, 183, 185
  breaches of privacy, 162-163, 172, 174, 175, 183, 214
  conspicuousness, 160, 174, 175, 176, 276

overpraise, 161-162, 174, 175, 176, 183, 278
ridicule, 160-161, 174, 175
social mistakes, 163-164, 174, 175, 183
See also Vicarious embarrassment
Embarrassment, Edelman model of, 171-172
Embarrassment, theories of, 169-175
    acute public self-awareness, 172-175
    appeasement, 170, 208, 275
    opinion of others, 169-170
    self-presentation, 170-172, 175, 176
    self-reference and evaluation, 172, 175
Empathy, 9, 11, 211, 235, 236-240, 244, 253, 254, 255, 276
    another's suffering and, 236
    distress and, 238-240
    gender differences, 237-238, 253-254
    perspective taking and, 148, 151, 236-237, 254, 255
    sociocentric, 245
    versus egoistic emotions, 243-245
    See also Altruism; Empathy, determinants of; Trait empathy
Empathy, determinants of, 240-243, 254
    empathy enhancers, 240-242
    empathy reducers, 242-243
Empathy, developmental theory of, 251
    motor mimicry, 251, 255, 277
Emphatic embarrassment, 159, 176, 276
Emphatic joy, 244, 245, 255, 276
    egocentric view of, 245, 276
Empirical self-concept, 258-259
Empty nest syndrome, 115
Ensembled individualism, 117
Entity theorists, 51-52, 85, 276
Evaluation, self-esteem and, 87
Evaluative embarrassment, 172
Evolution, altruism and, 250, 251-252
    inclusive fitness, 251
Exaggerated self-worth, 47-48, 83
Extension of self, 4, 21

Face, concept of, 200-201, 208, 276
Facial identity, 32
Focusing on oneself, 6
Foreclosure of identity, 113, 114, 119, 276
Future self, 267-268, 269, 272, 273, 276

Gender identity, 103, 104, 105, 119, 276
Gender identity scale for men, 103
Gender misidentification, 103-104
Generalized other, 148
Guilt, 8, 193, 201, 264
    embarrassment and, 158, 159
    emotions and, 193
    expiation of, 198, 208, 276
    generalized, 191-192
    in Japan, 207
    major cause of, 197
    private self and, 195-196
    religion and, 197-198
    responses, 188
    self-awareness and, 194-195
    self-cognitions and, 197
    self-labeling and, 207
    versus shame, 193-201
    See also Guilt, interpersonal theory of; Survivor guilt
Guilt, interpersonal theory of, 185-186, 277
    empathy in, 185
    fear of being excluded in, 185

Helping behavior:
    other-directed, 245, 277
    self-directed, 245
Hidden self, 2
High self-esteem, 84
    versus low self-esteem, 73, 75-76
Homosexuality, 106
    shame and, 178, 181
Homosexuals, 104
    body image and, 40
    negative identity and, 95-96, 97
    teasing and, 104
Hostility, 60, 61-62, 84, 85, 151, 276
Hypochondriacs, 28

Ideal self, 4, 9, 263, 264, 269, 273, 276
    seen by another, 264
Identity, 4, 7-8, 11, 14, 18-19, 21
    body image and, 31-32
    marriage and, 88
    medieval sources of, 110
    versus self-esteem, 87-89, 118

See also Personal identity; Social identity
Identity achievement, 114
Identity crisis, 115
Identity development, 111-116
  childhood through adolescence, 111-115
  maturity, 115-116
Identity diffusion, 113, 114, 119, 277
Identity moratorium, 113-114, 120, 277
Identity statuses, 113-114. *See also*
  Foreclosure of identity; Identity achievement; Identity diffusion; Identity moratorium
Identity theory, Erikson's, 113
Imaginary selves, 9
Impression management, 71, 270
Impulsives, 116
Incremental theorists, 52, 85, 277
Independent self, 117, 119
Independent thinking, self-esteem and, 72-73
Individualism, collectivism and, 116-118
Individualist culture, 116, 117, 119, 277
  in United States/Canada, 82, 83, 84
  versus collectivist culture, 82-83
Inner-directed, 109, 110
Inner life, 8, 11
Inner self, 8
Institutionals, 116
Interdependent self, 117, 119
Interdependent thinking, self-esteem and, 73
Internal state awareness, 138, 139, 140, 150
Introspection, 2
I-self, 5
I-self versus me-self, 3, 4

James's view of self, William, 3, 4, 20, 259. *See also* Material self; Social self; Spiritual self
Japanese self-consciousness, 150
Japanese self, 10

Koro, 43

Leadership, self-esteem and, 54
Looking-glass self, 3, 277
  definition, 22
Love:
  self-esteem and, 54, 79, 88

unconditional, 79-80
Low self-esteem, 84
  versus high self-esteem, 73, 75-76

Machismo, 179-180, 208, 277
Mastectomy, 277
  body image and, 33, 45
  shame and, 181
Material self, 3, 20, 277
  definition, 22
Me-not me boundary, 5, 19, 21
Merging, 249, 254
Me-self, 4
Midlife crisis, 115
Minnesota Multiphasic Personality Inventory (MMPI), hypochondria scale of, 28
Mirror image recognition, 15-17, 18, 19, 21, 124-127, 136, 167, 172, 277
  definition, 22
  in human developmental sequence, 16-17
  research, 16
Mirror image self, 148
Mortality salience theory of self-esteem, 81-82
Multiple personality, 108, 120, 277
Multiplicity in identity, 107-108

Negative identity, 95-96, 120, 277
  criminals and, 96
  hate groups and, 96
  sexual orientation and, 95, 96, 97
  See also Negative self
Negative self, 138, 151, 277. *See also* Negative identity
Negative self-evaluation. *See* Embarrassment; Shame
Novelty, 277

Obesity, body image and, 38, 42
Objective self-awareness, 140-142, 151, 277
Optimal distinctiveness theory, 108
Optimism, 60
Other-directed, 2, 22, 109, 110, 277

Ought self, 263, 264, 265, 266, 269, 272, 273, 277
   seen by another, 264

Panic attacks, 29
   treatment, 29
Parental attitudes, internalized, 277
Past self, 269, 272
Personal identity, 89, 100-109, 112, 118, 120, 278
   continuity and, 105
   private self, 102-104, 105
   public self, 100-102, 105
   sources, 118
   versus social identity, 89
   See also Personal self; Twins
Personality, 250
Personal self, 118
   versus social self, 116-118
Personal space, 212, 228-229, 233
   cultural variations, 229
   gender differences in, 229
   intimate zone, 228, 233, 277
   invasion of, 228
   personal zone, 228, 233, 278
Perspective taking, 148, 151, 236-237, 254, 255, 278
Pessimism, 84
Possible self, 267-269, 270, 272. *See also* Can self; Future self
Praise, self-esteem and, 55
Primitive self, 15-17, 21
   versus advanced self, 18, 19-20
   See also Body boundary; Double stimulation; Mirror image recognition
Primitive self-awareness, 174, 202
Privacy, 8-9, 173-174, 211-212
   clandestine activities, 173
   components, 229-232
   private self, 174
Privacy questionnaire, 229-232
   concealment factor, 230, 231, 232
   personal space factor, 230, 231, 232
   self-disclosure factor, 230, 231, 232
Private body awareness, 278. *See also* Private body consciousness
Private body consciousness, 26, 27
   downside, 28
   measuring, 26
   See also Hypochondriacs; Private body awareness
Private body self, 24-30
   aware-unaware, 26
   body boundary, 24-26, 275
   interior versus exterior focus, 24-26, 44
   neutral stimuli, 26-28
   stimuli accompanying anxiety, 28-30
Private identity, 102-104
   ambitions, 104
   daydreams, 102, 104
   fantasies, 102
   feelings, 102, 104
Private self, 10, 17
   religion and, 214
   self-disclosure and, 212, 213-214
   versus public self, 193-201
Private self-awareness, 124, 137-140, 143-145, 152, 194, 278
   development of, 146-147
   inducers, 143-144, 151, 277
   intensification, 144-145, 150
   private self-consciousness and, 126
Private self-consciousness, 27, 123, 125, 127, 128, 150, 152
   development of, 147-148, 150
   private self-awareness and, 126
   self-reports and behavior and, 129-131
   versus public self-consciousness, 134-137
   See also Internal state awareness; Self-reflectiveness
Private self-focus, 124-131
   versus public self-focus, 134-137
Propriate striving, 4, 21, 278
   definition, 22
Prosocial behavior, 173, 176, 278
Psychological extension of self, 5
Psychological privacy, 163
Psychotherapy, 2
Public body consciousness, 26. *See also* Public body focus; Public self
Public body focus, 25
   appearance of face, 35-36
   appearance of hair, 36-37
   appearance of torso, 37-38
   cosmetic surgery and, 36
   negativity toward, 35
   overall body appearance, 35-38

reconstructive plastic surgery and, 36
  See also Body builders
Public identity, 100-102, 105
Public self, 10, 30, 35-38, 194
  self-disclosure and, 212-213
  versus private self, 193-201
  See also Public body focus
Public self-awareness, 145-146, 152, 194, 278
  development of, 148-149
  perceptual feedback as inducer, 146, 278
  social attention as inducer, 145
Public self-consciousness, 26, 37, 131-134, 151, 152, 278
  appearance and, 131-132
  attention from others and, 132-134
  development of, 149-150
  hostility and, 133
  paranoia and, 133-134
  versus public self-consciousness, 134-137
  See also Public self-focus
Public self-focus:
  versus private self-focus, 134-137

Rape, shame and, 178
Rational coper, 4, 5
Reactance, 125
Reality testing, 24
Real self, 9, 263
Reciprocal altruism, 252
Reflective, 1
Relational self, 118
Religiosity, self-esteem and, 54
Representative intelligence, 20
*Re*presenting, 196, 208, 278
Respect, self-esteem and, 55
Rorschach ink blots, 24, 25, 45
  barrier responses to, 24, 25, 26, 44
  barrier scores, 24-25, 45, 275
  experiments, 24-25

Seclusiveness, 212
Self:
  concept of, 4-6
  defining, 5-6
  dimensions of, 9-14, 21
  elements of, 6-9
  historical views of, 1-4, 20
Self-accusations, 8

Self-actualization, 117
Self-affirmation theory, 64-65, 72, 74
Self as knower, 6
Self-aware, 1
Self-awareness, 124-127, 136-137
  development of, 146-150
  in psychological approaches, 121
Self-awareness/self-consciousness theories, 140-150. *See also* Control theory; Objective self-awareness; Private self-awareness; Public self-awareness; Self-consciousness theory; Self-relevance
Self-categorization theory, 108, 118
Self-centeredness, 80-81
Self-centeredness theory of self-esteem, 81, 84
Self-clarity, 262, 273, 278
Self-complexity, 107, 262, 273, 278
Self-concept, 9, 14, 272, 273, 278
  as theory, 261
  consistency and, 257, 258
  hierarchical, 258
  See also Empirical self-concept; Self-concepts
Self-concepts:
  academic, 258
  adaptive, 259
  generalized, 259
  material, 259
  nonacademic, 258
  personal, 259
  self/nonself, 259
  social, 259
Self-Conscious Affect and Attribution Inventory (SCAAI), 187, 188, 189
Self-consciousness, 8, 11, 14, 123, 124-127, 134-136, 172
  intensification of, 127-128, 141, 150
  self-knowledge and, 128-131, 131, 150
  See also Private self-consciousness; Private self-focus; Public self-consciousness
Self-Consciousness Questionnaire, 122-123, 137
  private self-consciousness items, 123
  public self-consciousness items, 123
Self-consciousness theory, 143-145, 151
  private self-awareness and, 143-145

public self-awareness and, 145-146
Self-consistency theory, 73
Self-contained individualism, 117
Self-digest, 268
Self-directed behavior, 6
Self-disclosure, 11, 14, 212-216, 229-232
  adolescent-parent, 219
  as confession, 217, 222, 232
  content of, 212-214
  for expression, 216
  for relationship development, 216-219, 222, 233
  for self-clarification, 217, 222, 232, 278
  for social comparison, 217, 222, 232
  for social control, 217
  for social validation, 216
  gender differences and, 226-227
  internal pressure and, 217-218
  motivation for, 216-221, 222, 232-234
  of romantic crush, 218
  private self and, 212, 213-214
  public self and, 212-213
  recipient of, 214-216
  reciprocity of, 219-220, 222, 224, 225, 233, 278
  risks, 222
  self-clarification of, 220-221, 278
  spousal, 219
  taping, 215-216
  trust and, 221, 225
  See also Blushing; Embarrassment; Self-disclosure, individual differences in
Self-disclosure, fever model of, 218
Self-disclosure, individual differences in, 221-226
  attachment style, 225-226, 233, 275
  disclosers, 223
  openers, 223, 233, 277
  self-consciousness level, 223-225
Self-discrepancies, 263-267, 273, 278
  actual/own and ideal/other, 264, 265
  actual/own and ideal/own, 264, 265, 272
  actual/own and ought/other, 264, 265
  among Japanese, 267
  ideal self versus ought self, 266
  depression and, 265, 266
  social anxiety and, 265
  undesired self, 263, 272, 273, 279
  See also Actual self; Ideal self; Ought self

Self-discrepancy theory, 263, 272. *See also* Self-discrepancies
Self-efficacy, 50, 85, 278
Self-enhancement, 70-74, 76, 84, 85, 278
  versus consistency, 71-74
  versus self-protection, 70-71
Self-enhancement theory, 74
Self-esteem, 4, 7, 14, 18, 19, 21, 47-48
  affective component in, 72
  body dysmorphic disorder and, 43-44
  cognitive mechanisms and, 67-76, 84
  confidence, 49, 66
  defending, 53
  elevating, 53
  fluctuations in, 77
  gender differences, 50, 56-58
  global, 12, 48, 66, 77, 78
  performance outcome and, 64-67
  stigma and, 58-59
  sources, 12
  top-down perspective on, 48
  unitary perspective on, 48
  versus identity, 87-89, 118
  worthwhileness, 49, 66
  See also Contingent self-esteem; Self-esteem, sources of; Vicarious self-esteem
Self-esteem, sources of, 48-59, 84, 87-88
  ability, 50, 56, 57, 87
  acceptance, 49
  achievement, 48, 49, 51-54, 84
  appearance, 48, 49-50, 56, 57, 77, 84, 87
  athletic competence, 77
  attention/affection from others, 48
  character, 84
  influence, 48, 49, 54, 84
  likableness, 48
  morality, 48, 54, 56, 57, 87
  peer likability, 77
  performance, 48, 51
  personal versus social, 57-58
  power, 87
  recognition, 52
  scholastic competence, 77-78
  skill, 51
  social influence, 56
  social rewards, 54-55, 56, 57, 84, 87
  standards, 50-51
  talent, 48, 51
  value of, 80-82

Subject Index

vicariousness, 55-56, 57, 84, 87
virtue, 49
  See also Altruism; Dominance; Leadership; Love; Praise; Religiosity; Respect; Vicarious self-esteem
Self-esteem, cognitive theories of, 74. *See also* Self-affirmation theory; Self-enhancement theory; Self-esteem maintenance; Self-verification theory; Social comparison theory
Self-esteem development, 76-80
Self-esteem maintenance, 74
Self-esteem questionnaires, 59-67. *See also* Hostility; Optimism; Pessimism; Shyness; Sociability; Social loneliness
Self-esteem theories, 81. *See also* Core-periphery theory; Mortality salience theory; Self-centeredness theory; Social dominance theory; Sociometer hypothesis; Terror management theory
Self-evaluation, 18, 21
Self-evaluation maintenance theory, 67-68, 85, 278
  extended, 68
  relevance in, 67-68
Self-focus, 6
Self-handicapping, 70-71, 85, 278
Selfhood, 1
Self-identity, 4
Self-image, 4, 21, 22, 278
Self-induced stimulation, 15
Selfishness, 252-252
Self-knowledge, 260-261
  accessibility to, 128-129
  conceptual, 260-261
  ecological, 260
  extended, 260
  interpersonal, 260
  private, 260
  private self-consciousness and, 131
Self-matching, 271
Self-Monitoring Questionnaire, 225
Self-presentation, 170-172, 176, 269-272, 273, 279. *See also* Drama metaphor
Self-protection, 84, 279
Self-recognition, 15, 17, 19
  in animals, 16
  See also Mirror image recognition
Self-reference issues, 129
Self-referential behavior, 167

Self-reflectiveness, 138, 139-140
  personality variables and, 138
Self-reflexiveness, 6, 21
  essence of, 8
Self-related behavior, defining characteristics of, 5-6
Self-relevance, 143
Self-schemas, 9, 257, 259-262, 273, 279
Self-schemata, 257, 267
Self-state representations, 264
Self-verification, 84, 85, 279
Self-verification theory, 73-74
Self-worth, 84, 85, 279
  true, 78
  versus confidence, 80
Sensory self, 19, 22, 279
Shame, 8, 177-178, 193
  as generalized emotion, 190-191
  bodily, 43
  child abuse and bodily, 43
  consequences of, 184, 185
  culture and, 200-201
  distinctive causes of, 198-201
  embarrassment and, 158, 159, 177
  emotions and, 193
  imagery and memory and, 196-197
  in Japan, 195
  public self and, 195-196
  reactions to, 184, 185, 188
  self-awareness and, 194-195
  self-labeling and, 177, 207
  specific, 192
  versus embarrassment, 177-178, 182-184, 185
  versus guilt, 193-201
  See also Shame, causes of; Vicarious shame
Shame, causes of, 178-182, 183, 185, 207, 214
  drunkenness, 179
  illegality, 178-179, 207
  impotence, 180
  lying, 179
  omission of socially expected behavior, 179
  public failure, 180-181, 183, 207
  sexual immorality, 178, 183, 207
  stigma, 181-182, 184, 199, 207, 208
  withholding child support, 180
Shame/embarrassment:
  conception of, 183-184

research, 182-183
Shame/guilt, development theories of, 201-203, 208
  attributions and self-consciousness, 201-202, 275
  See also Advanced self-awareness; Primitive self-awareness
Shame/guilt, evolutionary theories of, 203-207, 208
  appeasement, 203-205, 208, 275
  necessary conditions, 205-206, 207
  sufficient conditions, 206, 207
Shame/guilt, theories of, 207-208
  development, 201-203, 208
  evolutionary, 203-207, 208
  See also Shame/guilt, development theories of; Shame/guilt, evolutionary theories of
Shame reaction, 207
Shame versus guilt, dynamic theories of, 186-193
  attributional style, 189, 275
  ego-ideal/ego gap, 186, 208, 276
  guilt proneness, 187, 189, 191, 208, 276
  internalized parental attitudes, 186, 208
  modified psychoanalytic, 186-187
  psychoanalytic, 186
  shame proneness, 187, 189, 191, 208, 279
Shyness, 60, 61, 84, 168
Sociability, 60, 62
Social comparison, 67-69, 84
  downward, 69, 70
  upward, 69, 70
  See also Vicarious self-esteem
Social comparison theory, 74
Social dominance theory of self-esteem, 81
Social identity, 89, 90-100, 105-106, 118, 120, 247, 279
  dimensions of, 97
  motivation for, 108
  negative, 14
  rankings, 98-99
  versus personal identity, 89, 118
  See also Social identity, sources of
Social identity, sources of, 118
  ancestral family, 96
  children, 91, 96
  educational organizations, 93, 96
  ethnicity, 94, 97, 118
  extended family, 91-92
  fraternities/sororities, 92-93, 96, 97, 247

gangs, 96, 97
gender, 118
interpersonal roles, 118
kinship, 90-92, 97
marriage, 90, 96
nationalism, 95, 247
nationality, 97, 118, 247
organized social groups, 118
outcast groups, 118
parents, 90-91, 96
place, 95, 97
race, 96
religion, 94-95, 96, 97, 106, 118
vocation, 92, 96, 97, 114
See also Negative identity
Social identity theory, 89, 108-109, 118
Social interaction, drama and self in, 271-272
Socialization, 8, 22, 279
Social loneliness, 60, 61, 84, 85, 279
Social roles, 88, 120, 279
Social self, 2, 3, 20, 194
  versus personal self, 116-118
Sociometer hypothesis of self-esteem, 81, 82, 85, 279
Somatic interpretation model, 29
Spiritual self, 3, 20
St. Augustine, 1-2
Stigma, 208, 279
  group differences and, 58
  self-esteem and, 58-59
Survivor guilt, 199, 208
Symbolic interactionism, 3
Symbolic self theory, 269

Teasing, 149, 160-161, 169, 173
  body dissatisfaction and, 41
  body image and, 39, 40
  embarrassment and, 183
  homosexuals, 104
  provoking, 171
Terror management theory of self-esteem, 81, 84, 85, 279
TOSCA, 188, 189
Trait empathy, 244-245
Transsexuals, 32, 44, 45, 279
  body image scale for, 32
Transvestites, 32
Trivialization of identity, 110, 111
Twins, personal identity and, 101-102

Unified self, 118

Vicarious blushing, 156, 164
Vicarious embarrassment, 164-165, 174

Vicarious self-esteem, 55-56, 67, 85, 279
Vicarious shame, 181-182, 199

Western self, history of, 109-111

About the Author

Arnold Buss was trained as a clinical psychologist and has taught at the University of Pittsburgh, Rutgers University, and the University of Texas, where he still teaches. His work has been mainly in the areas of personality and social psychology. He is best known for theory and research on aggression, temperament, self-consciousness, and shyness. For several decades, he has been teaching a course on the self that includes topics such as body image, self-esteem, and identity. He is the author of 80 articles and book chapters, and this is his 12th book.